Smart Collaborative Identifier Network

Hongke Zhang · Wei Su
Wei Quan

Smart Collaborative Identifier Network

A Promising Design for Future Internet

 Springer

Hongke Zhang
National Engineering Laboratory for Next
  Generation Internet Technologies, School
  of Electronic and Information Engineering
Beijing Jiaotong University
Beijing
China

Wei Quan
National Engineering Laboratory for Next
  Generation Internet Technologies, School
  of Electronic and Information Engineering
Beijing Jiaotong University
Beijing
China

Wei Su
National Engineering Laboratory for Next
  Generation Internet Technologies, School
  of Electronic and Information Engineering
Beijing Jiaotong University
Beijing
China

ISBN 978-3-662-56986-3   ISBN 978-3-662-49143-0   (eBook)
DOI 10.1007/978-3-662-49143-0

Printed on acid-free paper

This Springer imprint is published by Springer Nature
The registered company is Springer-Verlag GmbH Berlin Heidelberg

Foreword I

I have known Prof. Zhang and his work for more than 10 years and as a collaborator on a recent project focusing on the future Internet. I am writing to provide my highest recommendation for publishing his proposed book on this subject at your esteemed press.

Professor Zhang is a highly innovative and persevering as well as respected scientist in Chinese academia. He has submerged himself in research on information networks for the past several decades. During that period, he spearheaded many national-level research projects sponsored by National Basic Research Program of China, National High-tech R&D Program and National Natural Science Foundation of China. He has made many significant achievements and inventions and published over 100 papers and several academic writings on this subject. He has also received many awards and recognitions.

It is worth noting that in recent years Prof. Zhang proposed and prototyped a novel future Internet architecture, called the Smart Collaborative Identifier Network, which has many attractive features. The proposed book, Smart Collaborative Identifier Network, is an excellent culmination of his work, which includes Prof. Zhang's latest research findings. There are many new ideas, concepts, and technologies in this proposed book, which will attract the interest of both academia and industry, fostering further advancement of future Internet research.

In short, given the excellence of the author, the topic, and the content, I strongly support the publication of this monograph without any reservation.

Sincerely,
Chunming Qiao
Professor, IEEE Fellow
Department of Computer Science and Engineering
University at Buffalo, SUNY, Buffalo, NY, USA

Foreword II

Prof. Hongke Zhang requested a letter of recommendation from me to support publishing his new monograph at your world-renowned press. As his acquaintance, I am pleased to comply with his request.

Prof. Hongke Zhang has applied himself to research on the communication network for many years. He has written numerous famous academic writings, including Principle and Technology of IPv6 Routing Protocol Stack, Mobile Internet Technology, Principle and Technology of Routers and so on. All of his research findings have been widely accepted. In recent years, he has received strong state patronages for several national-level projects from the National Basic Research Program of China ("973 Program"), National High-tech R&D Program ("863 Program") and National Natural Science Foundation of China. Certainly, he has obtained a series of significant academic achievements as well.

What distinguished him among his colleagues, I think, is his recent accomplishments in future Internet architecture, the Smart Collaborative Identifier Network, which theoretically solves the existing problems of the current Internet. Moreover, the feasibility and reliability of this novel Internet architecture has been demonstrated by the telecom industry. To spread these valuable ideas, Prof. Hongke Zhang has spent a lot of time and effort on writing this monograph. As far as I know, this book is the first one focusing on the future Internet architecture, mechanisms, and technologies. This book makes a detailed elaboration of the working principles, key technologies and prototype system of the Smart Collaborative Identifier Network. It also makes great contributions to promoting the development of the future Internet.

In summary, I have every reason to believe that this book will be an outstanding performance. I would greatly appreciate it if you give this book favorable consideration. Please feel free to contact me directly if more assistance is needed.

Sincerely yours,
Dr. Sy-Yen Kuo, IEEE Fellow
Distinguished Professor, Department of Electrical Engineering
National Taiwan University

Foreword III

I am very glad to write this reference letter in support of the publication of this monograph.

In recent years, the research on the future Internet architecture and mechanisms has become a most important topic in the area of the information network. As far as I know, there are many different proposals for the future Internet all over the world, such as CCN/NDN, DONA, PSIRP and so on. However, few monographs detailing the future Internet design can be found so far. This book, Smart Collaborative Identifier Network—A Promising Design of Future Internet, is the first great monograph especially about the future Internet. It introduces the clean-slate network architecture clearly, including the basic theories and advanced technologies. The Smart Collaborative Identifier Network has great potential to overcome the drawbacks of the current Internet and satisfy emerging demands of the future Internet.

The authors, Prof. Hongke Zhang and his team, have been devoted to the research on the future Internet for decades. Prof. Zhang has rich experience in the area of the future Internet. During the past decades, he has been the chief scientist for numerous national research projects, such as the "Basic Research on Theories of Smart and Cooperative Networks" founded by the National Basic Research Program of China ("973 Program"). He has also published several academic works concentrating on the technologies of the computer network, such as the Principle and Technology of Routers, Mobile Internet Technology, Principle and Technology of the Ipv6 Routing Protocol Stack and so on. This book is another great achievement of his recent research.

In a word, this book proposes a many new ideas, new concepts, and new technologies of the future Internet. In my opinion, this book has an important academic value and is also very significant for the deployment of the future Internet. I also hope that this book will make great contributions to the development of the future Internet.

Yours honestly,
Zhou Bingkun
Academician, Chinese Academy of Sciences
Tsinghua University, Beijing, China

Preface

Over the past few decades, the Internet, as a huge success, has permeated almost every aspect of our daily life. However, with its fast growth and development, the current settings of the Internet exhibit various shortcomings, for instance, the security problems, the lack of support of flexible services, the inability to provide mobility and the insufficient support of manageability. These shortcomings are serious obstacles to the further development of the Internet. Therefore, the networking research community has engaged in an ongoing conversation about how to move the Internet forward.

Arguments about whether researchers should focus on improving today's Internet architecture or on designing new network architectures, which are unconstrained by the current system, always exist. Jennifer Rexford from Princeton University first gave his viewpoint that a "clean-slate design is important for enabling the networking field to mature into a true discipline, and to have a future Internet that is worthy of society's trust." We believe this could be proven eventually. Furthermore, although there have been many improvements on top of the current Internet architecture, few, if any, can comprehensively, effectively and sustainably solve the aforementioned problems.

More and more researchers have recently reported that problems about the Internet originate mostly from the limitations of its primary design. Many efforts have been made worldwide to investigate and develop the future Internet technologies and systems. Furthermore, the research community and the telecom industry have started to explore the new approaches to build the future Internet, such as Future Internet Network Design (FIND), Future Internet Architecture (FIA) in the USA; Future Internet Research and Experimentation (FIRE) and FIRE + in the European Union. Now, designing and building up the future Internet frame has become one of the most important and urgent topics in the research field of information networks. Thanks to these efforts, remarkable progress has been made for the future Internet. However, a general and ultimate solution for the future Internet has yet to be introduced.

This book examines the recent research on the future Internet all over the world and introduces a promising design for the future Internet named by *Smart*

Collaborative Identifier Network (SINET). SINET is intended to address the main issues and defects existing in the current Internet architecture. In this book, we present SINET's basic theories and principles, a broad range of architectures, protocols, standards and future research directions. Over the last decade, a variety of theoretical models and industrial applications have demonstrated that SINET is able to manage most of the problems of today's Internet. Through the comprehensive experiments and practical verification, SINET offers impressive flexibility, security, mobility, manageability and efficient resource utilization.

The book consists of 13 chapters in total. To give a clear and all-round introduction to the SINET, the chapters are further categorized into three parts. First, we introduce the Theory and Principle of SINET in Part I, which includes Chaps. 1–6. With knowledge of the basic principle, we detail many key technologies of SINET in Part II, which consists of Chaps. 7–10. Finally, some applications and developments are discussed and analyzed in Part III, comprising Chaps. 11–13.

To profit the audience the most, we expect the readers to have basic knowledge of the current Internet architecture and a brief understanding of how the current Internet works. This book can be used as a reference for researchers and practitioners interested in or working in the field of Internet design and the future Internet architecture. The contents are also suitable for both graduate students and senior undergraduate students in the fields of computer science, information science, computer networks and communication engineering. We hope that this book will serve as a valuable blueprint and contribute to the future Internet. We also hope to attract more researchers worldwide in this community to exchange ideas and to build a more effective and powerful Internet collaboratively.

Beijing, China   Hongke Zhang
                                                                                          Wei Su
                                                                                        Wei Quan

Acknowledgements

Many researchers have assisted me technically in writing this book. I am very grateful. Without their help, the book might never have been finished. My deepest thanks go to Prof. Chunming Qiao (University at Buffalo, The State University of New York), Prof. Sy-Yen Kuo (National Taiwan University), Prof. Bingkun Zhou (Chinese Academy of Sciences), Prof. Youzhi Xu (Mid Sweden University) and Gidlund Mikael (ABB, Sweden), who were so kind as to fully support us in writing this book and give us many valuable suggestions. They are all experts in their respective fields.

I am also very grateful to Prof. Wei Su, Dr. Wei Quan and Dr. Jia Chen, who are all outstanding researchers in our team and helped greatly in the organization of the whole contents of this book (each of them contributed at least four chapters, Chaps. 1–4, Chaps. 5–8, Chaps. 9–13, respectively). Many other researchers have also assisted in various ways during the preparation of this book. I am thankful to Huachun Zhou, Deyun Gao, Yajuan Qin, Hongbin Luo, Changqiao Xu, Fei Song, Dong Yang, Ping Dong, Ying Liu, Hongchao Wang, Shuai Gao, Tao Zheng and Jianfeng Guan. They have shared many research ideas over the years, which are mostly included in this book, and/or also been a great help in pointing out errors in the texts, examples and algorithms.

My current students, Zhongbai Jiang, Ying Rao, Ru Jia, Fei Ren, Yakun Xu, Xiaojun Xie, Bosong Liu, Bingjie Han, Tongming Zhang, Chunqiu Shi, Yana Liu, Yun Zhao, Wei Huang and Peipei Jing, contributed as well by researching/preparing materials for several chapters and/or checking chapters and made numerous corrections. This book also refers to the works of several of my former students. To list them all would be impossible, but I would particularly like to thank Huaming Guo, Feng Qiu, Xiaoqian Li, Shuigen Yang, Ming Wan and Jianqiang Tang.

It was a pleasure working with the helpful staff at Springer. I thank my editor Dr. Celine Chang, Dr. XiaoLan Yao and Miss. Jane Li, who gave us great guidance in preparing this book, helped us improve the presentation, and guided us through the final production process. Working with them has been a wonderful experience.

Three anonymous book reviewers selected by Springer also gave us many insightful comments.

This book was supported by the National Basic Research Program of China (the 973 Program) under grant no. 2013CB329100, the National Natural Science Foundation of China (NSFC) under grant no. 61232017 and 61602030, the Project Funded by the China Postdoctoral Science Foundation under grant no. 2015M580970 and the Fundamental Research Funds for the Central Universities under grant no. 2015JBM009. In addition, Beijing Jiaotong University (BJTU) and National Engineering Laboratory for Next Generation Internet Technologies (NGIT) provided major support and a comfortable environment for preparing this book.

Last but not least, my greatest gratitude goes to my family. They have helped me in so many ways unconditionally, in particular my wife, who has taken care of everything at home and put up with me during the long hours that I have spent on this book. I dedicate this book to them.

November 2015   Hongke Zhang

Contents

Acronyms

AC	Authentication Center
ACK	ACKnowledge
ACN	ACcess Network
ADNT	Anomaly Detection based on Network Traffic
ADRM	Anomaly Detection Response Mechanism
AID	Access IDentifier
AID-RM	AID Resolution Mapping
ALT	Alternative Topology
ARPA	Advanced Research Projects Agency
ARPANET	Advanced Research Project Agency Network
ASR	Access Switching Router
BGP	Border Gateway Protocol
CCN	Content-Centric Networking
CERNET	China Education and Research Network
CID	Connection IDentifier
CID-RM	CID Resolution Mapping
CoA	Care of Address
CON	COre Network
CPS	Content Providing Server
CUSUM	Cumulative Sum
DDoS	Distributed Denial of Service
DHT	Distributed Hash Table
DONA	Data Oriented Network
DoS	Denial of Service
EU	European Union
FBD	Family Behavior Description
FIA	Future Internet Architecture
FID	Family IDentifier
FIND	Future Internet Design
FIRE	Future Internet Research and Experimentation

FP7	EU's Seventh Framework Program (FP7)
GSR	General Switching Router
HA	Home Agent
HIP	Host Identity Protocol
HTTP	Hyper Text Transfer Protocol
ICCC	Intelligent Central Control Component
ICT	Information Communication Technologies
IDMS	Identifier Mapping Server
IETF	Internet Engineering Task Force
IP	Internet Protocol
IRTF	Internet Research Task Force
ISP	Internet Service Provider
ISRS	Intelligent Service Resolution Server
KM	Kermack-Mckendrick
LISP	Locator/Identifier Separation Protocol
MIP	Mobile IP
MIPv6	Mobile IPv6
MN	Mobile Node
MOST	Ministry of Science and Technology
MR	Mobile Router
MTC	Mobile Terminal Component
NAT	Network Address Translation
NBD	Node Behavior Description
NDN	Named Data Networking
Net-Inf	Network of Information
NGIT	National Engineering Laboratory for Next Generation Internet Technologies
NID	Node IDentifier
NRS	Name Resolution Server
NSC	Network Switching Component
NSF	National Science Foundation
NSFC	National Natural Science Foundation of China
NSFNET	National Science Foundation Network
NSR	Network Switching Router
PIT	Pending Interest Table
PN	Provider Network
P2P	Peer-to-peer
QoS	Qualtiy of Service
RARS	Resource Adapting Resolution Server
RH	Resolution Handler
RID	Routing Identifier
RM	Resolution Mapping
RP	Rendezvous Point
RTT	Round-Trip Time
SAP	Service Access Point

SB	Service Binding
SBD	Service Behavior Description
SCTP	Transmission Control Protocol
SDN	Software Defined Network
SID	Service Identifier
SID-RM	SID Resolution Mapping
SINET	Smart Identifier NETwork
SIP	Session Initiation Protocol
SIR	Susceptible-Infectious-Removed
SIS	Susceptible-Infectious-Susceptible
SMS	Service Management System
STC	Stable Terminal Component
SYN	SYNchronous
TCP	Transmission Control Protocol
TCP/IP	Transmission Control Protocol/Internet Protocol
URL	Uniform Resource Locator
VAM	Virtual Access Module
VBM	Virtual Backbone Module
VCM	Virtual Connection Module
VSM	Virtual Service Module
XIA	eXpressive Internet Architecture

List of Figures

List of Tables

Part I
Theory and Principle

Chapter 1
Introduction

In this chapter, we first give an overview about the Internet, including its background, history and current research challenges. We then summarize the main contents of this book in the last section of this chapter. In particular, we present the background of the Internet and analyze the drawbacks to the traditional Internet design. Then, an overview of recent reported works on the future network is given. Finally, the book structure is enclosed at the end of this chapter.

1.1 Background of the Internet

The current Internet is a distributed interconnected system that supports a variety of heterogeneous networks and services [1]. After several decades of development, the Internet has become a critical infrastructure of our daily lives. In the technical sense, its achievements can be attributed to the *TCP/IP-based Internet* architecture, which was successfully designed and has been continuously improved. The history of the Internet can be divided into several stages with significant milestones. According to different concerns, scholars have given many different division results [2–4]. In general, the development of the Internet can be divided into four phases from its birth, shown in Fig. 1.1.

Phase One: Origin of the Internet. In 1969, the United States (US) *Advanced Research Projects Agency (ARPA)* invented a packet switching network, called *ARPANET* [5]. This technology was completely different from the circuit switching technology used in the traditional telecommunication networks. By the mid-1970s, researchers recognized that a single network was unable to satisfy the demands of heterogeneous content transmission. Then, the ARPA began to research on the interconnection of numerous networks. After that, the TCP/IP protocol was proposed and became the standard protocol of the ARPANET [6]. In general, the ARPANET is believed to be the origin of the Internet.

© Springer-Verlag Berlin Heidelberg 2016
H. Zhang et al., *Smart Collaborative Identifier Network*,
DOI 10.1007/978-3-662-49143-0_1

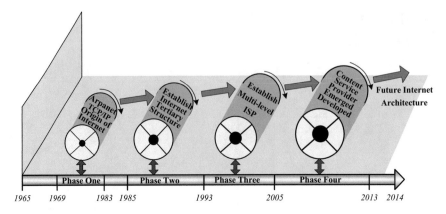

Fig. 1.1 Main development stages of the Internet

Phase Two: Three-level Structure of the Internet. By 1985, the *US National Science Foundation (NSF)* had built the National Science Foundation Network (NSFNET) [7] based on six large computing centers. The NSFNET mainly covered the universities and research institutes of the US. It was divided into three levels including the backbone network, regional network and local area network. This three-level structure gradually became the main part of the Internet. Afterwards, the NSF and other government agencies recognized the potential power of the Internet, and many organizations were encouraged to connect to the it. At that time, the Internet grew overwhelmingly in terms of scale and traffic. In addition, a series of related technologies and theories were also rapidly developed, such as the computer, communication and integrated circuit technologies.

Phase Three: Commercialization of the Internet. Up to 1993, in order to improve the communication quality of the Internet, the NSFNET was gradually divided into several *commercial backbones*, which were controlled and managed by different *Internet Service Providers (ISPs)* [8]. The ISPs managed and maintained the Internet by means of building communication lines and deploying network devices. They charged the users for the usage of IP addresses and link connections. This management model brought great economic benefits for the ISPs and supported the development of the Internet.

Phase Four: Application Proliferation and Mobile Services. In the twenty-first century, the Internet underwent two major evolutions. First, the Internet applications changed from traditional web browsing to content distribution and access [9]. Besides, many emerging network applications have appeared, such as social networks, cloud computing and online games, and so on. Second, with the rapid popularization of mobile terminals, the mobile Internet has undergone tremendous development. The demands of mobile services have also increased dramatically, such as mobile multimedia [10–12], vehicular services [13], location-based service (LBS) [14] and mobile payment [15, 16], and so on.

Therefore, the mobile Internet has gradually become an essential part of the Internet and boosted the reformation of the Internet industries.

Over the past decades, the Internet has achieved a huge success. By the end of 2014, the number of the Internet hosts has reached more than 1 billion. Nowadays, many researchers all over the world are still continually developing Internet technologies to build a more efficient and powerful future Internet.

1.2 Challenges for the Current Internet

The current Internet architecture was designed over 40 years ago for some primitive purposes, for example, data communications. Along with the development of the Internet, the scale of the network and the number of the network applications have increased dramatically. The workload and traffic of the Internet reach to an unforeseen level. In this context, the drawbacks of the Internet are magnified. Therefore, with the massive emergence of new user demands, the current Internet is facing many unprecedented challenges, such as security, mobility, scalability and resource utilization. Figure 1.2 shows several drawbacks and challenges of the current Internet.

Fig. 1.2 Drawbacks and challenges of the Internet

Security. The initial design of the Internet only aims at the *end-to-end data communication*, which supposes that this communication model is secure by default. Therefore, the security-related problems are not taken into account in the initial design. However, today, the Internet has become an open and public accessible network that anyone can access through different ways at anytime and anywhere. The current Internet is therefore vulnerable to malicious attacks, such as Denial of Service (DoS) attacks and virus programs.

Mobility. The original Internet merely considers the communication among fixed terminals. However, in recent years, the number of smart mobile terminals has increased dramatically. With the development of wireless technologies, the demands for the mobile Internet and services continue to increase. Therefore, mobility is another major challenge for the existing Internet. How to provide high-quality service in a high-speed mobile environment, i.e., the high-speed railway, has become a serious concern.

Scalability. Scalability is another serious concern to address. Specifically, the deficiency of the IPv4 address resources has become a barrier that obstructs the development of the Internet. Furthermore, the routing entries of the core network increase 1.3 times every 2 years. This directly leads to a low efficiency of routing entries. And the routers have to maintain a large number of routing entries. Moreover, the longest prefix-matching technology exacerbates the scalability problem [17, 18].

Resource Utilization. With the rising energy costs and alarm about global warming, there is a clear demand for developing an energy-efficient network as well as improving the power efficiency. According to the statistics, many network resources are wasted in the current Internet. The average link utilization in the backbone network is only around 30–40 % [19], and the utilization of the access network is even less than 10 % [20]. Therefore, it is essential to integrate the resource utilization into the design of the future Internet.

In order to alleviate the aforementioned challenges, researchers around the world have proposed many *evolutionary schemes*, which serve as ad hoc patches to the current Internet architecture. Moreover, *overlay technology* is also used to alleviate the current problems [21, 22]. The representative evolutionary schemes and technologies include the following:

- *Mobile IP (MIP)* solves the problem of mobility support [23];
- *IPsec* improves communication security [24];
- *Network Address Translation (NAT)* alleviates the shortage of IPv4 addresses [25];
- The *scalable routing system* ameliorates the problems of routing scalability [26].

Though the above solutions are able to address some challenges to a certain extent, they are all based on the original design of the Internet. These incremental patches have made the TCP/IP-based Internet architecture increasingly complicated without being able to completely remedy the problems. It largely restricts innovations and the deployment of novel applications. Meanwhile, the continuous deployment of the overlay networks and fixes makes the Internet architecture more

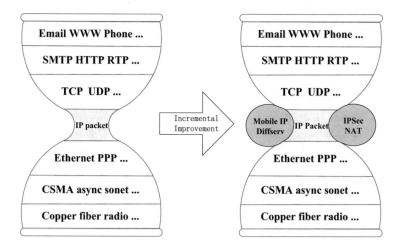

Fig. 1.3 Evolutionary transformation of the TCP/IP model

vulnerable to malicious attacks. To this end, the Internet model is transformed from a "*narrow waist*" to a "*prominent waist*" one, which is shown in Fig. 1.3.

The root cause of the aforementioned problems is that the existing Internet architecture is relatively "*static*" and "*rigid*." Under this architecture, few of the newly proposed solutions are able to break through the restrictions. It seems impossible for the Internet to satisfy the emerging demands of the information network, such as high speed, high efficiency, high throughput and pervasiveness. Therefore, research on the future network architecture has become a hot topic and a significant event in recent years. There has been increasing research effort on "clean slate" designs of the future Internet architecture [27–30].

1.3   Related Research on the Future Internet

Currently, many countries have launched numerous projects to support and develop research on the future Internet architectures and related technologies. In this book, instead of enumerating most of the national projects, we concentrate on introducing a few of them aiming at providing the readers with a basic understanding of the current state of this research field.

1.3.1   Research in the US

In 2005, the *Global Environment for Network Innovation (GENI)* [31] was launched in the US. It introduces the idea of virtualized slices. The purpose of GENI is to establish a large-scale testbed to evaluate the network architecture, applications and services. It provides researchers with a realistic environment to test clean-state designs. It also offers helpful guidance for the development of next-generation networks.

The first phase of GENI was started in October 2008. The objectives of the first phase include establishing a technical framework that supports various technologies and building end-to-end slices for cross-technologies. For the first objective, five control planes, including *DETER, PlanetLab, ProtoGENI, ORCA* and *ORBIT*, are selected through open competitive bidding. For the second objective, a variety of techniques are used to create a *virtual network topology* and *non-IP transmission technology*. These techniques include IP virtual private networks, Ethernet, MPLS and so on.

The second phase of GENI began in October 2009. Its main purpose is to improve the performance of integrated GENI prototype systems. Meanwhile, GENI launched two types of campus GENI program, which used *OpenFlow* technology and *WiMAX* technology, respectively.

The third phase was initiated in October 2010. Its main objective is to support the experimental infrastructure to achieve easy resource access, easy network connections and easy environmental configuration.

Currently, the main objectives of GENI include increasing the number of users of the GENI platform by providing better services and adding more nodes to expand the coverage of GENI.

In 2006, the US NSF also launched the "*Future Internet Design*" *(FIND) project* [32]. This project invested about $20 million to redesign the Internet to solve the existing problems. Its main purpose is to build a new generation network, including network architecture, theoretical principles and operating mechanisms.

In 2010, the US NSF further released the *Future Internet Architecture (FIA) program* [33]. FIA is the next phase of FIND. It aims to integrate the ideas of FIND into several overall architecture proposals. FIA sponsors four major projects, namely *Named Data Networking (NDN)* [34], *MobilityFirst* [35], *NEBULA* [36] and *XIA* [37].

NDN was originally proposed by Van Jacobson in 2009, named *Content-Centric Networking (CCN)*. In 2010, Lixia Zhang, and others, further improved the architecture of CCN and renamed it NDN. NDN transfers the concentration of existing networks from "where the content is" to "what concerns content users." By focusing on naming data's contents rather than their location, NDN assigns the first priority to the data. In this context, NDN has to address several technical problems including routing scalability, fast forwarding, network security and content privacy. This project also simultaneously develops the prototype system and applications for NDN protocols.

MobilityFirst is motivated by the current Internet, which is designed for interconnecting fixed hosts. This project aims to satisfy the demands for mass communication services of mobile devices. Some major challenges encountered by

MobilityFirst comprise the balance between mobility and scalability, delay tolerance, content caching and opportunistic data transmission. To deal with the above challenges, MobilityFirst introduces several new features including global name resolution, hop-by-hop transmission on the path, a caching-aware routing protocol and so on.

NEBULA intends to establish a cloud-computing network architecture. It proposes to build the core data network, which interconnects numerous data centers. NEBULA aims to design the future Internet embedded with security, availability, reliability, integration of data centers and so on. NEBULA also takes mobility into consideration by connecting the users to the nearest data center with a variety of access mechanisms.

XIA (eXpressive Internet Architecture) directly targets the security issues within its design. It aims to provide the intrinsic security by using self-certifying identifiers, the eXpressive IDentifier (XID). XIA also defines a set of building entities including the host, content, service and other potential entities. These entities communicate with each other using XID. By leveraging the XID, the communication is transferred into indirect content retrieval and no longer relies on particular hosts.

To continue the long-standing support for the research on the future Internet, the NSF launched the *FIA Next Phase (FIA-NP) project* in 2014. FIA-NP relies on and enhances the existing FIA designs. It aims to authenticate the previously funded FIA projects at a reasonable scale within a real network environment. FIA-NP sponsors three projects including the *MobilityFirst-NP Project*, the *NDN-NP Project* and the *XIA-NP Project* [38].

MobilityFirst-NP focuses on improving the existing designs to respond to recent technology changes and emerging service demands. Its research objects include mobile cloud services, context aware services, cellular-Internet convergence and content services.

NDN-NP consists of two research threads, i.e., Enterprise-level BAS/BMS and Device-side IoT. The Enterprise-level BAS/BMS concentrates on enterprise-level requirements for naming, device scalability, security and trust management. The Devie-side IoT focuses on creating embedded device implementations using NDN.

XIA-NP attaches great importance to the evaluation of network architectures, network environments, the design of control plane architecture and the application of XIA networks. Among the above research directions, the control plane architecture is the core direction.

Besides the above programs, NSF also launched the Computer and Network Systems (CNS) in 2012 to support research on computer systems and networking technologies. Moreover, US IGNITE was also launched in 2012 to foster the development of the next-generation network and accelerate US leadership in the adoption of software-defined networks. For the ease of presentation, Table 1.1 gives a brief list of the future Internet-related programs and organizations in the US.

Table 1.1 Future
Internet-related programs and
organizations in the US

Time	Program and organization
2005	GENI
2006	FIND
2010	FIA: NDN, MobilityFirst, NEBULA, XIA
2012	Computer and Network Systems (CNS)
2012	US IGNITE
2014	FIA-Next Phase: MobilityFirst-NP, NDN-NP, XIA-NP

1.3.2 EU's Research

In 2007, the EU launched the *Future Internet Research and Experimentation (FIRE) project* under the *EU's Seventh Framework Program (FP7)* [39]. This project plans to redesign the concept, protocol and architecture of the future Internet. It proposed a model of the future Internet and developed self-discipline communication methods without compatibility restrictions. The initial investment cost 40 million euros, which was used for research on the architecture, service mechanism and testbed platform of the future Internet. In 2010, the project entered into the second phase, in which 50 million euros was invested. The research scope of the second phase project was expanded, including the sensor network and cloud storage. In 2011, the project entered into the third phase, which concentrated on integrating the previous achievements. The fourth stage began in 2012, with 25 million euros invested. It focused on applications of the previous research accomplishments.

FIRE initially sponsored 15 sub-projects in total. These sub-projects can be divided into two categories. The first category focuses on modeling of future Internet. It aims to design the new architectures and key technologies of the future Internet. The other one concentrates on building the testbed to provide the experimental platform for network technologies such as a distributed and reconfigurable protocol structure, distributed services architecture, and embedded security technology. The funded projects are shown in Table 1.2.

In 2008, the Germans started the German Lab Project for Future Internet Studies, named G-LAB. The purpose of G-LAB is to drive the research on developing future Internet technologies. It aims to address the problem of the traditional Internet such as security, reliability and service quality. G-LAB consists of two major fields, i.e., the design and setup of experimental facilities and research studies on future Internet components. The first phase was launched in 2008 and lasted for 3 years. It targets the establishment of experimental facilities and studying the mechanisms and algorithms of the next generation network. The second phase was set up in 2009. Its main objective is to enhance the achievements of the first phase and expand the experimental platform. Additionally, Smart and Green Networks (SAGN) was also started in 2009 to promote the integration of the energy network and Internet.

Table 1.2 The projects funded by FIRE

Program type	Program name
Integrated project	Pan-Euro laboratory construction
	Open laboratory supporting future Internet research
Key project	Optimal network design and experiment
	Experimental cognitive distributed engine
	New communication network
	Smart antenna in a multimode wireless mesh network
	User-centric and seamless mobile mode of future Internet
	Nanometer data center
	Adaptable future network architecture, mechanism and experimental assessment
	Self-management cognitive future network principle
	Embedded end-to-end technology for next generation network
	Wireless sensor network testbed
Supplementary project	Infrastructure used for computing network architecture innovative research
Coordination and management project	Strategy working group
	Society-related network paradigm

In 2014, *Horizon 2020* was launched by the EU [40]. Horizon 2020 is the biggest EU research and innovation program with nearly 80 billion euros of funding available over 7 years. This project sponsors 22 research areas and nearly hundreds of research topics. Since the Internet has become the major basis for job creation and social progress, future Internet-related topics are included in Horizon 2020 under the area of ICT Research and Innovation. Future Internet-related topics include ten research topics, such as *Smart Networks and Novel Internet Architecture, Future Internet Research and Experimentation (FIRE+), Integrating Experiments and Facilities in FIRE+* and so on.

Among the above topics, Smart Networks and Novel Internet Architecture concentrates on the research on new Internet architectures and networking concepts that satisfy the up-to-date demands of information networks. The researches under this topic are expected to address novel issues such as information access and delivery, built-in security and privacy, generalized mobility and so on.

FIRE+ can be divided into three sub-topics, i.e., Research and Innovation Actions, Innovation Actions and Coordination and Support Actions. FIRE+ expects to achieve an experimental capability at the European level. Its final purposes are to build ten world-class experimental facilities and platforms and to develop common architectures across the various prototypes.

FIRE+ aims to support experiment-driven researches, which can be well served by the available infrastructures. This topic anticipates expanding the access to FIRE facilities and serving innovation-oriented experimentation, which were not previously supported by FIRE+. For ease of presentation, future-Internet-related research in the EU is listed in Table 1.3. The research can be referred to via [41].

Table 1.3 Future-Internet-related programs and organizations in the EU

Time	Program and organization
2007	Future Internet Research and Experimentation (FIRE)
2008	National Platform for Future Internet Studies (G-Lab)
2009	Smart and Green Networks (SAGN)
2012	FIRE (in Call 8)
2014	Horizon 2020, FIRE+
2015	5G Network Architecture

1.3.3 Research in China

China also attaches great importance to research on the next-generation information network. In recent years, the National 973 Program, the National 863 Program and the National Natural Science Foundation of China (NSFC) have sponsored many projects, some of which are listed as follows:

In 2006, the Ministry of Science and Technology (MOST) funded the 973 Project *"Fundamental Research on the Universal Network for Supporting Pervasive Services"* (2007–2011) [42–44] to support research on the architecture of the future information network. This project focused on the theory of a new information network, the integration of a heterogeneous network, the pervasive services of new network system as well as the credibility and mobility of the new network architecture.

In 2009, the MOST funded the 973 Project *"Basic Research on Architecture and Protocols of Next Generation Internet"* (2009–2013). This project studied the scalability, reliability, efficiency and manageability of a massive data transmission system through cross-domain routing. In the same year, the NSFC launched a key project called "Research on the Theory and Key Technology of the Future Internet System" (2009–2012).

In 2010, the MOST funded the 973 Project *"Model and Basic Theories of Information Services"* (2010–2014). The project took the expressivity and suitability of information services into account. In the same year, the National 863 Program launched "Research on Evolution Technology and System of Tri-networks Integration."

In 2011, the MOST funded the 973 Program *"Research on Key Mechanism of a Service-oriented Future Internet Architecture"* (2011–2015) [45] and "Research on the Architecture of the Reconfigurable Fundamental Communication Network" (2011–2015) [46].

In 2013, the MOST funded the National 973 Project *"Fundamental Research on Smart and Collaborative Networks"* (2013–2017) [47–49], which aimed to satisfy the demands for "high speed," "efficiency," "massiveness," and "ubiquity." This project focused on the theories of smart and cooperative networks, dynamic resource adaption and smart mapping mechanisms, and the game decision theory of complex network behaviors.

Besides these projects, the NSFC also launched several key projects including *"Research on the Architecture and Mechanism of the After-IP Network"* (2012–2016) [50] and *"Future Network System Architecture and Key Technologies"* (2013–2017) to research and explore the next-generation information network system. Table 1.4 gives a brief list of the future-Internet-related programs in China.

1.3.4 Research in Other Countries

Besides the above three territories, other countries are also making major contributions to the research on the future Internet.

In 2006, Japan launched the *AKARI* [51] (a small light in the dark pointing to the future) project. This project aims to design a new network architecture to eliminate the drawbacks of the existing Internet, and to complete the design of the future Internet. This project takes multiple issues into account such as energy consumption, natural disasters, health services and economic disparities. It proposes the following three principles as the core design principles for the future Internet.

Crystal synthesis: This is a thinning technology used in an integrated environment. It aims to keep the network architecture simple and plain when numerous functions modules are integrated. It follows the design principles of traditional Internet architecture.

Table 1.4 Future-Internet-related programs and organizations in China

Time	Program and project	Funds
2006	Fundamental Research on a Universal Network and Pervasive Service Internet Architecture	973
2009	Basic Research on the Architecture and Protocols of the Next-Generation Internet	973
2009	Research on the Theory and Key Technology of the Future Internet System	NSFC
2010	Model and Basic Theories of Information Services	973
2010	Research on Evolution Technology and the System of Tri-network Integration	863
2011	Research on the Key Mechanism of a Service-oriented Future Internet Architecture	973
2011	Research on the Architecture of the Reconfigurable Fundamental Communication Network	973
2012	An Information-centric Future Internet Architecture for Innovation	973
2012	Research on the Architecture and Mechanism of the After-IP Network	NSFC
2012	Future Network System Architecture and Key Technologies	NSFC
2013	Fundamental Research on Smart Collaborative Networks	973
2015	Future Universal Network Technologies and Applications	863

Table 1.5 Future-Internet-related programs and organizations in other countries

Time	Program and organization
2006	AKARI in Japan
2006	Future Internet Forum (FIF) in Korea
2009	Future Internet Research on a Sustainable Testbed (FIRST) in Korea
2010	Mobile Oriented Future Internet (MOFI) in Korea

Reality connection: This breaks the separation between network entities and real life, and it separates the physical and logical structures. Mutual authentication and traceability are also taken into account.

Sustainability and evolution: This means the future Internet is flexible enough to be ready for future changes.

Korea also has launched several projects for the future Internet. In 2006, the first *Future Internet Forum (FIF)* was started in Korea to promote research on the future Internet. In 2009, the *Future Internet Research on a Sustainable Testbed (FIRST)* was started. The primary purpose of this project is to explore the key technologies for the future Internet platform, including network virtualization and the control framework. This project also collaborated with the US GENI program. In 2010, *Mobile Oriented Future Internet (MOFI)* was also launched aiming at redesigning the Internet for the mobile-oriented environment. This project stipulated four design principles:

- the separation of the host ID and host location;
- ID-based communication and location-based routing;
- location query before data transmission;
- dynamic and distributed mapping between the identifier and location.

Table 1.5 gives a brief list of the future-Internet-related programs in other countries.

1.4 Candidate Technologies for Future Internet

With the indefatigable worldwide effort for the Internet, a promising research field has already come into being. Meanwhile, many popular technologies appear to be contributing to the future Internet architecture. Typically, four kinds of mainstream technologies are being widely researched currently: Information Centric Networking (ICN), the Software Defined Network (SDN), the Network Function Virtualization (NFV), and the Locator/Identifier Separation Protocol (LISP). These technologies are proposed to solve the problems of the current Internet from different viewpoints. Brief introductions and references about these technologies are described in the following subsections. More details about these technologies can be traced back to the related reports and research papers.

1.4.1 Locator/Identifier Separation Protocol (LISP)

The over-loading of Internet protocol (IP) addresses is an important reason for serious scalability problems. The *Locator/ID Separation Protocol (LISP)* [52] separates the IP address into two namespaces: *Endpoint Identifiers (EIDs)*, which are assigned to the end hosts, and *Routing Locators (RLOCs)*, which are assigned to the devices that make up the global routing system. The LISP need not change the end systems; just a little change of the Internet infrastructure can be appropriate. In the LISP, an EID is allocated to a host from an EID-prefix block associated with the edge network where the host is located. RLOCs are numbered from topologically aggregated blocks where the topology is defined by the connectivity of transit networks [53]. *Ingress tunnel routers (ITRs)/egress tunnel routers (ETRs)* are tunnel routers to encapsulate or de-capsulate packets. When an end host needs to contact another remote end host, it sends a normal IP packet encapsulated with the source EID and destination EID. When receiving a packet, the ITR encapsulates the packet with RLOCs and sends the packet out. Then, the packet will be routed to the ETR based on the RLOCs. The ETR strips the LISP header and forwards the packet to the destination host.

There are some representative LISP-alike schemes, such as *Six/One* [54], *Shim6* (Level 3 Shim for IPv6) [55], *MILSA* (Mobility and Multi-homing supporting Identifier Locator Split Architecture) [56], *GLI-Split* (Global Locator, Local Locator and Identifier Split) [57] and *HIP* (Host Identity Protocol) [58]. The comparison and analysis of these schemes are shown in Table 1.6.

1.4.2 Information Centric Networking (ICN)

To meet the users' increasing and changing demands, the communication mode should be changed from host-centric to information-centric. Therefore, *Information Centric Networking (ICN)* [9, 29] has been widely proposed and attracted increasing attention. ICN is based on *Named Data Objects (NDOs)*, such as web pages and videos. The ICN architecture includes in-network caching and multiparty communication through replication, thus facilitating the efficient and timely delivery of information to users. By introducing uniquely named data as a core

Table 1.6 Comparison and analysis of LISP-like schemes

	Scalability	Multi-home	Mobility	Identity mapping	Mapping location
Six/One	Support	Support	Support	Addressing rewriting	Network + host
Shim6	None	Support	None	Add the protocol layer	Host
MILSA	Support	Support	Support	Add the mapping layer	Network + host
GLI-Split	Support	Support	Support	Addressing rewriting	Network + host
HIP	None	Support	Support	Add the protocol layer	Host
LISP	Support	Support	None	Encapsulation	Network

Table 1.7 Features of ICN projects

	DONA	CCN	PSIRP	NetInf
Namespace	Flat	Hierarchical	Flat	Flat
Name-data integrity	Signature, PKI independent	Signature, external trust source	Signature, PKI independent	Signature or content hash, PKI independent
Human-readable	No	Yes	No	No
NDO granularity	Objects	Packets	Objects	Objects
Routing of NDO request	Name-based (via resolution handlers)	Name-based	NRS (rendezvous)	Hybrid NRS and name-based
Routing of NDO	Reverse request path or direct IP connection	Reverse request path using router state	Source routing using a Bloom filter	Reverse request path or direct IP connection
Transport	IP	Many including IP	IP/PSIRP	Many including IP
Evolution	No	NDN [63]	PURSUIT [64, 65]	SAIL [66], OpenNetInf [67]

Internet principle, ICN allows the Internet infrastructure to directly support this use. In addition, the data in ICN become independent from the location.

The ICN approach has been explored by a number of research projects, such as the Data-Oriented Network Architecture (DONA) [59], Content Centric Networking (CCN) [60], Publish-Subscribe Internet Routing Paradigm (PSIRP) [61] and Network of Information (NetInf) [62]. Based on existing research [9], the features of these projects are compared and summarized in Table 1.7.

1.4.3 Software-Defined Network (SDN)

The *Software-Defined Network (SDN)* is proposed to decouple the control logic from data planes, enabling a logically centralized and programmable control plane. Thus, the SDN can provide more efficient configuration and higher flexibility to accommodate innovative network designs.

SDN is currently attracting significant attention from both academia and industry [68]. A group of network operators created the Open Network Foundation [69] and promote SDN by standardizing the OpenFlow protocol [70]. On the academic side, the OpenFlow Network Research Center [71] has been created. In addition, the IETF and IRTF also make great efforts to standardize SDN technologies.

The OpenFlow comprises three key elements [72]: the switch, controller and interface protocol. Each switch consists of one or more flow tables and a group table, which perform packet lookups and forwarding. The switch communicates with the controller, and the controller manages the switch via the interface protocol. In other words, the controller can add, update and delete flow entries in flow tables.

Table 1.8 Programs and events about SDN

Time	Organization	Programs and events
2008	Stanford University, etc.	OpenFlow: Enabling Innovation in Campus Networks
2010	FP7 OFELIA	OpenFlow Testbed in the EU
2011	Open Networking Foundation (ONF)	SDN White Paper
2012	Open Networking Research Center (ONRC)	Protocol design, wireless and mobile applications of SDN
2012	ONF	SDN: The New Norm for Networks
2013	OPEN Daylight	Linux-based Open Source for SDN
2014	BII, ONF, ETSI, OPEN Daylight	Global SDN Technology Conference
2015	ONF, ETSI, China SDN Commission	Global Future Network and SDN Technology Conference

Before the advent of OpenFlow, there were already some programmable networking programs, such as Open Signaling [73], Active Networking [74], 4D Project [75], NETCONF [76] and ForCES [77]. Table 1.8 lists some significant SDN events.

1.4.4 Network Function Virtualization (NFV)

Network Functions Virtualization (NFV) [78, 79] is a newly proposed network architecture concept. It proposes to virtualize entire classes of network node functions into building blocks by evolving IT virtualization-related technologies. These virtual blocks may be flexibly connected or chained to create communication services. Table 1.9 lists some significant NFV events.

It is worth noting that NFV relies upon, but differs from, traditional virtualization techniques such as those used in IT enterprises. Instead of having custom hardware appliances for each network function, a virtualized network function may consist of one or more virtual machines running different software and processes, which are consolidated into industry standard high-volume servers, switches and storage, or even cloud computing infrastructure and data centers. The examples of NFV include virtualized load balancers, firewalls, intrusion detection devices and WAN accelerators [80].

Table 1.9 Programs and events related to NFV

Time	Organization	Programs and events
2014	ETSI	NFV virtualized basic architecture NFV software architecture NFV security research
2014	IETF, IRTF SDNRG	Data models for network functions virtualization, routing requirements Urban low-power and lossy networks

The research in [81] provides a simple but clear relation between NFV and SDN. NFV is complementary to SDN, but NFV can also be run independently. Figure 1.4 gives a brief summarization of the relations among NFV, SDN and other open innovations.

Although great potential value can be generated by combining the two concepts together, NFV can be implemented in the absence of SDN. It is worth noting that NFV also incorporates the idea of separation of the control and data plane and achieves good performance and compatibility by using existing deployments and maintenance procedures. Moreover, NFV also provides support for SDN and has the same objectives as the SDN to use commodity servers, switches and routers. The detailed comparisons are listed in Table 1.10.

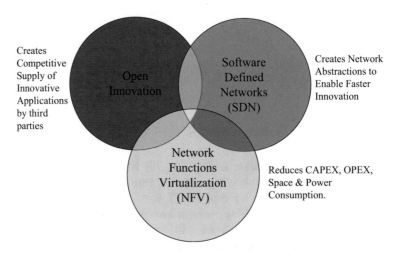

Fig. 1.4 Relations among NFV, SDN and other open innovations

Table 1.10 Comparison of NFV and SDN

Category	SDN	NFV
Aims	Separation of control and data, centralization of control and programmability of the network	Relocation of network functions from dedicated network equipment to generic servers
Target location	Campus, data center, cloud	Service provider network
Target devices	Commodity servers and switches	Commodity servers and switches
Initial applications	Cloud orchestration and networking	Routers, firewalls, gateways, CDN, WAN accelerators, SLA assurance
New protocols	OpenFlow	None yet
Formalization	ONF, ETSI, OPEN Daylight, BII	ETSI, IETF, IRTF, BII

1.5 About SINET

As mentioned above, the future Internet has become a hot research topic in the area of information communication technologies (ICT). However, the research on the future Internet is still a relatively fresh subject. Up to now, few of the current research outcomes have been able to provide an overall solution for the multiple drawbacks existing in the current Internet design. There are few books to introduce the theory and architecture of the future Internet. To fill this gap, this book is written as the first monograph concentrating on the overall design and theory of the smart future Internet.

This book not only summarizes the related research in the field of the future Internet, but also highlights the research achievements acquired by the *National Engineering Laboratory for Next Generation Internet Technologies* (abbreviated as *NGIT*) of China. The *NGIT* focuses on resolving the serious problems existing in the traditional Internet and makes efforts to establish theories of the future network architecture. In recent years, the *NGIT* has been funded by two *National 973 Programs* (the National Basic Research Program of China). During 2006 to 2011, the *NGIT* undertook the 973 Program project *Fundamental Research on the Universal Network for Supporting Pervasive Services*. In 2013, the *NGIT* received continued support from the 973 Program. The continued project is *Fundamental Research on Smart and Collaborative Network*. With the support of these funds, the *NGIT* proposed a novel future Internet architecture, which is named the *Smart Identifier NETwork (SINET)*.

This book integrates the theoretical research and relevant techniques of the above two 973 Program projects. With the efforts of a few decades, SINET has been designed to provide an *"immune system"* for defending the problems of the current Internet and aims to satisfy the multiple emerging demands including mobility, security, scalability and energy saving. SINET features autonomic identifier-based mappings and takes into account the network behaviors, smart service, resource adaption and component collaboration to build the future smart Internet. In the meantime, *NGIT* has developed many SINET-related devices to build the prototype and testbed, such as the Access Switching Router (ASR), General Switching Router (GSR), Identifier Mapping Server (IDMS), Multi-Connection Server, Multi-Connection User Terminal and so on.

1.6 Structure of This Book

This book is arranged into three parts: Part I Theory and Principle of SINET, Part II Key Technologies and Part III Applications and Development. They are further elaborated into 13 chapters in total. The content of each chapter is summarized in the following:

Part I Theory and Principle focuses on the foundations of SINET including topics related to the network reference model, basic principles and some performance evaluations. It comprises Chaps. 1–6.

Chapter 2 *Foundations of the Smart Identifier Network* gives an overview of the SINET by studying its fundamental principles and layered architecture. The basic reference model, four identifiers and three mappings models are introduced, respectively. Besides, seven main operation solutions are also discussed. Finally, some superiorities of SINET are analyzed in terms of the scalability improvement, mobility support, security enhancement, reliability guarantee and manageability. With knowledge of the foundations of SINET, the next chapter will introduce the details of the lower layer of the basic SINET model.

Chapter 3 *Principle of the Network Component Layer* includes the theory, functional design and key mechanisms of the Network Component Layer. It first introduces the contents of the Access IDentifier (AID) design, Routing Identifier (RID) design and identifier resolution mapping between AIDs and RIDs, which are basics in the Network Component Layer. Then, the routing and control management mechanisms in SINET are addressed in this chapter. The details of the upper layer of the SINET model follow in the next chapter.

Chapter 4 *Principle of the Pervasive Service Layer* concentrates on the theory, functional design and key mechanisms of the Pervasive Service Layer. The detailed design and model of the Pervasive Service Layer are presented with an emphasis on the Service IDentifier (SID), Connection IDentifier (CID) and the related resolution mapping schemes. Some operation mechanisms in the Pervasive Service Layer are also presented, including the service acquisition, service compatibility and connection management. In the next chapter, we will further develop the model with an advanced design.

Chapter 5 *Evolutions of* the *Smart Identifier Network* illustrates the advanced design of the SINET. A new layer named the Dynamic Resource Adaption Layer is proposed for dynamically adapting network resources upon service requirements. Smart functions have been designed into the Smart Pervasive Service Layer and Collaborative Network Component Layer to interact with the Dynamic Resource Adaption Layer. The new design proves that the SINET can solve many problems in resource utilization, information dissemination and energy efficiency. Furthermore, the SINET can support cloud computing and big data in a better way. Some specific analysis and experimental evaluations for the SINET principle are provided in the next chapter.

Chapter 6 *Analysis and Evaluations* presents the performance analysis of the SINET. Based on various experiments on the data set of campus network traffic, the performance of the SINET is simply analyzed in terms of mapping performance, routing scalability, security, service migration, SID resolution and so on. It shows that SINET outperforms the current Internet in various aspects to meet the emerging requirement of the future Internet.

Part II Key Technologies are devoted to the topics related to the main technologies used in the SINET including scalable routing technologies, an efficient mapping system, mobility management and security technologies described in Chaps. 7–10.

Chapter 7 *Scalable Routing Technologies in SINET* covers the scalable routing technologies of the SINET. Two kinds of routing approaches are explained in detail in this chapter, including path family-based routing and source identifier routing. In the next chapter, we will focus on another important part of the SINET: the mapping system.

Chapter 8 *Efficient Mapping System in the SINET* describes the efficient mapping in the SINET in detail. Two mapping systems are presented based on different data storage structures. The two systems are the DHT-based mapping system and the hierarchical mapping system. The performance demonstrates that the two mapping systems achieve good performance in terms of robustness, mobility and so on. Another important component of the SINET, the mobility management mechanism, is described in the next chapter.

Chapter 9 *Mobility Management in* the *SINET* consists of several solutions regarding mobility management in the SINET. We first examine several candidate schemes including network-based mobility management, the hierarchical mobility management scheme, mapping forwarding-based mobility management and the indirect-mapping-based mobility support mechanism. After the performance analysis, we compare each with its advantages and disadvantages. The proposed scheme outperforms every other scheme with its superior mobility management. Security is further considered in the next chapter.

Chapter 10 *Security Technologies in the SINET* addresses the security solutions employed in the SINET. Three mechanisms, namely the anomaly detection mechanism, the DDoS-preventing mechanism and the worm propagation-preventing mechanism, are proposed with the purpose of guaranteeing the security of the SINET. The simulated experimental results prove the high feasibility of the proposed mechanisms used in the Internet.

Part III Development and Applications draws special attention to SINET equipment development, SINET applications, transition solutions and future directions in Chaps. 11–13.

Chapter 11 *System Development of the SINET* is devoted to the design and development of the SINET system and its specific equipment. The design is represented in terms of the core function, topological structure and typical implementation. Meanwhile, how to develop the prototype system is also described in detail. Some tests and supporting applications are presented at the end of this chapter. The transition schemes are critical for the deployment on the basis of the current network's settings.

Chapter 12 *Transition Schemes to the SINET* discusses the transition scheme from the current network to SINET. A smooth transition scheme to solve the connectivity problem between the traditional network and the SINET is first presented, which is based on the ASR (access switching router). Additionally, a data-centric incrementally deployable transition scheme is proposed to support mobility or multi-homing. The superiority of the proposed schemes is verified via comprehensive experimental analysis. In the next chapter, we will list some typical applications of the SINET.

Chapter 13 *Applications* enumerates interesting topics and future research directions of the SINET. In addition, the significance of the future Internet, developing trends and hot research topics are discussed in this chapter.

References

1. Barab P (1964) On distributed communications networks. IEEE Trans Commun Syst 12(1):1–9
2. Leiner B, Cerf V, Clark D (2009) A brief history of the Internet. ACM SIGCOMM Comput Commun Rev 39(5):22–31
3. Xia R (2008) Progression of the Internet and the tendency for its future development XIA. Mech Manag Dev 23(6):172–173
4. Li L (1995) Computer network techniques and their progress. Telecommun Sci 11(12):51–55
5. Michael H (2015) ARPANET—the first Internet. http://www.livinginternet.com/i/ii_arpanet. htm. Accessed 1 June 2015
6. Yang P, Liu Y (2006) Anatomy of Internet architecture. Comput Sci 33(6):15–20
7. NSFNET (2015). http://www.nsfnet-legacy.org/. Accessed 1 June 2015
8. Living Internet (2015). NSFNET-National Science Foundation Network. http://www. livinginternet.com/i/ii_nsfnet.htm. Accessed 1 June 2015
9. Ahlgren B, Dannewitz C, Imbrenda C et al (2012) A survey of information-centric networking. IEEE Commun Mag 50(7):26–36
10. Xu C, Liu T, Guan J et al (2012) CMT-QA: quality-aware adaptive concurrent multipath data transfer in heterogeneous wireless networks. IEEE Trans Mob Comput 12(11):2193–2205
11. Colonnese S, Cuomo F, Melodia T (2013) An empirical model of multiview video coding efficiency for wireless multimedia sensor networks. IEEE Trans Multimed 15(8):1800–1814
12. Guan Z, Melodia T, Yuan D et al (2013) Jointly optimal rate control and relay selection for cooperative video streaming in wireless network. IEEE/ACM Trans Netw 21(4):1173–1186
13. Xu C, Zhao F, Guan J et al (2013) QoE-driven user-centric VoD services in urban multihomed P2P-based vehicular networks. IEEE Trans Veh Technol 62(5):2273–2289
14. Lien T, Lin Y, Shieh J et al (2013) A novel privacy preserving location-based service protocol with secret circular shift for K-NN search. IEEE Trans Inf Forensics Secur 8(6):863–873
15. Karnouskos S (2004) Mobile payment: a journey through existing procedures and standardization initiatives. IEEE Commun Surv Tutorials 6(4):44–66
16. Venkatesh J, Kumar DS (2012) Evaluation of mobile payment system and its service providers. Int J Multidiscip Res 2(4):118–123
17. Zhang W, Bi J, Wu J (2010) Scalability of Internet inter-domain routing. J Softw 22(1):84–100
18. Meyer D, Zhang L, Fall K et al (2015) Report from the IAB workshop on routing and addressing, RFC 4984. http://tools.ietf.org/html/rfc4984. Accessed 1 June 2015
19. Fisher W, Suchara M, Rexford J et al (2010) Greening backbone networks: reducing energy consumption by shutting off cables in bundled links. In: ACM SIGCOMM, 2010
20. Goma E, Canini M, Toledo A et al (2011) Insomnia in the access. In: ACM SIGCOMM, 2011
21. Mathieu B, Turong P, Peltier J (2012) Media networks. In: Mathieu B, Truong P, Peltier J et al (eds) Information-centric networking: current research activities and challenges. In: Moustafa H, Zeadally S (eds). CRC Press, pp 141–162
22. Louati W, Zeghlache D (2005) Network-based virtual personal overlay networks using programmable virtual routers. IEEE Commun Mag 43(8):86–94
23. Bhagwat P, Perkins C, Tripathi S et al (1996) Network layer mobility: an architecture and survey. IEEE Pers Commun 3(3):54–64
24. Oppliger R (1998) Security at the Internet layer. IEEE Comput 31(9):43–47
25. Egevang K (2015) The IP network address translation (NAT), RFC 1631. http://tools.ietf.org/ html/rfc1631. Accessed 1 June 2015
26. Zhang X, Liu Z, Zhao Y et al (2008) Scalable router. J Softw 19(2):1452–1464
27. Rexford J, Dovrolis C (2010) Future Internet architecture: clean-slate versus evolutionary research. Commun ACM 53(9):36–40
28. Pan J, Paul S, Jain R (2011) A survey of the research on future Internet architectures. IEEE Commun Mag 49(7):26–36

29. Xylomenos G, Ververidis C, Siris V et al (2014) A survey of information-centric networking research. IEEE Commun Surv Tutorials 16(2):1024–1049
30. Luo H, Zhang H, Zukerman M et al (2014) An incrementally deployable network architecture to support both data-centric and host-centric services. IEEE Netw 28(4):58–65
31. Global energy network institute (2015). http://www.geni.net/. Accessed 1 June 2015
32. Future internet design (2015). http://www.nets-find.net/. Accessed 1 June 2015
33. Future internet architecture (2015). http://www.nets-fia.net/. Accessed 1 June 2015
34. Zhang L, Estrin D, Jacobson V et al (2015) Named data networking (NDN) project. http://named-data.net/techreport/TR001ndn-proj.pdf. Accessed 1 June 2015
35. Mobility first future internet architecture project (2015). http://mobilityfirst.winlab.rutgers.edu. Accessed 1 June 2015
36. NEBULA project (2015). http://nebula.cis.upenn.edu. Accessed 1 June 2015
37. Expressive internet architecture project (2015). http://www.ce.cmu.edu/~xia. Accessed 1 June 2015
38. Dubrow A (2015) Moving towards a more robust, secure and agile internet. http://www.nsf.gov/news/, Press Release 14-065. Accessed 1 June 2015
39. FIRE (2015). http://cordis.europa.eu/fp7/ict/fire/overview_en.html. Accessed 1 June 2015
40. Horizon 2020 (2015). http://ec.europa.eu/programmes/horizon2020/en/area/ict-research-innovation. Accessed 1 June 2015
41. Digital Agenda for Europe (2015). http://ec.europa.eu/digital-agenda/en/future-internet. Accessed 1 June 2015
42. Zhang H, Su W (2007) Fundamental research on the architecture of new network—universal network and pervasive services. Acta Electronica Sinica 35(4):593–598
43. Dong P, Qin Y, Zhang H (2007) Research on universal network supporting pervasive services. Acta Electronica Sinica 35(4):599–606
44. Yang D, Zhou H, Zhang H (2007) Research on pervasive services based on universal network. Acta Electronica Sinica 35(4):607–613
45. Wu Q, Li Z, Zhou J et al (2014) SOFIA: towards service-oriented information centric networking. IEEE Netw 28(3):12–18
46. Lan J, Cheng D, Hu Y (2014) Research on reconfigurable information communication basal network architecture. J Commun 35(1):128–139
47. Zhang H, Luo H (2013) Fundamental research on theories of smart and cooperative networks. Acta Electronica Sinica 41(7):1249–1254
48. Gao S, Wang H, Wang K et al (2013) Research on cooperation mechanisms of smart network components. Acta Electronica Sinica 41(7):1261–1267
49. Su W, Chen J, Zhou H et al (2013) Research on the service mechanisms in smart and cooperative networks. Acta Electronica Sinica 41(7):1255–1260
50. Xie G, He P, Guan H et al (2011) PEARL: a programmable virtual router platform. IEEE Commun Mag 49(8):71–77
51. AKARI (2015). http://akari-project.com/. Accessed 1 June 2015
52. Fuller F, Meyer V, Lewis D (2013) Locator/ID Separation Protocol (LISP). IETF RFC 6830
53. Li X, Zhou H, Luo H et al (2014) HMS: a hierarchical mapping system for the locator/ID separation network. Comput Inform 32(6):1229–1255
54. Vogt C (2008) Six/one router: a scalable and backwards compatible solution for provider-independent addressing. ACM MobiArch workshop on mobility in the evolving internet architecture
55. Nordmark E, Bagnulo M (2009) Shim6: Level 3 multi-homing Shim protocol for IPv6. IETF RFC 5533
56. Pan J, Paul S, Jain R et al (2008) MILSA: a mobility and multi-homing supporting identifier locator split architecture for next generation Internet. IEEE global communication conference, New Orleans, USA
57. Menth M, Hartmann M, Kelin D (2010) Global locator, Local locator, and Identifier Split (GLI-Split). Technical Report 470, University of Wrzburg Institute of Computer Science
58. Moskowitz R, Nikander P (2006) Host identity protocol (HIP) architecture. IETF RFC 4423

59. Koponen T, Chawla M, Chun B et al (2007) A data-oriented (and Beyond) network architecture. SIGCOMM computer communications, October 2007
60. Jacobson V, Smetters D, James D. Thornton (2009) Networking named content. In: The 5th international conference on emerging networking experiments and technologies, New York, USA
61. Ain M, Trossen D, Nikander P et al (2009) D2.3–architecture definition, component descriptions, and requirements. PSIRP 7th FP EU-funded project
62. Ahlgren B (2010) Second NetInf architecture description. http://www.4ward-project.eu. Accessed 14 June 2015
63. Zhang L, Estrin D, Jacobson V et al (2010) Named Data Networking (NDN) project. Technical Report, 2010
64. Fotiou N, Nikander P, Trossen D, Polyzos G (2010) Developing information networking further. International ICST conference on broadband communications, networks, and systems (BROADNETS)
65. PURSUIT. http://www.fp7-pursuit.eu/PursuitWeb. Accessed 14 June 2015
66. Scalable and Adaptive Internet Solutions (SAIL). http://www.sail-project.eu. Accessed 14 June 2015
67. OpenNetInf. http://www.netinf.org/category/opennetinf. Accessed 14 June 2015
68. Nunes B, Mendonca M, Nguyen X et al (2014) A survey of software-defined networking: past, present, and future of programmable networks. IEEE Commun Surv Tutorials 16 (3):1617–1634
69. Open networking foundation. https://www.opennetworking.org/about. Accessed 14 June 2015
70. McKeown N, Anderson T, Balakrishnan H et al (2008) OpenFlow: enabling innovation in campus networks. ACM SIGCOMM Comput Commun Rev 38(2):69–74
71. Open Networking Research Center (ONRC). http://onrc.net. Accessed 14 June 2015
72. Open networking foundation (2012) OpenFlow Switch Specification Version 1.3.1 (Wire Protocol 0x04)
73. Campbell A, Katzela I, Miki K, Vicente J (1999) Open signaling for atm, internet and mobile networks. ACM SIGCOMM Comput Commun Rev 29(1):97–108
74. Tennenhouse D, Wetherall D (2002) Towards an active network architecture. ACM SIGCOMM Comput Commun Rev 37(5):81–94
75. Rexford J, Greenberg A, Hjalmtysson G et al (2004) Network-wide decision making: toward a wafer-thin control plane. ACM SIGCOMM Comput Commun Rev 37(5):81–97
76. Enns R (2006) NETCONF Configuration Protocol. RFC 4741
77. Doria A, Salim J, Haas R et al (2010) Forwarding and Control Element Separation (ForCES) Protocol Specification. RFC 5810
78. Noble S (2015) Network Function Virtualization or NFV Explained. http://wikibon.org/wiki/v/Network_Function_Virtualization_or_NFV_Explained. Accessed 14 June 2015
79. Chiosi M, Clarke D et al (2012) Network functions virtualization, White Paper, SDN and openflow world congress, October, 2012
80. ETSI Industry Specification Group (2014) Network functions virtualization: use cases. http://www.etsi.org/deliver/etsi_gs/NFV/001_099/001/01.01.01_60/gs_NFV001v010101p.pdf. Accessed June 2015
81. Pate P (2013). NFV and SDN: what's the difference? https://www.sdxcentral.com/articles/contributed/nfv-and-sdn-whats-the-difference/2013/03. Accessed June 2015

Chapter 2
Foundations of the Smart Identifier Network

In this chapter, we introduce the foundations of the SINET in order to allow the audience to understand the background and philosophy of the SINET. The two-layer-based primary reference model, three resolution mapping models and seven main operations are outlined as an overview of the SINET. The basic principles and workflow of the SINET architecture are the main topics of this chapter, through which the superiority of the SINET over the traditional Internet is indicated. Based on this chapter, the detailed principles of the SINET will be further given in Chaps. 3 and 4.

2.1 Problem Statement

The current Internet architecture was designed over 40 years ago only for some primitive purposes of data communications. Due to the limitations of technology at that time, the original design of the Internet did not consider many advanced requirements and functions. However, along with the massive emergence of new applications, the current internet is facing many unprecedented challenges, such as poor security, low mobility and high energy consumption. How to resolve these problems *comprehensively* and *effectively* in order to allow the Internet to meet the emerging demands of this community is a well-known major challenge.

We explore the root causes of the problems of the current Internet and conclude that it is what we call *triple bindings* that result in most of the existing Internet issues. These *triple bindings* make the Internet relatively *STATIC* and *RIGID*, which greatly restricts the development of the traditional Internet. The *triple bindings* refer to the resource/location binding (*r/l binding*), the user/network binding (*u/n binding*) and the control/data binding (*c/d binding*), respectively. Figure 2.1 illustrates the cause and effect related to the *triple bindings* and some of the problems in the current Internet.

© Springer-Verlag Berlin Heidelberg 2016   25
H. Zhang et al., *Smart Collaborative Identifier Network*,
DOI 10.1007/978-3-662-49143-0_2

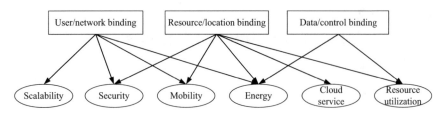

Fig. 2.1 The triple-binding and cased problems

Lately, many clean-slate Internet designs have been proposed to loosen or decouple the aforementioned bindings. However, most of the existing future Internet proposals only partially decouple the *triple bindings*. For example, CCN [1] and NDN [2] aim to decouple the service resources from their locations by using content-based addressing and in-path caching; LISP [3] and MobilityFirst [4] decouple user information from an access network by separating routing locators and user identifiers; SDN/OpenFlow [5] separates flow control from data transfer by using two different planes: the control plane and data plane.

It is worth noting that the three bindings are not entirely independent of each other. For example, mobility support issues are related to both the *u/n binding* and the *c/d binding*. And security problems may be affected by both the *r/l binding* and the *u/n binding*. Therefore, a *holistic approach* is needed to resolve the *triple binding*-related issues completely. The SINET is a collaborative future Internet architecture, which aims to provide an overall clean-slate design of the future Internet enabling the decoupling of the *triple bindings* completely.

Before introducing the Smart Identifier Network (SINET), we first mention the Identifier-based Universal Network (IUN) architecture, which is a foundation of the SINET. The IUN was proposed as the main achievement of the national 973 Program "Fundamental Research on the Universal Network for Supporting Pervasive Services" of the *NGIT*. Based on the IUN, the SINET was further supported with the fund of the second 973 Program "Fundamental Research on Smart Collaborative Network."

To help the readers better understand the design principles of the SINET, we define some of its basic technical terms. These technical terms will be consistently used in the following chapters.

The *COre Network (CON)* is in charge of transmitting the backbone data flow. The CON is usually operated and managed by the Internet Service Provider (ISP). In general, the CON can be divided into numerous different management domains. There are relatively small variations between these management domains. Additionally, an ISP can operate and manage multiple such management domains.

The *ACcess Network (ACN)* is a network between the CON edge interface and the user terminal equipment. The ACN may contain a single node or a fixed/mobile subnet (such as a campus network and an enterprise network). The user terminal equipment in the ACN is usually a source or destination node that generates the network data traffic.

The *Access IDentifier (AID)* is a unique identifier that denotes the identity of the terminal accessed to the network. When a terminal is connected to a network, it has at least one AID. Besides, the AID of the terminal will remain unchanged even if its location changes.

The *Routing IDentifier (RID)* is an identifier used for the working CON equipment. It is used for interconnecting different CON equipment and is used for the packet locating, addressing and forwarding in the CON.

The *Service IDentifier (SID)* is an abstract description of service resource information, which is used to uniquely represent a service resource datum (such as a video, a web page or a picture) or a service type (such as telephone or mail). In the SINET, the SID has a flat structure and does not change with the time and location of service providers.

The *Connection IDentifier (CID)* identifies the process of a user obtaining a service. Since the required service may be the combination of different services, such as a web containing multiple media, one CID may correspond to multiple network sources or destination nodes.

Resolution Mapping (RM) is used to generate the corresponding relationship between different identifiers, i.e., AID, RID, CID and SID. In detail, the SINET contains three kinds of RMs.

The *Access Switching Router (ASR)* is located at the edge of an ACN. It is responsible for the access of various fixed/mobile terminals and ad-hoc networks. Besides, the ASR is responsible for the authentication of terminal users and the mapping between AID and RID in the ACN as well as managing the user data forwarding in the CON.

The *General Switching Router (GSR)* is the backbone routing equipment in the CON, which is responsible for the unified routing and forwarding in the CON.

The *IDentifier Mapping Server (IDMS)* is used to manage and store the mapping rules and algorithms of the SINET. It is also responsible for disseminating the mapping rules and mapping processes to ASRs to achieve the resolution mappings.

The *Authentication Center (AC)* is used to perform the bidirectional authentication process when a node accesses the network. If the node passes the authentication, the packets from the nodes can be routed in the network. Otherwise, the packets will be discarded.

In the following chapters, we will elaborate how the SINET decouples the *triple bindings* of the current Internet and promotes a smart and collaborative Internet in both theory and practical applications.

2.2 Primary Reference Model

Over the past decades, the Internet and telecommunication networks both have obtained huge success, providing researchers with many useful and valuable suggestions. The research on the future Internet should absorb the advantages of the Internet as well as the telecommunication network [6, 7]. Before introducing the

SINET model, it is necessary to analyze and compare the essence of these two network architectures.

A traditional telecommunications network can be seen as a collection of terminal nodes, links and any intermediate nodes that are connected to maintain communications. The original telecommunication network was designed for *voice transmission*. This network architecture is composed of three parts, including the carrying network, service network and supporting network. The carrying network and supporting network constitute the network infrastructure and provide the basic network platform for services. The service network is usually used to provide a specific business, such as selecting a service, building connections and services.

Different from the traditional telecommunication network, the Internet was initially designed for *data transmission*. It is composed of a series of user access equipment, network switching/routing equipment and specific service servers. These network devices are connected through different media and together constitute the foundation of Internet communication. When users need to obtain the data through the Internet, the program of user terminals will first build connections with the corresponding servers. Then, the required data will be transmitted through the built end-to-end connections, such as the TCP and UDP connections. Finally, the data will be forwarded and routed according to the IP address of the corresponding data packet.

Based on the above analysis, we recognize that the above network architectures share several common features. The first one is that network equipment is interconnected to form a *network infrastructure*, in which all nodes are able to cooperate with each other through the corresponding mechanisms. The second is that the service requester and service provider are connected because of the service provision. They first build connection channels based on the network infrastructure before the data transmission. Then, the channel will be released after the termination of the service provision. Therefore, based on the above two features, we originally created the novel SINET architecture, which contains only two layers, the *Network Component Layer* and *Pervasive Service Layer*, by comparison with the *OSI reference model* [8] and *TCP/IP reference model* [9].

The Network Component Layer is in charge of accessing of all kinds of network terminals, routing/forwarding of data packets and providing a unified communication platform for network services such as data, voice and video. It corresponds to the *Physical Layer*, the *Data Link Layer* and the *Network Layer* in the traditional OSI reference model or the *Network Layer* and the *Network Layer* in the TCP/IP reference model. The Pervasive Service Layer is in charge of managing the service data resource and the unified control of network connections. It corresponds to the *Transport Layer*, the *Session Layer*, the *Presentation Layer* and the *Application Layer* in the traditional OSI reference model or the *Transport Layer* and the *Application Layer* in the TCP/IP reference model. The comparison and relationship of these three network architectures are shown in Fig. 2.2.

This two layer-based reference model absorbs the characteristic of the existing network architectures but removes their disadvantages. It simplifies the design of the network and improves the flexibility of the network design. Based on this

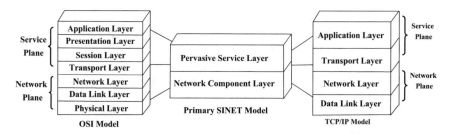

Fig. 2.2 The comparison of three network architectures

model, more detailed principles are derived from the current clean-slate future Internet designs [10–17] and are considered to overcome numerous drawbacks of the current Internet. Here, *eight main requirements* for the future Internet are listed as follows:

Information-/Data-Centric. While the current Internet was designed centering on hosts, its current major usage is data retrieval. Accordingly, there is an increasing consensus that the future Internet should be information-/data-centric. That is, content should be assigned the first priority and be processed independently.

Efficient Support for Mobility. With the rapid increase in the number of mobile devices, the future Internet architecture should efficiently support mobility.

Enhanced Security. The current Internet employs a default-on model and any host is able to send packets to a remote host, which makes the current Internet vulnerable to cyber attacks. Therefore, the future Internet should offer receivers the ability to control incoming traffic, especially to refuse unwanted traffic.

Enhanced Scalability. The future Internet should provide better routing scalability than the current Internet. The routing table size should be significantly less than that in the current Internet.

Efficient Support for Multi-homing. In multi-homing, a host (or network) is simultaneously attached to multiple networks. While the current Internet is cumbersome when supporting multi-homing since it causes serious routing scalability issues, the future Internet architecture is expected to support multi-homing efficiently.

Ease of Traffic Matrix Estimation. It is difficult to estimate traffic matrices in the current Internet. However, since traffic matrices are critical inputs to many aspects of network management such as traffic engineering and network provisioning, the future Internet should make it easy to precisely estimate traffic matrices in real time.

Deployability. Although we aim at a clean-slate design, the future Internet architecture should be deployed without incurring significant cost.

Encouraging Innovation. The future Internet architecture should allow each network to use its preferred network architecture and routing mechanism so that different network technologies can be simultaneously deployed and contested, thus encouraging innovation.

In the SINET, the Network Component Layer brings in the *Virtual Access Module (VAM)* and the *Virtual Backbone Module (VBM)*. The Pervasive Service Layer introduces the *Virtual Service Module (VSM)* and the *Virtual Connection Module (VCM)*. Meanwhile, four kinds of identifiers are introduced, i.e., the Service IDentifier (SID), Connection IDentifier (CID), Access IDentifier (AID) and Routing IDentifier (RID). To better cover the mentioned requirements, we establish the interaction between the two layers to connect four different function modules as shown in Fig. 2.3.

All the above modules are responsible for different network functions and building the basic functional units of the network communication.

The *VAM* carries out the AID-related functions, which are responsible for completing unified access of all kinds of network terminals such as the fixed networks, mobile networks and sensor networks. It is also responsible for providing data switching and forwarding in the ACN.

The *VBM* carries out the RID-related functions, which are responsible for switching, routing and forwarding of data packets, as well as maintaining the interconnection of network equipment.

The *VSM* carries out the SID-related mechanisms, which are responsible for the unified description, management of all kinds of network service resources and provision of a unified service interface for user application programs.

The *VCM* carries out the CID-related mechanisms, which are responsible for generating virtual access channels for specific network services according to the service demand and real-time network status. Meanwhile, it also determines the corresponding network service interface for data received from different connection channels.

Besides building the modules, how to organize them together to complete the communication efficiently and collaboratively is very important. The current

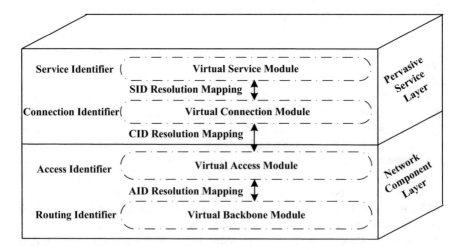

Fig. 2.3 Foundational reference model of the SINET

Internet adopts the logic interfaces to realize the connection between the upper-layer protocol entity and lower-layer protocol entity. Usually, this interface design is specific for a certain function and lack of flexibility. What is more, there is no unified description for the interactive information among different layers. With the rapid increase of the number of network services and the network facility complexity, this simple design cannot meet the requirements of the future Internet. In SINET [18–20], three kinds of resolution mappings are introduced to select the appropriate network routings to meet the requirements of providing different network services. The next section will illustrate the resolution mappings in detail.

2.3 Resolution Mappings

In the primary SINET reference model, the three different resolution mappings comprise AID Resolution Mapping (AID-RM), SID Resolution Mapping (SID-RM) and CID Resolution Mapping (CID-RM).

2.3.1 AID Resolution Mapping

AID-RM is used to generate the corresponding relationship among accessing (in ACN), switching and routing (in CON). This mapping is able to insulate the ACN from the CON and to protect the privacy information of the user terminal, including its identity and location.

Suppose the AID space set is $X = \left\{ x_i^{(j)} | i, j \in N \right\}$, where N is the natural number set, i represents a node, and j represents the jth AID of the node i. In the SINET, suppose that the number of access positions is Q and $X_q (X_q \subseteq X, 1 \le q \le Q)$ is the set of all AIDs in access position q. Similarly, suppose the RID space set is $Z = \{r_i | i \in N\}$ and $Z_q \subseteq Z$ represents the RID set used in access position q. Then, the *AID-RM* can be expressed as follows.

$$
\begin{bmatrix} Z_1(t) \\ \vdots \\ Z_q(t) \\ \vdots \\ Z_Q(t) \end{bmatrix} \triangleq \Omega \begin{bmatrix} X_1(t) \\ \vdots \\ Z_q(t) \\ \vdots \\ Z_Q(t) \end{bmatrix},
\tag{2.1}
$$

Here, $\Omega(\cdot)$ is the *AID-RM* function, which is used for completing the mapping transformation from the AID space to the RID space. Its inverse mapping $\Omega^{-1}(\cdot)$ will complete the mapping transformation from the RID space to AID space.

Additionally, Eq. 2.1 shows that Z_q and X_q are the functions of time t. The AID set X_q of all access nodes at the access location q will vary with the change of time t. After mapping $\Omega(\cdot)$, all the Z_q at access location q will also vary with the time t in the SINET.

AID-RM is an efficient design to separate the location information and identity information, and it can also solve the problems in the traditional network such as the routing scalability and node mobility. Besides, the design of the *AID-RM* successfully separates the access space and routing space. In the realization process of Eq. 2.1, we introduce the authentication mechanism to stringently check the mapping process. Consequently, the security of the CON is improved.

2.3.2 SID Resolution Mapping

SID-RM is used to generate the corresponding relationship between the network services and network connections to map the SIDs to CIDs.

In the SINET, the SID includes a set of kinds of service properties, such as $p_1, p_2, \ldots p_J$. For a service S, the SID is denoted as:

$$S \triangleq \phi\left[p_1^{(S)}, p_2^{(S)}, \ldots, p_J^{(S)}\right], \tag{2.2}$$

where $\phi(\cdot)$ denotes the SID generation operator; $p_j^{(s)}(1 \leq j \leq J)$ denotes the jth property of service S.

Suppose $S = \{s_i | i \in N\}$ is the SID space set, where N is the natural number set and i represents a node. We denote that the network service with a SID of $s_n(s_n \in S)$ is being obtained by node i as $s_i^n(s_i^n \in S)$. At the time t, all the services that node i is obtaining can be expressed as:

$$S_i(t) = \sum_n s_i^n d_i^n(t), \tag{2.3}$$

where $d_i^n(t)$ denotes whether node i is obtaining the network service $s_n(s_n \in S)$ at the time of t. The value of $d_i^n(t)$ is defined as:

$$d_i^n(t) = \begin{cases} 1, & \text{obtaining} \\ 0, & \text{not obtaining} \end{cases}. \tag{2.4}$$

Suppose $C = \{c_i | i \in N\}$ is the CID space set, where N is the natural number set. $C_m(t)$ denotes the CID set that is established for the on-going m-th service at time t. It is obvious that $C_m(t) \subseteq C(t)$.

Then, the process of SID resolution mapping can be expressed as follows,

$$
\begin{bmatrix} C_1(t) \\ \vdots \\ C_m(t) \\ \vdots \\ C_M(t) \end{bmatrix} \triangleq \Phi \begin{bmatrix} S_1(t) \\ \vdots \\ S_i(t) \\ \vdots \\ S_I(t) \end{bmatrix}, \tag{2.5}
$$

where I denotes the number of the nodes that are obtaining the service in the network, M represents the number of SIDs in the obtaining state, $\Phi(\cdot)$ achieves the transformation from the SID space to the CID space, and the inverse mapping $\Phi^{-1}(\cdot)$ achieves the transformation from the CID space to the corresponding SID space.

The design of the *SID-RM* solves the problem in the traditional Internet in which all the applications are tightly bound with specific network addresses and transport protocols. It is able to make a service independent from a specific network connection. Based on this design, network services are flexibly mapped to the specific CID. Then, the transport protocols and specific service nodes can be shielded, which provides an efficient service-oriented delivery process.

2.3.3 CID Resolution Mapping

CID-RM is used to generate the corresponding relationship between the source nodes and destination nodes, i.e., providing a network connection for an actual content transmission. *CID-RM* achieves the mapping from the CID space to AID space, which chooses the communication connections for network services. *CID-RM* is defined as:

$$
\begin{bmatrix} Y_1(t) \\ \vdots \\ Y_i(t) \\ \vdots \\ Y_I(t) \end{bmatrix} \triangleq \Psi \begin{bmatrix} C_1(t) \\ \vdots \\ C_m(t) \\ \vdots \\ C_M(t) \end{bmatrix}. \tag{2.6}
$$

where $\Psi(\cdot)$ represents the mapping function, which completes the transformation from CID to corresponding AID pairs during the service acquisition procedure. The inverse mapping function $\Psi^{-1}(\cdot)$ is used to map the corresponding AID pairs back to one connection CID during the process of acquiring network service. I denotes the number of nodes that are obtaining service; M is the total number of SIDs that are being obtained in the network; $Y_i(t)$ is a set of AID relation pairs when node i acquires network services at the time t, which can be expressed as follows:

$$Y_i(t) = \sum_{n=1}^{M} Y_i^n d_i^n(t).$$

$$= \sum_{n=1}^{M} \sum_{i,k,l} <x_i^{(j)}, x_k^{(l)}>_n d_i^n(t) \qquad (2.7)$$

Here, Y_i^n is a set of AID relation pairs used by node i to acquire the service s_n. $<x_i^{(j)}, x_k^{(l)}>_n$ denotes the existing connection channels between the AID $x_i^{(j)}$ of node i and the AID $x_k^{(l)}$ of node k when node i is acquiring service s_n. It is worth noting that $<x_i^{(j)}, x_k^{(i)}>_n$ may contain multiple sub-channels using different transport protocols.

CID-RM is a key design to connect the upper-layer services and lower-layer network resources. In the traditional Internet, the upper-layer services are all bound with the lower-layer network resource. This results in the problems of connection flexibility, application mobility and communication security, and so on. In the SINET, CID-RM is introduced to complete the mapping between connections and services, which has changed the process of traditional end-to-end connection control and is able to solve the aforementioned problems.

With the above three mappings, the network data stream generated for service $s_n (s_n \in S)$ will be delivered through corresponding nodes and links. The inverse mapping processes will be executed to determine which user application receives the service data when the data stream reaches the destination node. According to the preset optimal strategies, the mapping in each level is able to optimize and adjust the network behaviors dynamically based on the network status. To this end, the network will eventually establish appropriate connections to provide services for users, which greatly improves the network performance, such as the availability, security, reliability, controllability and manageability of the Internet. In a word, the different mapping functions $\Omega(\cdot), \Phi(\cdot)$ and $\Psi(\cdot)$ and their inverse mappings build a flexible control and management system for SINET.

2.4 Basic Operations

In SINET, all the network services are provided by three kinds of flexible mappings. In the following, we will illustrate the operations flow of SINET in detail, which is divided into seven basic procedures.

2.4.1   Node Access

As for a new Internet architecture, the intercommunication between the heterogeneous networks is an important metric of the network scalability. To this end, ACN
should support various kinds of network terminal nodes. Due to the different types
of networks, these nodes may have different AIDs with different forms and lengths.
To achieve the uniform access of various nodes with various types, a *unified AID
access control* is introduced in SINET for the access process. With this mechanism,
any node that requests to access the ACN needs to pass the node access control
process. Only for the trusted nodes will the data communications be allowed. If the
node passes the authentication, the ASR will be in charge of the mapping from AID
to RID and then provides the available resource for the following data routing and
forwarding in CON.

2.4.2   Service Registration

In the SINET, network services are managed uniformly according to the *SID
allocation*. Every service provider must *identify* its network services and *register*
them into the SID Management System (SMS). Then, these services will be looked
up and retrieved by users. During the registration, providers need to collect and
maintain the resource information of their own services as much as possible, such as
the service identifier, service description, service type, resource demand, resource
data and resource location. With the knowledge of the information, the provider
registers them into the SMS. After that, the SMS will disseminate the registration
information over the overall network by using the information exchange protocol
among different SMSs for the ease of the retrieval service.

2.4.3   Service Resolution

Generally speaking, the network node is not able to process the user descriptions of
the network service demands. Therefore, these verbal descriptions have to be
translated into machine language for the ease of processing. This translation process
is called the *service resolution*. In the SINET, the service resolution transforms the
keywords and *abstract* of verbal descriptions into the corresponding services stored
in the SMS. Then, the SMS sends back the essential service information, such as the
SID and service description, to user nodes according to the service registration and
other strategies. Because the SMS may store multiple services, which are matched
with the user's service demands, user nodes may receive multiple resolution results.
On this occasion, the final service needs to be manually chosen by the user or
automatically selected by the SMS.

Even though the service resolution is very important, it is not indispensable. This service resolution can be skipped in the following three situations:

- the application program in user node has been registered at the SMS;
- the information of the demanded network service is already known;
- the user node has cached the service information.

2.4.4   Connection Establishment

After the service resolution, the user has already got the SID of the demanded network service. Then, the user needs to establish the network connections to obtain the service. In the SINET, the user node first sends the service information to a Connection Identifier Management System (CMS) such as the SID. The CMS will generate the *corresponding CID* based on the mapping rules. Then, the CMS will transmit the AID of the service provider and the connection information, such as the transport protocol and congestion control, to the user, according to the preset strategies and current network state. After receiving the information from the CMS, the user node will send the connection request to the corresponding service provider according to the generated CID. When the service provider receives the request, it will complete the mapping from the CID to AID according to its network service and strategies such as the verification of the CID. Finally, a transmission channel of network data based on the acquired CID between user nodes and service nodes will be built.

2.4.5   Data Forwarding

During the acquisition of the network service, the mapping between the AID and RID is also necessary for the packets to pass through the CON. The packets are first routed to the ASR, which is at the edge of the ACN. The ASR will *map the AID* to the *RID* according to the service type, quality of service (QoS) and so on. The newly generated RID can be identified and routed by the devices of the CON. Then, the packets are routed in the CON to another ASR at the edge of the ACN. This ASR will map the RID of packets back into the AID. Eventually, the packets are routed and switched to the destination node. It is worth noting that the mapping between the AID and RID has four types: one to one, one to many, many to one and many to many. The four mapping types are determined by the service type, QoS and so on, providing support for the diversified routing.

2.4.6   Node Mobility

During the acquisition of the network service, the service may be interrupted because of the mobility of the user node. To prevent the service interruption, the node needs to complete the following mobile procedures. If the node does not move out of the ACN, the corresponding ASR, CON and correspondent node need not perform any operations. The nodes in the ACN communicate by the means of the flat routing method. If the node moves between different ACNs, the node will be connected to a new ASR. The newly connected ASR will generate a new AID for the node. Then, the ASR will register the mapping relationship at the AID mapping server, and the ASR will cooperate with the ASR of the correspondent node to optimize the subsequent packet transmission path.

2.4.7   Service Migration

Service migration, also called service movement, is a critical metric of *service universality* in the SINET. During the acquisition of service, the service node usually stops providing the service because of data movement, accidental failure and so on. After the user node detects the service interruption, it will adjust the mapping between the CID and AID to select another service node to obtain the service. Therefore, the network connection in the upper layer will remain the same. In this way, the influence of service migration on the upper layer application is avoided, and the service migration is therefore efficiently supported. Moreover, service migration also includes the situations that one of the two nodes in a communication link is changed to a third node or a third node is invited in the network service. For the above two situations, the CID of the network connection built for this service remains unchanged. Only the mapping relationship between the CID and AID needs to be changed.

2.5   Conclusion

This chapter introduces the initiation and fundamentals of the SINET. We first describe the foundational reference model of the SINET. Then, three kinds of resolution mappings are elaborated comprising the SID-RM, CID-RM and AID-RM. Based on the fundamental theory, we further introduce the basic operations of the SINET in terms of node access, service registration, service resolution, connection establishment, data forwarding, node mobility and service migration. All these elements constitute the operational foundations of the SINET. In the following chapters, we will further introduce the principle and technologies of the SINET.

References

1. Jacobson V, Smetters D, James D, Thornton (2009) Networking named content. The 5th international conference on emerging networking experiments and technologies, New York, USA
2. Zhang L, Estrin D, Jacobson V et al (2010) Named data networking (NDN) project. Technical report
3. Fuller F, Meyer V, Lewis D (2013) Locator/ID separation protocol (LISP). IETF RFC 6830
4. Mobility first future internet architecture project (2015). http://mobilityfirst.winlab.rutgers.edu. Accessed 1 June 2015
5. McKeown N, Anderson T, Balakrishnan H et al (2008) OpenFlow: enabling innovation in campus networks. ACM SIGCOMM Comput Commun Rev 38(2):69–74
6. Modarressi A, Mohan S (2000) Control and management in next-generation networks: challenges and opportunities. IEEE Commun Mag 38(10):94–102
7. Clark D (2002) A new vision for network architecture. http://www.isi.edu/know-plane/DOCS/DDC_knowledgePlane_3.pdf
8. Zimmermann H (1980) OSI reference model-the OSI model of architecture for open systems interconnection. IEEE Trans Commun 28(4):425–432
9. Feit S (1998) TCP/IP. McGraw-Hill School Education Group
10. NSFNET (2015). http://www.nsfnet-legacy.org. Accessed 3 June 2015
11. Future internet architecture (2015). http://www.nets-fia.net. Accessed 3 June 2015
12. Global energy network institute (2015). http://www.geni.net. Accessed 3 June 2015
13. Mobility first future internet architecture project (2015). http://mobilityfirst.winlab.rutgers.edu. Accessed 3 June 2015
14. NEBULA project (2015). http://nebula.cis.upenn.edu. Accessed 3 June 2015
15. Expressive internet architecture project (2015). http://www.ce.cmu.edu/~xia. Accessed 3 June 2015
16. FIRE (2015). http://cordis.europa.eu/fp7/ict/fire/overview_en.html. Accessed 3 June 2015
17. AKARI (2015). http://akari-project.com. Accessed 3 June 2015
18. Zhang H, Luo H (2013) Fundamental research on theories of smart and cooperative networks. Acta Electronica Sinica 41(7):1249–1254
19. Gao S, Wang H, Wang K et al (2013) Research on cooperation mechanisms of smart network components. Acta Electronica Sinica 41(7):1261–1267
20. Su W, Chen J, Zhou H et al (2013) Research on the service mechanisms in smart and cooperative networks. Acta Electronica Sinica 41(7):1255–1260

Chapter 3
Principle of Network Component Layer

In this chapter, we will focus on the theory, functional design and key mechanisms of the Network Component Layer. After a brief literature review, we introduce the AID design, RID design and the identifier resolution mapping between AID and RID, which are the basics of the Network Component Layer. Then, the routing mechanisms and some control and managing schemes are both presented in this chapter. The design aims to ensure that the network will have better performance in terms of security, scalability, mobility and so on. After reading this chapter, the readers are supposed to have a deeper understanding of the Network Component Layer in the SINET, especially the routing schemes using AID and RID, and the mutual mapping mechanism.

3.1 Related Work

To solve the problems arising from an irregular and unequal-length AID, there are two ways to achieve the interconnection between nodes in the traditional Internet. One way is to use traditional routing protocols (such as RIP [1] and OSPF [2, 3]) to diffuse the AID among all the ASRs in the ACN to obtain all the access node routing. Another way is to use the distributed hash algorithm (DHT) to preprocess the AID and adopt a new plane routing mechanism to achieve interoperability among access nodes. Although the deployment of traditional routing protocols is relatively simple, massive manual configuration work is required to achieve full interoperability. It is required to add a route entry for every access node. Cumbersome configuration will easily lead to errors. Manual configuration also makes it difficult to meet the demands of node mobility. Also, all routing nodes should learn and respond to all routing changes, which will result in low efficiency, long convergence time and other issues. In addition, traditional routing protocols currently only support IPv4, IPv6 and other specific AIDs and will be inefficient in adapting to AIDs with variable or unequal length. Therefore, in solving the problem

© Springer-Verlag Berlin Heidelberg 2016
H. Zhang et al., *Smart Collaborative Identifier Network*,
DOI 10.1007/978-3-662-49143-0_3

of different structure identifiers in hybrid routing, especially under the condition of an irregular identifier, more researchers are focusing on the study of a planarization route. Caesar et al. [4] have proposed a method that uses the plane host identifier for routing. In this method, the path can be built directly based on the network host identifier, avoiding the traditional routing protocols' reliance on the network layer protocol information for the location. Ray et al. [5] also provide a method of using a DHT-based address resolution in a mass Ethernet to solve the radio bandwidth occupation problem arising from address resolution and improve the expansibility. Kim et al. [6] describe a method applying a DHT algorithm to the mass Ethernet for packet switching. The implementation of plane address structure ensures the plug and play function in large enterprise network. However, this method only focuses on the data exchange in link layer packets and does not provide any effective routing forwarding mechanisms.

What is more, in the traditional Internet, as various nodes use the same address-based protocol, user nodes can initiate any packets toward other nodes, and the packet content is not limited to the network. As a consequence, there is huge safety risk in such architecture, and it is hard to achieve sustainable steady and effective work. Next, since the IP address in the traditional Internet has dual semantics, which represents the terminal identity and carries the location information at the same time. It is easy for hidden nodes in the network to follow and steal the data of the target node, which brings a huge safety threat to nodes and their privacy. In addition, the ambiguity of the IP address makes it difficult for the Internet to follow the routing scalability rule, which is also called Rekhter's law [7], where the address is allocated according to topology or topology is deployed according to address, which results in poor routing scalability. In the traditional Internet, packets are forwarded according to the IP address. The establishment of a connection between nodes and networks is also based on the IP address. When a node changes its location, the unchanged IP address will lead to unreachable transmission problems, while the changed IP address will lead to unrecognized connection problems. Such a contradiction is so irreconcilable that it will cause an insurmountable obstacle to providing better mobility support. For this reason, many identifier-based resolution mechanisms have been proposed, such as LISP [8, 9], SHIM6 [10, 11], HRA [12, 13], Hidra [14], SILMS [15–17], DHT-MAP [18], 4I [19] and ISMA [20, 21].

3.2 Identifiers and Mapping

In the previous chapter, we have presented a basic introduction of SINET's foundations. As mentioned before, the primary reference model of SINET consists of two layers, which are the Network Component Layer and Pervasive Service Layer. The Network Component Layer is responsible for unified access for terminals and global routing for packets; the Pervasive Service Layer is responsible for providing uniform services for requesters.

Specifically, the Network Component Layer is designed by using two virtual modules, named the *Virtual Access Module* and *Virtual Backbone Module*. Two kinds of identifiers and a mapping between them are embedded in these two modules. As shown in Fig. 3.1, AID is used in the Virtual Access Module, and RID is used in the Virtual Backbone Module, respectively. The interactions between the two modules are operated through the *Access Identifier Resolution Mapping (AID-RM)* between the AID and RID. In the following section, we will give a more detailed description of the design of the Network Component Layer.

The *Virtual Access Module* introduces the AID to represent the identity of the access terminal. Each terminal will be allocated one or more globally unique AIDs. Various networks and terminals can access the network in a uniform way, such as the fixed network, mobile network, sensor networks in the traditional Internet and access terminals in telecommunication networks. Therefore, it not only provides a solution for supporting various heterogeneous networks, but also extends the scope and variety of services.

The *Virtual Backbone Module* introduces the RID for generalizing the switching routing and addressing. When data packets enter the backbone network, the source AID is replaced with its internal RID in the ASR for data forwarding. When the packets reach the ASR at the corresponding end, the RID will be mapped back to the original AID.

Between these two modules, identifier resolution mapping is used to complete the mapping between the AID and RID. In this way, the AID will remain unchanged to maintain the connection even though the access networks and terminals change their positions. Besides, it can enhance the security. For example, it is difficult for hackers to analyze the user identity even if they capture the packet information during the data transmitting process, which therefore protects the privacy of users.

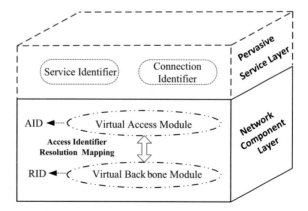

Fig. 3.1 Model of the network component layer in SINET

3.2.1 AID Formulation

Suppose X is a set of AIDs, which can be represented as an infinite set $X = \{X_1, X_2, \ldots, X_i, \ldots\}$. Each element represents a type of terminal with its own characteristics, which are different from other elements.

The AID of terminal n with a type i, which is denoted as $X_i(n)$, can be expressed by Eq. 3.1:

$$X_i(n) \triangleq \phi_i[a_1(n), a_2(n), \ldots, a_k(n)], \tag{3.1}$$

where $k \in \{1, 2, \ldots\}$, $a_k(n)$ means the k-th property of terminal n, and $\phi_i(\cdot)$ is the AID-generating function, which is dependent on the type i.

The presentation of all the elements in x can be deduced from Eq. 3.1, as shown in Eq. 3.2:

$$\begin{bmatrix} X_1(n) \\ X_2(n) \\ \cdot \\ \cdot \\ \cdot \\ X_i(n) \end{bmatrix} \triangleq \Phi \begin{bmatrix} a_{11}(n), a_{12}(n), \cdots, a_{1k}(n) \\ a_{21}(n), a_{22}(n), \cdots, a_{2k}(n) \\ \cdot \\ \cdot \\ \cdot \\ a_{i1}(n), a_{i2}(n), \cdots, a_{ik}(n) \end{bmatrix}_{i \times k}, \tag{3.2}$$

where the number of properties of set X_i is related to terminal type i, and Φ is the general description of $\phi_i(\cdot)$.

Based on the above descriptions, *the structure of AID* is not limited as *a plat form* or *a hierarchical form*. The comparison of two kinds of AID structures is shown in Table 3.1.

It is worth noting that the *IPv4/IPv6 format address* can be used as an AID as well. Although the AID can be with a flat or hierarchical structure, the compatibility with the current Internet is the most important feature. Therefore, in the SINET system implementation, the AID supports a structure similar to the IPv4 or IPv6 address. Based on this consideration, the AID has a length of 32 or 128 bits, which provides a good transitional solution from the current Internet to the SINET.

Table 3.1 Comparison of two kinds of AID structures

	Flat structure	Hierarchical structure
Advantages	• Easily allocated • Easy to use the hash value of the public key • Self-validation in asymmetric cryptographic algorithms [25]	• Easily aggregated • Small routing/mapping table • Easily compatible with IPv4/IPv6 addresses
Disadvantages	• Difficult to aggregate • A big routing/mapping table • With poor compatibility with IPv4/IPv6 addresses	• Fixed allocation way • Hard to construct the AID using an asymmetric cryptographic algorithm

Although the IPv4/IPv6 address can be divided into two parts, the network address and host address, this kind of AID can also be processed as a whole string with a flat structure by ignoring the hierarchical information.

In the detailed implementation, each ACN is allocated a series of AIDs with the same prefix. Each access terminal is assigned one or more globally unique AIDs. Notably, once the IP address is used as an AID in the SINET, some fields in the IP packet header must be reinterpreted to meet the requirements of the AID. Besides, only some key nodes in the CON, such as the ASR and IDMS, can perceive and process those fields. Terminals and other routing nodes do not need to perceive these special fields, where the AID can be processed as a common IP address.

If the AID is formatted as an IPv6 address with a length of 128 bits, the special attribute can utilize some bits from the reserved fields in the IPv6 address. If the AID is formatted as an IPv4 address with a length of 32 bits, the special attribute can select one bit from the IPv4 address except the first byte as its flag bit. This setting can avoid the conflict with the unicast/multicast flag of the IPv4 address. For example, there are two special attributes: the *identifier attribute* and *mobility attribute*. The identifier attribute is used to distinguish the AID from the RID. It facilitates the ASR in the CON in detecting the validity of packets for better safety assurance. The mobility attribute is used to distinguish a mobile terminal from a fixed terminal. It can help to decrease the information interaction among ASRs and IDMS and provide better support for the node mobility.

Although the AID can be expressed by a hierarchical structure, there are still some differences from the traditional Internet in the routing process. In the SINET, the AID represents the identity of the node, and it will remain unchanged when the node changes its position. Therefore, once a node leaves its original position and accesses another ACN, the routing entries of this AID cannot be aggregated. Therefore, the ACN must maintain the position of each access node. No matter how the routes change in the ACN, these changes cannot affect the stability of the global routing system in the CON according to the resolution mapping between the AID and RID.

3.2.2   RID Formulation

Suppose Z is the set of the RID, which can be represented as an infinite set $Z = \{z_1, z_2, \ldots z_m, \ldots\}$ ($m \in \{1, 2, \ldots\}$). Different from the set of the AID, Z is used for better addressing and forwarding in the CON.

In detail, Z can be divided into many subsets: $Z_1, \ldots, Z_n$, which represent different exchange routing types (like unicast, multicast or anycast.). This should satisfy the following relations $Z_i \subset Z, Z_i \neq \emptyset, \bigcup_{i=1}^{n} Z_i = Z, Z_i \cap Z_j = \emptyset$ ($i, j = 1, 2, \ldots, n; i \neq j$). Z_i can be expressed as Eq. 3.3:

$$Z_i = \{z | \varphi_i[p_1(z), p_2(z), \ldots, p_k(z)]\}, \tag{3.3}$$

where $p_k(z)$, $k \in \{1, 2, \ldots\}$ represents the k_{th} characteristic of element z, and $\varphi_i(\bullet)$ is the RID-generating function in set Z_i.

RID can be designed to be similar to the IPv4 or IPv6 address with a length of 32 bits or 128 bits to allow the SINET to maintain good compatibility with the current Internet. This hierarchical RID structure can assure the aggregation of the global routing table in the CON. It is worth noting that the address space of the RID is different from that of the AID. Using an IPv4/IPv6 address as both an RID and an AID at the same time is not allowed. With this design, some protocols such as HLP [22] can be used to enhance the scalability of the routing system in the CON.

In terms of routing in the CON, the SINET introduces four key functional entities: *IDMS, AC, ASR* and *GSR*. IDMS is primarily used to complete the management and maintenance of <AID, RID> mapping pairs. AC is responsible for recording the authentication information of the AID. When a node intends to access to the CON, it has to be authenticated before further actions, and then it is allowed to be assigned the <AID, RID> mapping information. The ASR is the connection point between the ACN and CON, which is responsible for the separation and mapping of the AID and RID; it thus plays a very important role in the SINET. GSR is responsible for the packet routing in the CON. Each GSR can be allocated by one or multiple RIDs without any knowledge of the AID information.

Each ASR in the CON is equipped with two types of interface: *the access network interface* and *core network interface*. The access network interface is an ACN-oriented interface, which is used to provide the network access capabilities for users. The core network interface is a CON-oriented interface for connecting other entities in the CON, such as the IDMS, AC and GSR. In order to communicate with other nodes, each access network interface and core network interface can be assigned an AID and an RID, respectively. Their relation is maintained by the resolution mapping in the IDMS.

3.2.3   Resolution Mapping Between AID and RID

As mentioned above, the AID resolution mapping process is significant for the routing in the SINET because of its necessity. There are many different resolution-mapping methods, including the one to one, the one to many, the many to one and the many to many. These mapping methods are all responsible for realizing the resolution mapping between the AID to RID [23]. It can also further combine the functions of the Virtual Access Module and Virtual Backbone Module together. Equations 3.4–3.7 describe four kinds of mapping principle adopted in the SINET.

One-to-One Mapping. Equation 3.4 represents a resolution mapping from one AID to one RID as follows:

$$\begin{cases} z_T(i)_{RID} \triangleq \Omega(x_{PQ}(i)_{AID}) \\ x_{PQ}(i)_{AID} \triangleq \Omega^{-1}(z_T(i)_{RID}) \end{cases},\tag{3.4}$$

where $z_T(i)_{RID}$ represents the RID in the routing process T of type i, $x_{PQ}(i)_{AID}$ represents the AID of terminal F in access position Q with type i, $\Omega(\cdot)$ is the mapping function to complete the mapping process from AID to RID, and its inverse mapping $\Omega^{-1}(\cdot)$ will do the reverse mapping. This resolution mapping can provide better support of safety and mobility.

One-to-Many Mapping. Similarly, one-to-many mapping can be formulated as Eq. 3.5:

$$\begin{cases} (z_1(i)_{RID}, z_2(i)_{RID}, \ldots, z_T(i)_{RID}) \triangleq \Omega(x_{PQ}(i)_{AID}) \\ x_{PQ}(i)_{AID} \triangleq \Omega^{-1}(z_1(i)_{RID}, z_2(i)_{RID}, \ldots, z_T(i)_{RID}) \end{cases}.\tag{3.5}$$

It represents a resolution mapping from one AID to multiple RIDs. Packets can be transmitted through multiple paths, reflecting the reliability design concept.

Many-to-One Mapping. The many-to-one mapping principle can be formulated as Eq. 3.6:

$$\begin{cases} z_T(i)_{RID} \triangleq \Omega(x_{11}(i)_{AID}, x_{22}(i)_{AID}, \ldots, x_{PQ}(i)_{AID}) \\ (x_{11}(i)_{AID}, x_{22}(i)_{AID}, \ldots, x_{PQ}(i)_{AID}) \triangleq \Omega^{-1}(z_T(x)_{RID}) \end{cases}.\tag{3.6}$$

It represents a resolution mapping from multiple AIDs to one RID to construct multicast paths for multiple terminals, theoretically proving that the identifier separation resolution-mapping algorithm can effectively support multicast.

Many-to-Many Mapping. The many-to-many mapping principle can be formulated as Eq. 3.7:

$$\begin{cases} (z_1(i)_{RID}, \ldots, z_T(i)_{RID}) \triangleq \Omega(x_{P1}(i)_{AID}, \ldots, x_{PQ}(i)_{AID}) \\ (x_{P1}(i)_{AID}, \ldots, x_{PQ}(i)_{AID}) \triangleq \Omega^{-1}(z_1(i)_{RID}, \ldots, z_T(i)_{RID}) \end{cases}.\tag{3.7}$$

It represents a resolution mapping from multiple AIDs to multiple RIDs. When a terminal owns multiple AIDs, it can access to the network through different access points and can be mapped to multiple RIDs. This design can be used to support the multi-homing naturally.

Taking Eqs. 3.4–3.7 into consideration, the general definition of AID resolution mapping can be concluded as Eq. 3.8:

$$\begin{bmatrix} z_1(i)_{RID} \\ z_2(i)_{RID} \\ \vdots \\ z_T(i)_{RID} \end{bmatrix} \triangleq \Omega \begin{bmatrix} x_{11}(i)_{AID}, x_{12}(i)_{AID}, \ldots, x_{1Q}(i)_{AID} \\ x_{21}(i)_{AID}, x_{22}(i)_{AID}, \ldots, x_{2Q}(i)_{AID} \\ \vdots \\ x_{P1}(i)_{AID}, x_{P2}(i)_{AID}, \ldots, x_{PQ}(i)_{AID} \end{bmatrix}_{P \times Q},\tag{3.8}$$

where each row in the right matrix represents different access positions of the same terminal, and each column represents different terminals that share the same access position.

Based on the AID resolution mapping defined in Eq. 3.8, we can conclude that the mapping mechanism can effectively solve the problems in terms of mobility, security and other issues. It can also support multiple routing schemes, i.e., multi-path transmission, multicast and multi-homing routing. Following this approach, not only the transmission efficiency can be improved, but also the error recovery capabilities can be enhanced through the introduction of redundant paths. Figure 3.2 illustrates the AID resolution-mapping mechanism in the SINET.

The principle of AID resolution mapping provides *a concrete foundation for the transition between the AID namespace and RID namespace*. This mapping can be achieved through various technologies such as *the identifier encapsulation and the identifier replacement*.

Identifier encapsulation means that the ASR at the source end (the data-transmitting side) will encapsulate one data packet header and insert the header into the original packet, where the source and destination are represented by the AID. In the new encapsulated header, the source and destination fields are filled with the RID, corresponding to the original AID. The ASR at the destination end (the data-receiving side) will remove this encapsulated header from data packets received before forwarding to the destination node in the ACN.

Identifier replacement means that the ASR at the source side will replace the source/destination AID in the packet header with the correspondent RIDs. The ASR at the destination end will conduct the reverse process before retransmitting the data packet to the destination node. Table 3.2 gives a comparison of identifier encapsulation and identifier replacement.

As shown in Table 3.2, the solutions of identifier encapsulation and replacement have their own advantages and disadvantages, respectively. The identifier replacement scheme will not bring an additional traffic burden and has natural superiority in the security and privacy assurance aspect. Although this method may bring some additional overhead for the ASR, it does not affect the performance very much because of the high processing rate of the current high performance hardware. Therefore, the SINET adopts the identifier replacement method to forward data packets in its implementation.

Fig. 3.2 AID resolution-mapping principle

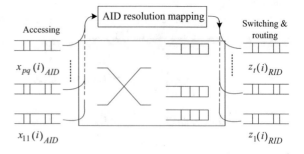

Table 3.2 Comparison of identifier encapsulation and identifier replacement

	Identifier encapsulation	Identifier replacement
Advantages	1. Lower the burden on the ASR and the mapping server in the CON 2. No need to do the one-to-one mapping between the AID and RID	1. No extra traffic or repartition issues 2. Can protect users' privacy and data security 3. Can provide effective support of node mobility
Disadvantages	1. Bring extra traffic and introduce the packet repartition issues 2. Lack of the safety assurance 3. Hard to support node mobility	1. Need an additional mechanisms to complete the mapping from the RID to AID 2. Add some overhead to the ASR

After determining the design of the AID, RID and their mapping methods, the overall design of the Network Component Layer in the SINET is completed. In the following, we will detail the routing principles in the SINET.

3.3   Mapping-Based Routing

3.3.1   Routing in the ACN

In the SINET, the separation design of the ACN and CON greatly enhances the scalability of routing. Since one single ASR has limited access capacity, if all nodes in the ACN directly access to the network through the ASR at the edge of the CON, the ASR will be overloaded [24]. In order to provide stable node access, we need to deploy more ASRs at the edge of the CON.

SINET allows end users to organize their own network and have further access to the CON through the ASR at the edge within a certain range. This also satisfies the development demands of the current Local Area Network (LAN) and enterprise network. Besides, the separation design of the ACN and CON is able to uniformly provide the access function, which can improve the network access utilization rate as well as the scalability in both the ACN and CON.

Compared with the traditional Internet, the biggest difference of the ACN in the SINET is that it easily supports access networks with different schemes. As for various access networks, the AID allocated to them may vary in length. In addition, unlike the traditional Internet, the IP address inside the network shares the same prefix; the SINET allows AIDs belonging to the same ACN to have almost no common rules. In this way, the prefix-based matching principle may no longer be valid. Although the host-based routing mechanism can realize the intercommunication among nodes in the ACN, under this circumstance, each node should store and maintain all host-related routing entries. This is a burden on management and will make it even harder to keep the synchronization among nodes. Therefore, flat format processing will be a better choice for the AID in the SINET.

In summary, the routing principles in the ACN can be concluded as follows:

Support Different Kinds of Terminals. Heterogeneous interconnection is the trend of future node communication. In the SINET, such interconnection is mainly achieved inside the ACN. There are many network nodes with different types and different medias in the ACN (such as those in the Ethernet, WiFi networks and wireless sensor networks). These nodes usually have different propagation vectors and different transport protocols. In the design of the ACN in the SINET, we must take all these factors into account. The routing equipment inside the ACN must have the ability to adapt to the interface and protocol of access nodes of different types.

Support Variable Length of AID. Due to the difference in access network type and node number, the length of the AID may vary with the number of network nodes. Actually, there is no need to assign a fixed-length AID. As for the nodes in individual or household sensor networks with small size, it is not suitable to assign an AID with a long length because of the limitations of storage and process resources. The length of the AID needs to be long enough to distinguish different nodes; thus, an AID with a length of 16 bits is perfect to satisfy the requirement. However, for those nodes in large-scale networks, such as campus or enterprise LAN, an AID with the length of 32 bits or longer is better. In fact, an AID with different lengths can represent different access spaces. This design allows the ACN in the SINET to have better scalability than those with fixed length.

Support Internal Mobility in the CAN. In the ACN, network nodes are allowed to change the access point within a certain range and can automatically adjust themselves to ensure the service continuity. The design of supporting internal mobile solutions should be neither too complex nor too expensive to avoid affecting the normal operation of the network. Based on the above descriptions, an irregular AID and unequal-length AID make the access identifier in the SINET show flattening characteristics. Combined with the network link state and the distributed hash routing, the SINET can solve many of the current problems, such as achieving quick access, exact forwarding and node mobility.

In order to make all packets routed in a unified lookup match, the SINET introduces the *preference_purpose_router* option to define the packet's destination router. Data packets can be precisely forwarded to the preset preferred router and then arrive at the final destination node. After receiving the data packets, routers in the ACN will first check whether the *preference_purpose_router* option is set. If so, the preset router generates the hash routing. Otherwise, it will generate the hash routing based on the destination node.

Figure 3.3 shows the communication process between terminal x and y. Assume that terminal x wants to send packets to terminal y; its access location information is stored in router R2, and the access location information of terminal y is stored in router R5. The packet forwarding process is as follows: (1) After receiving the packets from x to y, router R2 will carry out the hash routing based on the AID of y. According to the hash routing table, R2 will forward the packets to the next-hop node R3. (2) Then, router R3 will do a similar hash routing to find the next-hop router R6. (3) When packets arrive on router R6, R6 will find the next-hop node. In this step, R6 will find the next hop router R5 according to the relationship between the

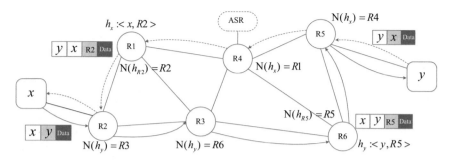

Fig. 3.3 Packet forwarding between access terminals in the ACN

node and access point of terminal y. Then, it will set R5 as the *preference_pur-pose_router* and forward the packet to R5. (4) After receiving the packets, router R5 will remove the *preference_purpose_router* option, search terminal y in its neighbor list and then forward the packet to y. If y needs to send packets back to x, the packet forwarding process is similar. The packets will be routed to router R1 according to the hash value of x's AID and then set the *preference_purpose_router* option to be R2 before forwarding to router R2. The packets will eventually arrive at x.

In reality, if x communicates with the external network terminal (assuming z) through the ACN, the packets should go through the ASR, which connects the two ACNs. They will also be routed according to the AID of z. When the packets arrive at the correspondent location management router, the router will set the *prefer-ence_purpose_router* option to be the border ASR since there is no information about z. When the ASR receives the packets, it will check its own neighbor list, mapping relationship and other information to decide how to deal with the packets next.

In the ACN, all the ASRs achieve the routing entry matching query based on the AID consistency. This mechanism can effectively achieve the unified access of the AID with different types/lengths and plane routing. Due to this distributed storage method, the corresponding relationship of the access nodes and access location is distributed to each router through the ACN to lower the burden on one single router. It can also support the node mobility inside the ACN.

3.3.2 Routing in the CON

In the CON, the ASR is responsible for maintaining the <AID, RID> mapping caching information, including *local user caching entries and correspondent node caching entries*. Local user mapping caching entries are related to nodes that are accessing and being authenticated currently. Such an entry will be valid for a long time until the node leaves or the network disconnects. Each local user mapping caching entry can be regarded as a part of the mapping information database. The correspondent node-mapping caching entries are related to nodes that have recently communicated with local nodes. Such an entry has a shorter valid time. When it is unused over a period of time, the mapping entry will be removed.

Packet processing and forwarding are the key features of the ASR in the CON. The ASR should first classify the packets and then process them according to their categories. There are three key attributes in packet classifications: the receiving interface, source identifier and destination identifier. There are two kinds of receiving interface: the interface on the ACN side and interface on the CON side, respectively, are expressed as the access network interface and core network interface. There are four kinds of source/destination identifier, respectively, namely the local AID, corresponding AID, local RID and corresponding RID. Under normal circumstances, the sources/destination identifier attributes are assigned by the packet sender. Considering that they may be intercepted by network attackers who conceal nodes' identities to conduct illegal behaviors, it is necessary to check the legality of these identifiers together with the attribute of the receiving interface. In local user mapping caching entries, we can find the AIDs/RIDs that are already allocated to local terminals. While in the correspondent node-mapping caching entries, we can find the AIDs/RIDs that are already allocated to the corresponding terminals.

Based on the combination of these three key attributes, the legality check can be achieved. Packets are not allowed to be mapped, routed or forwarded unless they have passed the legality check. Table 3.3 gives all these combinations, where "*" represents an arbitrary value.

In the legality check process, the first principle is that the source and destination identifiers at the access network interface are both AIDs. For the core network interface, they are both RIDs. This is the strict separation of the ACN from the CON in the SINET. Nodes in the ACN can only be allowed to send packets with the AID as their source and destination address, while nodes (except the ASR) in the CON can only be allowed to send packets with the RID as their source and destination address. Therefore, in Table 3.3, nos. 3, 4, 6, 7, 8, 9, 11 and 12 are all illegal. These packets will be regarded as fraudulent (or malicious attacks) and should be discarded directly.

As for no. 5, it corresponds to the situation in which an external terminal has ever communicated with the local terminal; its AID can be found in the correspondent node-mapping caching entries. However, when it moves to the local ACN, its packets should be dropped until it passes the authentication process by the current network.

As for no. 10, it corresponds to the situation in which a packet from a local terminal is arriving at the core network interface; it will be abandoned if the packet is forged or the CON is looped.

The remained four legal situations are:

The Line 1 is for the communication among local terminals, which can be directly forwarded through the access network interface.

The Line 2 is for the communication from the local terminal to external terminal; the packets should be forwarded through the core network interface after identifier mapping;

Table 3.3 Combination determination table

No.	Receiver interface attribute	Source identifier attribute	Destination identifier attribute	Legality
1	Access network interface	Local AID	Local AID	Legal
2	Access network interface	Local AID	Corresponding AID	Legal
3	Access network interface	Local AID	Local RID	Illegal
4	Access network interface	Local AID	Corresponding RID	Illegal
5	Access network interface	Corresponding AID	*	Illegal
6	Access network interface	Local RID	*	Illegal
7	Access network interface	Corresponding RID	*	Illegal
8	Core network interface	Local AID	*	Illegal
9	Core network interface	Corresponding AID	*	Illegal
10	Core network interface	Local RID	*	Illegal
11	Core network interface	Corresponding RID	Local AID	Illegal
12	Core network interface	Corresponding RID	Corresponding AID	Illegal
13	Core network interface	Corresponding RID	Local RID	Legal
14	Core network interface	Corresponding RID	Corresponding RID	Legal

Line 13 represents the packet from the external terminal; it should be forwarded through the access network interface after identifier mapping.

Line 14 represents the packet transmitted in the CON and will pass by the ASR in the CON; it should be forwarded through the core network interface. On this occasion, the ASR only plays a role as a common router.

Figure 3.4 shows the detailed procedure of how protocol stacks on the ASR will deal with the packets arriving at the CON. The procedure bases on the combination determination process are demonstrated in Table 3.3. In Fig. 3.4, there are two additional situations. One is for the packets from the ASR in the CON to itself; the packet will be transmitted to the upper layer in the protocol stack. The other is for the packet transmitted to the former local node, which has already moved. On this occasion, the packet should operate destination identifier mapping to the newest RID before being forwarded.

The whole process fully takes all possible packet categories into account. In the SINET, the "different category, different treatment" scheme is also the critical rule of the packet processing procedure on the ASR in the CON. Furthermore, this procedure will be improved along with future deeper research, such as new proposed commands or newly generated packet types, and so on.

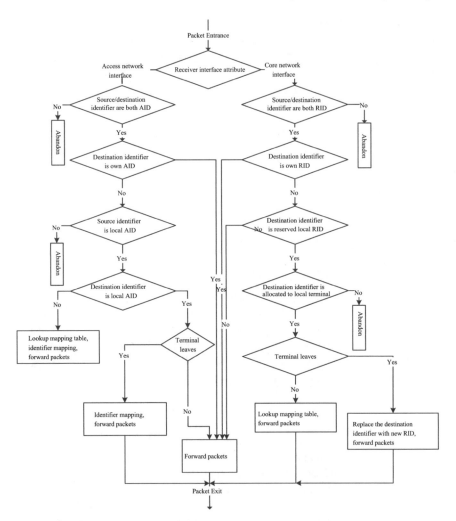

Fig. 3.4 Packets processing of ASR in CON

3.3.3 Flow of Packet Routing

Taking one-to-one identifier resolution mapping as an example, Fig. 3.5 shows the basic data exchange process in the SINET.

In Fig. 3.5, the communication is initiated by terminal A to terminal B; (1) when A gets into the coverage of the ASR in the CON, namely ASR_A, it will first receive the routing notification message from ASR_A. (2) A sends an access request to ASR_A. (3) ASR_A contacts the authentication center to do an authentication query of A. (4) If the authentication is passed, ASR_A will allocate an RID to A and then establish an <AID, RID> mapping information entry and save it to the local user

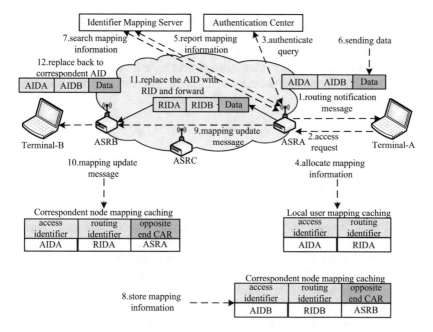

Fig. 3.5 Basic data exchange process of SINET

mapping caching. (5) ASR$_A$ will also report the mapping information to the identifier mapping server. (6) When A sends data to B, the packet source is the AID of A and the destination is the AID of B. (7) When ASR$_A$ receives the first packet from A to B, it will query the identifier mapping server to get the mapping information of B. (8) After obtaining the mapping information, ASR$_A$ will store mapping information in its correspondent node caching entries. (9) ASR$_A$ will obtain the RID of ASR$_B$ and send a mapping update message to ASR$_B$ to update the mapping information of A. (10) After ASR$_B$ has received a mapping update message, it will store the mapping information together with ASR$_A$ into its correspondent node caching entries. (11) ASR$_A$ will replace the source and destination AID of the packet with the correspondent RID and forward the packet. (12) After ASR$_B$ has received the packet, it will replace the source and destination RID back to the correspondent AID and forward it to B. In the end, B will receive the data from A. Among these steps, step 9 is to assist the ASR in completing AID mapping and solve the not carrying mapping information problem in the identifier replacement way.

In the ACN, terminals are only allowed to send packets whose source and destination are both AID or the packets will be directly discarded by the ASR. Therefore, malicious terminals are unable to attack the terminal in the CON who adopt the RID to communicate. What is more, the source and destination AID in packets are replaced to the RID in the CON. Any possible monitor cannot get the identity information, which better prevents passive attacks against terminals. RIDs, which represent the node location, are used in the CON; both communicators can only know each other's AID, which protects the location privacy of both sides. Moreover, there is no need for terminals to send information to an identifier mapping server. The identifier in the management layer is totally invisible to access nodes, which can further guarantee the safety of equipment on the management level.

3.4   Routing Control and Management

3.4.1   Control/Data Separation

In the SINET, there are many terminals with various access techniques. Therefore, AIDs have various types and lengths in the ACN. The CON is divided into the control plane and the data plane. The data plane is responsible for completing user packet forwarding, while the control plane is in charge of the access authentication, mapping management, routing calculation and other functions.

As shown in Fig. 3.6, the data plane is composed of a General Switching Router (GSR), while the control plane comprises the identifier mapping system, security authentication system and routing control system. Among them, the identifier mapping system is responsible for maintaining mapping information of all AIDs and RIDs to obtain access to the CON. The security authentication system is responsible for recording and maintaining authentication information for all registered terminals. The node authentication procedure can be achieved through the network control protocol described in Sect. 3.1.

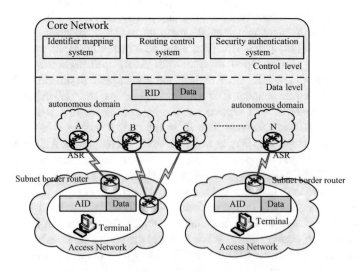

Fig. 3.6 Topology schematic diagram of the SINET

3.4.2   Routing Identifier Management

In the design of the SINET, the RID is the one of the most important elements in the CON. Without the RID, data packets cannot be forwarded inside the CON. To provide better forwarding performance, the ASR should be configured with the necessary RIDs. The allocation and management of RIDs are very important in CON routing. According to the current routing mechanisms, an unreasonable plan and random use of RIDs will result in routing entry expansion in the CON. Therefore, to avoid chaos in using RIDs, deploying an RID management server in the CON is required to schedule the resource forwarding procedure. On the other hand, the server can update, merge and reallocate the RID to reduce the size of the routing table in the CON in a timely manner. Furthermore, to achieve the one-to-many, many-to-one and many-to-many mapping between the AID and RID, different RID blocks need to be allocated different privileges, priorities and weights. For different RIDs, we can also adopt different routing calculation algorithms so that different RIDs can correspond to different physical paths.

3.4.3   Mapping Caching Management

During the mapping process, the ASR is responsible for the allocation, maintenance and management of the RID corresponding to the AID. It is also responsible for the mapping registration to the identifier mapping server and the query of the corre-spondent terminal's mapping relationship. But to make full use of network resources and accelerate the query rate, the ASR needs to cache the latest and recent <AID, RID>. The setting of the mapping cache will be conducive to reducing the bandwidth overhead of registration and query at the ASR. It also helps to lower the waiting time of packets in the mapping queue. Moreover, the ASR also needs to clear the cached mapping entries that have not been used for a long time. This time interval for updating the caches is very critical to the performance. The big mapping cache expired time will lead to large storage space demand on the ASR and may also affect the accuracy of the mapping relationship retrieval. Therefore, the SINET should make the tradeoff among network overhead, storage space, caching time and mapping accuracy.

3.4.4   Mobility Management

According to the principle of AID and RID mapping, when a node changes its location, it will get a new mapping relationship from new ASR. But in the meantime, the correspondent node cannot detect this variation, and it will forward packets according to the pristine mapping relationship. To minimize the packet loss, the original ASR needs to obtain the current mapping relationship. This process needs the participation of the identifier mapping server. When a node accesses the new ASR, the new mapping relationship will be registered to the identifier mapping server. To prevent continuous fast switching among multiple ASRs, the original ASR should delay removing the former mapping information while storing the new one. An update of the correspondent ASR is also needed to avoid redundant routing. For the identifier mapping system, supporting node mobility is a complex process. It requires carrying through research on the caching mechanism, especially the caching of the original mapping relationship, update mechanism and setting of the caching expired time.

3.5 Conclusion

This chapter presents the detailed design and working mechanisms of the Network Component Layer in the SINET, especially the routing principle and mapping management mechanisms.

The SINET divides the network into the ACN and CON. Different network identifiers are used separately in the ACN and CON, and they are bridged by a mapping management system. Nodes in the ACN cannot directly exchange data with nodes inside the CON, which brings many advantages. For example, nodes in the CON will not be easily attacked by nodes inside the ACN; hence, the security will be greatly improved. Besides, the separation design of ACN and CON can protect the node identity and node location. In other words, it is difficult to obtain the identity of source nodes and destination nodes through capturing packets in the CON, and it is difficult to learn the location of correspondent nodes in the ACN. In this way, the threats from the ambiguity of the IP address can be basically solved. The separation of identity information and location information can also avoid the scalability problem of network scale and the node mobility issues in the CON, which provides a basis for establishing a reliable routing architecture.

This chapter demonstrates that the Network Component Layer has many features different from the traditional Internet. For example, the introduction of the AID provides unified access to terminals/networks of different types. The separation design of the ACN/CON and the mapping from the AID to RID are able to better support mobility and improve the security and scalability of the SINET.

References

1. Malkin G (1998) RIP Version 2, RFC 2453. http://www.ietf.org/rfc/rfc2453.txt
2. Moy J (1998) OSPF Version 2, RFC 2328. http://www.ietf.org/rfc/rfc2328.txt
3. Colton R, Ferguson D, Moy J et al (2008) OSPF for IPv6, RFC 5340. https://www.rfc-editor. org/rfc/rfc5340.txt

4. Caesar M, Condie T, Kannan J et al (2006) ROFL: Routing on Flat Labels. ACM SIGCOMM Comput Commun Rev 36(4):363–374
5. Ray S, Guerin RA, Sofia R (2007) A distributed hash table based address resolution scheme for large-scale Ethernet networks. In: IEEE international conference on communications
6. Kim C, Caesar M, Rexford J (2008) Floodless in SEATTLE: a scalable Ethernet architecture for large enterprises. In: ACM SIGCOMM 2008
7. Meyer D, Zhang L, Fall K (2007) Report from the IAB workshop on routing and addressing, RFC 4984. http://www.ietf.org/rfc/rfc4984.txt
8. Mathy L, Iannone L, Bonaventure O (2008) LISP-DHT: towards a DHT to map identifiers onto locators. IETF Internet Draft, draft-mathy-lisp-dht-00. Accessed Feb 2008
9. Farinacci D, Fuller V, Oran D et al (2012) Locator/ID separation protocol (LISP). IETF Internet Draft, draft-ietf-lisp-22. Accessed Feb 2012
10. Nordmark E, Bagnulo M (2009) Shim6: level 3 multihoming shim protocol for IPv6, RFC 5533. http://www.ietf.org/rfc/rfc5533.txt
11. García-Martínez A, Bagnulo M, Van Beijnum I (2010) The Shim6 architecture for IPv6 multihoming. IEEE Commun. Mag 48(9):152–157
12. Xu X, Guo D (2008) Hierarchical routing architecture (HRA). In: the 4th Euro-NGI conference on next generation internetworks
13. Pan J, Jain R, Paul S et al (2009) Enhanced MILSA architecture for naming, addressing, routing and security issues in the next generation internet. In: IEEE International Conference on Communications
14. Wang N, Ma HL, Cheng DN et al (2009) Hidra: a hierarchical inter-domain routing architecture. Chin J Comput 32(3):377–390
15. Hou J, Liu Y, Gong Z (2009) SILMS: a scalable and secure identifier-to-locator mapping service system design for future Internet. In: Second international workshop on computer science and engineering
16. Abid N, Bertin P, Bonnin J (2011) SANA: a service-aware naming architecture for future Internet. In: 2011 IEEE Jordan conference on applied electrical engineering and computing technologies
17. Vu T, Baid A, Zhang Y et al (2012) Dmap: a shared hosting scheme for dynamic identifier to locator mappings in the global internet. In: 2012 IEEE 32nd international conference on distributed computing systems
18. Luo H, Qin Y, Zhang H (2009) A DHT-based identifier-to-locator mapping approach for a scalable internet. IEEE Trans Parallel Distrib Syst 20(12):1790–1802
19. Luo H, Wang H, Zhang H et al (2009) 4I: a secure and scalable routing architecture for Future Internet. Technical report, Beijing Jiaotong University, 2009
20. Dong P, Zhang H, Gao D et al (2007) ISMS-MANET: an identifiers separating and mapping scheme based internet access solution for mobile ad-hoc networks. In: Mobile ad-hoc and sensor networks. Springer, Berlin, pp 633–644
21. Dong P, Wang H, Zhang H (2008) An efficient approach to map identity onto locator. In: The 5th international conference on mobile technology, applications, and systems
22. Subramanian L, Caesar M, Ee CT et al (2005) HLP: a next generation inter-domain routing protocol. ACM SIGCOMM Comput Commun Rev 35(4):13–24
23. Stoica I, Morris R, Karger D et al (2001) Chord: a scalable peer-to-peer lookup service for internet applications. ACM SIGCOMM Comput Commun Rev 31(4):149–160
24. Skiena S (1990) Dijkstra's algorithm. In: Implementing discrete mathematics: combinatorics and graph theory with mathematica. Perseus Books, pp 225–227
25. Kovalenko IN, Kochubinskii AI (2003) Asymmetric cryptographic algorithms. Cybern Syst Anal 39(4):549–554

Chapter 4
Principle of the Pervasive Service Layer

In this chapter, we focus on the principle and operating mechanisms of the Pervasive Service Layer, which is responsible for providing service management, service acquisition and adaptive connection management. Related work on Internet services and applications is summarized at the beginning. The SID design, CID design, SID resolution-mapping mechanism and CID resolution-mapping mechanism are then introduced, respectively. Moreover, we also introduce the service acquisition mechanism, service compatibility mechanism and adaptive connection management designed in the Pervasive Service Layer. After reading this chapter, we expect the readers could have a full understanding of the Pervasive Service Layer in the SINET, especially the SID-based service acquisition, CID-based adaptive connection management and service compatibility mechanism.

4.1 Related Work

Since the 1970s, the scale of the Internet has grown dramatically. Nowadays, the Internet applications have been deployed all over the world. The Internet can be ranked as one of the most successful technologies. However, with the further development of the information network technique and increasing demands for network communication, the network services are also becoming increasingly diverse. The latest data show that the number of web pages that can be retrieved in the main search engines such as Google and Yahoo is up to 3.32 billion [7]. The number of secondary domain names registered on the existing major network system (DNS) reaches 136 million [8] (up to 10 July 2014). With the fast development of the Internet of Things and Cloud Computing, sensor network services and cloud computing-based services are definitely making the number of existing network services increase greatly. However, in the current network service

© Springer-Verlag Berlin Heidelberg 2016
H. Zhang et al., *Smart Collaborative Identifier Network*,
DOI 10.1007/978-3-662-49143-0_4

architecture, many problems still need to be resolved. Specifically, there are issues in network applications designed for specific terminals, such as bad compatibility and poor management.

In the traditional Internet, there are many typical network applications, such as FTP, web application, e-mail and network telephones. Each network application needs a specific service system. Moreover, different terminals with different systems need different applications. This redundant design leads to the waste of resources, which seriously influences the scalability of network service systems. It is not difficult to find that the traditional Internet lacks a unified description for service sources on the network application level, which leads to the situation where different network applications define their own description format and design their own acquisition process.

Recently, P2P business has taken up a large proportion of Internet traffic [9–11]. It shows that increasing demands for service concentrate on their own resources rather than require that from their host locations. On the contrary, in the traditional Internet, all of the services are host-oriented. If users want to get a certain resource, they need to find the location, that is to say, the IP address of the resource, and then the service in that location can be acquired.

To address this change, it has been considered the current trend in network service architecture to develop an Information Center Network (ICN), providing service-oriented resource acquisition for users [12–15]. The ICN has fundamentally solved the problems of the traditional Internet, such as low resource utilization, dynamic burst access, distributed denial of service (DDoS) [16] attack and defects of host-oriented security mechanisms. In particular, the encrypted data transmission channel and service certification security mechanism cannot authenticate service data from untrusted servers. However, the ICN is still in its initial stage, and one of its core contents is the name and resolution mechanism of service.

Besides, in the traditional Internet, descriptions such as the URL [17, 18] for network service resources are not enough to reflect the information of the requested connection in the acquisition process, such as service type, data size, bandwidth demand and optional transport protocols. This leads to the difficulty in providing effective Quality of Service (QoS) to satisfy network service demands during the acquisition process. Hence, it is difficult for the traditional Internet to provide a unified platform for pervasive service.

In this context, one of the most important tasks for the future network service is to create a pervasive service mechanism that can support multiple services to improve the controllability, manageability, availability and reliability of network resources. Numerous researchers have proposed different solutions from different viewpoints. The URN [19] is a permanent mechanism that does not rely on network locations. The HIP [20, 21] uses a flat and self-certified identifier to identify the terminal itself, but does not describe the resource. The SFR [22] proposes a permanent service identifier resolution mechanism based on the DHT. The DDNS [23] gives a way to map the network service identifier to the dynamic network addresses, which allows users to find the corresponding network resource in a timely manner even if the location changes. The INS [24] provides a solution for resources in the dynamic network. The DONA [12] proposes a routing mechanism based on names. Besides, I3 [25], TRAID [26], IPNL [27] and NDN [28] have different characteristics in obtaining services. Different from these solutions, the SINET originally creates a Pervasive Service Layer, which employs the SID, CID and their inter-mapping mechanisms to flexibly manage the service delivery.

4.2 Identifiers and Mappings

In the SINET, the Pervasive Service Layer contains two modules, the *Virtual Service Module (VSM)* and *Virtual Connection Module (VCM)*. As shown in Fig. 4.1, the SID and CID are used in the Pervasive Service Layer and Network Component Layer, respectively. Meanwhile, the *Service Identifier Resolution Mapping (SID-RM)* and *Connection Identifier Resolution Mapping (CID-RM)* are also presented in order to achieve the unified control and management of various services.

In the VSM, the SID is used to uniformly describe various network services and guarantee the Quality of Service (QoS). In the VCM, the CID provides a service-oriented connection. The SID-RM maps SID to multiple CIDs to support diversified network services and provide better mobility and security in the Pervasive Service Layer. The CID-RM maps the CID to multiple end-to-end paths in the Network Component Layer. Here, multiple end-to-end paths are established between access devices, which are different from the routing paths. Such identifier resolution mappings reflect the idea that one service can be mapped to multiple connections and paths, and repetitively it can build up the pervasive network services.

The most obvious advantage of the Pervasive Service Layer is that it efficiently supports the *pervasive service*. First, the SID uniformly identifies various services in different networks, which achieves the unified control and management of

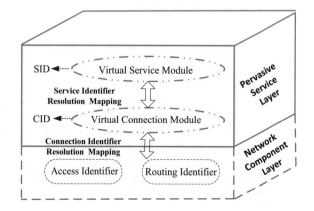

Fig. 4.1 Model of the pervasive service layer in SINET

services. Meanwhile, the CID is independent of the location. It will not change during the communication process and be able to provide stable and reliable network connection in mobile environments. Second, the SID-RM and CID-RM make the choice of network connection and transmission path flexible enough during the resource transmission process. The demands of pervasive service for multiple resource types and access methods are therefore satisfied. Finally, the CID provides the Pervasive Service Layer with a separated name space. Furthermore, the SID-RM and CID-RM separate the mapping between the service name and access location into two resolution processes, which will improve the efficiency of service provision.

4.2.1 SID Format

In the SINET, the SID is used to replace the current service identifier using the domain name to identify various services. The SID is a *flat identifier* with a specific lifetime, self-certification ability, fixed length and position-independent feature. Since a flat naming structure is non-hierarchical, it has no inherent structural limitations. Therefore, it does not depend on any specific structure and achieves the separation between the identifier and the location.

The SID can be obtained through hashing the keywords or content of the services. Common hash algorithms are MD-5 [1] and SHA-1 [2] with 128- and 160-bit hash values, respectively. Considering the large number of future network services, the SINET adopts the SHA-1 algorithm, and the length of the SID can be set as 160 bits. The SID provides a unique and persistent identifier for the service. It is mainly used for service discovery. However, the flat and non-semantic structure of the SID is not good at providing the rich descriptions of service and flexible service mapping. Thus, besides assigning an SID for a certain service, a service description structure is also included to constitute a complete service identifier information unit to provide a more comprehensive illustration. We will detail the service management in the following sections.

4.2.2 CID Format

In order to establish service connections, the Pervasive Service Layer introduces the CID to identify a connection. During the service connection process, both the service provider and the requester generate a CID. Then, these two CIDs form into a pair to *uniquely identify a service connection*.

Suppose Z is a set of CIDs. Theoretically, $Z = \{z_1, z_2, \ldots z_m, \ldots\}$ is an infinite set, where $m \in \{1, 2, \ldots\}$. z_i denotes the CID of the i-th connection and contains numerous connection attributes, such as QoS. It can be generated as:

$$z_i \triangleq \phi[a_1(i), a_2(i), \ldots, a_k(i)], \tag{4.1}$$

where $a_k(i)$ is the k-th ($k \in \{1, 2, \ldots\}$) attribute of the i-th connection; $\phi(\bullet)$ is the CID-generating function, which is dependent on the attributes of the i-th connection.

When two nodes in the SINET communicate with each other for the first time, a pair of CIDs is used to identify the connection. The CID pair can be described by an ordered pair $\langle z_i(m), z_j(n) \rangle$, where m and n denote the two nodes, and i and j are the numerical orders of the two nodes.

In the SINET, the RID denotes a node location. The CID represents a service connection. This design separates the terminal identity and its location. Moreover, it also simplifies the handover of communication links during the node movement. If a node moves to another location, only the RID is changed, and the CID remains the same. In this way, the communication connection will not be interrupted. Therefore, through the introduction of the CID, the SINET efficiently supports the mobility of the node.

4.2.3   Resolution Mapping Between SID and CID

In order to complete the mapping from the service to connection, we need to *build a connection between* the *VSN and VCM* and *establish the mapping relationship between the SID and CID*. Therefore, the *SID-RM* is designed. The mapping types of the SID-RM comprise of one-to-one simple mapping, one-to-many multi-connection mapping, many-to-one multi-stream mapping and many-to-many complex mapping. The one-to-one simple mapping is defined as:

$$< z_{XY}(h)_{CID}, z_{XY}(l)_{CID} > \triangleq \Phi \big(z_X(h)_{SID} \big), \tag{4.2}$$

where X is the service type; Y is the connection type; SID represents the service identifier; CID represents the connection identifier; h is the service requester; l is the service provider. One-to-one simple mapping maps the service $z_X(h)_{SID}$ requested by h to a connection $< z_{XY}(h)_{CID}, z_{XY}(l)_{CID} >$. This kind of mapping is similar to the service connection modes of the traditional Internet and telecommunication network, which are achieved by the TCP [3] or UDP [4] connection and circuit connection, respectively.

The one-to-many multi-connection mapping is defined as

$$\big(< z_{X1}(h)_{CID}, z_{X1}(l)_{CID} >, \ldots, < z_{Xn}(h)_{CID}, z_{Xn}(l)_{CID} > \big) \triangleq \Phi \big(z_X(h)_{SID} \big), \tag{4.3}$$

which maps a service $z_X(h)_{SID}$ to many connections. In Eq. 4.3, n denotes the number of connections. Such multi-connection mapping can accelerate the service data transmission. According to Eq. 4.3, we can construct the mapping model as

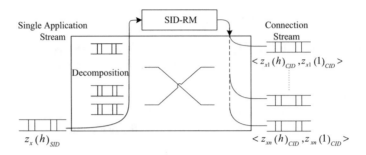

Fig. 4.2 One-to-many SID-RM model

shown in Fig. 4.2. Figure 4.2 shows that the data stream of one single application can be decomposed into multiple transmission connections.

The many-to-one multi-stream mapping is defined as

$$<z_{XY}(h)_{CID}, z_{XY}(l)_{CID}> \triangleq \Phi(z_{X1}(h)_{SID}, z_{X2}(h)_{SID}, \ldots z_{Xn}(h)_{SID}). \qquad (4.4)$$

Equation 4.4 denotes that the same service can be transported through different data streams, which have different types. However, such many-to-one mapping is essentially the same as the one-to-one mapping. This is because the service is first internally divided into several logical streams according to the data type. Then, these divided logical streams are mapped into different connections using the one-to-one mapping. For example, data with error control and data insensitive to error can be transmitted through different connections. This design is conducive to providing different connections for different data types, which greatly improves the transmission efficiency. The mapping model of Eq. 4.4 is shown in Fig. 4.3. Figure 4.3 shows that an application stream is classified into multiple streams according to the stream types, and all these streams will be mapped to the same connection.

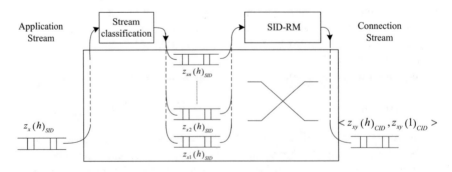

Fig. 4.3 Many-to-one SID-RM model

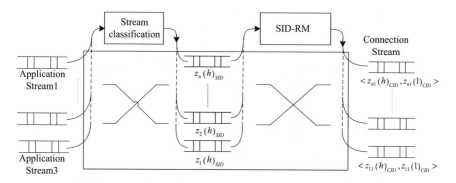

Fig. 4.4 Many-to-many SID resolution mapping model

$$
\begin{array}{c}
<z_{11}(h)_{CID},z_{11}(l)_{CID}>,\ldots,<z_{1m}(h)_{CID},z_{1m}(l)_{CID}> \\
<z_{21}(h)_{CID},z_{21}(l)_{CID}>,\ldots,<z_{2m}(h)_{CID},z_{2m}(l)_{CID}> \\
\vdots \\
<z_{n1}(h)_{CID},z_{n1}(l)_{CID}>,\ldots,<z_{nm}(h)_{CID},z_{nm}(l)_{CID}>
\end{array}_{n\times m}
\triangleq \Phi
\begin{bmatrix}
z_1(h)_{SID} \\
z_2(h)_{SID} \\
\vdots \\
z_n(h)_{SID}
\end{bmatrix}.
$$

$$(4.5)$$

Based on the Eqs. 4.2–4.4, the transmission between the multi-application and multi-connection is also designed, which is shown in Eq. 4.5. In Eq. 4.5, the service $z_n(h)_{SID}$ is divided into different streams with different types, and then it will be transmitted through multiple connections. Many-to-many complex mapping can also accelerate service data transmission and is able to process data streams of different types with different methods, which reflects the idea of pervasive service. The many-to-many complex mapping model is shown in Fig. 4.4.

4.2.4   Resolution Mapping Between CID and AID

The basic model of the SINET comprises of the Network Component Layer and Pervasive Service Layer. This kind of hierarchical design enables the independent characteristic of each layer. Due to the independence, each layer only needs to provide some interfaces for the others, without the information of the specific implementation method. In the SINET, the *CID-RM* acts as the interface and *connects the VCM in* the *Pervasive Service Layer with Network Component Layer.* The CID-RM is also responsible for achieving the mapping between the connection and routing path. Due to the independence of the two layers, the Network Component Layer can be abstracted as a routing path for the connection in the Pervasive Service Layer. Hence, the CID-RM does not include the one-to-one or

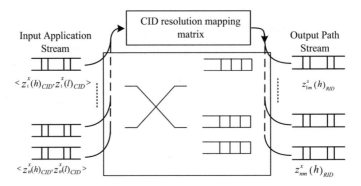

Fig. 4.5 Many-to-many CID resolution mapping model

one-to-many mapping; it only includes the many-to-one mapping and many-to-many mapping.

The many-to-many CID-RM is defined as

$$
\begin{array}{c}
z_{11}^X(h)_{RID}, z_{12}^X(h)_{RID}, \dots, z_{1m}^X(h)_{RID} \\
z_{21}^X(h)_{RID}, z_{22}^X(h)_{RID}, \dots, z_{2m}^X(h)_{RID} \\
\vdots \\
z_{n1}^X(h)_{RID}, z_{n2}^X(h)_{RID}, \dots, z_{nm}^X(h)_{RID}
\end{array}_{n \times m}
\triangleq \Psi
\begin{bmatrix}
< z_1^X(h)_{CID}, z_1^X(l)_{CID} > \\
< z_2^X(h)_{CID}, z_2^X(l)_{CID} > \\
\vdots \\
< z_n^X(h)_{CID}, z_n^X(l)_{CID} >
\end{bmatrix}, \qquad (4.6)
$$

where X represents a certain service; h denotes the client; l represents the server; n and m are the variables; and $\Psi(\bullet)$ is the generation function, which is responsible for mapping the connections between terminal h and terminal l for service X to the routing paths. Based on Eq. 4.6, Fig. 4.5 illustrates the many-to-many CID-RM model. The multiple input connections are mapped to multiple paths through CID-RM.

The many-to-many CID-RM enables the Network Component Layer to provide service for the Pervasive Service Layer. In addition, due to the existence of multiple connections, the transmission efficiency and reliability can also be significantly improved. If a connection is interrupted, another connection will be immediately in place and the data transmission can be recovered in a short time. Nevertheless, this mechanism is absent in the traditional Internet.

4.3 Services Management

In this section, a newly proposed service-oriented resource acquisition mechanism in the SINET is introduced with the goal of realizing the unified management, service mobility and resource security.

4.3.1 Generation of SID

In the SINET, the goal of the Pervasive Service Layer is to provide friendly, reliable and secure services for users. The target of naming and identifying a service is to provide useful service interfaces for the large number of network applications so as to flexibly describe and transport network resources. Therefore, the *scalability*, *flexibility* and *security* are the main consideration factors that matter in the SID. Scalability of the SID means that the SID space can not only describe the existing network services, but also describe the ever-increasing network services and types. Besides, it must have the ability to meet the potential demands of services for the SID for a long time. The flexibility of the SID means that the SID should be able to identify network services by themselves and should not be influenced by the time and location changes of network service so as to provide consistent and friendly service interfaces for different terminals and networks. Security of the SID means that the SID cannot be denied permanently and uniquely represents the specific network service so as to provide a reliable basis for security in the provision and acquisition of network services.

By considering the above three demands, the SID should possess the following two characteristics. First, the SID must be able to represent a *unique network resource*, such as documents and web pages. Second, the SID should be a *permanent identifier* of network resources and will not change with time and location. Therefore, the SINET adopts a consistent distributed hash table (DHT) algorithm to generate the SID. Because the length of the SID determines the number of network services that the SID space can accommodate, we first assume that the hash value of the DHT algorithm is with a length of n bits. Moreover, the hash algorithm has a flat characteristic. It satisfies the design requirements that services are permanent, unique and independent of time and location.

In SINET, the generation function of SID is defined as:

$$SID = Hash(PKEY, NAME, [Abstract], [Content]), \qquad (4.7)$$

where *PKEY* is the public key announced by the network service publisher, which is used to verify the accuracy and completeness of the SID information in the registration and resolution process; [●] means the optional parameter; *Name* is the name of the network service; *Abstract* is the abstract or explanation information of the network service, while *Content* is the content of the network service. Both *Abstract* and *Content* are chosen based on the specific network service type.

During the process of generating the SID, *Abstract* and *Content* are set as optional contents mainly due to the fact that there are various types of network services. For example, for the file resource, such as a song, a movie or a document, its SID generation process will contain the network resources content. For network services with potential resource data, the potential content cannot be predicted in advance. Therefore, it can only be described by the SID. For example, for a live broadcast show, the content will not be involved in the generation process of the

Fig. 4.6 Process of
generating the SID

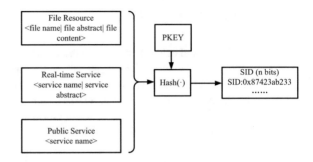

SID. Furthermore, for other kinds of network services whose resource data are unknown, such as voice call and email, the abstract description of such a service is not necessary. Therefore, the generation process of such an SID does not contain the abstract and content. The generation process of the SID for different service types is shown in Fig. 4.6.

In the real-time implementation of the network services, because of the existing market competition mechanism, sometimes we need to distinguish network services provided by different service providers. In this case, we just need to extend the service name, which can be expressed as <service name | service provider> [service abstract].

Some examples are given as follows:

- Live TV show: <news channel | CCTV> [introduction]
- Email: <email | Google>
- Voice call: <voice call | China Mobile>
- Instant message: <QQ chatting | Tencent>

The design of the SID allows network resources to obtain a permanent and unique identifier. However, the hash value is flat and non-semantic. It cannot describe the differences among network services, which makes it difficult to allocate network resource for users and map the SID to CID in the process of service acquisition. Therefore, it still needs other auxiliary information during the SID generation process. The SID information unit formed by the SID and service description is shown in Table 4.1.

For a network service, the field marked * is indispensable, while other fields are optional. Without special configuration, these fields are with default settings. Each field in Table 4.1 is explained in details as follows.

- SID: n-bits hash value of a network service;
- Service Name: name of a service;
- Service abstract: simple introduction information of a network service, the default value is *NULL*;
- Keywords: SID public key provided by the provider of a network service, the default value is *NULL*;
- Type: type of a network service, the default type is *file*;

Table 4.1 SID information
unit format sample

SID*	0 × 87423ab233...... (n-bits)	
Service name*	Service name	
Service abstract	An introductive information of service	
Keywords	Like example, SID, structure	
Public key*	PKEY	
Type	File	
Provider*	AID*	Limit rules
	AID 1	RULE 1
	AID 2	RULE 2
	......	......
	AID x	RULE x
Service parameters	[Type, QoS, Rate, ...]	
Valid time	2008.2.1 00:00:00-2015.2.1 00:00:00	

- Provider: service node providing the network service;
- AID: the identifier provided by service node for a service, at least one;
- Limit rules: limit conditions for each AID provided by the service node, the default value is *NULL*;
- Service quality: QoS guarantee conditions needed in the service acquisition process, the default value is NULL;
- Valid time: effective lifetime of a network service, the default value is *permanent*.

4.3.2   Management of SID

In the service system of the SINET, all network services indexes are managed and maintained by the *SID resolution system* via *their indexes*. A network service can only be used after its corresponding service node registers its SIDs at the SID resolution system. And this registration makes the network service available to be queried and used by other network users.

As shown in Fig. 4.7, the SID resolution server can be divided into two parts: the SID proxy and distributed SID resolution server. The SID proxy maintains all information of the network services provided for external users, including locations of the network resources, and attribute descriptions of the network service. It is also responsible for cooperating with the upper layer server to complete the registration, maintenance and retrieval of the SID information. The distributed SID resolution

Fig. 4.7 Architecture of the
SID resolution server

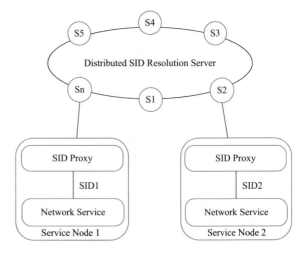

Fig. 4.8 Schematic diagram
of the SID registration process

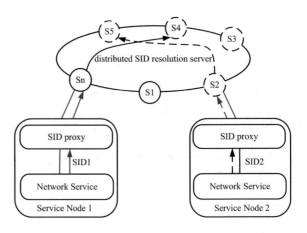

server maintains the SID information of network services registered by service
nodes and couples the information of the same network services from different
nodes to provide service resolution.

As shown in Fig. 4.8, if Service Node 1 needs to register a webpage file *index.
html* to the SID resolution server, then the specific process can be expressed as
follows:

* According to the corresponding SID application programs, Node1 generates the
  SID1 for the webpage based on the generation process of the SID described in
  Sect. 4.2.1;
* Node 1 reconstructs the SID1 into SID information units through the SID
  application program and registers the location of webpage POS1 and informa-
  tion about service terminal application program APP1 to the SID proxy;

- The SID proxy of Node 1 saves the information unit of SID1 and sends the registration request for the SID1 to the SID resolution server in the upper layer (if Node 1 has configured the upper SID resolution server, node 1 will not send this request). At the same time, the SID proxy monitors the change of the status of file *index.html* according to the registered location information;
- Suppose Node 1 had configured the upper SID resolution server Sn. If Sn receives the SID registration request from Node 1, it will check its registration authority first. If Node 1 has the authority, Sn will return the registration response and complete the registration of SID1. If not, Sn will discard the SID registration request from Node 1.
- After receiving the SID1 information unit from Node 1, Sn will save it to all of the distributed servers in the network (suppose it is finally saved in service S4) based on the specific distributed algorithm.

After this procedure of registration, the webpage *index.html* provided by Node 1 can be resolved and retrieved by other nodes. Additionally, SID2 provided by the service Node 2 can also be registered at the corresponding SID proxy, such as server S2 and server S5.

In the process of SID registration, the SID proxy or server combines the registration information from different sources in which SIDs might be the same. To this end, the server needs to extend the AID and the restriction rules of the providers. Moreover, the SID proxy also needs to record and monitor different network resources and corresponding service responding procedures.

After the SID registration process, the service node together with its registered SID allows other nodes to obtain correct and valid services. The contents need to be maintained including the changes of resource location, network application, AIDs, restriction rules, valid time and network service information. Once some information of the SID changes or the service provider releases its services, the SID resolution server in the upper layer will respond to the relevant change and update the new services. Meanwhile the updating procedure of the network resource location and the running responding programs will both be suspended.

4.3.3   *Resolution of SID*

In the traditional Internet, users usually cannot remember all the network links or the corresponding IP addresses of the network resources. Users get used to depending on the built-in network application information, like the DNS [5] or some third-party search engines, e.g., Google, to request the network resources. In the SINET, it is hardly possible to remember all the network resources and their affiliated information for users. What is more, the *SID is not readable*. Therefore, the *SID resolution system* provides a complete resolution process. The main objective of the SID resolution system is to transform the service to specific a SID

Fig. 4.9 SID resolution process

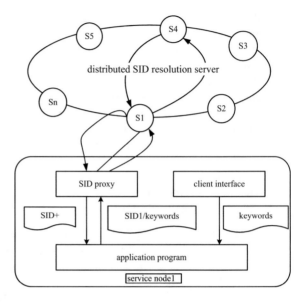

and complete the query process of SID resolution. Therefore, the corresponding SID and other affiliated information can be used by the clients.

The resolution process of a specific SID is shown in Fig. 4.9. For instance, a user wants to browse the webpage index.html by Node1. Before this user reaches the network resources, the SID can only be resolved by searching the keywords of the service because the client does not know the service content. The specific resolution process is shown as follows.

- Client inputs the keywords of needed network resources through the given user interface;
- Corresponding network application programs construct a specific SID to resolve the query message including the keywords. Then, the messages are sent to the SID proxy of Node 1;
- The SID proxy first searches the record tables and cached contents to check whether the keywords match with the provided services. If the keywords are matched, the SID and affiliated information will be returned. Then, the resolution process is completed. If not, the SID proxy will send the recursive request to the SID resolution server S1 at the upper layer;
- S1 uses the distributed algorithm to send the resolution request to server S4;
- S4 retrieves the corresponding SID item. Then, based on the restriction rules, the SID information that is allowed to be visited by Node 1 will be returned to S1;
- After receiving the resolution response, S1 will forward the response to the SID proxy of Node 1;
- The SID proxy of Node 1 will cache these items and then send them to the application program until the end of the resolution process.

When requesting the network services, clients may directly use the application programs bounded with the fixed SID. However, the application programs may contain incomplete information causing the failures of accessing the network services for clients. Therefore, the accurate SID resolution process is still necessary, which is similar to the above procedure. After clients obtain the demanded network resources at the SID, the service acquisition process will be followed.

4.3.4   Services Acquisition Flow

Based on the model of the Pervasive Service Layer, the uniform treatment mechanism is designed and shown in Fig. 4.10. In Fig. 4.10, the *SID uniform manager* is responsible for uniformly and globally managing the registration and acquisition of the SID. User2 and Client2 are service providers, and User1 and Client1 are service requesters. The *unified treatment mechanism* is divided into the following four stages:

Service Registration can be abstracted into a triple information group, namely the AID, SID and Service Description. The AID is the concept proposed in the Network Component Layer. It can represent the identity information of the communication terminal. The SID is used to identify a service. It can also be used to listen and establish a service connection. The Service Description is a user-friendly

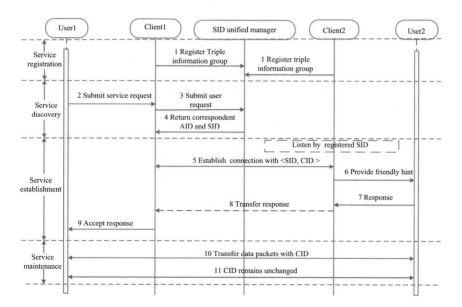

Fig. 4.10 Workflow of uniform treatment in the pervasive service layer of the SINET

description of service features and performance, which reflects the preference of the user. The service provider is responsible for registering the corresponding triple information group to SID uniform manager so as to complete the service registration.

The Service Discovery procedure comprises of three processes. First, the service requester submits the needed service description to the SID unified manager. Second, the SID uniform manager gets the corresponding triple information group from the registered services. Third, the SID uniform processer returns the corresponding AID and SID back to the users. The key point in the service discovery procedure is that the SID uniform manager gets the corresponding three-dimensional information from registered services.

Service Establishment contains two processes. First, a service provider uses its own registered SID to perform the connection listening. Second, a service requester establishes the service connection with the service provider based on the corresponding CID. This stage involves a handshake and authentication mechanism to establish the connection.

Service Maintenance is responsible for integrating the switched data packet flows from the two communication sides. To this end, the traditional Internet uses a socket [6] composed of the IP address and port number, while the SINET introduces the AID to distinguish the data packet flows.

Working mechanisms of the Pervasive Service Layer in the SINET are illustrated as follows. First, through the naming rules of the SID, it provides the unified identifier for various services. This unified identifier achieves the uniform service scheduling and provides support for various services. Then, if a user node needs to access a service, the service can be located through the SID query mechanisms performed by the SID resolution system. The located service is able to establish one or multiple connections with the VCM and construct a mapping relationship with the CID through the SID-RM. According to the various features of the resource, the types of connections are also different. Moreover, numerous sub-connections can also be provided for the complex resources. In this way, the reliability of the connection can be guaranteed. In the following, a connection can be mapped into one or multiple paths in the Network Component Layer through the CID-RM. The multi-paths not only improve the connection reliability, but also increase the transmission efficiency. Eventually, the resource exchange can be completed.

The novelty of uniform treatment in the Pervasive Service Layer is reflected in these three aspects. First, it introduces the third-party SID uniform manager so that the service provider can change the SID at any time only by the means of re-registration. Second, it introduces the AID generated from local independent random numbers, which separates the service connection from service maintenance. Therefore, the privacy data packets can be protected effectively. Third, the AID is separated from the host location, which avoids the service interruption in the mobile environment.

4.4   Services Compatibility

Although the pervasive service system in the SINET brings many advantages, the application of novel network technologies and the deployment of new network devices cannot come into being overnight. They still need a long period of transition. To make full use of the advantages of the SINET, it is necessary to develop network applications in the new service acquisition mode.

However, the number of traditional network applications is too large to modify all the applications to support new architecture patterns of network services. Therefore, it is necessary to design a *compatibility mechanism* to facilitate the deployment of the Pervasive Service Layer. Generally speaking, a compatibility mechanism should follow the below principles:

- *Gradualness*: the compatibility mechanism should sustain the coexistence of new network applications and traditional network applications. With the development of new network applications, the traditional ones will be gradually replaced.
- *Universality:* in terms of traditional applications, the compatibility mechanism should be pervasive. In other words, it should meet all or most of the traditional applications. Moreover, it does not need to use different methods to meet different applications.
- *Simplification:* the design of the compatibility mechanism should be as simple as possible so as to avoid the introduction of too much operation latency.

The compatibility mechanism proposed in this section is based on the *extension of the traditional socket interface*. The socket is an integrated set of API interfaces provided by the TCP/IP protocol stack. The socket was initially designed for the UNIX system. Due to its excellent properties, it is also applied to other operating systems, such as Linux and Windows.

The typical workflow of the socket is described as follows:

- The server starts, and the service application calls the socket() to create a socket and returns a file descriptor;
- The service application calls bind() and connects the socket with the local network address to set the address for providing service;
- The service application calls listen (). Then, the service application prepares for socket interception and sets the length of the client request queue in the meantime;
- The server waits for the client connection;
- After establishing a connection through socket (), the client sends a connection request to the server by calling connect ().
- If the server monitors the connection request from the client, its service application will call accept () to accept the request and establish the connection. Otherwise, it will return to (4) and continue to wait.
- When the connection is established, the server and client will call read () and write () to send and receive network service data.

- When the data transmission is finished, the server and client will call close () to close the socket.

Based on the above descriptions, we can see that traditional web applications need to specify the network address and address type when acquiring the network services. Therefore, this kind of service acquisition is host-oriented. In the SINET, however, the service acquisition is service-oriented. In order to support the applications in the traditional Internet and SINET, we need to extend the function of the traditional socket. The structure of the pervasive service stack of the compatibility mechanism is shown in Fig. 4.11.

In order to realize the backward compatibility of the socket(), it is extended to the *socket (SID, ...)*, which is used to judge the number of input parameters in a specific implementation. If the number is 1, it will be implemented by the service-oriented socket mechanism of the SINET. If the number is 3, it will be implemented by the mechanism of the traditional Internet.

In SINET, to guarantee the quality of service acquisition, QoS information is needed. However, the establishment of the socket only contains one SID, without containing the QoS information of web resources. Therefore, it is required to add the service quality *SO_QOS* to end the socket.

Socket Listen. In the traditional socket function *listen ()*, the parameters are the socket descriptor and the length of the client's request queue. The function interfaces need not to be modified in the SINET, but it should add the necessary operations according to the service acquisition mechanism for implementation.

On the server side, calling *listen ()* represents that the server begins to provide service, and it needs to register the provided resources to the SID resolution server.

Socket Bind. Traditional socket function *bind ()* is used for assigning network addresses to the provided services. In the SINET, it can still be used to assign the AIDs to the service provider or requester. When the service provider calls *bind ()*,

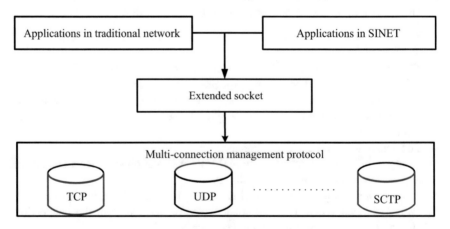

Fig. 4.11 The structure of the pervasive service stack in the SINET

the bound identifier needs to be consistent with the registered AID. When the requester calls *bind()*, the bound address is the AID that they use during service acquisition process.

Socket Connect. Parameters of traditional socket function *connect ()* include the network address of server and some other information. But this information has nothing to do with establishing service-oriented connections in the SINET. During the establishment of the connection, we just need to start the corresponding socket function *connect (fd)*, where *fd* is the file descriptor of the service socket. Therefore, it can be extended to *connect (fd, …)* like the *socket(SID, …)*, which is used to judge the number of input parameters in a specific implementation.

In the SINET, the establishment of a connection is quite complex. The function body of the *connect ()* needs to be added with the necessary operations to achieve the mapping between the SID and CID. Meanwhile, the generated CID also needs to negotiate with providers to establish a transport channel. The detailed procedure is shown in Sect. 4.2.

Socket Accept. The socket function *accept ()* is used for selecting clients from the request queue to establish new socket connections for the communication between servers and clients. It can still be used in the SINET by adding the additional verification process to check the validity of the connection request from clients. The detailed procedure is shown in Sect. 4.2.

Socket Close. The socket function *close ()* is used to close the socket descriptor, and it can be used in the SINET without any modifications.

Next, we will explain the workflow of this mechanism through an instance of network communication, which is shown in Fig. 4.12.

As shown in Fig. 4.12, compared with the traditional socket communication, many changes are made for the establishment and connection of the socket. Moreover, a small number of changes also take place for the listening socket. The remaining socket functions are the same. The above instance also shows that service acquisition in the SINET can be achieved, and support for the traditional Internet is also sustained after the modifications.

Based on the extended socket, the compatibility mechanism proposed in this chapter matches the previously described principles well.

- In the compatibility mechanism, the expansion of the socket retains the original functions, which guarantees that the traditional applications can still be used, and the new applications of the SINET can be deployed and implemented.
- The modifications and expansions of the socket in the compatibility mechanism are aimed at system kernel and library functions. It is irrelevant to the specific application, which ensures the universality in network applications.
- Based on the compatibility mechanism, the coexistence of the traditional application and SINET application can be achieved easily just through upgrading the kernel and changing the library functions.

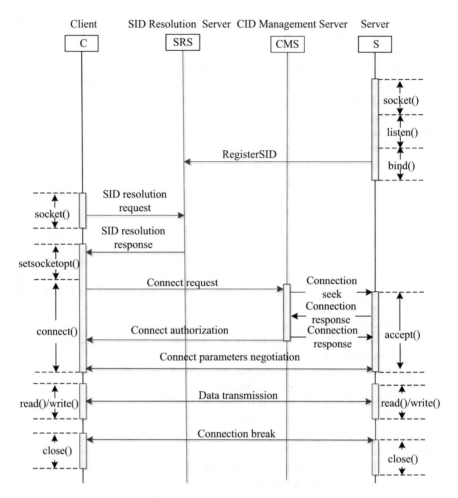

Fig. 4.12 Process for the network communication procedure based on the extended socket

4.5   Connections Management

The VCM in the Pervasive Service Layer introduces the *CID* to *establish and maintain the appropriate session connection* for each service until the termination of service. The CID is used to achieve the mapping from the network application to transport protocol and maintain the network connection. During the service acquisition process, the CID of each connection remains unchanged. In the realistic network service process, the corresponding network service establishes one or more connections with the VCM and the mapping relationship with the CID through the SID-RM. In addition, the service is able to select the appropriate connection type according to the resource characteristics and network environment conditions. For complex resources, the network service can provide numerous sub-connections to ensure the reliability of the connection. Then, a connection is mapped into one or more network channels through the SID-RM. Finally, a network service acquisition in the SINET is conducted.

In the SINET, the CID is also used to distinguish the different network service processes. Thus, it is necessary to ensure the uniqueness of the CID for different network services. In order to generate a unique CID, the consistent hash algorithm is used based on the connection information. Furthermore, the bit number of the hash value determines the space that the CID can accommodate. In order to facilitate the computer processing, we assume the bit number is n, and it is recommended that $n \geq 16$ to ensure the compatibility with the existing port number. The parameters of the hash algorithm are $<SID, AID_S, AID_C, k, QoS>$. The meanings of these parameters are shown as follows:

- SID: service identifier to distinguish different services;
- AID_S: access identifier of the server, which uniquely identifies the service provider;
- AID_C: access identifier of the client, which uniquely identifies the service requester;
- k: the number of established connections;
- QoS: parameters of service quality information, including the service type, QoS level, data transfer rate, minimum latency and bandwidth.

CID provides a unique identifier for the network service process, which does the favor of addressing the connection problems. However, in order to handle the flexibility, mobility and security problems in the network connection, it is still necessary to design a *signal and data negotiation mechanism*. Figure 4.13 shows the design of adaptive connection management. Different from the end-to-end transport protocol, a central control device named the CID Management Server (CMS) is introduced in the adaptive connection management. As shown in Fig. 4.13, SRS is SID Resolution Server. S1 and S2 are the two application servers to provide services with the same SID. C is a client.

The specific workflow of adaptive connection management is shown as follows:

Step 1: Application servers S1 and S2 register network services to SRS. The registration information comprises the SID, QoS, AID and service range Sub. Both the S1 and S2 are able to provide the service whose identifier is SID.

Step 2: Client terminal C uses the SID to query the SRS whether the service is available.

Step 3: SRS sends a set of servers that can provide the appropriate service back to the client. The set of servers is the AID_{S1} and AID_{S2} in Fig. 4.6.

Step 4: Client terminal C requests the CMS to get the necessary CID. The request information comprises of the SID, QoS, AID_C, AID_{S1} and AID_{S2}.

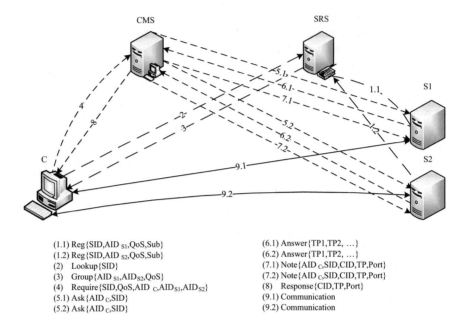

(1.1) Reg{SID,AID $_{S1}$,QoS,Sub}   (6.1) Answer{TP1,TP2, ...}
(1.2) Reg{SID,AID $_{S2}$,QoS,Sub}   (6.2) Answer{TP1,TP2, ...}
(2)   Lookup{SID}   (7.1) Note{AID $_C$,SID,CID,TP,Port}
(3)   Group{AID $_{S1}$,AID$_{S2}$,QoS}   (7.2) Note{AID $_C$,SID,CID,TP,Port}
(4)   Require{SID,QoS,AID $_C$,AID$_{S1}$,AID$_{S2}$}   (8)   Response{CID,TP,Port}
(5.1) Ask{AID $_C$,SID}   (9.1) Communication
(5.2) Ask{AID $_C$,SID}   (9.2) Communication

Fig. 4.13 Design of adaptive connection management

Step 5: CMS asks the application server for the information of the lower layer that is necessary to complete the service, such as the available transmission protocols.

Step 6: The application server sends the needed information to the CMS.

Step 7: CMS sends the generated CID, transport protocol type, port number and other information to the application server.

Step 8: CMS sends the generated CID, transport protocol type, port number and other information to the client.

Step 9: The client establishes a connection with the server through the CID, transport protocol type, port number and other information received.

In the service acquisition process, users will get the corresponding SID through a third-party service system. Based on the SID and other relevant information, CMS will consult and generate the corresponding CID. Then, the CID and related information will be synchronized between communicating entities.

Inside the CMS, the CID and the mappings of <SID, CID> and <CID, AID> are stored in the database. According to the monitoring and management of the CMS, network administrators can be aware of and control the current network connection status. Therefore, the above design can effectively solve the problems of establishing service in the current network.

The CID and connection management mechanism provide a potential communication mechanism that guarantees the network application session migration. However, abundant information needs to be dealt with during the application

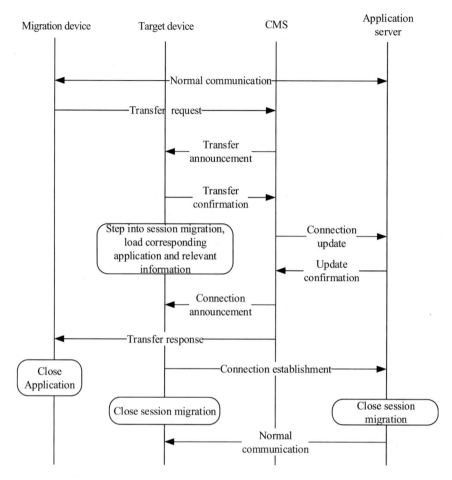

Fig. 4.14 Flow chart of the application session migration process

migration process. Hence, a special session information-caching module is also designed to cache the established session connection. The application session migration process is shown in Fig. 4.14.

Step 1:   The migration device sends the request to the CMS to perform the migration of the CID connection to the target device.

Step 2:   CMS verifies the CID. If the verification is successful, CMS will send the CID connection request to the target device. Otherwise, the process will be closed.

Step 3:   The target device verifies the CID. If the verification is successful, the target device will return the permission information to the CMS. Meanwhile, the target device will enter into the session migration status. Then, the corresponding application programs will be started and the relevant information including status information and user information will also be loaded into the programs. If the verification is unsuccessful, this progress will be closed.

Step 4: CMS updates the CID information at the application server.

Step 5: The application server receives the update request and verifies the information at first. If the CID is right, the server will return confirmation to the CMS and transform the session connection into a migration state.

Step 6: CMS receives the confirmation and sends the CID, transport protocol, port number and other information used by the application server to the target device. Meanwhile, the CMS sends corresponding response information to the migration device to confirm the request.

Step 7: The target device sends a network connection request to the application server according to the information disseminated by the CMS. When the connection is established, the migration will be closed. Then, the migration device changes to a normal session connection state.

Step 8: When the application server receives the connection request from the migration device, it will check its validity and then configure the communication protocol.

Step 9: The application server sends network resources to the target device and terminates the session migration state. Then, the migration process is finished.

4.6 Conclusion

This chapter includes the detailed design and working mechanisms of the Pervasive Service Layer in SINET, presenting specifically the service acquisition, service compatibility and adaptive connection management mechanisms. The introduction of the SID and CID and two resolution mapping mechanisms can achieve central control and management of various services, provide pervasive network services, support the mobility and improve the security of the SINET. In the next chapter, we will examine the open problems in SINET and introduce the advanced model of SINET1.

References

1. MD5. http://en.wikipedia.org/wiki/MD5. Accessed 7 June 2015
2. SHA-1. http://en.wikipedia.org/wiki/SHA-1. Accessed 7 June 2015
3. TCP. http://en.wikipedia.org/wiki/TCP. Accessed 7 June 2015
4. UDP. http://en.wikipedia.org/wiki/UDP. Accessed 7 June 2015
5. Domain Name System. http://en.wikipedia.org/wiki/Domain_Name_System. Accessed 7 June 2015

6. Berkeley sockets. http://en.wikipedia.org/wiki/Berkeley_sockets. Accessed 7 June 2015
7. The size of the World Wide Web. http://www.worldwidewebsize.com. Accessed 7 June 2015
8. WEBHOSTING.INFO. http://www.webhosting.info/domains/globalstats/totaldomains/. Accessed by 7 June 2015
9. Karagiannis T, Broido A, Brownlee N et al (2004) Is p2p dying or just hiding? IEEE globecom telecommunications conference
10. Karagiannis T, Broido A, Faloutsos M et al (2004) Transport layer identification of P2P traffic. The 4th ACM SIGCOMM conference on Internet measurement
11. Karagiannis T, Papagiannaki K, Faloutsos M (2005) BLINC: multilevel traffic classification in the dark. ACM SIGCOMM Comput Commun Rev 35(4):229–240
12. Koponen T, Chawla M, Chun B et al (2007) A data-oriented (and beyond) network architecture. ACM SIGCOMM Comput Commun Rev 37(4):181–192
13. Ahlgren B, D'Ambrosio M, Dannewitz C et al (2008) Design considerations for a network of information. The 2008 ACM CoNEXT conference
14. Jokela P, Zahemszky A, Arianfar S et al (2009) Lipsin: line speed publish/subscribe inter-networking. ACM SIGCOMM Comput Commun Rev 39(4):195–206
15. Jacobson V, Smetters D, Thornton J et al (2009) Networking named content. The 5th ACM international conference on emerging networking experiments and technologies
16. Denial-of-service_attack. http://en.wikipedia.org/wiki/Denial-of-service_attack#Distributed_attack
17. Hoffman P (2005) The telnet URI scheme, RFC 4248. http://www.ietf.org/rfc/rfc4248.txt. Accessed 7 June 2015
18. Hoffman P (2005) The gopher URI scheme, RFC 4266. http://www.ietf.org/rfc/rfc4266.txt. Accessed 7 June 2015
19. Uniform resource name. http://en.wikipedia.org/wiki/Uniform_resource_name. Accessed 7 June 2015
20. Moskowitz R, Nikander P, Jokela P et al (2006) Host identity protocol (HIP) architecture, RFC 4423. http://www.ietf.org/rfc/rfc4423.txt. Accessed 7 June 2015
21. Moskowitz R, Nikander P, Jokela P et al (2008) Host identity protocol, RFC 5201. http://www.ietf.org/rfc/rfc5201.txt. Accessed 7 June 2015
22. Walfish M, Balakrishnan H, Shenker S (2004) Untangling the Web from DNS. The 1st conference on symposium on networked systems design and implementation
23. Vixie P, Thomson S, Rekhter Y et al (1997) Dynamic updates in the domain name system, RFC 2136. http://www.ietf.org/rfc/rfc2136.txt
24. Adejie-Winoto W, Schwartz E, Balakrisshnan H et al (1999) The design and implementation of an intentional naming system. ACM SIGOPS Oper Syst Rev 34(2):22
25. Stoica I, Adkins D, Zhuang S et al (2004) Internet indirection infrastructure. IEEE/ACM Trans Netw 20(2):205–218
26. Cheriton D, Gritter M (2000) TRIAD: a new next-generation Internet architecture. www.cs.umd.edu/class/spring2007/cmsc711/papers/triad.ps. Accessed 7 June 2015
27. Ramakrishna PF (2001) IPNL: a NAT-extended internet architecture. ACM SIGCOMM Comput Commun Rev 31(4):69–80
28. NDN: Named Data Networking. http://named-data.org/index.html. Accessed 7 June 2015

Chapter 5
Evolutions of SINET

In order to provide emerging services and improve network performance, SINET is evolving to become more intelligent, dynamic and adaptive. In this chapter, we will give in-depth descriptions and discussions of the evolutionary architecture of SINET. Particularly, a new layer named the *Dynamic Resource Adaption Layer* is introduced for dynamically adapting network resources according to service requirements. In addition, two domains, namely the *entity domain* and *behavior domain*, are introduced to improve the flexibility of entity naming and descriptions in different layers. This novel "three layers and two domains" network reference model is introduced in Sect. 5.1. In Sect. 5.2, the Collaborative Network Component Layer is presented. Then, Sect. 5.3 introduces the Smart Pervasive Service Layer mechanism. The Dynamic Resource Adaption Layer is further elaborated in Sect. 5.4. Finally, Sect. 5.5 concludes this chapter.

5.1 Evolutionary Reference Model of SINET

Based on the fundamental reference model mentioned in Chap. 2, an evolutionary network reference model is further proposed for SINET to dynamically adapt network resources for services [1–3]. The network model comprises of three layers, namely: *Smart Pervasive Service Layer*, *Dynamic Resource Adaption Layer* and *Collaborative Network Component Layer*. It also contains two domains called *Entity Domain* and *Behavior Domain*. The network reference model is shown in Fig. 5.1.

In this architecture, the *Smart Pervasive Service Layer* is responsible for the naming and description of services. The *Dynamic Resource Adaption Layer* dynamically adapts network resources and builds network families by perceiving the service demands and network status so as to satisfy the service demands and improve the quality of experience. The *Collaborative Network Component Layer* is responsible for the storage and transmission of data. Meanwhile, the Collaborative

© Springer-Verlag Berlin Heidelberg 2016
H. Zhang et al., *Smart Collaborative Identifier Network*,
DOI 10.1007/978-3-662-49143-0_5

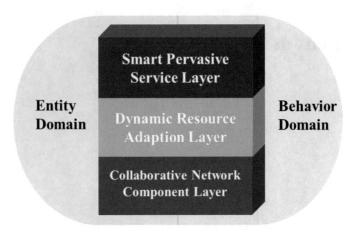

Fig. 5.1 Evolutionary reference model of SINET

Network Component Layer is also responsible for the network components'
behavior perceiving and aggregation. The *Entity Domain* includes the naming of the
service, network family and component. The *Behavior Domain* represents the
description of the service, network family and component. In the Dynamic
Resource Adaption Layer, the entities in the entity domain are generated, according
to the behavior domain decision, which leads to *the separation of* the *control plane
from the data plane* in SINET.

At the same time, smart and collaborative functions have been designed into the
Smart Pervasive Service layer and *Collaborative* Network Component layer to
interact with the *Dynamic* Resource Adaption layer. With these enhanced functions,
SINET can achieve the *decoupling of the three bindings thoroughly*. With these
features, SINET further resolves the scalability, mobility, security and controllability issues that have been partially solved in the SINET fundamental model.
Furthermore, SINET can solve the problem of resource utilization, energy efficiency, and support of cloud computing and big data transmission.

As shown in Fig. 5.2, *Service IDentifier (SID)* is introduced as a unique and
independent namespace to name a smart service in the Entity Domain, which is
used to separate the resource and location of services. *Family IDentifier (FID)* is
used to name a network family. *Node IDentifier (NID)* is used to name a network
component device. The Entity Domain leverages FID and NID to avoid the
"control and data binding." In the Behavior Domain, *Service Behavior Description
(SBD)*, *Family Behavior Description (FBD)* and *Node Behavior Description (NBD)*
are used to provide further descriptions of SID, FID and NID, respectively. They
are widely used in the enhanced mapping process in SINET, which is shown in the
following. Three intelligent mapping functions are proposed, namely: F1, F2 and
F3. F1 chooses the appropriate network families according to the service demands.
F2 matches the network components of a network family with the service demands.
F3 achieves the behavior aggregation of network components by using an
intra-family cooperation mechanism.

Figure 5.3 shows the relationship between the SINET fundamental model (introduced in Chap. 2) [4–6] and evolutionary model. For the SINET evolutionary model, the SID includes the basic service information contained in the fundamental model of SINET. Additionally, emerging service types, such as Computing Service, Storage Service and Software Service, are also included [7]. CID is considered as a special case of FID. In CID, the connection is *static* for each communication process [8]. While for SINET, FID is *adaptively* and *dynamically generated*. AID and RID in the fundamental model of SINET *belong to* the NID in SINET. They can be considered as NID residing in different topologies.

The operational principles of SINET are shown in Fig. 5.4. Between the Smart Pervasive Service Layer and Dynamic Resource Adaption Layer, SINET deploys an *inter-family collaboration* mechanism through *behavior matching*. In the Behavior Domain, the behavior-matching mechanism maps SBD to FBD to find the optimal family function module for a smart service. Then, the selected network families operate collaboratively according to the inter-family collaboration mechanism. In addition, SINET employs an *intra-family cooperation mechanism* by using a *behavior-aggregation* mechanism between the Dynamic Resource Adaption Layer and Collaborative Network Component Layer. The behavior aggregation mechanism is used to map FBD to NBD to find the optimal set of network nodes. Then, the network nodes in a family cooperate together according to the intra-family cooperation mechanism. Through the aforementioned mechanisms, SINET is able to dynamically adapt network resources to various service demands to satisfy the demands of pervasiveness and smartness.

The workflow of SINET is shown in Fig. 5.5. First, service providers register SIDs and SBDs. Second, a service client requires the SBD, looks up the service and

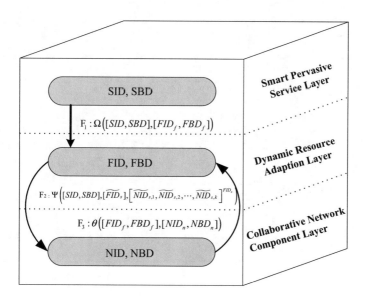

Fig. 5.2 Enhanced mapping models

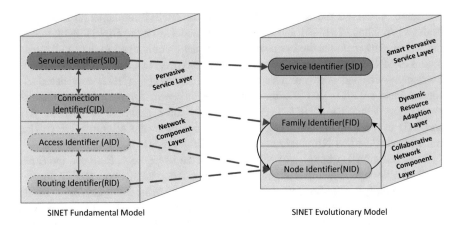

SINET Fundamental Model   SINET Evolutionary Model

Fig. 5.3 Relationship between SINET fundamental model and evolutionary model

selects the specific SID and SBD. Then, SINET will match the selected SBD with
the FBD to perform the mapping between SID and FID. The FID and FBD of the
selected network family are confirmed. Third, the network components are aggregated to different network families according to NBD. Then, SINET will analyze
the needed SBD and chosen NBD to select the optimal network components.

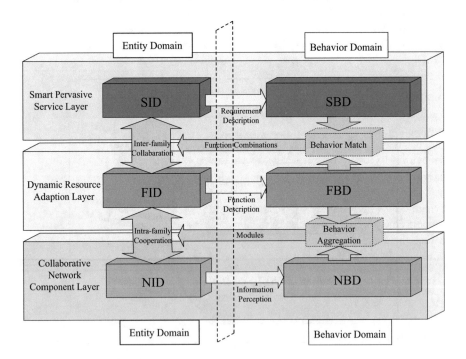

Fig. 5.4 Principle of SINET

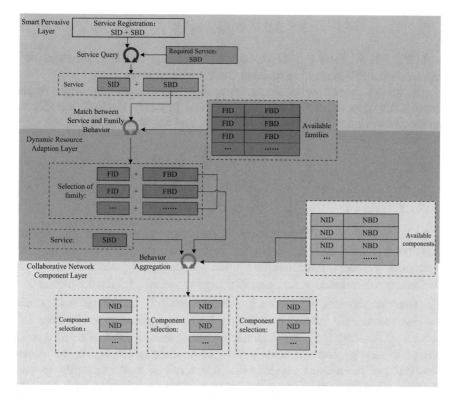

Fig. 5.5 Workflow of SINET

Finally, the service client will acquire the service through the chosen network components.

To summarize, by introducing the Dynamic Resource Adaptation Layer, the control and data planes of SINET are separated. By introducing the entity domain and behavior domain, SINET can easily perceive service demands and network behaviors. By applying the three enhanced mappings, SINET can adapt network families and components smartly to provide services. Meanwhile, SINET deploys a behavior-matching mechanism and behavior-aggregation mechanism to achieve dynamic adaption and collaborative allocation of network resources. SINET can support emerging service types, improve the utility ratio of network resources and reduce the energy consumption of the network.

5.1.1   Smart Pervasive Service Layer Model

In order to provide smart and pervasive service for the client, SID is introduced and defined as follows:

$$SID \triangleq \Phi(S_{type}, S_{data}). \tag{5.1}$$

In Eq. 5.1, S_{type} and S_{data} represent the service type and service content; $\Phi()$ represents the SID-generating function (such as SHA1, etc.).

The SBD is introduced to denote the service properties. SBD provides further descriptions of service based on service naming. Typically, the SBD includes the topology description, performance description and functionality description. It is defined as follows:

$$SBD \triangleq \begin{bmatrix} \{b_L^{ST}, b_C^{ST}, \ldots\}_T \\ \{b_Q^{SP}, b_B^{SP}, b_D^{SP}, b_L^{SP}, b_M^{SP}, \ldots\}_P \\ \{b_T^{SF}, b_N^{SF}, b_S^{SF}, b_P^{SF}, \ldots\}_F \end{bmatrix}. \tag{5.2}$$

In Eq. 5.2, T, P and F correspond to the *topology* description, *performance* description and *functionality* description, respectively. Among them, the topology description includes service location b_L^{ST} and service cache location b_C^{ST}, and so on. Performance description includes quality requirement b_Q^{SP}, bandwidth requirement b_B^{SP}, delay requirement b_D^{SP}, packet loss requirement b_L^{SP} and the optimal communication means b_M^{SP}, and so on. Function description includes: service type b_T^{SF}, version b_N^{SF}, credibility b_S^{SF} and provider signature attribute b_P^{SF}, and so on. Among them, the service location and service cache location represent the device description of the network service node, which can be used to identify network location information. Service type is the type of business service, such as voice, video, images, documents and so on. Service credibility attributes include users' perceptual evaluation and feedback information of other services. The version information is used to describe the version number when the service provider releases a new version based on an unchanged service identity. The provider signature is for security reason, with which the authenticity and reliability of the information can be ensured.

The mapping mechanism between SID and FID is introduced in the Smart Pervasive Service Layer. This mapping mechanism matches the SBD with all of the FBDs. It finds the optimal network family for the smart service.

The mapping between SID and FID is shown as follows:

$$\begin{bmatrix} FID_1' \\ FID_2' \\ \ldots \\ FID_s' \end{bmatrix} \triangleq \Omega \left([SID, SBD], \begin{bmatrix} FID_1, FBD_1 \\ FID_2, FBD_2 \\ \ldots \\ FID_f, FBD_f \end{bmatrix} \right). \tag{5.3}$$

In Eq. 5.3, $\widetilde{FID_1} \sim \widetilde{FID_s}$ are FIDs of the selected network families. The vector $[SID, SBD]$ denotes the SID and SBD. FID_i and FBD_i are the FID and FBD of Network Family i, which is generated in advance. There are f candidate family modules. $\Omega[]$ is the match mapping function.

In summary, the Smart Pervasive Service Layer uses SID and SBD to name, register, query and match services, and the mapping between SID and FID provides a necessary basis for the allocation of network resources. This can lead to the improvement of the user experience.

5.1.2 Dynamic Resource Adaption Layer Model

The Dynamic Resource Adaption Layer uses FID to name a network family. The network families' division is based on behavior descriptions. The network family divisions are different according to different kinds of behavior. Thus, the classification is the most important attribute of the family. When the network families are formed, each family will have a certain behavior similarity, thus forming family-specific behavior characteristics. According to the family classification and behavior characteristics, a network family can be identified, and the FID is defined as follows:

$$FID \triangleq \varphi(F_T, F_P, F_F). \tag{5.4}$$

In Eq. 5.4, F_T represents the topology behavior. F_P represents the performance behavior. F_F represents the functionality behavior. $\varphi(\bullet)$ represents the family identifier-generating function.

In order to describe the family behaviors, the Dynamic Resource Adaption Layer uses FBD, which is a further description based on FID. It mainly contains three aspects, namely *topology*, *performance* and *functionality*. For example, according to the topological properties, the network family can be divided into two main groups: the core network family and access network family. The two main families can be further subdivided into sub-families according to their specific locations. According to the performance properties, the family can also be divided into several main groups: the high-performance group, performance group and low-performance group. Meanwhile, these main groups can also be further subdivided according to specific parameters such as high bandwidth, low latency and other ethnic groups. According to functionality properties, the family can be divided into several main groups: server, transmission equipment, sensors, storage, smart management, service registry query and IO adapters, and so on. All the families can be further subdivided according to specific information. When the network device function increases, the families can continue adding new groups at the same time. According to the family classification and behavior characteristics, the network family can be identified.

FBD can be defined as follows:

$$FBD \triangleq \begin{bmatrix} \{b_L^{FT}, b_N^{FT}, b_D^{FT}, b_R^{FT}, \ldots\}_T \\ \{b_B^{FP}, b_D^{FP}, b_L^{FP}, b_S^{FP}, \ldots\}_P \\ \{b_T^{FF}, b_F^{FF}, b_S^{FF}, b_M^{FF}, \ldots\}_F \end{bmatrix}, \tag{5.5}$$

in which, T, P and F correspond to the topology behavior, performance behavior and functionality behavior, respectively. For FBD, topology behavior includes: family location b_L^{FT}, the number of components within family b_N^{FT}, component distribution within network family b_D^{FT} and neighboring family relations b_R^{FT}, and so on. Performance behavior includes: bandwidth b_B^{FP}, delay b_D^{FP}, packet loss b_L^{FP}, stability b_S^{FP} and so on. Functionality behavior includes: family type B_T^{FF}, family function b_F^{FF}, security level b_S^{FF} and mobility b_M^{FF}, and so on.

The resource adaption layer analyzes the service demands from the upper layer and network resource of the lower layer, and then it selects the appropriate network family and components for the service. In this way, the resource utility ratio can be improved, and the service can be retrieved smartly.

The mapping between NID with SID and FID is shown as follows:

$$\triangleq \Psi \left([SID, SBD], \begin{bmatrix} \widetilde{FID}_1 \\ \widetilde{FID}_2 \\ \cdots \\ \widetilde{FID}_s \end{bmatrix}, \left\{ \begin{matrix} \left[\widetilde{NID}_{1,1}, \widetilde{NID}_{1,2}, \ldots, \widetilde{NID}_{1,i} \right]^{FID_1} \\ \left[\widetilde{NID}_{2,1}, \widetilde{NID}_{2,2}, \ldots, \widetilde{NID}_{2,j} \right]^{FID_2} \\ \cdots \\ \left[\widetilde{NID}_{s,1}, \widetilde{NID}_{s,2}, \ldots, \widetilde{NID}_{s,k} \right]^{FID_s} \end{matrix} \right\} \right). \tag{5.6}$$

$$\left\{ \begin{matrix} \left[\widetilde{NID}_{1,1}, \widetilde{NID}_{1,2}, \ldots, \widetilde{NID}_{1,a} \right]^{FID_1} \\ \left[\widetilde{NID}_{2,1}, \widetilde{NID}_{2,2}, \ldots, \widetilde{NID}_{2,b} \right]^{FID_2} \\ \cdots \\ \left[\widetilde{NID}_{s,1}, \widetilde{NID}_{s,2}, \ldots, \widetilde{NID}_{s,c} \right]^{FID_s} \end{matrix} \right\}$$

In Eq. 5.6, $\left[\widetilde{NID}_{s,1}, \widetilde{NID}_{s,2}, \ldots, \widetilde{NID}_{s,c} \right]^{FID_s}$ represents the network component of network family s. $\widetilde{FID}_1 \sim \widetilde{FID}_s$ are the Family Identifiers of the selected family module by Eq. 5.3. The vector $[SID, SBD]$ denotes the SID and SBD of the requested service. $\left[\widetilde{NID}_{s,1}, \widetilde{NID}_{s,2}, \ldots, \widetilde{NID}_{s,c} \right]^{FID_s}$ denotes the network components of the network family s, which are selected by the inter-family collaboration function. $\Psi[]$ represents the behavior match function. This equation indicates that the network family, as well as the components in it, is selected to transmit data for users by means of behavior matching, which takes into account of the FBD of a network family, network component behavior and the service demand. Therefore, the network resource can be adapted collaboratively, and the network will be more efficient.

5.1.3 Collaborative Network Component Layer Model

In the Collaborative Network Component Layer, *network components* are defined as the devices to achieve one or more functions such as collection, generation, storage, forwarding, reception and computing of data. NID is proposed to identify a network component, which is defined as

$$NID \triangleq \omega\left(N_{type}, N_{device}\right). \tag{5.7}$$

In Eq. 5.7, N_{type} denotes types of network components (transmission nodes, storage nodes, etc.), N_{device} denotes information of network components, and $\omega()$ denotes the NID-generating function.

NBD is introduced to denote the node properties. NBD provides further descriptions of components based on information perception. Typically, the NBD includes the *topology* description, *performance* description and *functionality* description.

The NBD can be defined as follows:

$$NBD \triangleq \begin{bmatrix} \{b_L^{NT}, b_P^{NT}, b_R^{NT}, b_C^{NT}, \ldots\}_T \\ \{b_B^{NP}, b_D^{NP}, b_L^{NP}, b_S^{NP}, \ldots\}_P \\ \{b_T^{NF}, b_F^{NF}, b_C^{NF}, b_S^{NF}, \ldots\}_F \end{bmatrix}. \tag{5.8}$$

In Eq. 5.8, T, P and F represent topology behavior, performance behavior and functionality behavior, respectively. For NBD, topology information includes component location b_L^{NT}, component affiliation b_P^{NT}, component adjacency b_R^{NT}, connectivity b_C^{NT} and so on. Performance information includes bandwidth b_B^{NP}, delay b_D^{NP}, packet loss b_L^{NP}, stability b_S^{NP} and so on. Functionality information includes component type b_T^{NF}, component function b_F^{NF}, operator b_C^{NF} and security level b_S^{NF}, and so on.

The behavior aggregation mechanism compares the NBD with FBD to find the most appropriate network components. In the Entity Domain, the intra-family cooperation mechanism interconnects the network components in order to achieve the selecting of network components within the network family.

The mapping between FID and NID is shown as follows:

$$\left\{ \begin{bmatrix} \widetilde{NID}_{1,1}, \widetilde{NID}_{1,2}, \ldots, \widetilde{NID}_{1,i} \end{bmatrix}^{FID_1} \\ \begin{bmatrix} \widetilde{NID}_{2,1}, \widetilde{NID}_{2,2}, \ldots, \widetilde{NID}_{2,j} \end{bmatrix}^{FID_2} \\ \cdots \\ \begin{bmatrix} \widetilde{NID}_{s,1}, \widetilde{NID}_{s,2}, \ldots, \widetilde{NID}_{s,k} \end{bmatrix}^{FID_s} \right\} \triangleq \theta \left(\begin{bmatrix} FID_1, FBD_1 \\ FID_2, FBD_2 \\ \cdots \\ FID_f, FBD_f \end{bmatrix}, \begin{bmatrix} NID_1, NBD_1 \\ NID_2, NBD_2 \\ \cdots \\ NID_n, NBD_n \end{bmatrix} \right).$$

$$\tag{5.9}$$

In Eq. 5.9, FID_f and FBD_f are the FID and FBD of the network family f. NID_n and NBD_n are the NID and NBD of the network component n. $\left[\widetilde{NID}_{s,1}, \widetilde{NID}_{s,2}, \ldots, \widetilde{NID}_{s,k}\right]^{FID_s}$ represents the network component of the network family s. $\theta[]$ is the behavior aggregation function. This equation indicates that network components are selected for the network family by perceiving the information of network components and performing behavior aggregation.

5.2 Collaborative Network Component Layer Mechanisms

In this section, the collaborative network component layer mechanism is introduced. By applying the model and mechanisms in the Collaborative Network Component Layer, the concern of information dissemination and energy efficiency of the current Internet can be solved. In the following, we will elaborate the smart network component design, a dynamic storage management mechanism and an adaptive energy-saving mechanism, respectively.

5.2.1 Smart Network Component Design

Network components of the future Internet mainly include: the *Network Switching Router Component (NSR)*, *Network Switching Component (NSC)*, *Intelligent Service Resolution Server (ISRS)*, *Resource Adapting Resolution Server (RARS)*, *Intelligent Central Control Component (ICCC)*, *Content-Providing Server (CPS)*, *Stable Terminal Component (STC)*, *Mobile Terminal Component (MTC)* and so on. *ISRS* is mainly applied for analyzing service requirements and performing service matching. *RARS* is mainly responsible for dynamical adaptation between services and network resources through behavior matching (inter-family collaboration). *ICCC* is mainly responsible for the internal management within a family by using behavior aggregation (intra-family cooperation). *NSC* is used for data forwarding. *NSR* is mainly responsible for the transmission and storage of data. In the following, we elaborate the system design of NSR.

Figure 5.6 shows the typical design of NSR. This model includes two main features. First, the memory module is introduced in the component data plane, which is used to dynamically store network data and adapt the resources according to service popularity so as to support cloud computing and cloud service. Second, the modularized virtual technology and separation mechanism between the control

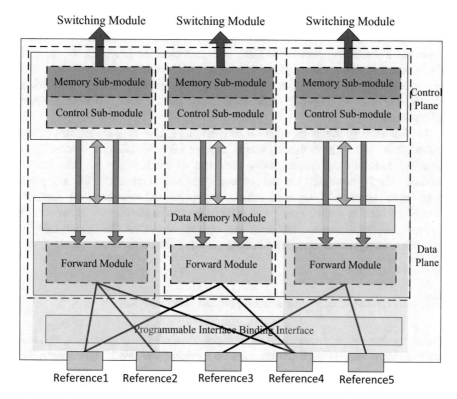

Fig. 5.6 Design of NSR

plane and data plane allow components to perceive their own conditions and regroup function modules in flexible ways so as to optimize network performance and reduce energy consumption.

As shown in Fig. 5.6, the typical network component model includes the component *control plane and data plane*. The control plane includes a memory sub-module and control sub-module. The memory sub-module is used to perceive the status information of the network component, store reachability information, path status information, path reliability information and performance information. In addition, it can be used to obtain and store the SID and SBD from the data level. The control sub-module is used to control data forwarding according to memory sub-module information.

The data plane includes the data memory module and forward module. The data memory module is used to store the contents of service, which is important for efficient information dissemination and acquisition [9–11]. The forward module is used to forward data. When the data flow through the forward module, the memory module stores the contents of service according to the requests of the control plane and sends SID and SBD to the control plane. When the same service is requested again, the network component can extract the data from the data plane according to the information of the control plane and provide the nearest service to the user. This can successfully avoid high energy consumption and long delays in acquiring remote services to improve user experience and achieve efficient resource utilization.

In this model, the component is divided into several sub-modules. These sub-modules can be recombined, which improves the flexibility of data transmission. For example, the control sub-module can recombine with the data forward module, which formulates several switching modules supporting different protocols. On the other hand, separating the control plane and data plane can make the data plane turn to sleep mode when having no data transmission. However, the control plane still remains aware of the network status for the achievability of network topology, thus ensuring the energy saving of the network.

5.2.2 Dynamic Storage Management Mechanism

Based on the collaborative network component model, we propose a dynamic storage mechanism to store the contents of services in network components. The mechanism supports acquiring service information residing in the network component, so that the network can access the nearest service and improve network performance. The storage mechanism is shown in Fig. 5.7 and is explained in the following.

- Data flow through the data forward module.
- Forward module transmits the data to the control sub-module.

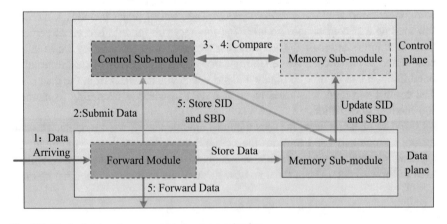

Fig. 5.7 Typical network component storage mechanism

- The control sub-module transmits the SID and SBD to the control memory sub-module.
- The control memory sub-module compares the SID and SBD with its storage information and provides the result to the control sub-module.
- The control sub-module decides whether to store the content with the SID by analyzing the received result based on the corresponding control plane algorithm. If the data need to be stored, they will be stored in the data memory module, and the SID and SBD are returned to the memory sub-module within the control plane. Then, the data are forwarded. Otherwise, the data are forwarded directly to the next component.

In addition, the control module can carry out a variety of operations for the data memory sub-module, such as adding, deleting, updating, sorting and so on. When the stored data have not been accessed for a long time, the control module can delete them. When the version of the stored data needs to be updated, the control module can inform the data memory module for data updating.

5.2.3   Adaptive Energy-Saving Mechanism

In the current network, the router does not support sleep mode, with only the "on" and "off" mode enabled [12, 13]. Even if link utilization is low, it still remains a working status, resulting in high energy consumption. To achieve the network component sleep mode, the separation of the control plane and data plane is proposed based on the component network mode so as to reduce energy consumption.

When link utilization is low, SINET will start the network component energy-saving mechanism. Particularly, the internal structure of network components is reconstructed, and network traffic is smartly transferred to one or a few of line cards according to the demand of different business volumes. The other idle line cards can be put to sleep mode to reduce energy consumption.

When the components are in sleep mode (no data forwarding), its configuration information is stored in control module, which can ensure their existence. This can ensure the network topology is unchanged, reducing a large number of routing updates. On the other hand, this can also shorten the wake up time of components from sleep mode, ensuring the rapid response to emergencies.

The "sleep" mode is different from the "off" mode, as the components in sleep mode can still send limited kinds of packets (such as "hello" packets) to ICCC. When ICCC receives such packets, it is informed that the component is in sleep mode, and no data packets are forwarded to the sleep component. ICCC collects and processes the sensed status information of all the components and calculates the corresponding sleep policy. When the network traffic increases, ICCC will calculate a new sleep policy according to the status information and wake up the corresponding network components.

5.3 Smart Pervasive Service Layer Mechanisms

This session introduces the mechanism of the Smart Pervasive Service Layer. The Smart Pervasive Service Layer is responsible for the service naming, service describing, service caching and service sensing, and so on. Figure 5.8 shows the Smart Pervasive Service Layer model of SINET. SID is used to achieve unified service naming and description and also to achieve the separation between resources and location. SBD is introduced to denote the service properties. It is used to describe the multi-dimensionality and multi-granularity of service requirements so that the network infrastructure can provide better support for different service requirements. SID mapping is used to conduct dynamical matching among the aggregation of network components in the service and adaption layer, achieving smart coupling among network infrastructures.

The mechanism of the Smart Pervasive Service Layer mainly includes *service naming and description, service registration and query, service resource caching methods* and *service dynamics sensing methods*. The Smart Service Pervasive Layer solves the issues of the current network shown in the following three aspects. First, a unified description and naming for the service are proposed to reduce the complexity of information delivery and improve compatibility and control and management. Second, the *separation of service resources and location* can be achieved in a rigid delivery model for better information retrieval. Third, the dynamic matching between the network infrastructure and service is proposed to achieve the quality of experience for multi-dimensional and multi-granularity of services.

Fig. 5.8 The smart pervasive service layer model of SINET

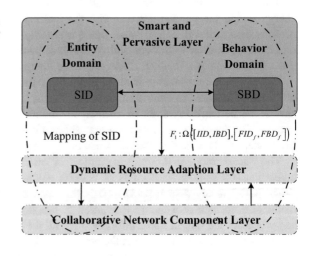

5.3.1   Service Naming and Description

In order to provide smart and pervasive service for clients, SID is introduced as a unified name to describe a service. SID includes the service types in the fundamental SINET, such as data, voice, video and so on. In addition, emerging service types, such as computing services and storage services, are also included. Considering the large number and different types of service, a flat SID will have serious scalability challenges [14, 15]. Therefore, SINET distinguishes the service according to various attributes. The network generates a hierarchical SID to ensure its scalability. The common network service classification is shown in Table 5.1.

As shown in Table 5.1, SID can be generated by using multiple service attributes. For example, if the type of service is e-commerce, the credibility of the content provider is good, and if the network belongs to China Unicom, then its SID will be generated according to number 2, 4 and 6 in Table 5.1. The generating function of SID can be determined according to the actual network environment and needs.

Table 5.2 is a further description of service type in Table 5.1. In addition, certain attributes of network service are subjective, such as service reliability and so on. The classification of these attributes needs to consider the specific application

Table 5.1 Classification of service

Classification index	Classification standard	Types
1	Area	Domestic; international
2	Content/ISP credibility	Excellent; good; fair; poor
3	Credibility	Excellent; good; fair; poor
4	Provider	China Education and Research Network; China Telecom; China Unicom
5	Category	Education; culture; arts; broadcasting; film and television; agriculture; forestry; scientific research
6	Type	Details shown in Table 5.2

Table 5.2 Typical service types

Service type		
	Access service	Virtual space
	E-commerce	VoIP
	Broadband multimedia	Online game
	BBS	Blog
	Instant message	Homepage
	Email	Uploading and downloading
	Message service	WWW
	Online video	Others

environment. For example, if high reliability of services is required in certain scenarios, the granularity of classification needs to be further refined.

Notably, the network service classification in Table 5.1 and the service type in Table 5.2 merely illustrate some examples of service attributes. These tables do not contain all services.

The naming and description of services not only achieve unified control and management of multi-dimensional and multi-granularity, but also scalability. In addition, SBD is introduced to denote the service properties. SBD includes the topology description, performance description, functionality description and so on, defined in Eq. 5.2. Thus, SBD, on the basis of the SID, can accurately describe the features and attributes of service, which lays a necessary foundation for the network nodes to support smart services.

5.3.2   Service Registration and Query

In SINET, the naming of SID can achieve the separation between the service resource and location. When a user requests a certain service, the service providers need to register the provided services so that the user can query the services. The service registration and query system are shown in Fig. 5.9. The details of the working process are described as follows.

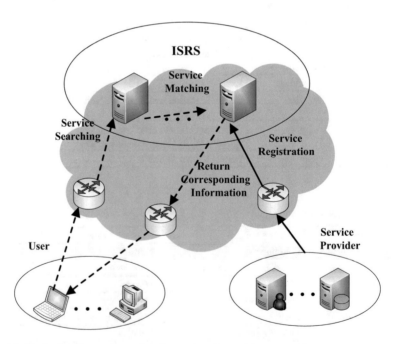

Fig. 5.9 Design for the service registration and query system

First, the service provider must register the SID and SBD in the system. Second, when a user requests a certain service, he or she may send three types of request message, which are shown as follows: (1) an accurate service request message, which provides the SID directly; (2) a service description request message, which provides SBD information; (3) a mixed service request message, which provides partial information of the SID and SBD. Subsequently, ISRS looks up the SID and SBD according to the required service through a certain algorithm. Then, the ISRS returns the results to the user by choosing the satisfactory service.

In the practical network environment, in order to achieve the above objectives, it is necessary to establish an ISRS for each network family to manage the services provided by its own or its subordinate network families, shown in Fig. 5.10.

During the service registration process, the service providers must send SIDs and SBDs of the provided services to ISRS for its network family. The ISRS stores the information in the local database and sends a registration message to the connected ISRS.

During the service query process, when a user wants to acquire a certain service, it needs to send service lookup request to the local ISRS. The user may send a quest of the precise SID, an SBD or a combination of partial attribute information belonging to SID and SBD. Then, the local ISRS begins to match the request in the SID Query Module. If the SID can be exactly matched, and the local ISRS can provide the service required by the user, the ISRS provides the service to the user directly and returns the SID and SBD. Conversely, if the local network cannot provide the service needed by the user, it will forward the request to a higher level ISRS until the service is located. Then, the SID and SBD are returned.

ISRS plays an important role in SID registering and querying. Therefore, the reliability and scalability of the system in the large-scale network must be considered seriously. For reliability, the system can use a redundancy program in the actual deployment. For scalability, the system can use hierarchical distributed deployment to achieve hierarchical management, which can improve its scalability in a large-scale network environment.

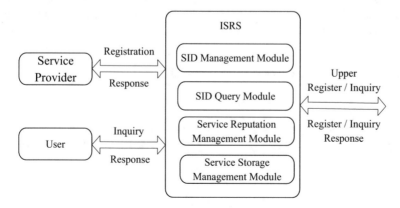

Fig. 5.10 Working process of service registration and query

5.3.3   Service Resource Caching

In traditional networks, service resources basically are stored centrally. With the development of triple play and other services, defects of such models are increasingly exposed. When a large number of users are accessing video service resources, large amounts of network bandwidth and routing devices will be consumed. This seriously affects normal operations of networks and greatly reduces the user's experience.

SID is introduced as a unique and independent namespace that names a service independent of its location. Thus, SINET can select appropriate service resource caching methods according to service resource properties and user preferences. The caching methods include centralized caching and distributed caching.

For example, services with a relatively small amount of data such as mail can still use the centralized storage mode. Services with a large amount but a lower user access frequency can also use the centralized mode. Services with a large amount and a high user access frequency can use a distributed caching mode. Table 5.3 shows a typical service resource caching strategy. The actual service resource caching strategy needs to consider the multi-dimensional demands from the user and multi-dimensional service attributes.

In the following, the distributed caching method of service resources for video service is illustrated. Figure 5.11 shows the caching method for video service resources. In this figure, there are two kinds of components, which are the NSC and Service Caching Component (SCC). The latter is mainly used for caching services. The local SCC nearest to the client stores hot video services, which are highly accessed. When a user accesses a video service that does not exist in the local SCC, the user can access the upper level SCC. If the service is still not hit, the user can continue to access the upper level SCC until the video server is reached.

Caching the representative services and data in SINET can provide the nearest service for users. This caching mechanism can greatly reduce the network service delay and traffic load so as to effectively improve the resource utilization. However, considering the limitation of network resources and randomness of service in the actual network, the mechanism needs to be further optimized, such as the fragmentation caching of service resources.

Table 5.3 A typical service resources caching method

User access frequency	Low	High
Service resource size		
Large (high bandwidth consumption)	Centralized caching	Distributed caching
Small (low bandwidth consumption)	Centralized caching	Distributed caching

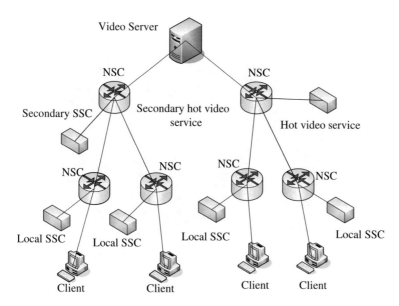

Fig. 5.11 Distributed caching method of video service resources

5.3.4   Service Dynamics Sensing

In order to enhance the quality of experience, a service dynamics sensing method is studied to scientifically obtain the changes in the service requirement and service behavior. The service-aware mechanisms of SINET mainly consist of the following four aspects:

- Service providers should obtain and measure the needs of users and provide personalized service for users according to the user's service request behavior.
- Network components forward user's service requests and send the SID and SBD to the ISRS, which analyzes the service request distribution and measures the service popularity to determine their popularity rating.
- Network components obtain the flowing data, extract the corresponding SID and SBD and determine whether or not to cache the service according to the popularity rating. If yes, the network component sends a message to the ISRS and registers its SID and SBD. Then, the system analyzes the received information and selects the appropriate network components to provide services in order to get a good user experience. In Fig. 5.12, ISRS selects network components NID_1 and NID_2 to provide the nearest service for users.
- Network components receive the changes of service behavior and exact the corresponding SID, providing a necessary basis for rational allocation of network resources.

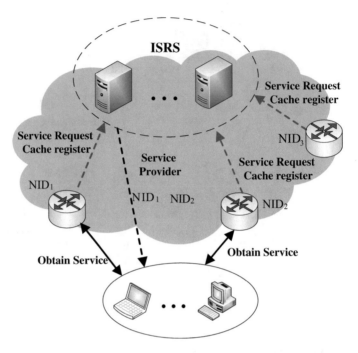

Fig. 5.12 Service dynamics sensing mechanism

5.4 Dynamic Resource Adaption Layer Mechanisms

In this section, the Dynamic Resource Adaptation Layer mechanism is introduced. The Dynamic Resource Adaptation Layer dynamically adapts network resources and configures network families by means of obtaining service demands and network behavior to satisfy the service demands and improve the quality of experience. By applying the dynamic resource adaptation layer mechanism, the control and data plane can be separated and network resource utilization can be optimized. Dynamic resource adaption is achieved by inter-family collaboration and intra-family cooperation, which are cross layer designed. And in this section, we introduce inter-family collaboration and intra-family cooperation mechanisms, respectively.

5.4.1 Inter-family Collaboration

The *inter-family collaboration* establishes the mapping between SID and FID through behavior matching to seek the best network family functional module to coordinately manage network resources and to achieve resource dynamic adaptation. The behavior mapping between SID and FID is shown in Eq. 5.3.

We further illustrate inter-family collaboration with an example shown in Fig. 5.13. The name of a video service is assumed to be SID_1, the required bandwidth is set to be b_1, the maximum delay is set to be d_1, and the credibility is set to be s_1. Then, the SBD is defined as follows:

$$SBD_1 = \begin{bmatrix} 0 \\ \{b_1, d_1\} \\ \{i_1\} \end{bmatrix}. \tag{5.10}$$

Suppose there are three family modules in the network, and their respective FID and FBD are (FID_1, FBD_1), (FID_2, FBD_2) and (FID_3, FBD_3). The behavior-matching mapping function $\Omega[\ ]$ is a bandwidth constraint function that can choose the minimum path family first. Besides, the family FID_3 has the maximum bandwidth and minimum path. Thus, the matching result is FID_3; that is, family FID_3 is chosen to provide service. It can be concluded through the above analysis that in order to provide smart and pervasive service for a client, the mapping between SID and FID provides a necessary basis for the allocation of network resources and offers improved user experience.

The inter-family collaboration is achieved by using RARS, which collects the behavior of network families, analyzes the service demands and performs behavior-matching mechanisms. Then, the control information is sent to each

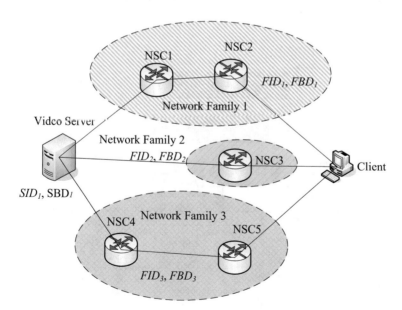

Fig. 5.13 Mapping between the service and family

family ICCC for selecting the best available components through intra-family cooperation, which is further introduced in the following section.

5.4.2   Intra-family Cooperation

The *intra-family cooperation* refers to the establishment of information interaction mechanisms for network components within the family through behavior aggregation to allow the network components to interconnect with each other better. The intra-family cooperation mechanism and its relationship with inter-family collaboration are illustrated in Fig. 5.14. Within each family, an ICCC or multiple ICCCs exist for collecting the behavior information for the network component. The behavior aggregation mechanisms are generated in the ICCC and are then sent to the network components. In addition, the ICCC within the family can communicate with the RARS for receiving the collaboration control information generated by using dynamic behavior matching in the inter-family collaboration process.

By establishing the inter-family collaboration among network families, the network resources are allocated with great flexibility. Thus, the utilization of network resources is improved. By applying intra-family cooperation, family self-healing is achieved to increase the robustness of the network. The inter-family collaboration and intra-family cooperation in the Dynamic Resource Adaption Layer of SINET enable control and data plane separation, leading to a high network resource utilization ratio, easy manageability of network resources and increased network robustness.

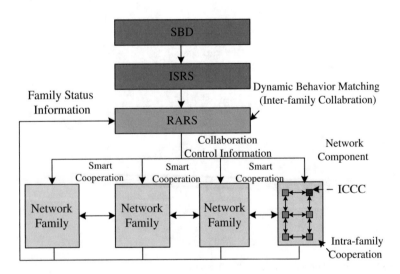

Fig. 5.14 Intra-family cooperation and inter-family collaboration

5.5 Conclusion

In summary, this chapter introduces the evolutionary architecture of SINET and mechanisms for the Collaborative Network Component Layer, Smart Pervasive Service Layer and Dynamic Resource Adaptation Layer. In the evolutionary model of SINET, the Dynamic Resource Adaptation Layer is introduced to achieve the separation of the control and data plane. The entity domain and behavior domain are brought for improving the feasibility of perceiving service demands and network behavior. Three enhanced mappings are proposed to smartly adjust network families and components to provide services. Meanwhile, SINET deploys the behavior-matching mechanism and behavior-aggregation mechanism for inter-family collaboration and intra-family cooperation to achieve dynamic adaption and collaborative allocation of network resources. By applying the above mechanisms, emerging service types are supported with high efficiency, the utility ratio of network resource is improved, and the energy consumption of the network is reduced. The above benefits of the evolutionary model will be further elaborated in the next chapter.

References

1. Zhang H, Luo H (2013) Fundamental research on theories of smart and cooperative networks. Acta Electronica Sinica 7:1249–1254
2. Su W, Chen J, Zhou H, Zhang H (2013) Research on the service mechanisms in smart and cooperative networks. Acta Electronica Sinica 7:1255–1260
3. Gao S, Wang H, Wang K, Zhang H (2013) Research on cooperation mechanisms of smart network components. Acta Electronica Sinica 7:1261–1267
4. Zhang H, Su W (2007) Fundamental research on the architecture of new network—universal network and pervasive services. Chin J Electr 41(7)
5. Dong P, Qin Y, Zhang H (2007) Research on universal network supporting pervasive services. Chin J Electr 41(7)
6. Yang D, Zhou H, Zhang H (2007) Research on pervasive services based on universal network. Chin J Electr 41(7)
7. Velte Toby, Velte Anthony, Elsenpeter Robert (2009) Cloud computing, a practical approach, 1st edn. McGraw-Hill Inc, New York, NY, USA
8. Luo H, Zhang H, Zukerman M et al (2014) An incrementally deployable network architecture to support both data-centric and host-centric services. IEEE Netw 28(4):58–65
9. Koponen T, Chawla M, Chun BG, Ermolinskiy A, Kim KH, Shenker S, Stoica I (2007) A data-oriented (and beyond) network architecture. ACM SIGCOMM Comput Commun Rev 37 (4), 181–192 (ACM)
10. Jacobson V, Smetters DK, Thornton JD, Plass MF, Briggs NH, Braynard RL (2009) Networking named content. In: Proceedings of the 5th international conference on emerging networking experiments and technologies. ACM, pp 1–12
11. Ahlgren B, Dannewitz C, Imbrenda C, Kutscher D, Ohlman B (2012) A survey of information-centric networking. Commun Mag IEEE 50(7):26–36
12. Fisher W, Suchara M, Rexford J (2010) Greening backbone networks: reducing energy consumption by shutting off cables in bundled links. In: Proceedings of the first ACM SIGCOMM workshop on green networking. ACM, pp 29–34

13. Bolla R, Bruschi R, Franco D, Cucchietti F (2011) Energy efficiency in the future internet: a survey of existing approaches and trends in energy-aware fixed network infrastructures. Commun Surv Tutorials IEEE 13(2):223–244 (Second Quarter 2011)
14. Xylomenos G, Ververidis CN, Siris VA, Fotiou N, Tsilopoulos C, Vasilakos X, Katsaros KV, Polyzos GC (2014) A survey of information-centric networking research. Commun Surv Tutorials IEEE 16(2):1024–1049 (Second Quarter 2014)
15. Bari MF, Chowdhury S, Ahmed R, Boutaba R, Mathieu B (2012) A survey of naming and routing in information-centric networks. Commun Mag IEEE 50(12):44–53

Chapter 6
Analysis and Evaluation of SINET

In order to evaluate the superiorities of SINET, its performance is evaluated by a thorough comparison with the recent network solutions. In this chapter, we focus on the analysis and evaluation of SINET. Specifically, in Sect. 6.1, some potential superiorities of SINET are discussed in theory from several different aspects, including scalability improvement, mobility support, security enhancement, support of cloud services, network robustness, resource utilization, manageability and energy efficiency. In Sect. 6.2, some experimental analyses are introduced to prove the performance of SINET, including mapping performance, routing scalability, security, services migration and SID resolution mapping. Section 6.3 concludes this chapter. This chapter illustrates that SINET outperforms the current Internet in various aspects and is able to meet the emerging requirements of the future Internet.

6.1 Analysis of SINET Superiorities

Currently, there have been many reported novel solutions for the future Internet, such as CCN/NDN [1], MobilityFirst [2], LISP [3] and SDN/NFV [4–6]. Each of these solutions is targeted to focus on overcoming only one or a few certain drawbacks appearing in the current Internet, but no solution has considered them in a complete way. For example, CCN/NDN focuses on improving the quality of content delivery by using name-based forwarding and in-path caching. However, Kuipers et al. have stated that the name-based routing in CCN/NDN will aggravate the problem of routing scalability [7]. For another example, LISP focuses on the lower network functions to achieve the separation of control and forwarding and does not care much about the upper applications, making it difficult to define a uniform naming for all kinds of services [3]. SDN concentrates on offering the ability to control and program the network through centralized network management, decoupling the control plane and the data plane, while NFV aims to offer the ability to reduce the device costs by leveraging hardware with high generality and

© Springer-Verlag Berlin Heidelberg 2016
H. Zhang et al., *Smart Collaborative Identifier Network*,
DOI 10.1007/978-3-662-49143-0_6

IT virtualization technologies. SDN and NFV create new opportunities as well as challenges for traditional service-chaining policy [8]. However, the increasing deployments of middle boxes and NFV-based services result in the complexity of flow management [9].

The underlining reason for the above problems is that the existing available technology is not able to solve the triple binding at the same time. As shown in Table 6.1, LISP is able to solve the user/network separation problem by separating the IP address into routing location and node identity. However, resource/location separation or control/data separation is not supported. NDN is able to support resource/location separation by using uniform hierarchical naming to break the relation between resource and location [10]. However, user/network separation is not supported since the Data Packets will be transmitted back according to the routing path of the Interest Packets, which leads to the dependence on location [10]. In addition, control/data separation is not supported because of the smart and dynamic forwarding plane design. SDN/NFV is able to support the control/data separation. However, user/network separation or resource/location separation are not supported.

SINET is designed to *be immune to* the problems exiting in the current Internet, such as scalability, mobility, security and so on, *by decoupling the triple bindings*. SINET is not only able to reserve the advantages of many novel future Internet proposals, but also to remedy the drawbacks when each single future Internet proposal is used. Generally speaking, SINET is able to provide solutions for user/network separation, resource/location separation and control/data separation. Thereby, the scalability, mobility and security can be enhanced. In addition, the cloud service, network robustness and resource utilization, network manageability and energy efficiency can be better supported. In the following, the superiorities of SINET are analyzed respectively.

6.1.1 Scalability Improvement

With the development of the Internet, the scalability problem is becoming increasingly serious [11, 12]. This problem is mainly caused by *user/network binding* and is concerned with multiple aspects, such as the network scale and ability to support new applications. In SINET, multiple mapping mechanisms provide efficient support for the network scalability. Here, we analyze SINET's scalability from two aspects: network scale and the ability to support emerging applications.

Table 6.1 Comparisons of LISP, NDN, SDN/NFV and SINET

	LISP	NDN	SDN/NFV	SINET
User/network separation	✓	✗	✗	✓
Resource/location separation	✗	✓	✗	✓
Control/data separation	✗	✗	✓	✓

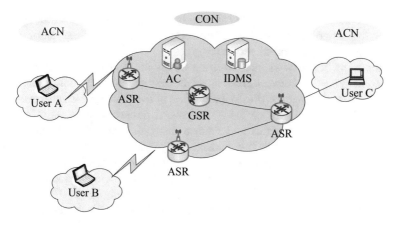

Fig. 6.1 The separation between ACN and CON

First, network scale is mainly reflected in the number of network nodes and links. Normally, the complexity of the network is proportional to the square of the amount of network nodes or links. The change of this amount will directly affect the complexity of network operation, management and maintenance. In SINET, the *AID-RM separates the network into two spaces*, named ACN and CON, which are shown in Fig. 6.1. In ACN, the AIDs are used, and in CON the RIDs are used. Due to this separation, the number of routings in CON will not be directly affected by the number of AIDs. Therefore, the complexity of the network can be reduced in CON, and hence the scalability is improved on some level.

Second, SINET is able to support new applications including emerging network technologies and service types. The "*narrow waist*" model employed by the traditional Internet simplifies the network applications. However, it brings difficulty in supporting the applications of emerging network technology. Moreover, network applications depending on the traditional Internet are difficult to adapt to the development of new technologies in the network layer and transport layer. To overcome this problem, SINET adopts an open design concept. It is able to take the network technology and transmission technology as two important properties when the demander and the provider negotiate and build network connections. Additionally, SINET also provides uniform service naming, behavior description mechanisms and uniform virtual interfaces for the network applications to promote the application of new technologies. Therefore, the scalability can be greatly improved in SINET.

6.1.2   Mobility Support

The mobility in SINET includes two aspects, i.e., *network mobility* and *service mobility*. The network mobility denotes the ability to provide services for mobile nodes. The service mobility, also called service migration, refers to the ability to transfer the on-going services to other sources in an authorized range without influencing the acquisition of services.

In terms of the network mobility, the traditional Internet is designed for the wired communication between fixed hosts. It lacks support for wireless and mobile services. The main reason is due to the *binding of user/network*. In other words, the traditional Internet is based on the IP address. If the access location of a node is changed, the IP address of this node is also changed. Hence, the IP address-based communication link has to be re-established to provide the service. However, users cannot always tolerate the duration of service interruption used for re-establishing the communication link. As shown in Fig. 6.2, SINET provides a good solution for mobility support. In SINET, *the user and network are designed to be decoupled*. The AID remains the same during the movement of a node. To this end, *the end-to-end network connection does not need to be rebuilt*. Because of the AID-RM, the change of access locations only influences the mapping between the AID and RID, without affecting the network service and the network link in the upper layer. In other words, SINET makes the network mobility transparent to the network link. Therefore, as long as the new mapping relationship can be generated in a short time, the network service can be provided without any interruption. Then, the network data generated by the node can be routed in CON uninterruptedly. It is worth noting that the mapping between the AID and RID can be distributed controlled by the IDMS, which makes the delay in generating a new mapping relationship small enough to satisfy the demands of network services.

From the view of the service mobility, the traditional Internet only supports the mobility of a small number of services. The main problem is due to the *binding of resource and location*. In SINET, the service resource and location are decoupled.

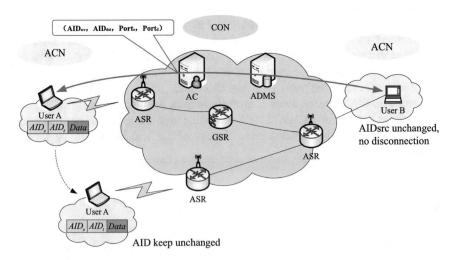

Fig. 6.2 The solution to the mobility problem

CID and CID-RM are used to make it convenient to fully support the mobility of network services. In detail, each service has a unique SID, which will not be modified once it is produced. When the service mobility occurs, the SID is not changed but the CID is updated by using of the CID-RM. This process provides a useful solution for the support of service mobility. Besides, during the service providing, both service providers and service requesters can be adjusted dynamically, such as the replacement, addition, deletion and so on. This design allows the network services to provide efficiently in highly mobile environments.

6.1.3 Security Enhancement

In the original design of the traditional Internet, it is believed that terminal nodes have high credibility. In general, terminal nodes can access to the Internet as long as IP addresses and other information are configured correctly. Therefore, malicious users can attack any node in the network by sending an extremely large number of packets. The main reason behind the security problem is *user/network binding* and *resource/location binding*. Besides, the traditional Internet does not check the information of the source nodes when routing the packets. One terminal node is able to attack the targets and forge another node. Last but not the least, the traditional Internet is an open network environment, such as the public WiFi network. Since the IP address contains both the identity and location information, users always suffer from serious information leakage by accessing a malicious network.

The improvement of network security in SINET originates mainly from several critical mechanisms concerning the aspects of *user/network decouple and resource/location decouple*, which include the *security access control mechanism, separation between ACN and CON, multi-level controllable identifier mapping mechanisms* and the *SID/NID decouple algorithm*. These designs resolve the important and serious security problems in the current Internet by enhancing the control of malicious users and improving the security of CON.

In SINET, AID represents the identity of a node. It remains unchanged once a node accesses a network. Due to the invariance property of AID, numerous security-related mechanisms are integrated with AID. The first one is the AID allocation mechanism. Since AID is tightly bounded with the node identity, AID-based network behaviors are easily tracked by the network administrator. It greatly increases the difficulty of network attacks and deters hackers to a certain extent.

Besides, in SINET, *an access control mechanism* is also designed based on AID. The access control mechanism is performed by the AC and IDMS. As shown in Fig. 6.3, AC strictly authenticates the nodes and verifies the legality of nodes. IDMS checks the validity of the ASR. Only if both the node and the ASR pass the access control process will the network provide the demanded resources for the requesters, such as allocating the RID. Otherwise, the node cannot connect with the ASR to acquire the services. This authentication mechanism ensures the authenticity of the access node and ASR. It is important for tracking network security events and the control of node behavior, and so on.

The *separation between ACN and CON* is another key characteristic of the SINET. The separated ACN and CON are operated in two different identifier spaces, i.e., AID space and RID space. The AID denotes the node identity information and is dedicated to the ACN. The RID represents the terminal position information and is only used in CON. The packets with AID sent out by the users of the ACN can only be routed within the ACN. These packets cannot be routed to the CON except by the mapping between the AID and RID. Additionally, during the mapping process, the ASR will also check the packets to identify the legality. The same procedure also happens to the packets sent out from the CON. This mechanism efficiently prevents DDoS attacks. As shown in Fig. 6.4, if the attacker wants to perform the DDoS attack on other node, the ASR will check the AID of the data packets. If the packets are identified as malicious packets, then they will be discarded. Otherwise, the packets will be routed in CON. Therefore, this kind of design greatly improves the security of CON.

In SINET, all the network services have to be completed through *multiple secure mapping processes*. These mapping processes play good roles as firewalls and improve the network security on a full scale. The AID-RM separates ACN and CON. In this way, the information of access nodes is absent in the CON. At the same time, the nodes in CON are not able to get the information of two access nodes. It is even impossible for the two access nodes to know each other. Thus, the privacy of access nodes is well protected, such as the identity and access location.

Additionally, the *separation between SID and NID* makes it difficult to attack a particular service provider. Different NIDs might provide the same service and can be generated by different mapping rules. This design greatly reduces the probability of a network attack for a specific service. Moreover, the mapping between the FID and SID is able to provide multiple-level secure transmission paths. Consequently,

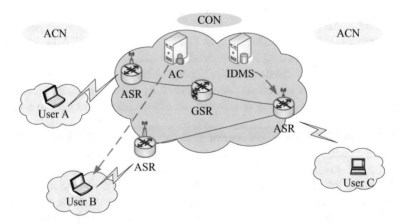

Fig. 6.3 The access control of SINET

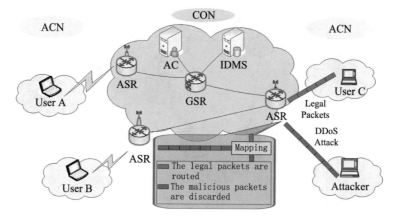

Fig. 6.4 DDoS prevention in SINET

the parallel transmission and the uncertainty of network providers considerably reduce the probability of information stealing by the third-party in the network. In this way, the security of network data service can be further guaranteed.

6.1.4 Support of Cloud Service

In recent years, emerging service types have been developing at a rapid speed, such as cloud service [13]. Large amounts of data are generated because of the emerging service, which makes it difficult for the network to deliver such data. The main reason is the *coupling between the resource and location*. In SINET, the Smart Pervasive Service Layer mechanism makes it possible to achieve *resource and location separation*.

The service resources can be disseminated within the network as shown in Fig. 6.5. Therefore, when an end customer (user A) requests a specific service, the data can be cached and adapted on the network component. Then, when another customer (user B) requests the same information, he or she will easily acquire this resource from the network component that has already been cached. Thus, users can access resources nearby instead of always obtaining service from the provider. Such separation of resource and location can lead to faster and efficient data retrieval. In addition, the Dynamic Resource Adaptation Layer mechanism dynamically adapts network resources and configures network families by means of a matching service and network behaviors so as to further enhance the service provision. Therefore, cloud services can be well supported in SINET.

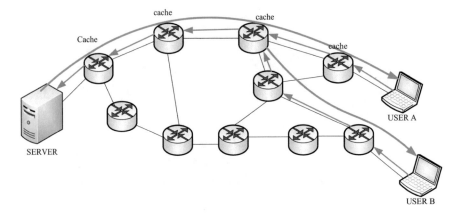

Fig. 6.5 Data retrieval process in SINET

6.1.5   Network Robustness and Resource Utilization

In the current Internet, the network is usually vulnerable to link failures, and resource utilization is low. The main reason is *binding of the resource/location and data/control plane*. In SINET, network robustness and a high resource utilization rate can be achieved by *decoupling the resource/location and data/control* through the multi-dimensional mapping between SID and CID and inter-/intra-family cooperation mechanisms.

Redundant backup is the most direct and effective method to improve the network robustness. However, it usually necessitates a large amount of equipment and network links, and so on. Therefore, redundant backup is difficult to implement under most circumstances. However, SINET is able to support the redundant backup without increasing the network cost. Additionally, the support for redundant backup also proves SINET has a high rate of utilization of network resources.

In SINET, due to the *separation of resource and location*, numerous CIDs can be generated for a SID, and the CID-RM also maps one CID into multiple AIDs for a network service. It is obvious that this design reduces the reliance on a single node during the service acquisition. Moreover, even if the CIDs are mapped to only one AID, SINET is also able to provide transmission redundancy. This is because there are several communication channels for the mapping between CID and AID. In other words, one connection can be established through different communication channels. Then, different transmission protocols and queue control algorithms can also be used. Therefore, the reliability of network service can improve a lot.

In addition, as shown in Fig. 6.6, the flexible mapping algorithm of AID-RM maps an AID into numerous different RIDs. Different RIDs have different network properties, which results in the different transmission paths in the CON. These transmission paths can be used together or used alone. Therefore, the redundant

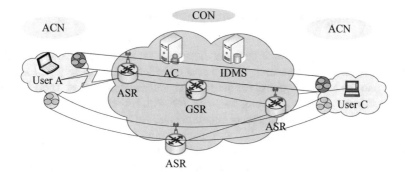

Fig. 6.6 Redundant transmission paths

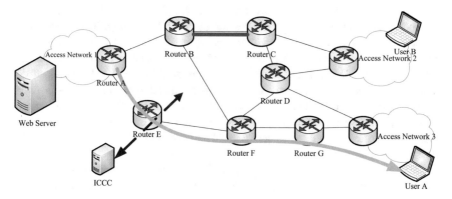

Fig. 6.7 Network resource adaptation

transmission paths can be established by the generated RIDs for a service. Then, the reliability of the network is further improved.

Besides the aforementioned methods, because of the *control and data plane separation* supported in the Dynamic Resource Adaption Layer, the network connection generated for a service can also be adaptively adjusted to find out the optimal transmission paths during the service acquisition. Due to the limited network resources, such as the bandwidth, the network link might be congested, which results in the limitation for providing high-quality service to end customers. When the link is highly congested or fails, as shown in Fig. 6.7, the network component may inform such changes to the central controller ICCC. Then, inter-/intra-family cooperation mechanisms can be performed centrally to recalculate the optimal available route. This dynamic adaption for transmission paths can provide the support for network robustness and the enhance resource utilization ratio.

6.1.6   Manageability and Energy Efficiency

The traditional Internet is initiatively designed for end-to-end communication, which only takes the data transmission into consideration. It merely performs the simple and predesigned control for the specific nodes and protocols. Therefore, it is hard to achieve smooth and complex operation with respect to the whole network for emerging network management requirements, such as energy efficiency. The main reason behind this is the triple binding (user/network binding, resource/location binding, data/control binding). In SINET, the manageability and energy efficiency can be enhanced through *decoupling of the three bindings*.

First, the *introduction of identifiers and mapping mechanisms* (decouple user/network binding) makes the network entities controllable and improves energy efficiency. Moreover, the management of mapping rules and mapping processes is directly controlled by the IDMS, as shown in Fig. 6.8. Thus, the IDMS can directly execute energy-efficient mapping rules for each AID mapping. This is also conducive to the controllability and manageability of the SINET. In addition, the mapping between AID and RID also completes the management of CON routing resources. Carefully designed mapping rules are able to achieve the balanced distribution of inter-domain network traffic, fine-grained intra-domain traffic engineering [13], multi-homed connection of access users [13, 14] and energy efficiency, and so on. It is worth noting that the utilization rate of the network resources can also be raised by guaranteeing the controllability and manageability of SINET.

Second, the control of SID mapping mechanisms (*resource/location separation*) is also capable of improving the manageability and energy efficiency of SINET. Through the control of SID mapping, SINET achieves the management of network services. Moreover, services are able to disseminate all around the network, and users can access to nearby resources. Therefore, the service providing can be effectively controlled by the carefully designed SID-RM, and thus the energy for data transmission can be significantly reduced [15, 16].

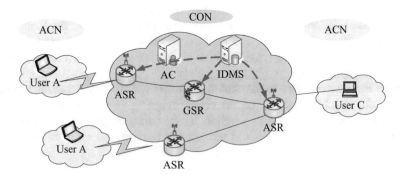

Fig. 6.8 The management of mapping rules

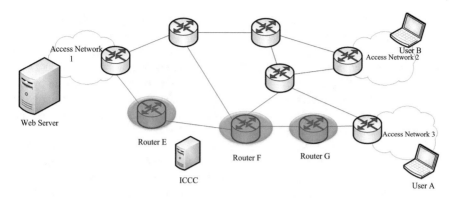

Fig. 6.9 Energy efficiency enhanced by control and data plane separation

Third, in SINET, *control and data planes are designed to be separated.* Therefore, the controller within the family (ICCC) can dynamically perceive the status of the network and make decisions on how to adapt network resources. Meanwhile, the ICCC can acquire the demand for network resources and deploy the energy-efficient data transmission algorithm. In addition, network components can be easily set to "work" or "sleep" with the aid of the ICCC.

As shown in Fig. 6.9, when user A and user B from the access network are visiting the web server in the access network, the ICCC will deploy an optimized path to connect the two users with the web server. Meanwhile, the controller will tell the router E/F/G to sleep since they are not being used, so as to save as much energy as possible. When the network status changes, the controller will recalculate these routers, and the router E/F/G may be awakened.

6.1.7 Summary

In summary, SINET is able to provide solutions for decoupling the triple bindings. SINET employs three layers to be in charge of different entities' information such as network services, network functions and network components, respectively. These entities are managed and handled separately. At the same time, they can be flexibly mapped to each other. This decentralized design achieves the decoupling of the "triple bindings" as follows.

In the Smart Pervasive Service Layer, SID is used to uniquely identify a service (such as a video streaming service). Each service also has an SBD, which is used to denote its extended properties, including service type, service cache, provider signature and provider location, and so on. These attributes can be used to classify and correlate various services. Therefore, it not only ensures the uniqueness of a service, but also specifies the varied features of a service by combining the SID and SBD. Based on this design, the *resource/location binding* can be naturally eliminated in SINET. For example, a certain service owning one SID may have multiple caches and providers (including different signatures and locations). The information is recorded in its SBD. When this service is requested, any one of the providers has a chance to respond to the request. Then, one or more providers will be selected according to the actual situation, e.g., the traffic load experienced by the providers and distance between the provider and the requester. This implies the requester only cares about the service required, but not its locations. Therefore, the *resource/location binding* can be decoupled in SINET.

In the Collaborative Network Component Layer, NID is used to uniquely identify a network node or component such as a router, server, proxy, sensor or even an interface. In addition, NBD is used to further extend NID by providing more detailed characteristic descriptions. Similar to SBD, NBD includes the node location, software, storage size, processing capacity, hardware type and so on. By utilizing a unique NID and a series of NBDs, SINET is able to manage and schedule the network nodes precisely based on upper requirements, e.g., the bandwidth and traffic control. It is worth noting that when a network node moves, its location information stored in NBD updates constantly, but its NID will not be changed. Based on this, no matter which one access network is connected, the user can be identified uniquely by using NID. To this end, the end-to-end communication links can be kept easily or re-established quickly without the NID reconfiguration. Then, the *user/network binding* can be easily removed in the SINET architecture.

In the Dynamic Resource Adaption Layer, FID is used to identify a network function group (such as the mobility support group, energy saving group and content caching group), which controls and manages numerous network nodes with the same function. Additionally, FBD describes the characteristics of a network function group, including group size, function, composition, capacity, affiliation and so on. By leveraging FID and FBD, the Dynamic Resource Adaption Layer is in charge of the resource adaption for service demands in the upper layer as well as the control decision for network components in the lower layer. Two essential mappings are adopted in the Dynamic Resource Adaption Layer to tightly connect the Smart Pervasive Service Layer and the Collaborative Network Component Layer. It is worth noting that the flow control and the data forwarding are separated in SINET thanks to the function group decision in the Dynamic Resource Adaption Layer. Thus, SINET inherently further resolves the *control/data* binding problem.

The above analysis explains how SINET is able to address the triple binding-related issues completely. This decoupled design provides significant benefits to improve the network performance in terms of scalability improvement, mobility support, security enhancement, support of cloud service, network robustness and resource utilization enhancement, and energy efficiency support.

6.2   Evaluation of SINET Performance

To further analyze SINET, we perform theoretical evaluation of the key performance of SINET in this section. SINET performance is evaluated quantitatively in
terms of mapping performance, routing scalability, security, service migration and
SID resolution mapping.

6.2.1   Experimental Dataset

To assess the performance of SINET [17–19], the network logs of the campus
network of Beijing Jiaotong University are analyzed. The campus network center
manages and maintains the network operations. It records all of the communication
data of the entire campus network. The campus network is connected to the Internet
through two export links. One is connected to the China Education and Research
Network (CERNET) [20]. The other is connected to China Telecom [21]. The
bandwidths of the two export links are all 1 Gbps. The network structure is shown
as in Fig. 6.10.

The network logs of the campus network are continuously collected for 24 h.
They include the timestamp, source address, destination address, source port,
destination port, packet number and so on. Considering the symmetry of the data
stream in terms of source address and destination address, this section only focuses
on the packets sent out of the campus network.

In the network logs, the packets involve 13,233 local addresses and 2,129,337
remote addresses. Figure 6.11 shows the number of the local and remote addresses.
It can be observed that the address number directly changes with day and night.
From 8 a.m., the address number increases dramatically. Then, the local address
number fluctuates at around 3000, and the remote address number is around 30,000.
After 11 p.m., the address number decreases rapidly because most of the users stop
using the Internet. Figure 6.11 also shows that the changing patterns of local

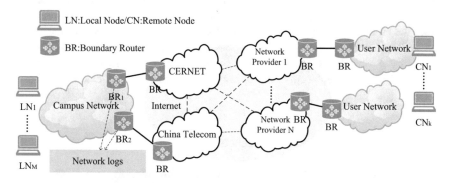

Fig. 6.10   The network structure for evaluating SINET

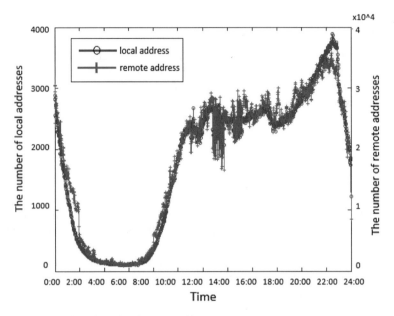

Fig. 6.11 The number of local and remote addresses

address and remote address numbers are similar. The remote address number is around ten times bigger than the local address number.

6.2.2 Mapping Performance Analysis

Identifier and Locator Separating mapping is one of the critical mechanisms of SINET. It is concerned with the communication link, data transmission delay, quality of service and so on. It is safe to say that the efficiency of separating mapping directly influences the performance of SINET. Therefore, this section focuses on the statistical analysis of separating mapping based on real network logs since the efficiency of separating mapping has a significant relation with the size of the address space and number of packets with a certain address. In the following, we analyze the characteristics of the packets related to the local and remote addresses, and carry out a curve fitting [22], which will give a guide to the design of SINET.

6.2.2.1 Local Address-Related Packets

The distribution of the local-addresses-related packets. Figure 6.12 shows the distribution of the local-address-related packets, i.e., these packets are all sent out from the devices with local addresses. As presented in Fig. 6.12, about 10 % of local addresses send fewer than 1,000 packets. Meanwhile, around another 10 % of local addresses send more than 20,000 packets. This means most local addresses send more than 1,000 and fewer than 20,000 packets.

To further analyze the packet distribution, the local addresses are rearranged in the order of the number of related packets, and then Fig. 6.13 is plotted, which shows the normalized distribution of the packets sent by local addresses. As shown in Fig. 6.13, local addresses sending more than 20,000 packets account for nearly 10 % of the total local addresses. The number of packets sent by these 10 % of local addresses accounts more than 60 % of the total packet number. Meanwhile, more than 50 % of local addresses send less than 10 % of packets. It is worth noting that the curve of Fig. 6.13 obeys the Pareto principle [23, 24].

The arrival interval distribution of the packets sent by local addresses. As proposed in [25, 26], the source AIDs and destination AIDs have to be mapped into corresponding RIDs. This mapping is performed by the ASR. However, this mapping process is different among arrived packets. The ASR has to repeatedly query the AID mapping server for every arrived packet. This repeated query process seriously increases the delay of packets and reduces the mapping efficiency. To solve this problem, a common method is to cache the mapping entries in the ASR. This method necessitates the arrival pattern of packets, because the arrival pattern directly relates to the hit probability and cache capacity.

For a given local address, the *packet interval* is defined as the period during which the local address does not send any packet. In this way, the distribution of the packet interval for the entire local addresses is derived. The distribution is shown in Fig. 6.14. Based on Fig. 6.14, it can be conjectured that the distribution obeys Zipf's law [27, 28].

In order to verify this conjecture, curve fitting is performed. Assuming the variable X denotes the packet interval, X obeys Pareto distribution [29, 30]. Pareto

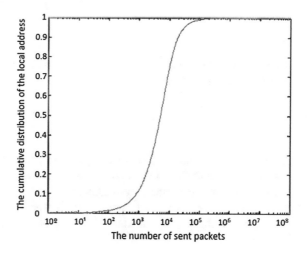

Fig. 6.12 The distribution of the local-address-related packets

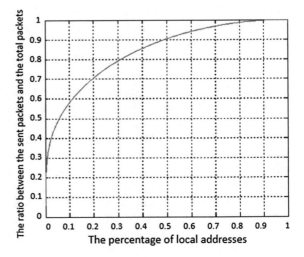

Fig. 6.13 Distribution of the packets sent by local addresses

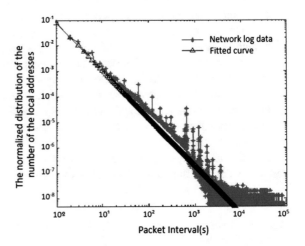

Fig. 6.14 The distribution of packet interval

distribution is the Zipf's distribution in discrete data statistics. The probability density function of X is:

$$f(x) = \begin{cases} \alpha \frac{x_m^\alpha}{x^{\alpha+1}} & when\ x > x_m \\ 0 & when\ x < x_m \end{cases}. \tag{6.1}$$

In Eq. 6.1, $x_m\ (x_m > 0)$ represents the minimum value of X; α is a positive parameter. To make the fitted curve close to real data, optimal x_m and α are needed. So, it is essential to estimate the x_m and α according to the real network logs. Let $x = (x_1, x_2, \ldots, x_N)$ denote the sample of X, where N is the number of samples. According to Eq. 6.1, the likelihood function of x_m and α is:

$$L(x_m, \alpha) = \prod_{i=1}^{N} f(x_i) = \prod_{i=1}^{N} \alpha \frac{x_m^{\alpha}}{x_i^{\alpha+1}} = \alpha^N x_m^{N\alpha} \prod_{i=1}^{N} \frac{1}{x_i^{\alpha+1}}, \tag{6.2}$$

Then, we calculate the logarithm of Eq. 6.2:

$$\ell(x_m, \alpha) = \ln[L(x_m, \alpha)] = \ln(\alpha^N x_m^{N\alpha} \prod_{i=1}^{N} \frac{1}{x_i^{\alpha+1}})$$

$$= N \ln \alpha + N\alpha \ln x_m - (\alpha+1) \sum_{i=1}^{N} \ln(x_i) \tag{6.3}$$

As shown in Eq. 6.3, $\ell(x_m, \alpha)$ is a monotonically increasing function with respective to x_m. Since $x > x_m$, the maximum likelihood parameter estimation of x_m is:

$$\hat{x}_m = \min_i x_i, \ where \ 1 \le i \le N. \tag{6.4}$$

Equation 6.4 means that the maximum likelihood estimation of x_m is the minimum value of the samples, that is, 10^{-5}. To derive the maximum likelihood estimation of α, compute the partial derivative of Eq. 6.3 and let the computed partial derivative equal to 0:

$$\frac{\partial \ell(x_m, \alpha)}{\partial \alpha} = N\alpha^{-1} + N \ln x_m - \sum_{i=1}^{N} \ln(x_i) = 0. \tag{6.5}$$

Then, the maximum likelihood estimation of α is obtained:

$$\hat{\alpha} = \frac{N}{\sum_{i=1}^{N} [\ln(x_i) - \ln \widehat{x}_m]}. \tag{6.6}$$

Based on Eqs. 6.1–6.6 and the samples of X, the fitting function is calculated as:

$$f(x) = \begin{cases} \frac{0.0778}{x^{1.863}} & when \ x > 10^{-5} \\ 0 & when \ x < 10^{-5} \end{cases}, \tag{6.7}$$

where x denotes the packet interval.

As compared in Fig. 6.14, the fitted curve is close to the actual data. The fitting result also demonstrates the distribution pattern of the packet interval obeys Zipf's law.

Based on the above analysis, it can be concluded that the distribution of the packets sent by local addresses obeys the Pareto principle and the distribution of packet interval obeys Zipf's law. The two conclusions are important to the caching strategy design of ASR. This is because it is necessary to set a Time to Live

(TTL) for the cached mapping entries. If the entry is used again within the TTL, the TTL will be recounted from zero and the entry will be reserved. Otherwise, this entry will be deleted. However, if the TTL is too long, the caching space will become too large. The caching efficiency will be reduced because the entry is seldom used in a long duration. On the contrary, if the TTL is too short, the hit-probability of the caching strategy will also be reduced and the performance of caching will therefore be impaired. Consequently, it can be observed that the TTL is tightly bound to the distribution of packet interval and the distribution of packets. In other words, the distribution of the packets sent by local addresses and the distribution of the packet interval provide a theoretical foundation for the design of the caching strategy.

6.2.3   Remote Address-Related Packets

In the real network environment, remote addresses are usually related to mobile communications. Moreover, mobile nodes usually communicate with multiple remote addresses at the same time. To satisfy the demand of handover delay and improve the efficiency of separating mapping in mobile communication, ASR needs to update the mapping entries between the mobile nodes and the remote addresses timely. This will increase the network overhead and the workload of ASR. Therefore, analyzing and learning about the relationship between the nodes and remote addresses is of great importance to improve the efficiency of separating mapping, especially for the mobile communications.

The distribution of remote address-related packets. Figure 6.15 shows the normalized distribution of remote-address-related packets. By adopting the statistic approach used in Fig. 6.12, the remote addresses are rearranged in the order of the number of related packets. Then, the relationship between the number of remote addresses and the number of received packets is derived. It is obvious that more than 90 % of packets are sent to less than 10 % of the total remote addresses. Meanwhile, less than 10 % packets are disseminated to more than 90 % remote addresses.

Figure 6.16 further presents the cumulative distribution of the packets that are sent to a single remote address. It can be observed that more than 96 % of remote addresses receive fewer than 100 packets. In addition, around 35 % of remote addresses receive only one packet. For this kind of remote address, the TTL of the cached mapping entries is meaningless. When the cache of mapping entries is designed, the frequently used entries should be cached first. And the cache time should be adjusted according to the usage frequency.

The average number of remote addresses related to a single local address. In the separating mapping mechanism, the ASR also needs to cache the mapping entries of remote addresses. To evaluate the number of caching entries, the relationship between the time and the average numbers of remote addresses related to a single local address should be derived based on network logs. The statistical result

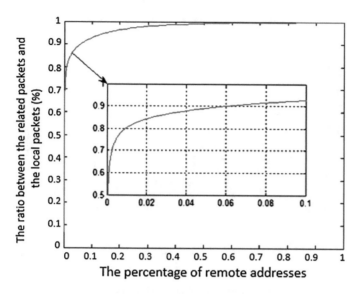

Fig. 6.15 The overall distribution of remote-address-related packets

Fig. 6.16 The distribution of the packets that are sent to a single remote address

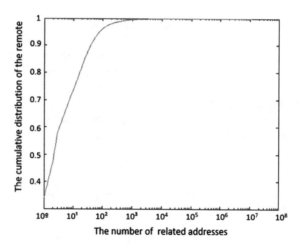

is shown in Fig. 6.17. As shown in Fig. 6.17, the fluctuation range of the average number is [7, 23]. The mean of these average numbers is 10. This result also verifies the conclusion that the remote address number is around ten times more than the local address number, which is observed from Fig. 6.11.

The probability distribution of remote-address-related packet intervals. As in the above analyses, the packet interval directly influences the TTL of the cached entries. Adopting the method used in Fig. 6.14, the distribution of the packet interval related to remote addresses is derived and is shown in Fig. 6.18.

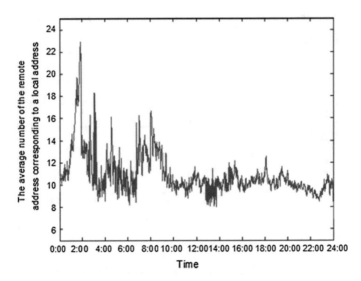

Fig. 6.17 The average number of remote addresses related to each single local address

As shown in Fig. 6.18, the distribution of the packet interval obeys Pareto distribution. Through curve fitting, the probability density function is computed as:

$$f(x) = \begin{cases} \frac{0.2981}{x^{1.573}} & when\, x > 10^{-5} \\ 0 & when\, x < 10^{-5} \end{cases}, \tag{6.8}$$

where x denotes the packet interval.

In order to explore more information, the three remote addresses that receive the most packets are selected. The three remote addresses are Sina [31], Google [32]

Fig. 6.18 The probability distribution of remote-address-related packet intervals

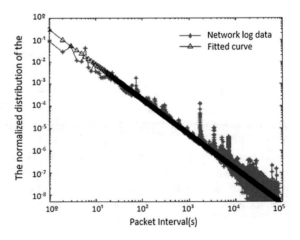

Fig. 6.19 The distribution of packet intervals for typical applications

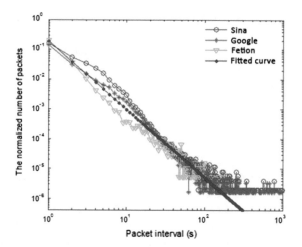

and Fetion [33], respectively. The packet intervals of the three remote addresses are presented in Fig. 6.19.

The probability distribution is calculated as:

$$f(x) = \begin{cases} \frac{0.1881}{x^{2.284}} & when\,x > 10^{-5} \\ 0 & when\,x < 10^{-5} \end{cases}, \qquad (6.9)$$

where x denotes the packet interval.

Just as in the analysis in Sect. 6.2.2.1, the above analysis also provide the theoretical basis for the design of the caching strategy of ASR in terms of the remote address-related packets. Moreover, because of tight connections between the remote addresses and mobile network, the conclusions derived from the above analysis will also influence the application of SINET on mobile networks.

6.2.4   Routing Scalability Analysis

The scalability is one of the important challenges for the traditional Internet. In recent years, the routing entries have increased rapidly, resulting in a considerable increase in the routing tables of routers. This also gives rise to the sharp decrease of routing lookup efficiency. The scalability problem seriously hinders the development of the traditional Internet. Therefore, this section focuses on the scalability analysis of routing in the SINET. In this section, the scalability is analyzed from the view of the memory cost and the routing delay of routers. The analysis results demonstrate that the SINET is able to efficiently resolve the scalability problem.

Memory Cost. To simulate the SINET, the network topology and network address assignment of Beijing Jiaotong University campus network are used. This campus network contains 42 routers and 36,322 addresses. Among these 42 routers, two are the core nodes, which are connected mutually. The remaining routers are connected to the two core nodes, respectively. These addresses occupy 20 Classless Inter-domain Routing (CIDR) [34] network segments. In SINET, routers store the routing entries, which represent the relationship between the AIDs and access locations. By performing the MD-5 hash [35] for the network addresses, the number of routing entries of each router is obtained (Fig. 6.20).

As shown in Fig. 6.20, the number of routing entries ranges from 3 to 3361. If the routers configure the hash ring according to the current number of routing entries, there will be huge distances among the access locations of each node. A feasible solution is first to arrange all the available addresses according to the corresponding hash algorithm. Then, it determines the AIDs with equal distance hash values. Eventually, it configures the routers according to the selected AIDs. In this way, the storage overload of routing devices can be balanced.

In addition, according to the scale of the current campus network, assume that each routing entry occupies a space of 40 bytes. Even in the worst case, 1.5 Mbytes are enough for routers to save all of the routing entries. The balanced overhead of routers will only be tens of kilobytes. This amount is very small and does not influence the performance of ordinary network devices much.

Routing Delay. In SINET, packets usually experience two logical phases during the routing in a subnet. The first one refers to the packets that are routed from the source node to a management router. The management router usually stores the locations of destination nodes. The second one refers to the packets that are routed from the management router to the destination node. Based on this process, the packet transmission delay is computed as follows:

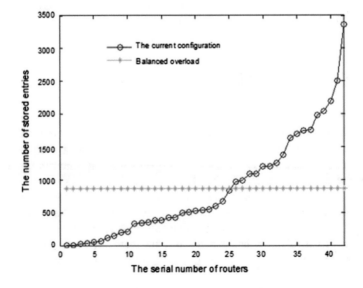

Fig. 6.20 The number of routing entries

$$T_{delay} = t_s + T_{MR} + T_{LR} + t_d, \tag{6.10}$$

where t_s denotes the time for routing the packets from the source node to the access router of the source node, T_{MR} denotes the time of routing the packets from the access router of the source node to the management router, T_{LR} denotes the time of routing the packets from the management router to the access router of the destination router, and t_d denotes the time of routing the packets from the access router of the destination node to the destination node. According to the similarity of the routing process, the following two assumptions are made: $t_d \approx t_s$ and $T_{MR} \approx T_{LR}$.

According to the Chord algorithm, the number of logic hops is $Hop_{logic} \leq \log_2(N)$ [36], where N denotes the node number. Thus, T_{MR} can be calculated as $T_{MR} = t_h * stretch * Hop_{logic}$, where $stretch$ is the scaling factor; t_h denotes the delay of one hop in the actual network. The scaling factor is the ratio between the number of logic hops and actual physical hops. By leveraging Eq. 6.10, the transmission delay is computed as:

$$\begin{aligned} T_{delay} &= 2 * t_h * (1 + stretch * Hop_{logic}) \\ &\leq 2 * t_h * (1 + stretch * \log_2(N)) \end{aligned} \tag{6.11}$$

Assume the link delay of the ACN is 1 ms and the scaling factor is 3. T_{delay} is calculated as less than 35 ms according to Eq. 6.11. This result is acceptable for the normal behaviors of the campus network.

In addition, there is always a management router, which maintains the mapping entries between the AID and the access location. As long as the mapping entries are updated in a timely manner, the terminal communication will not be affected by the change of the access locations of mobile nodes. Based on the neighbor discovery process, the access router is able to discover and update the location of the mobile terminals in the subnet. Therefore, the routing is also conducive to the support of mobility.

In conclusion, the memory cost and routing delay of routers are acceptable for ordinary network devices and normal network operations. Moreover, the existence of a management router also contributes to addressing the mobility problem. Therefore, the routing mechanism employed by SINET has good scalability in terms of both the router memory cost and routing overhead, which leads to better performance than the current routing system.

6.2.5 Security Analysis

In the traditional Internet, the Denial-of-service (DoS) attack is a critical threat. For the DoS attack, the IP address and port number of the targeted server are essential. After acquiring the IP address and port number, numerous malicious hosts coordinate to consume the bandwidth or resources of the server, causing it to deny service to its legitimate users. To prevent the DoS attack, listening to the port as well as acquiring the traffic anomaly is a common method used in the traditional Internet.

In SINET, it is no longer necessary to publicly listen to the port because of the introduction of the SID. The service mechanism in SINET efficiently supports the intrinsic listening on a multi-port in a single server. In other words, the application server that provides services is able to generate several listener ports according to the negotiation of the CID. However, the CID is allocated by the CID management server when the user requests the corresponding service. Users do not know the CID in advance. Meanwhile, SID enables several application servers to provide the same service. When the user requests a service, the servers that provide the corresponding service are selected by the mapping system. So, the uncertainty of the service providing the server and intrinsic multi-port listening mechanism can effectively prevent the DoS attacks.

To analyze the positive influence of the CID and adaptive connection management mechanism on network security, the port attack is selected as an example. In the traditional Internet, the attackers first need to learn about the security vulnerabilities of a network service. Then, the attackers have to determine the protocol and port of the service according to the well-known port. Eventually, the attacker will send a large number of scanning packets to the port so as to consume the resource excessively and even implant the virus program. However, the SINET leverages the service-oriented acquisition process, the CID-based transmission protocol and port negotiation mechanism. These advanced functions provide the network service with numerous alternative transmission protocols. Moreover, the port numbers of these protocols are variable. It is difficult for the attackers to determine the right port. Therefore, the SINET greatly reduces the probability of being attacked by the aforementioned method. Assume there are m kinds of transmission protocols for a service. The available port for each transmission protocol is denoted as $n_i(1 \leq i \leq m)$. The probability of being attacked is computed as:

$$P_{success}[k] = 1 - \left(1 - \frac{1}{\sum\limits_{i=1}^{m} n_i}\right)^k, \tag{6.12}$$

where k denotes the number of packets sent by the attacker.

In order to further describe the security support of the SINET, the statistical analysis is shown in Fig. 6.21 according to Eq. 6.12. Assume the transmission protocols are TCP and UDP and there are 2^{16} available ports for each protocol, that is $m = 2$ and $n_1 = n_2 = 65536$. As shown in Fig. 6.21, if the services are provided based on the given protocol and port in the traditional network, the probability of being attacked is 1. On the contrary, in SINET, if the number of packets sent by

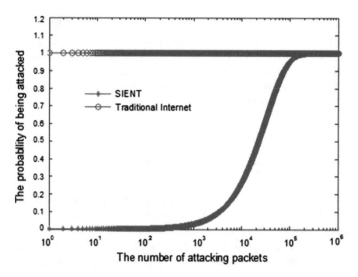

Fig. 6.21 The probability of being attacked

attackers is less than 10^4, the probability of being attacked in SINET is much less than that of the traditional network.

In conclusion, the CID and adaptive connection management mechanism are able to effectively prevent the port attack. What is more, due to the employment of the advanced functions, SINET naturally achieves better performance in terms of security than today's Internet.

6.2.6   Services Migration Analysis

Service migration refers to the change of service resource location. Service migration has perplexed Internet service providers for a long time. Because service is bound with the location in the traditional Internet, the efficiency of service acquisition for users will be reduced greatly after the change of service location. However, in SINET, the binding between the service and location is broken by the CID. This makes the service migration feasible and efficient.

To prove the feasibility and efficiency of service migration, the session migration system of network applications based on the CID and CID management mechanism is established. The system consists of three PCs, a CID management server and a WAN simulator. One of the PCs simulates the video-on-demand server, and the other two PCs simulate the clients. The three PCs are connected to the WAN simulator. The two clients repeatedly request the video during the service migration. The service migration experiment is performed 20 times. The experimental result is shown in Fig. 6.22. In this experiment, the recovery of the application state and delay of the WAN simulator are not taken into consideration. Through analyzing the packets collected from the video-on-demand server, the migration of the entire video application only consumes around 100 ms. That is, the delay of the video is around 100 ms. This result satisfies the delay requirement of the streaming media service, which is 100–200 ms.

6.2.7   SID Resolution Mapping Analysis

With the overwhelming proliferation of network services, the feasibility of SID resolution mapping has important implications for the service management and deployment of SINET. This section concentrates on the analysis of feasibility from the view of the scalability of SID and link cost of the SID resolution mapping system. The analysis result demonstrates the SID resolution mapping is theoretically viable.

SID Scalability. To provide the network resource and service with a unique SID, the SID space should be scalable enough. According to the report from China Internet Network Information Center [37], the number of Chinese Internet webpages was more than 60 billion by July 2010. This number is still on the rise at the rate of 78.6 %. Moreover, the average number of webpages for each website is 31,414 and is growing at the rate of 202 %.

According to the above statistics, it can be concluded that the growth pattern of information obeys the exponential growth law. Suppose the number of network resources and services equals the number of network links, and the number of

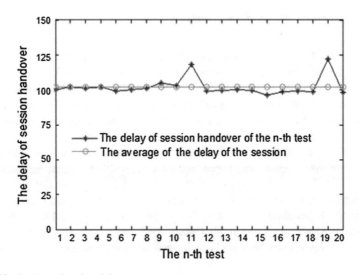

Fig. 6.22 Session migration delay

network links is assumed to be 10^{15}. If the SID space is able to accommodate these network resources and services, the bit number for SID is computed as:

$$2^n \geq 10^{15}, \tag{6.13}$$

where n denotes the bit number. Therefore, n should be greater than 50. Considering the definition of SID, this is easy to satisfy by using the hash functions with a large number of bit digits, such as SHA-1 [38].

Link Cost. To test the feasibility of the SID resolution mapping system, a model is established to evaluate the link cost of the SID resolution mapping system. The link cost includes three parts. The first part is the cost of maintaining the distributed SID resolution system. This is called the fixed cost. The second is the link cost of host nodes. The third is the cost of generating a new SID and updating the original SID. For ease of description, the notations and their corresponding definitions are provided and are shown in Table 6.2.

In the SID resolution system, suppose the average loads of the server are generated by the resolution request of user nodes and the SID update. Then, the average link load L for each server is calculated as:

$$
\begin{aligned}
L &= L_i + L_r + L_u \\
&= 8 \times \left[m \cdot f \cdot \log_2 N + \frac{N_p \cdot r \cdot \max(r_1 \cdot r_2)}{N} + \frac{N_u \cdot u}{24 \times 3600 \times N} \right].
\end{aligned} \tag{6.14}
$$

Based on the statistical analysis of network logs, the parameters of Eq. 6.14 are set as: $m = 128$, $f = 1/300$, $N_p = 10^{10}$, $r_1 = 512$, $r_2 = 1024$, $N_u = 10^{10}$ and

Table 6.2 Notations of SID resolution system

Notation	Definition
L	Overall cost of a single server link (bit/s)
L_i	Fixed cost of a single server link (bit/s)
L_r	Resolution cost of a single server link (bit/s)
L_u	Updating cost of a single server link (bit/s)
N	Number of service nodes in the SID resolution system
m	Average size of the status-maintaining packet between servers (byte)
f	Status maintaining frequency between servers (Hz)
N_p	Number of user nodes in the entire network
r	Arrival rate of the SID resolution request for single user nodes
r_1	Average size of the SID resolution request packet
r_2	Average size of the SID resolution response packet
u	Average size of the SID resolution update packet
N_u	Updated data size of the global SID each day
$\max(x, y)$	The maximum value x of and y

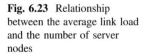

Fig. 6.23 Relationship between the average link load and the number of server nodes

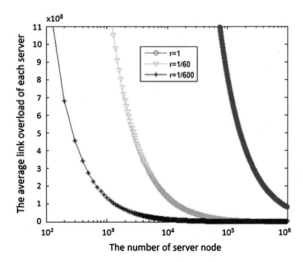

$u = 512$. Then, the relationship between the average link load L and the number of server nodes is obtained and shown in Fig. 6.23.

According to Fig. 6.23, when the link load reaches 0.5 Gbps, which is half of the tolerance capacity, the numbers of needed servers are derived under different arrival rates, i.e., $r = 1/600$, $r = 1/60$ and $r = 1$. The corresponding numbers are 300, 1300 and 110,000, respectively. To satisfy the maximum number of request and link redundancy demands, the number of server nodes should be chosen as 10^6. This means that one server serves 10^4 user nodes, which is theoretically feasible.

In conclusion, based on the above analyses, the SID resolution mapping possesses the merit of scalability, and the link cost for SID resolution is also acceptable. So, it can be asserted that the SID resolution mapping is theoretically feasible.

6.3   Conclusion

This chapter mainly gives an in-depth analysis of SINET in terms of the superiorities and performance. The superiorities of SINET are first analyzed from various perspectives. It has been shown that by decoupling the triple bindings, SINET can outperform the current Internet in terms of scalability, mobility, security, support of cloud service, network robustness and resource utilization, and manageability and energy efficiency. Then, a statistical analysis of the key performance of SINET is given comprising mapping performance, routing scalability, security, services migration and SID resolution mapping, which further demonstrate the benefits of SINET. According to these analysis results, it can be concluded that SINET outperforms the current Internet in various aspects, which provides a great possibility to meet the emerging requirements of the future Internet.

References

1. Jacobson V, Smetters D, James D. Thornton (2009) Networking named content. In: The 5th international conference on emerging networking experiments and technologies. New York, USA

2. Mobility first future internet architecture project (2015). http://mobilityfirst.winlab.rutgers. Accessed 1 June 2015

3. Farinacci D, Fuller V, Meyer D, Lewis D (2013) The locator/ID separation protocol (LISP), IETF RFC 6830, January 2013

4. Nunes B, Mendonca M, Nguyen X et al (2014) A survey of software-defined networking: past, present, and future of programmable networks. IEEE Commun Surv Tutorials 16 (3):1617–1634

5. Noble S (2015) Network function virtualization or NFV explained. http://wikibon.org/wiki/v/ Network_Function_Virtualization_or_NFV_Explained. Accessed 14 June 2015

6. Chiosi M, Clarke D et al (2012) Network functions virtualization, White paper, SDN and OpenFlow world congress, October, 2012

7. Adrichem N, Kuipers F (2013) Globally accessible names in named data networking. In: IEEE INFOCOM

8. Ding W, Qi W, Wang J et al (2015) OpenSCaaS: an open service chain as a service platform toward the integration of SDN and NFV. IEEE Netw 29(3):30–35

9. Wood T, Ramakrishnan K, Hwang J et al (2015) Toward a software-based network: integrating software defined networking and network function virtualization. IEEE Netw 29 (3):36–41

10. Zhang L, Estrin D et al (2013) Named data networking (NDN) project NEN-0001. Palo Alto Research Center, Technical report

11. Zhang W, Bi J, Wu J (2010) Scalability of internet inter-domain routing. J Softw 21:2524–2541

12. Meyer D, Zhang L, Fall K, et al (2007) Report from the IAB workshop on routing and addressing, RFC 4984. http://tools.ietf.org/html/rfc4984. Accessed 3 June 2015

13. Toby V, Anthony V, Robert E (2009) Cloud computing, a practical approach, 1st edn. McGraw-Hill Inc, New York

14. Awduche D, Chiu A, Elwalid A et al (2002) Overview and principles of internet traffic engineering, RFC 3272. http://www.ietf.org/rfc/rfc3272.txt. Accessed 3 June 2015

15. Abley J, Lindqvist K, Davies E, et al (2005). IPv4 multihoming practices and limitations, RFC 4116. http://www.ietf.org/rfc/rfc4116.txt. Accessed 3 June 2015

16. Chen J, Zhou H (2014) Cooperative energy efficient management scheme for multimedia information dissemination. Int J Distrib Sens Netw

17. Zhang H, Luo H (2013) Fundamental research on theories of smart and cooperative networks. Acta Electronica Sinica 41(7):1249–1254

18. Gao S, Wang H, Wang K et al (2013) Research on cooperation mechanisms of smart network components. Acta Electronica Sinica 41(7):1261–1267

19. Su W, Chen J, Zhou H et al (2013) Research on the service mechanisms in smart and cooperative networks. Acta Electronica Sinica 41(7):1255–1260

20. CERNET (2015). http://www.edu.cn/HomePage/english/cernet/index.shtml. Accessed 3 June 2015

21. China Telecom (2015). http://en.chinatelecom.com.cn. Accessed 8 June 2015

22. Levy E (1959) Complex-curve fitting. IRE Trans Autom Control 4(1):37–43. doi:10.1109/ TAC.1959.6429401

23. Pareto principle (2015). http://en.wikipedia.org/wiki/Pareto. Accessed 3 June 2015

24. Chen Y, Chong P, Tong M (1994) Mathematical and computer modelling of the Pareto principle. Math Comput Model 19(9):61–80

25. Luo H, Wang H, Zhang H, Qin Y et al (2009) 4I: a secure and scalable routing architecture for future Internet. Technical report, Beijing Jiaotong University

26. Dong P (2008) Research on the scalable routing architecture based on separating and mapping of identity and locator. Ph. D thesis, Beijing Jiaotong University
27. Newman M (2005) Power laws, Pareto distributions and Zipf's law. Contemp Phys 46 (5):323–351
28. Zipf's law (2015). http://en.wikipedia.org/wiki/Zipf%27s_law. Accessed 3 June 2015
29. Pareto distribution (2015). http://en.wikipedia.org/wiki/Pareto_distribution. Accessed 3 June 2015
30. Arnold B (2008) Pareto distribution. Wiley
31. Sina (2015). http://en.wikipedia.org/wiki/Sina_Corp. Accessed 8 June 2015
32. Google (2015). http://en.wikipedia.org/wiki/Google. Accessed 8 June 2015
33. Fetion (2015). http://en.wikipedia.org/wiki/Fetion. Accessed 8 June 2015
34. Fuller V, Li T, Yu J, etc. (2015). Classless inter-domain routing (CIDR): an address assignment and aggregation strategy. http://www.hjp.at/doc/rfc/rfc1519.html. Accessed 3 June 2015
35. Rivest R (1991) The MD5 message-digest algorithm. http://tools.ietf.org/html/rfc1321. Accessed 6 June 2015
36. Stoica I, Morris R, Liben-Nowell D et al (2003) Chord: a scalable peer-to-peer lookup service for Internet applications. IEEE/ACM Trans Networking 11(1):17–32
37. CNNIC (2011) Statistical report on internet development in China. http://www.cnnic.net.cn/hlwfzyj/hlwxzbg/hlwtjbg/201206/t20120612_26718.htm. Accessed 4 June 2015
38. SHA-1 (2015). http://en.wikipedia.org/wiki/SHA-1. Accessed 3 June 2015

Part II
Key Technologies

Chapter 7
Scalable Routing Technologies of SINET

As a future Internet architecture, SINET creates several new rules to support scalable routing, such as identifier/locator separation and intra-/inter-domain routing separation. In this chapter, we mainly discuss the scalable inter-domain routing technologies in SINET. Related work on advanced routing technologies is summarized at the beginning. Two kinds of inter-domain identifier-based scalable routing in SINET are introduced. One is the path family-based routing mechanism, and the other is the source identifier routing mechanism. Both of them can be flexibly applied to different applications with the specific routing techniques. At the end of this chapter, a summary of the two routing mechanisms is included.

7.1 Related Work

The current Internet routing system is facing serious scalability problems. In recent years, there have been a growing number of efforts. It is believed that the routing scalability problem will increase the *"clean slate"* designs of the Internet architecture. Since the current Internet is built around the "narrow waist" of the IP, the authors of [1–3] reported changing the IP-centric architecture to the information-centric architecture. Some researchers [4, 5] advocated that a future Internet should be designed to encourage innovations. In [6], authors mainly focus on designing an Internet that provides better support for the mobility and security.

In addition, pathlet routing [7] lends the idea of using path segments for inter-domain routing to the path family-based routing. Some researchers [8] proposed using autonomous system (AS) numbers for inter-domain routing to replace IP prefixes. Since AS numbers could not be split into sub-prefixes for finer granularity, adopting AS numbers can only reduce the route table size, but will increase the difficulty of traffic engineering. [9] made use of some auxiliary bits to subdivide an AS. [9] proposed multiple AS-prefix mappings, but they all result in the route table growth again. Furthermore, [10, 11] use the negotiation between the

© Springer-Verlag Berlin Heidelberg 2016
H. Zhang et al., *Smart Collaborative Identifier Network*,
DOI 10.1007/978-3-662-49143-0_7

destination AS and source AS to control the flow of their incoming traffic. However, the idea of "negotiating" is only limited to neighboring ASs. [11] first proposed the idea of explicit coordination, which makes the upstream ASs register their flows with all the downstream ASs that the flow passes through. Although [11] adopts this idea to the Source Identifier routing mechanism, registering each traffic flow with all the downstream ASs leads to a mass of traffic states and consumes too much bandwidth. SINET borrows the ideas of using self-certifying node identifiers from [6, 12].

7.2 Path Family-Based Routing

7.2.1 Design and Mechanism

The *path family-based routing mechanism* relies on an important network component family, named the *path family*. The path family is negotiated by adjacent domains. To allow the readers to easily follow the content, this section starts with a brief background about the path family and *Path Family Identifier* (*PIDs*).

In SINET, the Dynamic Resource Adaption Layer is in charge of perceiving the service demands from the upper Smart Pervasive Service Layer and controlling the components in the bottom Collaborative Network Component Layer. In the Dynamic Resource Adaption Layer, the *Family Identifier* (*FID*) is used to identify a network family, which is comprised of many special network components with the same function for a certain purpose. The path family is a collection of components used for building the transmission paths between different domains. *PID can be seen as a kind of FID*. For each path family, PIDs are used to name paths between domains. The idea of a path family-based routing mechanism is the coupling service location and inter-domain routing while decoupling them from forwarding.

By using the path family-based routing mechanism, adjacent domains could negotiate the number of paths between them. For a given path, its PID is also negotiated, but the PID must be unique in both domains. In addition, for the purpose of enhancing security [14], the PID between two domains is randomly chosen and known only by the two domains. The PIDs between two domains are not advertised to pass through the Internet, which makes it difficult for attackers to correctly guess them. Therefore, the security is further improved. In default, the length of PID is 32 bits, but optimizing this length is acceptable in accordance with different requirements. Usually a longer length of PID leads to higher bandwidth consumption, but it is more secure.

To support a large-scale network, just like the Internet, SINET can be performed among numerous *Autonomous Systems* (*ASs*). In each AS of SINET, there is at least one *Identifier Mapping Server* (*IDMS*) and one *Intelligent Central Control Component* (*ICCC*). IDMS is responsible for mapping between AIDs and RIDs, and ICCC is mainly responsible for the internal resource management, including the smart routing policy, component adjustment, traffic control and so on. Furthermore, these ASs constitute different hierarchical tiers (Tier-1, Tier-2, Tier-3), and each AS could be a provider, customer or peer to any other AS.

Here, we further take an example to illustrate the path family-based routing mechanism, which is shown in Fig. 7.1. The domains D2 and D3 negotiate two paths P2 and P3, as indicated by the bold solid lines. For a path that begins at a domain, the ICCC and the ASR maintain the path's end point located at the domain and the domain identifier at which the other endpoint is located. (All the Rns in Fig. 7.1 are the simplified form of ASRn.) Moreover, the inter-domain routing table of R4 is shown at the upper right corner in Fig. 7.1.

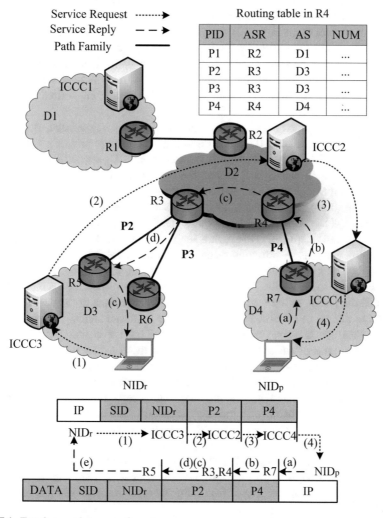

Fig. 7.1 Topology and message format

Through the service registration mechanism, ICCC stores all the locations and reachability information of all SIDs. Each ASR maintains an inter-domain routing table. When a service requester (NID_r) wants to obtain a service represented by an SID, it sends out a service request message to its local ICCC, and the request message is shown as in message format (1). The service request message should contain the SID and the requester's NID. If the ICCC cannot find an entry for the SID, it first chooses a provider ICCC and a path (PID) destined to the chosen domain. The ICCC then appends the PID of the chosen path onto the service request message and sends it to the chosen ICCC; the request message is shown as in message format (2). If the ICCC finds out at least one entry for the SID, it chooses an entry based on its local policy. If the node contained in the entry is in the same domain with the ICCC, the ICCC directly forwards the service request message to the node using the routing mechanism adopted by this domain. If the node is in another domain, the ICCC chooses a path toward that domain. The ICCC appends the PID of the chosen path onto the service request message and forwards the service request message to the service provider, which is shown as in message format (4). In Fig. 7.1, the thin dotted arrow illustrates how a service request message is forwarded from a requester to a provider hosting the desired service data represented by an SID.

When the provider (NID_p) receives the service request message, it gets three kinds of information: the SID of the desired content, the requester's NID and the inter-domain paths to be used to reach the requester. NID_p encapsulates the desired service/data with a header that carries the requester's NID, SID and PIDs. The encapsulated message is shown as in message format (4). For every path that begins at a domain, the ASRs and the ICCC in the domain maintain the end point of the path located at the domain and the domain identifier at which the other endpoint is located. The provider (NID_p) then sends the packets to the ASR associated with the first PID by using its own routing mechanism. The packet is then forwarded by the ASR to the other end of the first path. When the other end of the first path receives the packet, it strips out the PID at the outermost layer, gets the second PID and forwards the packet to the next ASR. Ultimately, the packets of the desired service, which are named as an SID, will be sent to the requester (NID_r).

The bold dotted arrows in Fig. 7.1 illustrate how the desired data message is forwarded from a provider to a requester. When the provider (NID_p) receives the service request message, it first encapsulates the desired data with a header that contains the SID, requester's NID_r and PIDs. For example, domain D3 and D4 use IPv4 for local routing, and then the provider (NID_p) encapsulates the packet with an outer IP header, as illustrated in message format (a). The packet will be forwarded to node R7 by IP routing. R7 then strips out the outer IP header and sends the packet to path P4, as illustrated in message format (b). When node R4 receives the packet, it looks up its routing table and knows that the next ASR for P4 is R3. When the packet is passed to R5, R5 encapsulates the packet with an outer IP header, as illustrated by the message format (e). Ultimately, the desired data are sent to the NID_p.

7.2.2   *Performance Evaluation*

To validate the path family-based routing mechanism and evaluate its performance, a Linux-based prototype system is built.

The network topology of the prototype system is shown in Fig. 7.2, which consists of 2 domains and 11 nodes, including 1 requester, 2 service providers, 2 ICCCs and 6 ASRs. The 11 nodes are placed in D1 and D2. Each domain has one provider, one ICCC and three ASRs. All the ASRs are simplified as Rn. As mentioned above, each domain in SINET is free to adopt its intra-domain routing mechanism. In this experiment, the NID of each node can be represented by its IP address. Therefore, D1 and D2 use IPv4 addresses and IPv6 addresses for local routing, respectively. The two domains are connected by two paths: PID1 between node R3 in D1 and node R4 in D2 and PID2 between R2 in D1 and R5 in D2. The IP addresses of each node are shown in Fig. 7.2. The PID tables of all nodes are manually configured. In the experimental process, every service provider registers 50,000 SIDs at its local ICCC. The local ICCC then forwards the registration messages to the other ICCC. Thus, every ICCC stores 100,000 SID entries. The datum corresponding to every SID is 1024 bytes. Each service request message is replied to by one data packet. The requester sends service request messages for SIDs randomly chosen from the 100,000 SIDs to ICCC. We have run the experiment for 1000 s. We conclude that the intervals between subsequent service request

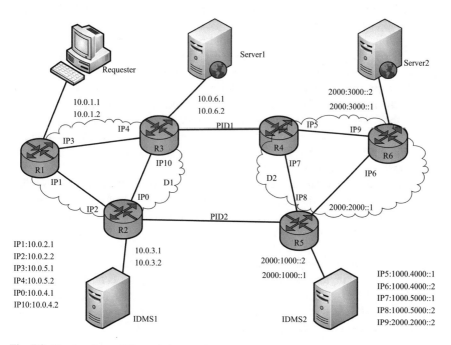

Fig. 7.2 The topology of the prototype system

Fig. 7.3 The delay in
processing request messages
in ICCC1. Reprinted from
Ref. [19], with permission
from IEEE

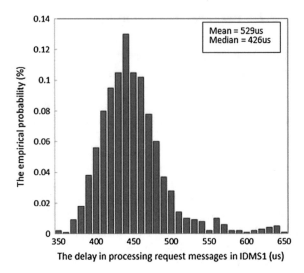

messages follow the exponential distribution, and the mean of the intervals equals to 1 ms. In addition, for the contents provided by server 2, ICCC1 chooses the path PID1with the probability of 0.7 and path PID2 with the probability of 0.3.

Figure 7.3 shows the distribution of the delay for processing service request messages at ICCC1. The processing delay ranges from 0.35 to 0.65 ms. The mean and median of the delay are 0.529 and 0.426 ms, respectively. If an ICCC is able to process 40,000 service request messages, the delay for processing a service request message will be 25 ms. In the experimental process, all the packets are forwarded as expected, which not only verifies the correctness of the path family-based routing, but also demonstrates its feasibility in the small-scale deployment.

After demonstrating the feasibility and the overall performance, we will further analyze the performance of the path family-based routing mechanism in detail, from four aspects, i.e., scalability, multi-homing, mobility and traffic matrix estimation.

Scalability. The scalability of the path family-based routing mechanism is determined by two factors: the routing table size and the number of SIDs whose uppermost domain must be able to handle.

In the path family-based routing mechanism, an ASR maintains two routing tables: the intra-domain routing table and inter-domain routing table. Because the domains are free to adopt the preferred routing mechanism by themselves, the size of the intra-domain routing table is well under control.

In order to get the inter-domain routing table size, the paths that connect the domain to the domain's parent/customer/peer domains are maintained by a router in a domain. For example, AS174 [13] had at most 4060 neighbors on 1 August 2013. Therefore, even if two domains have ten PIDs, the inter-domain routing table size is 40,600 at most. It is well known that it is significantly less than the current global routing table size (more than 480,000 as of 1 August 2013).

The literature [14] shows that *Resource Handlers* (*RHs*) in DONA are capable of processing *REGISTER* and *FIND* messages if DONA is deployed at the scale of the current Internet. Compared with DONA, which only caches contents on RH, SINET is able to cache contents on all nodes within a domain. Considering this fact, SINET can cache more contents than DONA in a domain that adopts a path family-based routing mechanism. Therefore, the number of messages that an ICCC needs to process can be reduced. Accordingly, the processing overhead of ICCCs in a path family-based routing mechanism should be less than that of RHs in DONA.

Multi-homing. The path family-based routing mechanism is able to efficiently support the multi-homing. When a new path is added between two networks, the PIDs are not advertised throughout the Internet. Thus, the inter-domain routing tables of other networks would not be affected. Although the ICCC in a network may register some SIDs to the ICCC in other networks, this does not increase the number of SIDs that top-level networks need to deal with. So it does not affect the scalability of the whole Internet. When a host has two interfaces connecting to two different ASs, the host can decide by itself to which network a service request message should be forwarded so as to make the best use of multi-homing. However, when the host has decided to forward a service request message to network, the ICCC in this network can decide where to forward the service request message based on its local policy.

A multi-homed host is able to control its incoming traffic by forwarding service request messages to different providers, because packets forwarding across domains is based on paths. The above nature of service request messages makes it easy for multi-homed hosts to achieve fine-grained traffic engineering and then makes the best use of multi-homing. This section evaluated the capability of path family-based routing mechanisms in efficient support of traffic engineering.

Figure 7.4 shows the number of packets on path PID1 and path PID2. The number of packets passing path PID1 is about 350 packets per second. The number of packets passing path PID2 is about 150 packets per second. It can be seen that, as described before, ICCC1 chooses path PID1 with 70 % probability and path PID2 with 30 % probability when it forwards service request messages for contents provided by Server 2. This implies the path family-based routing mechanism can efficiently support traffic engineering.

Mobility. A mobile node, which holds a datum, can unregister from the previous ASR and register at another ASR. When the registration state is installed at the new ASR and the related ICCC, subsequent service request messages for these data will be forwarded to this new ICCC. According to what we have discussed before, if a mobile node wants a piece of content, it will resend a service request message that is routed to a copy of the desired data nearby. What is more, the mobility management approach of the domain could address the mobility within a domain. When a consumer host roams from domain A to domain B, there will be a mobility anchor in domain A, which is in order to maintain communications. Therefore, the packets sending to the host can be first routed to the anchor. On the other hand, the host is able to know the PID from domain A to domain B, when a source host roams from domain A to a neighboring domain B. Accordingly, host A should first append one

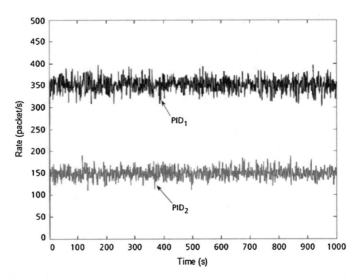

Fig. 7.4 The number of packets on path PID1 and PID2. Reprinted from Ref. [19], with permission from IEEE

PID onto the outer header of the packets indicating the path from domain A to domain B, when it sends out a packet. This way, the packets are first sent from domain B to domain A and then forwarded to the corresponding node.

Traffic Matrix Estimation. The path family-based routing mechanism has the ability to accurately estimate the *traffic matrices* (*TM*) in real time [15]. Each ASR in a domain maintains a routing table including all PIDs in the domain and the neighboring domain, and the egress ASR connects through the PIDs. When a new packet arrives at an ASR, the ASR first determines whether the provider is in the same domain or another domain. If the provider is in the same domain, the ASR can determine the NID of the provider. Otherwise, the ASR can determine the PID and the egress ASR destined to another domain. Accordingly, to obtain the traffic matrix from an ASR to any other node in the network, the ASR only needs to count these packets (sizes) that contain the PID. Then, to estimate the traffic matrices of a domain, each ASR in the domain must estimate the traffic matrix from the ASR to other ASRs in the domain and report its traffic matrices to the ICCC. These tasks can be done in real time, and we can obtain the accurate traffic matrix, which is a critical input to many network functions such as traffic engineering, capacity provisioning and anomaly detection.

The traffic matrix estimation in the current Internet is based on the *OpenFlow* technique. Some accomplishments are achieved, and many problems exist as well. First, the large amount of flow information has to be shipped to a centralized location for the correlation. Second, it is difficult to estimate the traffic matrices at a high speed in a timely manner. Finally, many approaches proposed for estimation traffic matrices in the current Internet are inflexible because their accuracies depend on the unknown traffic volumes.

However, the traffic matrix estimation in the path family-based routing mechanism outperforms that in the current Internet:

- By adopting the path family-based routing mechanism, the traffic matrices in SINET are efficiently estimated by the ASRs in parallel.
- By adopting the path family-based routing mechanism, the traffic matrices can be estimated in a timely manner in SINET, since a router is able to estimate the traffic matrix at a line speed when it forwards the data packets.
- The path family-based routing mechanism makes it easy to accurately estimate the traffic matrices without making any assumption, because routers estimate traffic matrices when they forward data packets and all the packets are counted.

The overhead of the traffic matrix estimation is acceptable according to Ref. [15], since the switches in OpenFlow also count the number of packets they forward. In SINET, ASRs are responsible for maintaining entries for PIDs. [13] shows that on 14 October 2013 the largest AS degree is 4131. If an AS has two PIDs with each of its neighbor ASs, the maximal number of PIDs that an AS has is less than 10,000. That is to say, the number of PIDs in a SINET is acceptable. Moreover, in the inter-domain routing table, an entry contains three fields: the PID, the number of packets and the number of bytes to the PID. Each field has a length of 32 bits. Each entry has a length of 96 bits. Thus, an ingress ASR needs at most 120,000 bytes of memory space, which is fairly small when compared with the routers in current Internet.

Figure 7.5 shows the estimated traffic matrices from ASR3 to ASR1, from ASR2 to ASR1, from ASR6 to ASR5 and from ASR6 to ASR4 in the prototype system shown in Fig. 7.2. It can be observed in Fig. 7.5 that the traffic from ASR3 to ASR1

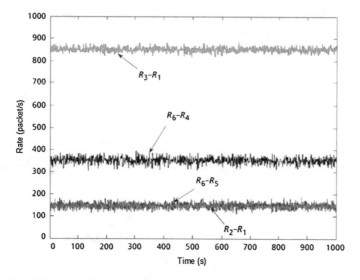

Fig. 7.5 The TM estimated from the prototype system. Reprinted from Ref. [19], with permission from IEEE

is about 850 packets per second; the traffic from ASR6 to ASR4 is about 350 packets per second; the traffic from ASR2 to ASR1 is about 150 packets per second; the traffic from ASR6 to ASR5 is about 150 packets per second. It is worth noting that these numbers match with the actual traffic matrices very well. For example, the actual traffic from node R6 to node R5 is 150 packets per second because the number of service request messages sent to ICCC2 is 500 per second and 30 % of the replying data packets are sent to PID2. The actual traffic from ASR6 to ASR4 is 350 packets because the number of service request messages sent to ICCC2 is 500 per second and 70 % of the replying data packets are being sent to PID1. These results demonstrate the accuracy of the path family-based routing mechanism in estimating traffic matrices.

To further evaluate the performance of traffic matrix awareness of the path family-based routing mechanism, this section compares it with the *OpenFlow* mechanism. Specifically, this section use the *OpenTM* approach proposed in [16] to estimate the traffic matrices. A prototype system as illustrated in Fig. 7.6 is built, which is comprised of four ASRs denoted as A, B, C and D, four end hosts and an ICCC. We assume that the four end hosts work as four domains, which are denoted as D1, D2, D3 and D4, for the path family-based routing mechanism in SINET, and the four routers constitute a domain D5, as illustrated by the dotted circle in Fig. 7.6 The PIDs between D5 and the other four domains are shown in Fig. 7.6.

When the prototype system is running, D1 sends data packets, which belong to nine different flows to D3. Nine flows are randomly generated, whose durations follow a uniform distribution between 30 and 50 s. When a flow terminates, another flow is sent out after a period (the duration also follows the uniform distribution between 20 and 40 s). Each flow sends out ten data packets per second. The size of a data packet is also fixed to 60 bytes. An OpenFlow controller polls the switches once every 25 s. The default value for a switch to remove a flow entry from its flow table is set to be 20 s. Similarly, an ASR in SINET estimates the traffic matrix from node A and node C and reports the estimated traffic matrix to the ICCC once every 25 s.

Figure 7.7 shows the real traffic matrix and the estimated traffic matrices by using the OpenTM approach and the path family-based routing mechanism. Figure 7.7 shows that the estimated traffic matrix with the path family-based

Fig. 7.6 The prototype system topology for TM estimation. Reprinted from Ref. [15], with permission from IEEE

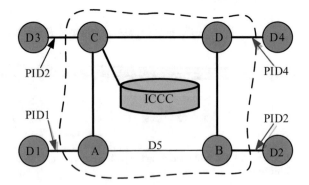

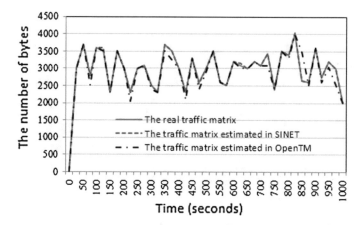

Fig. 7.7   The real and estimated TM. Reprinted from Ref. [15], with permission from IEEE

routing mechanism still matches very well with the real traffic matrix, which out-performs the traffic matrix estimated with OpenTM, because OpenTM has the drawback [16] that it cannot accurately estimate the traffic matrix if the duration between two consecutive polls is larger than the default value for a switch to remove a flow entry, while the path-family based routing mechanism has no such that drawback.

7.3   Source Identifier Routing

7.3.1   Design and Mechanism

In *Source Identifier Routing mechanism*, the inter-domain routing is based on multiple *Autonomous System* (*AS*) paths. In addition, the ASR controls the traffic across multiple paths for finer granularity by using source routing. In the SINET framework, the CON is separated from the ACN. Therefore, the ACN acts as a source or sink for data packets, and the CON transmits and forwards the packets across the network.

For the ease of description, this section first gives an example of the network topology in SINET with the Source Identifier routing mechanism. As shown in Fig. 7.8, in ACN1, the host NID_A intends to send a packet to a destination host NID_B in ACN3. When a packet from NID_A reaches ASR1, ASR1 will consult the ICCC1 to determine the RID of ASR4. After that, ASR1 encapsulates its own RID as the source and ASR4's RID as the destination in header of the packet. Then, ASR1 sends out the packet. After receiving the packet, ASR4 decapsulates the header, forwards the packets to ACN3 and further forwards to NID_B. It is worth

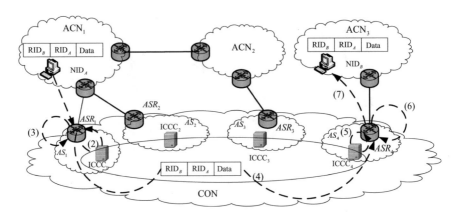

Fig. 7.8 The network topology in SINET. Reprinted from Ref. [20], with permission from IEEE

AS Number	Intra-domain Routing Identifier

Fig. 7.9 Structure of the address in CON. Reprinted from Ref. [20], with permission from IEEE

noting that AS can choose any kind of suitable intra-domain routing. Therefore, this section does not define the structure of the address in ACN.

The structure of the Source Identifier routing address of CON is shown in Fig. 7.9. The first part of the structure is the AS number of the AS, which is the unique identifier of the AS. The second part is the Intra-domain Routing Identifier of the local device. The AS number is a global unique identifier and is issued by an international organization. The Intra-domain Routing Identifier is a local unique identifier in the AS. The Intra-domain Routing Identifier is managed by each AS. The AS can flexibly organize the local Intra-domain Routing to fit the global Intra-domain Routing.

The *Network Layer Reachability Information* (*NLRI*) is also added to the structure address, which is called $PATH_{AS}$. The definition of $PATH_{AS}$ is the hash value of the AS path. For example, there is a path pass through the three ASs, which are AS_A, AS_B and AS_C. Therefore, the $PATH_{AS}$ of this path is the hash value of AS_A, AS_B, and AS_C. $PATH_{AS}$ is a global unique identifier of the path. Therefore, $PATH_{AS}$ carries reachability information of the network layer. However, this is not a prefix, but an AS number in the address. Other attributes of the address are the same as *BGP*. Multiple paths with the same AS destination can be exchanged between the source and the destination, without replacing any previous paths.

In the current Internet, an AS stores a large number of prefixes and sub-prefixes. Moreover, it also sends multiple update messages. However, other ASs could receive multiple messages but are not able to aggregate them again. This is because the large number of prefixes and sub-prefixes results in the large size of the routing

Fig. 7.10 Structure of the
packet header in CON.
Reprinted from Ref. [20],
with permission from IEEE

Version	$\cdots$ Standard IP Head $\cdots$	
$\cdots$	Flag	PATH$_{AS}$
AS Number of Destination		
Local Identifier of Destination		
AS Number of Source		
Local Identifier of Source		

table and update messages, while in SINET the AS has the ability to control the size of the routing table and number of routing updates. This is because a source could withdraw a path by sending the withdrawal message. AS is able to decide on the number of paths to a destination according to the local policies.

In SINET, to support the multi-path routing, four-tuple entries with the form of [destination AS, PATH$_{AS}$, outgoing interface, next hop PATH$_{AS}$] is proposed. The PATH$_{AS}$ represents the hash of the AS path from the current AS to the destination AS. The next hop PATH$_{AS}$ represents the hash value of the AS path from the next hop AS to the destination AS. The structure of the packet header in CON is shown in Fig. 7.10. The source and destination Local Intra-domain Routing Identifier (hereafter referred to as the Local Identifier) is used for intra-domain routing in source and destination ACNs. The PATH$_{AS}$ is used for the AS path selection at the inter-domain level. The Flag is used for routers to determine whether the path can be changed. The Version field is used to prepare for subsequent upgrade.

Figure 7.11 shows the actual forwarding process in the CON of SINET. The router first matches PATH$_{AS}$ using flat lookup. If there is an exact match of PATH$_{AS}$, the router forwards the packet to the outgoing interface. When the packet leaves the current AS to the next hop AS, the PATH$_{AS}$ in the packet is replaced by the next hop PATH$_{AS}$. When the network connection fails, there may not be a match of PATH$_{AS}$, and the router can use the destination AS Number to forward the packet or discard the packet, according to its policies. If PATH$_{AS}$ is the hash value of the destination AS, the packet will arrive at the destination AS. Then, the Local Identifier of destination and the intra-domain routing will be used to forward the packets to the destination.

When receiving a packet, ASR1 will get the RID of the destination ASR4 from the mapping system. There may be more than one path, so ASR1 must choose one AS path for the packet.

7.3.2   Performance Evaluation

In this section, we will evaluate the scalability and reliability of Source Identifier routing using real Internet topology data [17].

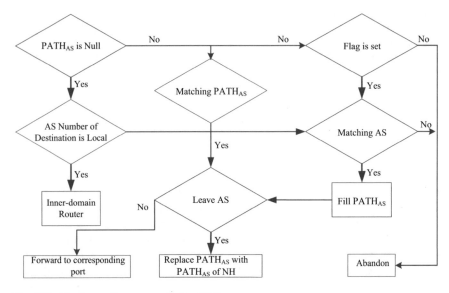

Fig. 7.11 The forwarding process in the CON

Scalability. This section adopts the data from RouteViews [18] to evaluate the scalability of the Source Identifier routing mechanism. The data set was recorded from February 2004 to March 2009. This section compares the Source Identifier routing mechanism with three other schemes: the intra-domain/inter-domain separation mechanism, ACN/CON separation mechanism and routing mechanism in the current Internet.

Figure 7.12 shows that the ACN growth is more significant than that of the CON.

Fig. 7.12 Incremental changes of the Internet

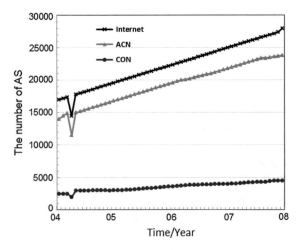

Figure 7.13 shows that 85 % of ASs in the Internet are in ACN and the other 15 % are in CON.

Figure 7.14 shows the rising tendency of the FIB entries in ACN, CON and the Internet.

As shown in Fig. 7.15, it is clear that the number of the independent AS path increases more quickly. Figure 7.16 also shows that the AS path in CON accounts for 21 % of all AS paths in the Internet.

Figure 7.17 shows the number of routing updates in the CON and Internet.

Figure 7.18 shows that the routing updates in CON account for 48 % of the whole Internet. The number of routing updates in CON can be seen as the number of routing updates in the ACN/CON separation scheme. The number of

Fig. 7.13 The percentage of CON and ACN

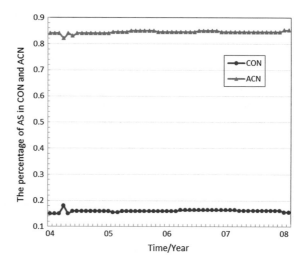

Fig. 7.14 Rising tendency of FIB entries

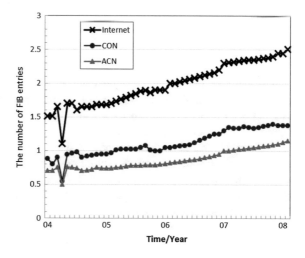

Fig. 7.15 Increase changes
of the AS path

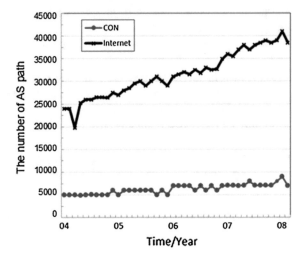

Fig. 7.16 Increase changes
of the number of AS paths

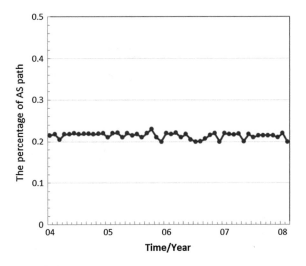

independent AS paths in the Internet can be seen as the number of routing updates
in the intra-domain/inter-domain separation scheme. The number of independent
AS paths in CON can be seen as the number of routing updates in the path
family-based routing mechanism.

Reliability. Based on the AS topology data on 1 June 2009 [17], we analyze the
reliability of the Source Identifier routing mechanism. The topology has 33,531 ASs
with 144,838 peer-peer relationships and 126,124 customer-provider relationships.
In CON, there are only 5,032 ASs, including 64,348 peer-peer relationships and
27,504 customer-provider relationships.

Fig. 7.17 Changes in routing updates

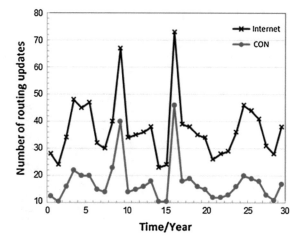

Fig. 7.18 The percentage of AS paths

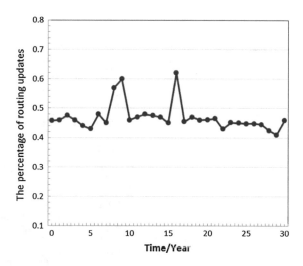

We also conduct an experiment to compute the multiple route paths for a destination. The paths are classified into three types: customer paths, peer paths and provider paths. The three paths are used with different priorities. The customer paths have the first priority. Then, the peer paths will be used if the customer paths are not available and are followed by the provider paths. AS is free to choose the route within each preference class. It does not advertise the routes to another peer or provider. Moreover, the AS is able to choose the destination randomly. Each time, an AS selects the k top paths in the corresponding class. If there are no more than k paths in the class, all the paths will be chosen. The k paths have different next hop ASs. For each neighboring AS, only one path will be chosen. In this experiment, k can be 1, 2, 4, 6. Because k takes various values, the paths (the average path number) that each AS gets in the FIB table are shown in Fig. 7.19.

Fig. 7.19 Average path
number with different k.
Reprinted from Ref. [20],
with permission from IEEE

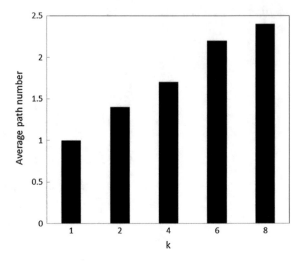

Fig. 7.20 Probability of link
failure. Reprinted from Ref.
[20], with permission from
IEEE

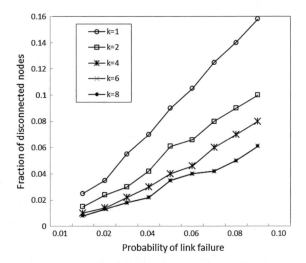

If k is not less than 6, we get more than 100 % paths for each AS in average.
Thus, the number of FIB entries we get is little more than 1,000, which is much less
that the current number of 300,000. Therefore, the AS can deliver the traffic more
efficiently if AS gets more paths.

To evaluate the reliability of the Source Identifier Routing mechanism, the path
links are randomly cut off with probability p. Then, we check whether the ASs fail.
The fraction of disconnected nodes for each value k and p is shown in Fig. 7.20. It
can be seen clearly that even one more path could greatly improve the reliability.

7.4 Conclusion

This chapter introduces two kinds of identifier-based scalable routing in SINET: the path family-based routing mechanism and source identifier routing mechanism. The path family-based routing mechanism can satisfy many attractive features, such as enhanced security, scalability, multi-homing, efficient support for mobility and traffic engineering. Source identifier routing changes the scaling behavior and uses the routing on $PATH_{AS}$ to build multiple paths between the source AS and destination AS. The source identifier routing mechanism has the ability to control the traffic across multiple paths using source routing for finer granularity. The source identifier routing mechanism outperforms the current Internet in terms of scalability and reliability. Both of them have their advantages and can be applied to actual development according to different requirements.

References

1. Nordstrom E, Shue D, Gopalan P et al (2012) Serval: an end-host stack for service-centric networking. In: Proceedings of the 9th USENIX conference on networked systems design and implementation, San Jose, CA
2. Jacobson V et al (2009) Networking named content. In: Proceedings of ACM CoNEXT'09, December 2009, Rome, Italy
3. Xylomenos G, Smetters D, Thornton J et al (2009) A survey of information-centric networking research. In: Proceedings of the 5th international conference on Emerging networking experiments and technologies, pp 1–12
4. Koponen T, Shenker S, Balakrishnan H et al Architecting for innovation. ACM SIGCOMM Comput Commun Rev 41(3):24–26
5. Chuang J (2011) Loci of competition for future internet architecture. IEEE Commun Mag 49 (7):38–43
6. Raychaudhuri D, Nagaraja K, Venkataramani A (2012) MobilityFirst: a robust and trustworthy mobility-centric architecture for the future internet. ACM SIGMOBILE Mob Comput Commun Rev 16(3):2–13
7. Godfrey P, Ganichev I, Shenker S, Stoica I et al (2009) Pathlet routing. ACM SIGCOMM Comput Commun Rev 39(4):111–122
8. Subramanian L, Caesar M, Ee C (2005) HLP: a next generation inter-domain routing protocol. ACM SIGCOMM Comput Commun Rev 35(4):13–24
9. Kastenholz F (2002) ISLAY: a new routing and addressing architecture. IRTF, Internet Draft
10. Mahajan R, Wetherall D, Anderson T (2005) Negotiation-based routing between neighboring ISPs. In: Proceedings of the 2nd conference on symposium on networked systems design and implementation, pp 29–42
11. Mahajan R, Wetherall D, Anderson T (2004) Towards coordinated interdomain traffic engineering. In: Proceedings of third workshop on hot topics in networks
12. Andersen D, Balakrishnan H, Feamster N et al (2008) Accountable internet protocol (AIP). ACM SIGCOMM Comput Commun Rev 38(4):339–350
13. BGP peer report (2015). http://bgp.he.net/report/peers. Accessed 12 June 2015
14. Koponen T, Chawla M, Chun B et al (2007) A data-oriented (and beyond) network architecture. In: Proceedings of the 2007 conference on applications, technologies, architectures, and protocols for computer communications, Kyoto, Japan

15. Luo H, Chen Z, Cui J, Zhang H (2014) An approach for efficient, accurate, and timely estimation of traffic matrices. Proceedings of the INFOCOM WKSHPS, Toronto, Canada
16. Tootoonchian A, Ghobadi M, Ganjali Y (2010) OpenTM: traffic matrix estimator for OpenFlow networks. In: Proceedings of 11th international conference on passive and active measurement, Zurich, Switzerland, pp 201–210
17. Zhang Y (2015) Internet AS-level topology archive. http://irl.cs.ucla.edu/topology/. Accessed 12 June 2015
18. University of Oregon RouteViews. http://archive2.routeviews.org/. Accessed 12 June 2015
19. Luo H, Chen Z, Cui J, Zhang H, Zukerman M, Qiao C (2014) CoLoR: an information-centric internet architecture for innovation. IEEE Netw Mag 28(3):4–10
20. Guo H, Gao S, Zhang H (2009) Towards a scalable routing architecture for future internet. IEEE Netw Infrastruct Dig Content (IC-NIDC): 261–265
21. Chen Z, Luo H, Cui J, Jin M et al (2013) Security analysis of a future internet architecture. In: Proceedings of the 21th IEEE international conference on network protocols (ICNP), Gottingen, Germany, pp 1–6
22. Quoitin B, Bonaventure O et al (2005) A cooperative approach to inter-domain traffic engineering. Next generation internet networks, pp 450–457

Chapter 8
Efficient Mapping System of SINET

As introduced previously, SINET supports two AID formats, namely aggregate AID and flat AID. Similarly, two mapping systems corresponding to the two different AIDs are presented in this chapter: the DHT-based mapping system (DHT-MAP) and the hierarchical mapping system (HMS). DHT-MAP and HMS are both overlay systems built to perform the mapping between AIDs and RIDs. Basically, the DHT-MAP is designed to map the flat AIDs into RIDs, while the HMS is designed to support aggregate AIDs. DHT-MAP is an AID-to-RID mapping scheme based on the distributed hash table (DHT) algorithm, whereas HMS has two levels: the upper level is responsible for storing the global mappings between AID prefixes and ASs; the bottom level is in charge of maintaining the mappings of AID-to-RID in an AS. The two kinds of efficient mapping approaches of SINET are thoroughly introduced in this chapter as well.

8.1 Related Work

As an identifier/locator separation framework, SINET has to face a critical challenge: how to perform the mapping service. SINET is a network architecture that adopts the idea of identifier/locator separation. It divides the IP address namespace into an Accessing Identifier (AID) and Routing Identifier (RID). Then, an identifier mapping system is needed to provide an appropriate RID for any given AID. In SINET, the Identifier Mapping Server (IDMS) plays that role. The IDMS is not a single device, but a distributed system. There have been several proposals to address this issue, each with its advantages and disadvantages.

In [1, 2], each AS maintains a default resolver to store global identifier-to-locator mappings, and the identifier is aggregatable. This approach can only be applied to small-scale networks. The authors of [3] propose a LISP alterative topology (LISP-ALT). In LISP-ALT, identifier-to-locator mappings are stored at distributed resolvers, and identifier reachability information is propagated by an overlay

© Springer-Verlag Berlin Heidelberg 2016
H. Zhang et al., *Smart Collaborative Identifier Network*,
DOI 10.1007/978-3-662-49143-0_8

infrastructure. Researchers of [4] borrow the ideas from [3], but improve the organization of the overlay infrastructure into a strict hierarchy mode. In [5], the researchers suggest identifier-to-locator mappings, but only limited to an IP-alike structured identifier. In [6], the authors suggest using bidirectional Protocol Independent Multicast (PIM) [7] trees to propagate the identifier-to-locator reachability information. LISP-DHT in [8] is another approach toward a DHT mapping system, where the resolver stores the mappings for a set of continuous identifiers and uses the highest one as a key. However, LISP-DHT cannot be applied to flat identifiers.

Researchers in [9] propose LISP+ALT to store the mappings in a distributed manner. LISP+ALT is an overlay system to propagate identifier-prefix reachability information using BGP. LISP-TREE [10] is based on DNS. In this approach, identifier blocks are assigned to the levels of the hierarchy by following the current IP address allocation policies. LISP+ALT and LISP-TREE are all hierarchical architectures.

8.2 DHT-Based Mapping System

8.2.1 Basic Concepts

Before introducing the DHT-based mapping system, some related terms and notations are provided.

AID-to-RID mapping is a binding between the AID and the RID. It is stored in ASR and can be used to determine the corresponding RID for any given AID.

Egress ASR is an ASR used to receive packets from CON, replace the RID header by the AID header and send new packets into ACN. When the egress ASR receives a packet whose destination address in the header is the ASR's local RID, it replaces the RID header by a corresponding AID based on its AID-to-RID mapping table.

Ingress ASR maintains the recently used AID-to-RID mappings. Each AID-to-RID mapping corresponds to a timer. If the timer exceeds the predetermined threshold, the ingress ASR will remove the AID-to-RID mapping from its local mapping table. If the ingress ASR receives a packet with an AID destination, it will perform an AID-to-RID mapping lookup through the mapping service and then prepends an optimum RID. It is worth noting that an ingress ASR may also be an egress ASR, and vice versa.

Resolver is an important element of IDMS, which is placed in the CON. Resolver maintains a mapping table storing AID-to-RID mappings and timers for each mapping. It is responsible for resolving RIDs after receiving mapping requests from ASRs. If the timer of an AID-to-RID mapping exceeds the predefined threshold, the AID-to-RID mapping will be removed from the mapping table in the resolver. One resolver may have one or more RIDs. It is worth noting that the RID of a resolver should be known by ASRs, other resolvers and forwarders.

A *mapping request* is sent to the resolver if an ingress ASR receives a new packet that will be routed to an AID address. Then, a resolver returns an RID corresponding to the AID to the request ingress ASR.

AID-to-resolver mapping indicates that the resolvers store the AID-to-RID mappings for a given AID. Thus, it is a binding between the AID and the resolver that stores some AID-to-RID mappings and resolves RIDs for AIDs upon request.

Forwarder is an important element of IDMS, which is responsible for storing AID-to-resolver mappings and forwarding the mapping requests for a given AID to the resolver that stores the required AID-to-resolver mapping. Each forwarder has two mapping tables. One is the main mapping table. The other one is the backup mapping table. Each AID-to-resolver mapping has a corresponding timer, which is stored in the forwarder. The forwarder removes the AID-to-resolver mapping from its main mapping table if the timer exceeds the predefined threshold. In addition, each forwarder maintains a preference for every AID-to-resolver mapping.

The illustration of the DHT-based Mapping System in SINET is shown in Fig. 8.1. The network topology consists of ACNs, CONs and a DHT-based mapping system. For ease of description, CONs can be seen as provider networks that provide data forwarding services. ACNs can be seen as customer networks that are the sources and sinks of traffic. Note that a customer network may connect to more than one provider network and may directly connect to another customer network. End hosts identified by AIDs are located at ACNs. End host's AID is always consistent, even in a mobile environment. When an end host sends out a packet, the

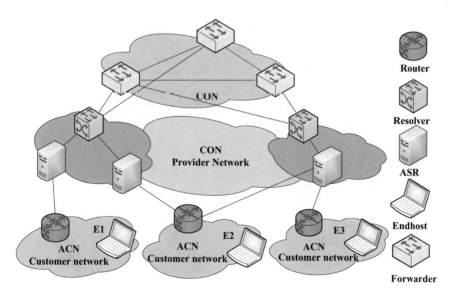

Fig. 8.1 Illustration of the DHT-based mapping system. Reprinted from Ref. [24], with permission from IEEE

end host's AID is attached to the source field and the destination host's AID is attached to the destination field. After an end host sends out a packet, the packet is routed to its local ingress ASR. The ingress ASR performs an AID-to-RID mapping lookup through a mapping service and then replaces the AID header by the corresponding RID. Then, the packet will be passed into CON. CON only uses RIDs to route packets from their ingress ASRs to egress ASRs. In CON, there are one or more resolvers in every AS, and each resolver maintains the AID-to-RID mappings for AIDs of all local hosts. Furthermore, in an AS, ASR knows the RID of the local resolver, and each resolver knows the RID of its nearest forwarder.

8.2.2 Registration in DHT-Based Mapping System

When the source field attaches to a new end host, the ingress ASR should assign an AID-to-RID mapping for the end host and register this mapping to the resolution system. A registration process is used to illustrate the DHT-based mapping system. The basic registration process is described as follows, with the help of the example shown in Fig. 8.2.

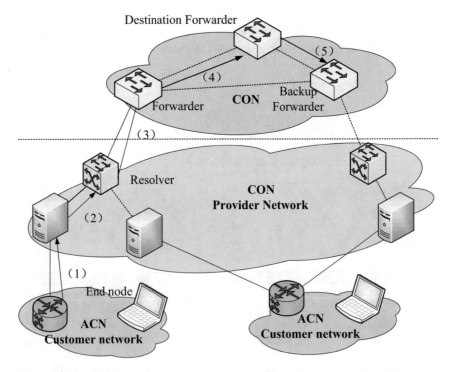

Fig. 8.2 The registration process. Reprinted from Ref. [24], with permission from IEEE

First, the message (1) is sent out from the end host to the ingress ASR. The message (1) includes the AID of the end host and indicates that it will access the CON through that ingress ASR.

Second, when receiving the message, the ingress ASR first lookups in its mapping table to check whether there is a related AID-to-RID mapping. If the ingress ASR has maintained this mapping, it continues to check whether the RID (in this AID-to-RID mapping) is local or not. If the RID belongs to this ingress ASR, the ingress ASR just needs to update the timer for this mapping. If the ingress ASR does not maintain the related AID-to-RID mapping or the desired RID belongs to another ASR, the ingress ASR should assign an RID for the AID and store the new AID-to-RID mapping to its local mapping table. After setting up a new mapping, the ingress ASR sets up a timer for this mapping and sends the mapping (2) to the resolver in the same AS.

Third, when mapping (2) arrives at the resolver, the resolver updates the timer for the AID-to-RID mapping according to the following steps. The resolver first checks whether there is a related mapping for the AID. If so, the resolver simply adds the new AID-to-RID mapping to its mapping table and does not need to send out an AID-to-resolver mapping to the CON, because the resolver has sent such a message before. During these processes, there may be multiple AID-to-RID mappings in the resolver for an AID. If that AID-to-RID mapping is not in the mapping table of the resolver, the resolver should add that mapping to its mapping table and set a timer for it. Thus far, the resolver has published an AID-to-resolver mapping and set a preference to the AID-to-RID mapping. Then, the AID-to-resolver (3) will be sent to the nearest forwarder.

Fourth, when AID-to-resolver mapping arrives at the forwarder, the forwarder hashes the AID to a point P. If the point P reaches its destination forwarder, the next step will be performed. If P is not in its own zone, the forwarder will send the mapping to a neighbor that is close to the point P. This process continues until the mapping (4) reaches its destination forwarder.

Finally, when this AID-to-resolver mapping arrives at the destination forwarder, the forwarder stores this mapping in its main mapping table. Then, this mapping will be sent to its backup forwarder (5). The backup forwarder (5) will store this mapping in its backup mapping table.

Sometimes, a multi-homed end host could connect to CON through multiple ASs. Each AS has to register one AID-to-resolver mapping to the forwarder. Thus, a forwarder stores multiple AID-to-resolver mappings for one multi-homed AID. When a mobile node leaves from an ASR, the ASR may detect the movement. Moreover, the mobile node is also able to send a message to indicate this movement. Then, the ASR has to send an unregistered message to the source resolver. When receiving this unregister message, the source resolver will remove the AID-to-RID mapping for the end host. After that, the unregister message would be sent from the resolver to the forwarders.

8.2.3   Resolving in DHT-Based Mapping System

When a packet with a destination AID_{dst} arrives at the ingress ASR, the ASR looks up the routing table whether or not there is a related AID-to-RID mapping for AID_{dst}. If the ingress ASR cannot find a related mapping in its local memory, the ASR will adopt a resolving process to find an RID for an AID. As shown in Fig. 8.3, the resolving process is described as follows.

First, the mapping request (1) is sent out by the ingress ASR to the local resolver. This section defines the resolver consulted by an ingress ASR as source resolver.

Second, when receiving the mapping request (1), the source resolver seeks in its local AID-to-RID mapping table to find whether there is a mapping for the required AID. If there is not a related mapping, the resolver should forward the mapping request to its nearest forwarder (2). If there is a related mapping, go to Step 6.

Third, when receiving the mapping request (2), the forwarder hashes the AID in the mapping request into the point P. If the point P is not in the forwarder's own zone, the forwarder should forward the mapping request to the neighbor (3), which is close to the destination forwarder. If the point P is in its own zone, then go to Step 4.

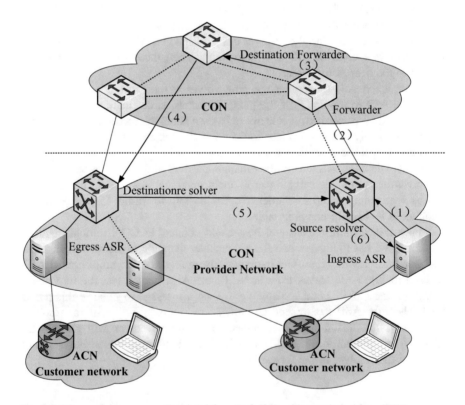

Fig. 8.3 The resolving process. Reprinted from Ref. [24], with permission from IEEE

Fourth, upon receiving the mapping request, the destination forwarder seeks a desired AID-to-resolver mapping in its main mapping table, which records the desired RID stored. After having found the AID-to-resolver mapping, the destination forwarder sends the mapping request to the destination resolver of the AID (4).

Fifth, after receiving the mapping request, the destination resolver replaces the AID and sends the data packet to its egress ASR. The destination resolver then sends the AID-to-RID mapping (5) to the source resolver.

Eventually, after receiving the AID-to-RID mapping, the source resolver first stores this AID-to-RID mapping into its mapping table and passes the new mapping to the ingress ASR (6). After receiving the AID-to-RID mapping, the ingress ASR stores this mapping into its local mapping table. Then, if the ingress ASR receives the same mapping request again, the ingress ASR simply encapsulates them without consulting others.

8.2.4   Evaluation and Analysis

Scalability. The DHT-based mapping system could have good scalability to support the AID/RID separation in the SINET, even if the number of AIDs may be as large as 10^{14}. This means that the number of people on the earth can be as large as 10^{10} and every person can occupy 10^4 AIDs. Each forwarder in the DHT-based mapping system only stores its routing table, the coordinate zone, the backup node of each neighbor and the coordinate zone of each backup node in $2d$ coordinate neighbors. In the routing table of each forwarder, if d is fixed, the information is fixed and does not vary with the number of forwarders as well as the number of AIDs. The AS may maintain multiple resolvers, which can be viewed as a super-resolver. A single ASR does not need to store many AID-to-RID mappings.

The campus network of Beijing JiaoTong University (with about 40,000 users) is used as an example to illustrate the scalability. If we set an ingress ASR at the edge of the campus network, when the cache timeout is set as 30 min, the ingress ASR needs to store about 200,000 AID-to-RID mappings. It is different from the current Internet, which must store all mappings at the same router. If the number of end hosts in an ACN increases, we can simply add ASRs so that each ASR deals with a small part of the end hosts. Therefore, there is no scalability problem for ASRs.

Resolution Delay. The DHT-based mapping system has the ability to keep the resolution delay at an acceptable level, even if it needs to support a large number of AIDs.

The resolution delay of a resolution request comprises nine parts, and they are denoted as T_1, T_2, ..., T_9. Assume $T_1 = 5$ ms. This denotes the propagation delay from an ingress ASR to its resolver. At the source resolver, the AID-to-RID mapping lookup delay is defined as T_2, and $T_1 = 1$ ms. The propagation delay from the source resolver to its closest forwarder is defined as T_3, and T_3 equals 10 ms.

The propagation delay is defined as T_4. The AID-to-resolver mapping lookup delay in the destination forward is defined as T_5, and T_5 equals 1 ms. The propagation delay from the destination forwarder to the destination resolver is defined as T6. The AID-to-RID mapping lookup delay at the destination resolver is defined as T_7. The propagation delay from the destination resolver to the source resolver is defined as T_8. The propagation delay from the source resolver to the ingress ASR is defined as T_9, and T_9 equals T_1. The values of T_6 and T_8 are the average end-to-end delay between two randomly chosen end hosts in the current Internet and [25] demonstrates that $T_6 = T_8 = 115$ ms.

The resolution delay T can be calculated by Eq. 8.1:

$$T = \sum_{i=1}^{9} T_i = 249 + T_4, \tag{8.1}$$

where T_4 is determined by the number of hops in the CON, and T_4 is dependent on the number of forwarders.

The number of AIDs is denoted as N. The required number of forwarders is denoted as n, and it is determined by the forwarders' storage space, request process ability and requests' arrival rate. In order to calculate the storage space requirement, we set AID as 160 bits long [11]. RIDs are set as 128 bits long (IPv6-alike 128-bit). In addition, since it has been reported that subscribing to more than four homes does not benefit a host [12], an AID is set to attach to four ASs and related to four resolvers. For each AID-to-resolver mapping, a timer and a preference are maintained by ASRs. The timer and the preference need a storage space of 16 bits.

With the above assumptions, the storage space required to store the AID-to-resolver mappings for an AID is 100 bytes.

Then, the total storage space required to store the AID-to-resolver mappings is $100 * N$ bytes. If the AID-to-resolver mappings are evenly stored at the forwarders and a single forwarder has K GB storage space, the required number of forwarders would be $100 * N/K$. This can be calculated by Eq. 8.2:

$$n = 100 * \frac{N}{K}. \tag{8.2}$$

The required number of forwarders to process the requests is dependent on the capability of forwarders. In this section, the forwarders are able to forward M requests/s, and Pa denotes the percentage of mappings per second. That is to say, $Pa * N$ is the number of resolution requests sent into the CON system per second. Notice that for a d-dimensional space that is partitioned into n equal zones, the average routing path length in the CON system is $(d/4) * (n^{1/d})$ hops. The DHT-MAP needs to deal with $Pa * N * (d/4) * (n^{1/d})$ messages. Assume that the arrival of all request messages at a forwarder obeys the Poisson distribution, and the messages are evenly distributed to all forwarders. Therefore, each forwarder is able to forward M requests per second, and M can be calculated by Eq. 8.3:

$$M > \frac{Pa * N * d * n^{1/d}}{4n}. \tag{8.3}$$

Equation 8.3 can be changed to Eq. 8.4:

$$n > \{Pa * d * N/(4M)\}^{\frac{d}{d-1}}. \tag{8.4}$$

The required number of forwarders would be calculated as:

$$n > \max\left\{100 * N/K, [Pa * d * N/4M]^{\frac{d}{d-1}}\right\}. \tag{8.5}$$

Next, we will discuss the storage space of a single end node. In [13], a Sun modular data center is able to provide a storage space of 3,000 terabytes, where four such end hosts are needed to store the AID-to-resolver mappings even if the number of AIDs is as large as 10^{14}. In this section, Google cluster technologies can be used to organize end hosts with normal storage capability to store those AID-to-resolver mappings to keep a low searching delay [14]. The average number of hops (denoted by h) that a request may pass through in the CON would be calculated by Eq. 8.6:

$$h = \frac{d * n^{1/d}}{4} > \left(\frac{d}{4}\right)^{\frac{d}{d-1}} * \left(\frac{Pa * N}{M}\right)^{\frac{d}{d-1}}. \tag{8.6}$$

In the current Internet, a router can forward 10^8 packets per second. A Power-Hammer P640 router is able to forward 934 mega packets per second [15]. Therefore, M could be set as 10^8.

When $N = 10^{14}$, Pa varies from 0.0001 to 0.01; d varies from 4 to 10. The average number of hops that a request may pass through in the CON is plotted in Fig. 8.4. When $N = 10^{14}$, $Pa = 0.01$ and $d = 8$, the average number of hops in the CON is about 8. However, Pa is less than 0.001 in practice. So, the average number of hops that a request may pass through in the CON would be less than 6.

Furthermore, when Pa varies from 0.001 to 0.01, N varies from 10^{10} to 10^{14}. When d equals 8, the average number of hops a request may pass through in the CON is plotted in Fig. 8.5. When $N = 10^{10}$, $Pa = 0.01$, the average number of hops is only about 2. In addition, if the number of AIDs increases to 10^{11}, the average number of hops only slightly increases to about 3. Since a resolution request may pass through 2 to 6 hops in CON, T_4 varies from 230 to 690 ms.

With the help of Eq. 8.1, we can calculate the resolution delay T varies from 479 to 939 ms. In addition, by using the techniques such as "increasing reality" and "caching" proposed in 0, T could be lower. Furthermore, when a new AID-to-RID mapping is added onto the ASR resolves, the mapping could be used by other users during a certain duration.

Number of Resolution Requests in the Practical Environment. In this section, the simulation is based on the real data traces collected from the campus network of the Beijing JiaoTong University during the week of 12 October 2008.

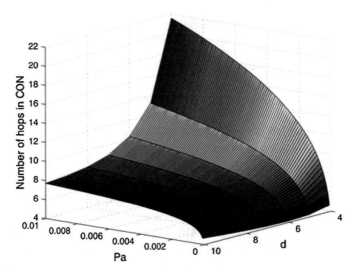

Fig. 8.4 Average number of a request hops when N = 1014. Reprinted from Ref. [24], with permission from IEEE

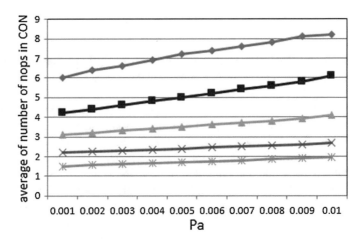

Fig. 8.5 Average number of a request hops when Pa varies. Reprinted from Ref. [24], with permission from IEEE

The campus network includes about 40,000 users, and 13,000 of them are active every day. The network is connected to the Internet through a border router, which can provide the Netflow measurement facility to collect the traffic. We assume that the border router can be regarded as an ingress ASR. The considered IP addresses can be regarded as AID-to-RID mappings, and we set a timer for each mapping. Then, we evaluate the number of AID-to-RID mappings cached at the border router. If the IP address is not used by any flow until the timer exceeds the cache timeout, the item is removed from the cache. If the IP address is used before the cache timeout, the timer for the item is reset to zero.

In the campus network, all the end hosts, from different sources, may send multiple packets to the same destination. For any two consecutive packets, there is an interval between the two packets. The cumulative distribution function of packet intervals is shown in Fig. 8.6. We can see that about 97 % of packet intervals are less than 3 min, and about 99 % are less than 30 min.

We set the cache timeouts to be 3 and 30 min, respectively. The numbers of items in the cache are shown in Fig. 8.7. We can see that the number of items in the cache increases with the increase of cache timeouts.

When the cache timeout is set as 3 min, there are at most 40,000 items in a cache. While if the cache timeout increases to 30 min, the number of items in the cache increases to about 200,000.

This number is acceptable for ingress ASRs for the following reasons:

- The lookup delay at ingress ASRs would be fairly small. Because AIDs are flat, an ingress ASR does not need to do the longest prefix matching, but only the accurate lookup. A simple accurate lookup is at least five times faster than the longest prefix matching [11].
- Since ingress ASRs are placed at the edge of the network, they only need to process a small number of packets.

In Fig. 8.7, it is evident that the number of items in the cache is different between day and night. When the cache timeout is 3 min, the number of items in the cache at night is about 2000–3000 while that during the day is about 1300–1400.

When a packet arrives at an ingress ASR, the ASR should look up the desired RID in its cache. If there is no desired RID, the ASR should send a resolution request to the resolution system. So, the duration of the cache timeout significantly impacts the number of resolution requests.

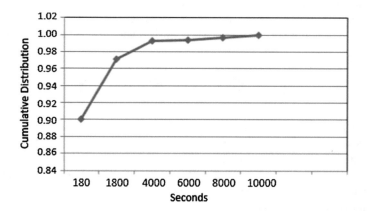

Fig. 8.6 The cumulative distribution function of a packet interval

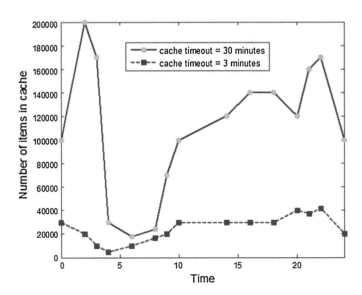

Fig. 8.7 Number of items in the cache

The number of cache misses/minute for different cache timeouts is shown in Fig. 8.8. When the cache timeout is 3 min, that number is 4780 on average through the whole day. When the cache timeout is 30 min, the number of cache misses/minute reduces to about 2330 on average through the whole day. Furthermore, the number of cache misses is also different between day and night. As shown in Fig. 8.8, when the cache timeout is 30 min, the number of cache misses at night is about 309 on average while that during the day is about 2747 on average.

If a resolving request has a length of 200 bytes and cache timeouts are 3 and 30 min, the average numbers of resolving requests are 4780 and 2330 per second. Thus, the required bandwidth is 7.648 Mbps and 3.728 Mbps, respectively. Since the bandwidth of the campus network's outgoing link is 1 Gbps, the message overhead of sending resolving requests is fairly small. Therefore, Pa is calculated as:

$$Pa = \frac{the\ number\ of\ cache\ misses/minute}{60 * 40,000}, \tag{8.7}$$

where 40,000 is the total number of users (i.e., IP addresses) in our campus network. Notice that we do not use the number of active users since we are interested in the ratio of the number of cache miss over the total number of AIDs.

It can be derived from Eq. 8.7 that Pa equals to 0.001992 when cache timeouts are 3 min and equals to 0.000971 when cache timeouts are 30 min. That is to say, Pa is fairly small on average.

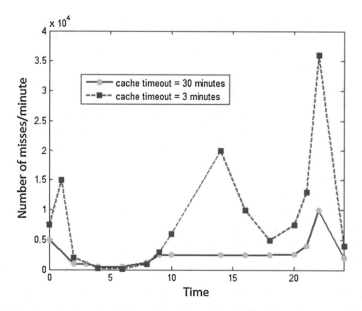

Fig. 8.8 Number of cache misses/minute for different cache timeouts

When the cache timeout is 3 min, Pa is 0.002673 on average. When the cache timeout increases to 30 min, Pa reduces to 0.001145, which proves that Pa is also very small during the day.

It is worth noting that the actual Pa would be lower, because the resolver could store the AID-to-RID mappings that have been recently used. Therefore, the resolver could directly resolve the AID-to-RID mappings for some requests without others.

In a word, the DHT-based mapping scheme maps flat AID into RID, which sets a resolver that stores the AID-to-RID mappings for the end hosts that attach to the AS. The resolver then registers an AID-to-RID mapping to the CON to indicate where one can find an AID-to-RID mapping. The DHT-based mapping system has good scalability and low resolution delay.

8.3 Hierarchical Mapping System

8.3.1 Basic Concepts

In SINET, the *Hierarchical Mapping System* (*HMS*) is built to complete the mapping between aggregatable AIDs and RIDs. HMS is an overlay system built to store the mapping information [26].

As shown in Fig. 8.9, the HMS has two levels: the upper level is responsible for storing the global mappings between AID prefixes and ASs; the bottom level is in charge of maintaining the mappings of AID-to-RID in an AS. Some related concepts are stated as follows.

The Mapping Server is responsible for storing the local mapping information of AID-to-RID in an AS in a distributed manner.

Forwarder is an agent in an AS to aggregate the AIDs. An AS can have one or more forwarders. The forwarder accomplishes *AID-prefix-to-Forwarder mapping* between AID prefixes and forwarders and reports the mappings to the Resolvers. If the AS has only one forwarder, the AID-prefix-to-Forwarder is actually the mapping of AID-prefix-to-AS.

Resolver is used to store the global mapping information of AID-prefix-to-Forwarder. The resolvers include an inter-AS mapping system to exchange AID-prefix-to-Forwarder mappings.

Forwarder and resolver are located in CON, and each one has at least one RID. They can be new entities added to the network or virtual functions running at the routers.

In the bottom level, each AID could be a flat identifier, and the mapping system is organized by *One-Hop DHT*. (One-Hop DHT is a distributed hash table maintaining a full routing table to achieve one hop lookup.) There are two primary reasons for using the One-Hop DHT to organize the Mapping Servers in the bottom level of SINET: First, one-hop DHT could implement fast lookup, which can make

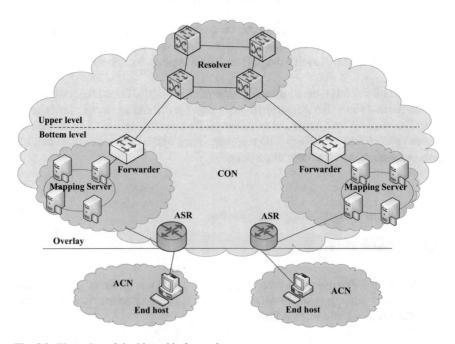

Fig. 8.9 Illustration of the hierarchical mapping system

sure that 99 % of lookups will be successful on the first attempt [16]. Second, the routing table in each node can be kept small, and the lookup is efficient, since the number of mapping servers in an as is not very large. In the mapping system, the mapping servers are rather stable; thus the network churn's low rate is suitable for one-hop DHT. In addition, the organization of mapping servers can be changed to other architectures.

The lookup in the upper level is very fast. In the upper level, the AID-prefix-to-Forwarder mappings in the resolvers are propagated like BGP. The mappings in the upper level are rather stable. If there is only one forwarder in an AS, the AID prefixes can be highly aggregated without considering the address space deaggregation in an AS. Then, the mapping changes within an AS will not impact the upper level.

8.3.2   Registration in HMS

When a new end host joins into the ingress ASR, the ingress ASR first assigns an RID to it and then registers the mapping to HMS. When an end host sends packets to the local ASR, the ingress ASR looks up the desired RID. If the ingress ASR cannot find the required AID-to-RID mapping in its local cache, it will resolve the mapping in HMS.

The basic registration process is shown in Fig. 8.10. After the end host AID attaches to an ingress ASR, the ingress ASR assigns an RID to it and registers the AID-to-RID mapping to the mapping system.

First, the ingress ASR reports the AID-to-RID mapping to the mapping server.

Second, after receiving the AID-to-RID mapping, the mapping server first stores the mapping, and then hashes the AID and forwards the mapping to the destination mapping server.

Third, the mapping server performs an aggregation on the AIDs and reports the AID prefixes to the forwarder in the same AS. It is worth noting that the mappings in mapping servers are local information within an AS.

Fourth, after receiving messages from all the mapping servers in an AS, the forwarder aggregates the AIDs, publishes the AID-prefix-to-Forwarder mapping for each AID prefix and reports the mapping to the resolver. Notice that the mappings in forwarders are local information within an AS.

Finally, after receiving a new mapping, the resolver propagates the information to other resolvers. Therefore, all the resolvers maintain a global AID-prefix-to-Forwarder mapping table and store the global information of the whole network.

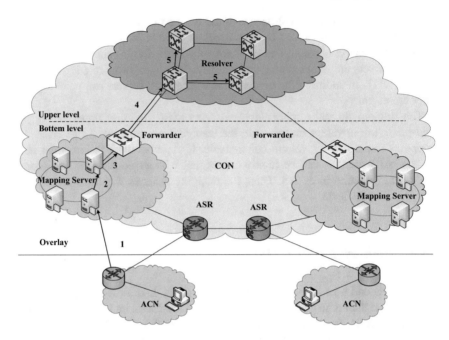

Fig. 8.10 The registration process

8.3.3 Resolving in HMS

In this section, we take the following scenario as an example to illustrate the resolving in HMS. If an end host identified by AID_Y wants to communicate with an end host identified by AID_X, AID_Y sends the request message to the local ingress ASR. If there is the desired mapping in its mapping table, the ASR encapsulates the packet and sends the packet out. If the ASR does not find the desired mapping, it will resolve the mapping of AID_X in HMS. The resolving process is shown in Fig. 8.11.

First, a map request message, which includes the AID_X and the RID of the ingress ASR, is sent to its default mapping server from the ingress ASR.

Second, after receiving the mapping request, the mapping server will look it up in its local mapping database. If AID_X is a local node, the mapping server just supplies the RID for AID_X. If AID_X is not a local node, the mapping server hashes the AID_X and forwards the mapping request to the destination mapping server in the AS.

Third, after receiving the mapping request from the mapping server, the destination mapping server looks up the RID for AID_X in its mapping table. If AID_X is a local node, the destination Mapping Server can supply the AID-to-RID mapping for AID_X. If not, the destination mapping server forwards the mapping request to the default resolver.

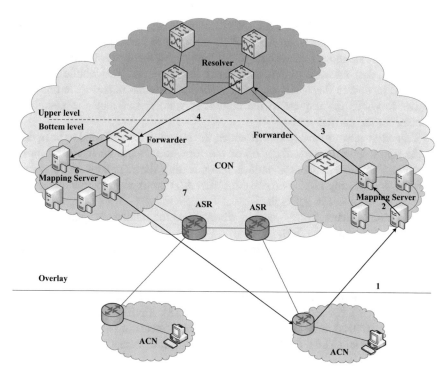

Fig. 8.11 The resolving process

Fourth, by using the longest prefix matching, the resolver finds the AID-prefix-to-Forwarder mapping for the desired AID_X. Then, the resolver forwards the mapping request to the forwarder in the mapping.

Fifth, the forwarder, which is chosen through the above process, randomly forwards the mapping request to a mapping server in its AS.

Sixth, the mapping server hashes the AID_X and forwards the mapping request to the destination mapping server in the destination AS.

Finally, the destination mapping server sends a reply, which includes the AID-to-RID mapping for AID_X to the ingress ASR. The ASR stores the AID-to-RID mapping in its cache and maintains a timer for the mapping. After that, the subsequent packets can be handled directly without resolving in HMS.

8.3.4 Evaluation and Analysis

Mobility and Multi-homing. By adopting the HMS, the mobility of the end host does not cause mapping changes in the upper level. In other words, HMS can efficiently support mobility.

In HMS, if a new mobile node (MN) moves in an AS, it has no effect on the upper level. It just updates the AID-to-RID mapping in the mapping servers. When the Mobile Node moves across between different ASs, the forwarder in the new AS sends an update message to the forwarder in the home AS. The mobile node does not need to update the resolvers. After receiving the map request, the home forwarder forwards the request to the current forwarder, and then the mapping is resolved in the current AS.

If an edge network changes its provider, the mappings do not need to be updated in the upper level because the RID of the forwarder is not changed. In another situation, if an edge network is multi-homing, namely the edge network connects to multiple ASs, it only needs one entry for each AID prefix in the upper level. Thus, the load of resolvers is not high.

Mapping Entries. In this section, we evaluate the number of mapping entries needing to be stored in HMS.

SINET separates the network into CONs and ACNs. CON consists of GSRs, ASRs (identified by RIDs) and some network management entities. ACN comprises individual hosts identified by AIDs. The mapping system needs to store AID-to-RID mapping items for AIDs. Therefore, HMS needs to organize the mappings for ACNs. Borrowing ideas from [17, 18], SINET can be classified into transit ASs (CONs) and stub ASs (ACNs). Some prefixes in the transit AS are not for transit service. Thus, CON is constituted by the IP boxes associated with the transit services.

This section considers all the ASs including the transit ASs and stub ASs to analyze the number of prefixes by using the BGP data from the RouteViews Oregon Collector [19]. In the bottom level, the HMS stores the AID-to-RID mappings. The number of AIDs in an AS decides the load of the mapping servers.

RIB data of the RouteViews Oregon Collector on 1 October, 2010 is taken as a sample to analyze the number of prefixes that each AS announces.

Figure 8.12 shows the cumulative distribution function (CDF) of the number of prefixes announced by an AS. As shown in [20], the average number of hosts of each AID prefix is about 1000. While 42.52 % ASs only need to manage 1000 AID-to-RID mappings, and more than 99 % ASs, the mapping servers announced fewer than 134,000 AIDs. In addition, combining several ASs together to organize the Mapping Servers could increase the resource utilization rate. The largest number of prefixes announced by one AS is 4,481,000.

Multi-homing and traffic engineering lead to a large number of address space fragmentations in the routing system. In HMS, the forwarders are responsible for aggregating the AID prefixes in an AS and reporting them to the upper level. The resolvers only store the AID-prefix-to-AS mapping if there is only one forwarder in an AS. This is similar with the Classless Inter-domain Routing (CIDR) approach [21].

A Linux-based operating system is built to perform the aggregating function. We take a sample of the first day for each month from October 2006 to October 2010. The aggregating function is running until there is no prefix to be aggregated. After

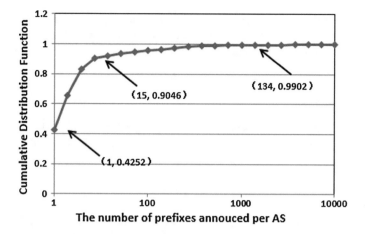

Fig. 8.12 CDF of the number of prefixes announced per AS

that, multi-homing prefixes are counted, which can further decrease the number of mapping entries in the resolvers.

Figure 8.13 shows that three kinds of prefixes, i.e., the number of prefixes in the global routing table, are aggregated after getting rid of the multi-homing prefixes. As shown in Fig. 8.13, the number of mappings of the routing table size reduces from $2.1 * 10^5 - 3.5 * 10^5$ to $1.5 * 10^5 - 2 * 10^5$ after being aggregated, decreasing by about 60 %. About $2 * 10^5$ multi-homing prefixes can be further minimized, and the curve is very close to the aggregated one. In addition, the curves also reveal that the mapping table in the upper level grows more slowly than the global routing table, which also proves that HMS is scalable.

Mapping Updates. In this section, we estimate the mapping updates at the bottom level, which are sent to the forwarder caused by the mobility. Assuming that

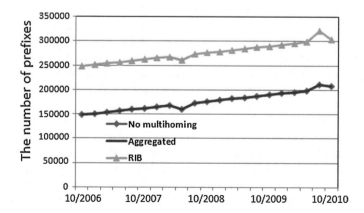

Fig. 8.13 The number of prefixes

there are n ingress ASRs in an AS, the area that each ingress ASR covers is s. The MNs move with an average speed of v. Thus, the rate r for an MN moving across an ingress ASR [22] can be calculated by Eq. 8.8:

$$r = \frac{4v}{\pi\sqrt{s}}. \tag{8.8}$$

The MN's movement direction is uniformly distributed over $[0, 2\pi]$. The border crossing rate λ for an MN out of an AS can be calculated by Eq. 8.9:

$$\lambda = \frac{4v}{\pi\sqrt{ns}}, \tag{8.9}$$

The rate λ for an MN staying in the same AS can be calculated by Eq. 8.10:

$$\mu = r - \lambda = \frac{4v}{\pi\sqrt{s}} * \left(1 - \frac{1}{\sqrt{n}}\right). \tag{8.10}$$

If there are x MNs in an AS, the number of micro mobility m causing mapping updates in the bottom level can be calculated by Eq. 8.11:

$$m = x^*\mu = \frac{4xv}{\pi\sqrt{s}} * \left(1 - \frac{1}{\sqrt{n}}\right). \tag{8.11}$$

The number of macro mobility M that needs to send update messages to forwarders is calculated by Eq. 8.12:

$$M = x * \lambda = \frac{4xv}{\pi\sqrt{ns}}. \tag{8.12}$$

The number of updates per minute is shown in Fig. 8.14. Since the average number of hosts is about 1000 per prefix [23], we set $x = 10,000$ and $n = 1,000$, which is enough to evaluate the performance of HMS. As shown in [22], the parameters could be set as follow: $s = 10$ km^2. If 10^3 ingress ASRs and 10^4 MNs are in an AS, the mapping updates in the bottom level per minute are about 650, and the updates sent to the forwarder per minute are about 21. In this way, the mobility management keeps the mappings in the upper level stable, and the resolution in HMS is accurate. Thus, HMS can support mobility efficiently.

Mapping Efficiency. In this section, we evaluate the number of map requests sent to the HMS. Traces of the traffic from and to the BJTU campus network were collected to help the evaluation. BJTU campus network connects to the ChinaNet and CERNET through a border router (2G links), which supports the Netflow measurement facility to collect the traffic trace. The Netflow measurement facility provides some records including the information about the time stamp, source and

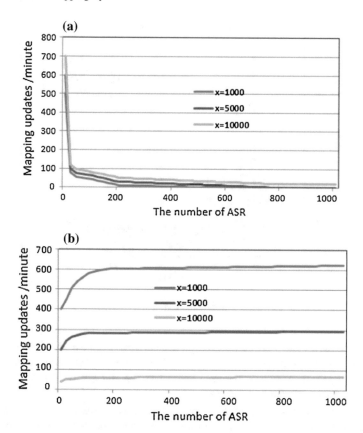

Fig. 8.14 Mapping updates per minute

destination IP addresses, and the size of the packets. We sampled the traffic from 0:00 a.m. to 23:59 p.m. on 12 October 2008.

This section regards the border router as an ingress ASR and the IP addresses as AIDs. The ingress ASR caches the AID-to-RID mappings during the cache time. Let ρ denote the percentage of packets that need to send mapping requests to HMS; ρ can be calculated by Eq. 8.13:

$$\rho = \frac{packets\ to\ be\ resolved/minute}{packets\ received\ by\ ingress\ ARS/minute}. \tag{8.13}$$

where ρ is related to the cache timeout of the ingress ASR. If the cache timeout is large, the ingress ASR can store more AID-to-RID mappings, which results in fewer mapping requests.

We set the ingress ASR's cache timeout as 3, 30 and 60 min, respectively. The evaluation results of ρ are shown in Fig. 8.15. When the cache timeout is 3 min, ρ is less than 5 % during the daytime and less than 15 % at night. Therefore, the

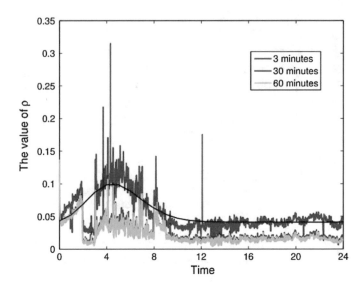

Fig. 8.15 The percentage of packets to be resolved

HMS wild not increase the complexity of the network because only 5 % of packets are issuing a mapping request. In addition, the values of ρ are almost equal when the cache timeout is 30 and 60 min. Therefore, the ingress ASR's cache timeout should be set to 30 min to keep the load of HMS very small.

As shown in Fig. 8.15, ρ reaches the largest value in the early morning. Using the fminsearch function in Matlab [8] under an unconstrained nonlinear optimization [9], a good fit between the time t and ρ, where t is the integer, is calculated by Eq. 8.14:

$$\rho = 0.3279 \ast \left(\frac{5^t \ast e^{-5}}{t!} \right) + 0.0411. \tag{8.14}$$

The black curve in Fig. 8.15 shows the fitting function when the cache timeout is 3 min.

8.4 Conclusion

This chapter introduces two kinds of mapping systems, namely the DHT-based mapping system and the hierarchical mapping system, corresponding to different kinds of AIDs.

The DHT-MS maps flat AIDs into RIDs. It sets a resolver in each AS to store the AID-to-RID mappings for the end hosts that attach to the AS. The resolver then registers an AID-to-resolver mapping to forwards. The DHT-MS has the significant benefits of supporting flat AIDs, good scalability and low resolution delay.

The HMS has two levels. In the bottom level, a one-hop DHT is used to store the AID-to-RID mappings within an AS. It can achieve one hop lookup in an AS. In the upper level, HMS propagates the global mapping information between AID prefixes and ASs using a protocol like BGP. HMS can aggregate the fragmentized prefixes in an AS, thus decreasing the size of the mapping table. The number of mapping entries in HMS grows more slowly than the routing table size, which allows HMS to possess high scalability. In addition, the mobility management in HMS keeps the mapping table in the upper level stable, allowing HMS to support host mobility efficiently. We also evaluate the number of map requests sent to HMS, which shows that the HMS has low overhead.

References

1. Jen D, Meisel M, Massey D, Wang L, Zhang B, Zhang L (2007) APT: a practical transit mapping service, IETF Internet draft
2. Whittle R (2007) IVIP (internet vastly improved plumbing) architecture. IETF Internet draft
3. Farinacci D, Fuller V, Meyer D (2007) LISP alternative topology (LISP-ALT). IETF Internet draft
4. Brim S, Chiappa N, Farinacci D, Fuller V, Lewis D, Meyer D (2007) LISP-CONS: a content distribution overlay network service for lisp. IETF Internet draft
5. Lear E (2008) NERD: a not-so-novel EID to RLOC database. IETF Internet draft
6. Brim S, Farinacci D, Meyer D, Curran J (2007) EID mappings multicast across cooperating systems for LISP. IETF Internet draft
7. Handley M, Kouvelas I, Speakman T, Vicisano L (2007) Bidirectional protocol independent multicast (BIDIR-PIM). IETF Internet Standard, RFC 5015
8. Mathy L, Iannone L, Bonaventure O (2008) LISP-DHT: towards a DHT to map identifiers onto locators. IETF Internet draft, draft-mathy-lisp-dht-00.txt
9. Fuller V, Farinacci D, Meyer D, Lewis D (2013) LISP alternative topology (LISP-ALT). IETF RFC 6836
10. Jakab L, Cabellos-Aparicio A, Coras F, Saucez D, Bonaven-ture O (2010) LISP-TREE: a DNS hierarchy to support the LISP mapping system. IEEE J Sel Areas Commun 28(8):1332–1343
11. Andersen D, Balakrishnan H, Feamster N, Koponen T, Moon D, Shenker S (2008) Accountable internet protocol (AIP). Proc ACM SIGCOMM '08
12. Akella A, Pang J, Shaikh A, Maggs B, Seshan S (2004) A comparison of overlay routing and multihoming route control. Proc ACM SIGCOMM '04
13. Sun Microsystems (2009). http://www.sun.com/products/sunmd/s20/specifications.jsp. Accessed June 2015
14. Augbarroso L, Dean J, Holzle U, Web search for a planet: the google cluster architecture. IEEE Micro 23(2):22–28
15. Harbournetworks (2009). http://www.harbournetworks.com. Accessed June 2015
16. Gupta A, Liskov B, Rodrigues R (2004) Efficient routing for peer-to-peer over-lays. In: 1st symposium on networked systems design and implementation (NSDI 2004), California, USA
17. Dhamdhere A, Dovrolis C (2008) Ten years in the evolution of the internet ecosystem. In: Proceedings of internet measurement conference (IMC 2008), Vouliagmeni, Greece

18. Oliveira R, Zhang B, Zhang L (2007) Observing the evolution of internet AS topology. In: ACM conference of the special interest group on data communication (SIGCOMM 2007), Kyoto, Japan
19. The RouteViews project. http://www.routeviews.org. Accessed June 2015
20. Menth M, Hartmann M, Hofling M (2010) FIRMS: a future internet mapping system. IEEE J Sel Areas Commun 28(8):1326–1331
21. Fuller V, Li T (2006) Classless inter-domain routing (CIDR): the internet address assignment and aggregation plan. RFC 4632
22. Kong K, Song M, Park K, Hwang C (2004) A comparative analytical study on the performance of IP mobility protocols: mobile IPv6 and hierarchical mobile IPv6. In: The 2nd international conference on advances in mobile multimedia (MoMM'2004), Bali, Indonesia
23. Menth M, Hartmann M, Hofling M (2010) FIRMS: a future internet mapping system. IEEE J Sel Areas Commun 28(8):1326–1331
24. Luo H, Qin Y, Zhang H (2009) A DHT-based identifier-to-locator mapping approach for a scalable Internet. IEEE Trans Parallel Distrib Syst 20(12):1790–1802
25. Ratnasamy S, Francis P, Handley M, Karp R, Shenker S (2001) A scalable content-addressable network. Proc ACM SIGCOMM'01
26. Xiaoqian LI, Zhou H, Luo H et al (2013) HMS: a hierarchical mapping system for the locator/ID separation network [J]. Comput Inform 32(6):1229–1255

Chapter 9
Mobility Management in SINET

In this chapter, we introduce four mobility management schemes available in SINET's architecture. SINET facilitates mobile nodes' locator changes at any time without disrupting the ongoing communication sessions. Thus, it can support efficient mobility, global routing scalability and location privacy. This chapter is organized as follows. Section 9.1 summarizes the related work on mobility management. Section 9.2 presents the network-based mobility management mechanism. Section 9.3 discusses the hierarchical mobility management mechanism. Section 9.4 proposes the location management in mapping-based forwarding. Section 9.5 describes the indirect-mapping based mobility support mechanism, and Sect. 9.6 concludes this chapter.

9.1 Related Work

In current Transmission Control Protocol/Internet Protocol (TCP/IP) stacks, the IP address carries too much information, including both identifiers and locators of a Mobile Node (MN). From the perspective of the application, the IP address is used to identify a host. From the perspective of routing, the IP address indicates the current topological location of a host. When an MN moves into a new subnet, it must configure a new IP address. As the transport layer connection with the old IP address is disrupted, the MN has to re-establish connections. As a result, the dual roles of the IP address make it difficult to support mobility.

With the boom of wireless technology in all its forms, wireless technology has been one of the most transforming and empowering network technologies to come along. The most obvious consequence of wireless is mobility. However, the current Internet was originally designed for end-to-end communications between statically located terminals and could not support the mobility well. To support mobility, the IETF (Internet Engineering Task Force) has proposed plenty of protocols, including MIPv4 [1] and MIPv6 [2].

© Springer-Verlag Berlin Heidelberg 2016
H. Zhang et al., *Smart Collaborative Identifier Network*,
DOI 10.1007/978-3-662-49143-0_9

The host-based MIPv4/v6 protocols have several drawbacks, including slow handoff [3], triangle routing, disclosure of location privacy [4], disclosure of the management node's address, i.e., HA, MN and third parties, and messages overhead on wire/wireless links between MN and HA.

One of the most important issues in today's Internet is routing scalability [5, 6]. That is, the routing table in the Default Free Zone (DFZ) grows to a level where it directly influences the routing performance. To address the issue, many organizations including the IETF LISP group [7] and IRTF (Internet Research Task Force) RRG (Routing Research Group) have agreed to the idea of separating the node's identity from its topological location. The ID/Loc (identifier/locator) separation is supposed to be a basic component in the new-generation Internet architecture, which can reduce the routing table size in the DFZ, improve traffic-engineering capabilities and natively support mobility [8]. There are several solutions, such as LISP [9], HIP (Host Identity Protocol) [10] and MILSA [11, 12], proposed to perform the ID/locator split-based scheme.

In a network with locator/identifier separation, a critical challenge is how to design a mapping system that maps identifiers onto locators. While many mapping systems have been proposed in the literature [13–21], they mainly focus on how to distribute/retrieve mapping information. In addition, they all directly or indirectly assume that, when an end host attaches to a tunnel router, the mapping registered to the mapping service for the end host is the mapping from the identifier of the end host onto the locator of the ASR. As a result, when the end host roams from one ASR to another, it is necessary to update the identifier-to-locator mapping for the end host to keep the end host reachable.

9.2   Network-Based Mobility Management (NMM)

The current Internet was originally designed for static hosts. Such targets lead to bad support of mobility [22, 23]. Some existing proposals for solving the mobility problems are host-based schemes, where the Mobile IP (MIP) is a typical paradigm. MIP guarantees the logical reachability irrespective of the host location by using the Home Address (HoA) and Care of Address (CoA), respectively [24]. The HoA is used to identify an MN, and the CoA represents the location information of an MN for packet routing. By using the separation function between the HoA and the CoA, MIP can keep transport connections alive and support global roaming.

However, there are some problems in MIP. First, MIP does not protect the home network equipment and MN's location privacy. In MIP, the Home Agent (HA) address can be obtained by a MN, and the MN's location information can be acquired via a correspondent node (CN). This design results in HAs and MNs being easily attacked. Second, as a host-based mobility management protocol, MIP requires MNs to participate in mobility-related signaling. Therefore, MIP consumes a considerable amount of wireless resources. Third, MIP lacks a global location manager, so that it does not offer good controllability and manageability.

9.2.1 Overview of NMM

Above all, the host-based schemes require users to participate in the mobility management. As the users' behaviors are hard to control by network operators, it is difficult for network operators to manage their network. Accordingly, it is necessary to develop a network-based scheme that can satisfy the needs of service providers.

This section proposes a network-based mobility management scheme (NMM) in SINET, which decomposes IP addresses into AIDs and RIDs and uses a mapping approach to support host mobility and network mobility, in which the Mobile Router (MR) takes charge of MN to participate in the mobility management. In NMM, it deploys the location management and the handoff management in the core network. The design is used to satisfy the requirement of route optimization, fast handoff, location privacy and routing scalability. It can also reduce the message overhead and traffic overhead on wireless links.

9.2.2 NMM Solution

NMM is able to support intra-domain mobility and inter-domain mobility. We define intra-domain mobility as MN moves from an Access Switching Router (ASR) to another in the same Internet Service Provider (ISP) domains. It can be simply supported by local mobility methods that are similar to CIP [25] and Hawaii [26] and will not cause the remapping of AID and RID. The handoff delay is on the order of milliseconds [27], and it can be ignored in intra-domain mobility.

Inter-domain mobility means that MN moves from one ISP domain to another. NMM uses the separating and mapping schemes to support inter-domain mobility. We denote the previous ASR as ASRp, the new ASR as ASRn and the corre-spondent node's (CN) ASR as ASRcn. Figure 9.1 shows the inter-domain handoff procedure. When an MN moves from its ASRp to ASRn, (1) it receives the "ASR advertisement" with ASRn's AID from ASRn. (2) After the movement detection, MN sends the "access request" to ASRn. (3) ASRn authenticates and assigns a new <AID, RID> mapping for MN and reports this mapping to the IDentifier Mapping Server (IDMS). (4) After receiving the "mapping report," IDMS updates its mapping record and notifies ASRp about the new mapping of MN. During the handoff procedure, the AIDs of MN stay unchanged, and the connection established between MN and CN will not be interrupted.

After the inter-domain handoff, the packets sent by CN to MN will follow the path CN- > ASRcn- > ASRp- > ASRn- > MN, which is not the shortest path. As shown in Fig. 9.2, we adopt a traffic-driven scheme to achieve the route optimization. When ASRp receives the first packet from CN to MN, it detects that the MN has moved away, and then ASRp sends the "ASR mapping update" including the new mapping of MN to ASRcn. Alternatively, when ASRn receives the first packet from MN to CN, ASRn will inform ASRcn about the new mapping

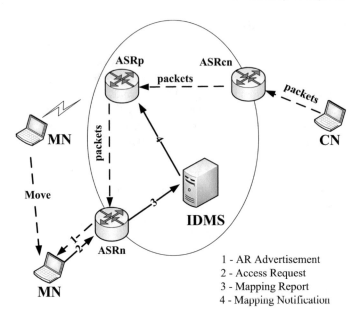

1 - AR Advertisement
2 - Access Request
3 - Mapping Report
4 - Mapping Notification

Fig. 9.1 Inter-domain mobility in a single ISP domain

of MN by sending the "ASR mapping update." Once ASRcn gets the new mapping of MN, the packets sent from CN to MN will follow the optimal route.

In summary, NMM provides an efficient solution to support the network mobility. When a customer network moves from one ASR to another, only the MR is aware of the movement. The MR and the ASR will communicate with each other

Fig. 9.2 Route optimization

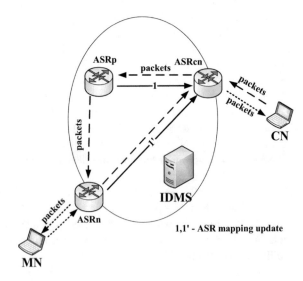

1,1' - ASR mapping update

by using their AIDs instead of a CoA. The MR will require the ASRp to reassign new mappings for the nodes inside the moving network. The nodes in the moving network are no longer aware of where their network attaches. All the connections based on AIDs will not be interrupted.

9.2.3 Evaluation

This section will present the evaluation of HMM on location privacy, routing scalability and wireless links overhead.

Location Privacy. In MIP, the location privacy problems include [28]: (1) disclosing the CoA to peers and (2) revealing the HoA to on-lookers.

In NMM, a packet is routed by AID between MN and ASR, whereas the routers in the core network use RID to forward it. Thus, (1) peers can only get the AID of an MN that does not contain location information. The RID of MN that contains the location information is hidden inside of the core network and does not disclose it to peers. (2) The AID and RID of MN will not be revealed to the on-lookers simultaneously. The on-looker in the core network can only get the RID of MN but cannot get the <AID, RID> mappings. As a result, they cannot get the location information of a given node.

Routing Scalability. The Internet consists of a large number of transit networks and customer networks containing hosts that are attached to the backbone [29].

In NMM, the customer networks and core network are clearly separated, and a mapping service is used to link these two spaces. Thus, the RID blocks assigned to the customer networks can be used to improve aggregation and reduce the number of globally visible prefixes greatly.

Wireless Links Overhead. Since wireless links have limited resources compared with wired links, this part focuses on the impact of wireless links overhead. In NMM, only two kinds of protocol messages need to be transmitted on wireless links. However, almost all the Mobile IPv6 (MIPv6) messages need to be transmitted on the wireless links. Tables 9.1 and 9.2 show these protocol messages together with their sizes.

As shown in Tables 9.1 and 9.2, in the normal Layer 3 (L3) handoff, the number of messages needing to be transmitted on wireless links is $N_{NMM\_MsgNum} = 2$ by NMM, and the total bytes of these messages are $N_{NMM\_MsgSize} \geq 104$. The number of messages needing to be transmitted on wireless links is $N_{MIPv6\_MsgNum} = 11$ by MIPv6, and the total bytes of these messages is $N_{MIPv6\_MsgSize} = 616$. The ratio between the numbers of messages NMM and MIPv6 is shown by Eq. 9.1, and the ratio between the sizes of NMM and MIPv6 is shown by Eq. 9.2.

Table 9.1 NMM messages and corresponding sizes

Messages	Bytes
AR advertisement	56 + Bytes of options
Access request	48 + Bytes of options

Table 9.2 MIPv6 messages
and corresponding sizes

Messages	Bytes
RS	48 + Bytes of options
RA	56 + Bytes of options
NS	64 + Bytes of options
BU to HA	52 + Bytes of mobility options
BA from HA	52 + Bytes of mobility options
HoTI	56 + Bytes of mobility options
CoTI	56 + Bytes of mobility options
HoT	64 + Bytes of mobility options
CoT	64 + Bytes of mobility options
BU to CN	52 + Bytes of mobility options
BA from CN	52 + Bytes of mobility options

$$N_{NMM\_MsgNum}/N_{MIPv6\_MsgNum} \leq 2/11 \approx 18.18 \,\% \qquad (9.1)$$

$$N_{NMM\_MsgSize}/N_{MIPv6\_MsgSize} \leq 104/616 \approx 16.88 \,\% \qquad (9.2)$$

Comparing Eqs. 9.1 and 9.2, on wireless links, NMM messages overhead are much smaller than those of MIPv6. It is illustrated that NMM can achieve the MN battery conservation by reducing the messages processed by MN. Furthermore, NMM adopts the identifier-mapping scheme to transfer packets, while the packets in MIPv6 will be encapsulated with a 40-byte IPv6 header by a tunnel. Otherwise, the packet will get the addition of a 24-byte routing header as the IPv6 extension header.

In the Internet, nearly 100 % of Internet packets are 1500 bytes or less. Almost 75 % of Internet packets are smaller than the typical TCP maximum segment size of 552 bytes. Calculated with 1500 bytes, the Internet traffic will be increased by $40/1500 \approx 2.67 \,\%$ and $24/1500 \approx 1.6 \,\%$ by the MIPv6 tunnel and extension header, respectively. Calculated with 552 bytes, the Internet traffic will be increased by $40/552 \approx 7.25 \,\%$ and $24/552 \approx 4.35 \,\%$ by the MIPv6 tunnel and extension header, respectively. As a result, NMM will not increase any traffic by adopting the identifier-mapping scheme for the Internet.

9.3 Hierarchical Mobility Management (HMM)

In the traditional TCP/IP stacks, the IP address not only represents the identifier but also the location of a node. Therefore, it cannot provide global roaming seamlessly. To address this problem, MIP uses dynamical CoA and HoA to denote MN's location and identifier, respectively. However, such a separation of MIP cannot support manageability, routing scalability [30, 31] and location privacy. This section proposes a novel Hierarchical Mobility Management scheme (HMM) based on the SINET architecture to resolve these problems in MIP. The HMM architecture consists of a separate logical management plane, which manages the identifier-to-locator mapping and user plane, which is responsible for transmitting the data packets.

9.3.1 Overview of HMM

The HMM architecture is shown in Fig. 9.3, which includes two planes: the management and user planes. The management plane is an overlay network and consists of a set of IDMSs. These IDMSs manage AID-to-RID mapping entries and resolve the mapping request messages. This section divides the user plane into a number of mapping domains (MDs). Each MD is managed by the corresponding IDMS and consists of some ASRs.

The main function of the ASR is to replace the AID with the RID. The ASR takes charge of managing the mapping-related signaling messages on behalf of MNs, and it is also used to route and forward data packets as the router does in today's Internet.

IDMS is used to manage AID-to-RID and AID-to-IDMS mappings and resolve the mapping request messages. There are two tables in the IDMS: the AID-to-RID mapping table for users currently staying in its MD and the AID-to-IDMS table for finding the home IDMS (HIDMS), which stores the AID-to-RID mapping. After receiving the AID-to-RID mapping request message, the HIDMS returns the mapping to the IDMS. The IDMS informs the ASR, and the ASR maps the AID to the RID. The ASR stores the MN's AID-to-RID mapping in it, and the subsequent packets can replace the AID/RID directly.

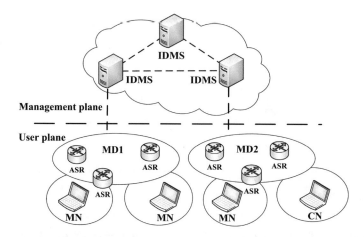

Fig. 9.3 The architecture of HMM. Reprinted from Ref. [2], with permission from Springer

9.3.2 HMM Solution

HMM divides the global Internet into a number of MDs and assumes each autonomous system (AS) is an MD, which is managed by different ISPs. In intra-domain mobility, a MN moves within the same MD. Meanwhile, we call it inter-domain mobility if the MN moves among different MDs. This section details the mobility handoff procedure in intra- and inter-domain, respectively.

Intra-domain Mobility. Figure 9.4 illustrates the message flows for HMM in the intra-domain mobility scenario. First of all, an MN moves to the ASR2 and sends an Access Message (AM) to the ASR2 (step 1). ASR2 receives the message and sends a mapping registration message containing the AID and RID of MN to the IDMS (step 2). The IDMS adds the mapping entry of the MN and responds to the ASR2 (step 3). Then, the ASR2 sends an access response message (ARM) to the MN (step 4). If the MN enters this MD for the first time and the domain is not its HIDMS, the IDMS should send a mapping registration message to the MN's HIDMS.

When a CN is communicating with the MN, it sends the packets to the ASR3 using its AIDs and MN's AIDs as the packets' source and destination addresses (step 5). After acquiring the MN's RID from the IDMS (step 6 and step 7), the ASR3 replaces the packets' AID with RIDs and forwards them to the ASR2 (step 8). ASR2 receives the packets and then sends them to the MN (step 9).

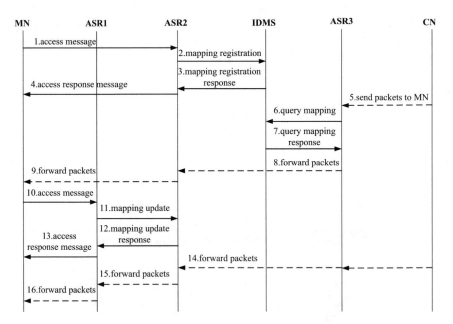

Fig. 9.4 Message flows of the location management scheme in intra-domain mobility. Reprinted from Ref. [2], with permission from Springer

When the MN attaches into the ASR1 within the same MD, it sends an AM to the ASR1 (step 10), and the ASR1 sends one mapping update message to the ASR2 (step 11). The ASR2 responds to the update message (step 12) and establishes a tunnel between ASR1 and ASR2. Then, the ASR1 sends an ARM to the MN (step 13). We regard the ASR2 as the local agent of MN. MN's AID-to-RID mapping does not need be changed as long as the MN is still in this MD. All the packets from other MD destinations to the MN pass through the ASR2 and then are forwarded to the ASR1 by the tunnel. In this way, the signaling overhead can be reduced significantly since the mapping information in the remote ASR3 and the HIDMS need not be changed.

For the ongoing communication, packets are still forwarded to the ASR2 (step 14). ASR2 strips the RID header and encapsulates them with the tunnel header, and it then forwards the packets to the ASR1 by tunnel (step 15). Finally, the packets are received by the MN (step 16).

If the MN moves to another new ASR that still belongs to the same MD, a new tunnel between the ASR2 and the new ASR will be established. Meanwhile, the old tunnel between ASR1 and ASR2 will be deleted. For intra-domain mobility, the ASR2 is still the agent of the MN in this MD, and it is not necessary to update the IDMS and the ASRs of CNs.

Inter-domain Mobility. The HMM scheme in the inter-domain mobility scenario is shown in Fig. 9.5. Assume that the MN has performed the handoff from the ASR2 to the ASR1 as shown in Fig. 9.4. Then, the MN moves from the ASR1 in the MD1 to the ASR3 in the MD2 and sends an AM to the ASR3 (step 1). As an

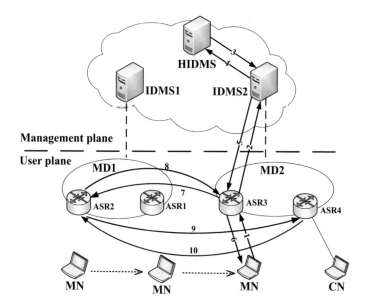

Fig. 9.5 The location management scheme in inter-domain mobility. Reprinted from Ref. [2], with permission from Springer

agent in the MD2, the ASR3 adds the MN's mapping entry in its local table and then sends a mapping update message to the associated IDMS2 (step 2). The IDMS2 looks up its AID-to-RID table to find the MN's HIDMS and sends a location update message to the HIDMS (step 3). The HIDMS updates the AID-to-RID mapping and responds to the IDMS (step 4). After that, the IDMS sends an update response message to the ASR3 (step 5). Then, the ASR3 sends an ARM to the MN (step 6). When ASR3 acquires the address of ASR2 from the IDMS2, it sends a location update message to the ASR2 (step 7). Then, the ASR2 notifies the ASRs of CNs' mapping information (step 8). Through the above procedures, it achieves a fast handoff recovery and avoids sending more messages to the mapping system since ASR3 will directly forward the packets.

Hereafter, the ASR2 sends a message to the ASR4 to update the new MN's mapping information in the ASR4's mapping table (step 9). When ASR4 gets the new mapping, packets destined to MN are directly routed to the ASR3 instead of passing through the old ASR2. Thus, the scheme can avoid triangle routing and achieve route optimization. Finally, the ASR2 removes the MN's mapping entry from its mapping table and inter-domain mobility ends.

9.3.3   Evaluation

In this section, we develop an analytical model to study the signaling overhead in HMM. Table 9.3 shows the main parameters and their descriptions.

Table 9.3   System parameters and their descriptions

Notations	Descriptions
c_{mt}	The transmission overhead between the MN and ASR
c_{nt}	The transmission overhead between the CN and ASR
c_{as}	The transmission overhead between the ASR_A and IDMS
c_{ac}	The transmission overhead between the ASR_A and ASR_{CN}
c_{at}	The transmission overhead between the ASR_A and ASR
c_{aa}	The transmission overhead between the ASR_As
c_{ss}	The transmission overhead between the IDMS and IDMS
a_n	The processing overhead at node (including MNs and CNs)
a_t	The processing overhead at ASRs (including ASR_As)
a_s	The processing overhead at IDMSs
λ_c	The rate of session arrival at the MN
λ_m	The frequency of crossing the ASR's boundary
ρ	The calling-to-mobility ratio
N_{cn}	The arrange number of CNs that are communicating with MN
$\beta(i)$	The probability that there are i ASRs crossings during two consecutive incoming calls

Assume that each MN may randomly move between N subnets and an MD consists of k subnets. In the HMM, we assume each ASR is a subnet. MNs will move to the other subnets with the same probability 1/(N-1). We term the action of each MN moving out of a subnet as "a movement" [32]. The probability of moving out of an MD at the Mth movement is

$$p_m = \frac{N-k}{N-1} \bullet \left(\frac{k-1}{N-1}\right)^{m-2}, \quad 2 \le m \le \infty. \tag{9.3}$$

The expectation of M is

$$E[M] = \sum_{m=2}^{\infty} m p_m = 1 + \frac{N-1}{N-k}. \tag{9.4}$$

For intra-domain mobility, when an MN moves among ASRs in the same MD, the MN sends an access message to the new ASR and then receives the response message. Next, the new ASR sends a location update message to the agent ASR (ASR$_A$), and then the ASR$_A$ sends a response message to the ASR. Each message contains the transmission overhead and the processing overhead. The location update overhead of intra-domain mobility is shown as

$$U_{intra} = 2c_{mt} + a_n + a_t + 2c_{at} + 2a_t. \tag{9.5}$$

For inter-domain mobility, the messages flows are shown in Fig. 9.5. Thus, the location update overhead is calculated as

$$U_{inter} = 2c_{mt} + a_n + a_t + 2c_{as} + a_t + a_s + 2c_{ss} + 2a_s + 2c_{aa} + 2a_t + N_{cn} \\ * (2c_{ac} + 2a_t). \tag{9.6}$$

To compare and analyze the location overhead of HMM, we develop the same analytical model in the MIP [33] and Hierarchical MIP (HMIP) [34, 35] to compare with the intra-domain mobility and inter-domain mobility in HMM, respectively. The local Mobility Anchor Point (MAP) domain in HMIP is equal to the MD in HMM. The MN executes the HMIP when moving in the same MAP domain. Otherwise, when an MN moves to another MAP domain, it performs MIP. Meanwhile, it is assumed that the MAP and Home Agent (HA) correspond to the ASR$_A$ and HIDMS.

The location update overhead for HMIP is

$$U_{hmip} = \underbrace{2c_{mt} + a_n + a_t}_{1} + \underbrace{2(c_{mt} + c_{at}) + a_n + a_t}_{2}, \tag{9.7}$$

where term 1 represents the access message and response message between the MN and access router (AR), and term 2 describes the location update message and response message between MN and MAP.

The location update overhead for MIP is shown in Eq. 9.8.

$$U_{hmip} = \underbrace{2c_{mt} + a_n + a_t}_{1} + \underbrace{2(c_{mt} + c_{at} + c_{ss}) + a_n + a_s}_{3} + \underbrace{N_{cn} * [2(c_{mt} + c_{ac} + c_{nt}) + 2a_n]}_{4},$$

$$(9.8)$$

where term 3 shows the location registration message and response message between MN and HA, and term 4 represents the location update message and response message between MN and CN.

It is supposed that during two consecutive incoming calls, the MN moves to new subnets for i times, and its probability distribution is $\beta(i)$. In HMM, $1/E(M)$ is the average probability of moving out of an MD at each movement. $\lfloor i/E(M) \rfloor$ is the number of times of inter-domain movement, and $\lfloor i - i/E(M) \rfloor$ is the number of times of intra-domain movement. The total location update overhead of the HMM is

$$U_{HMM} = \sum_{i=0}^{\infty} \left\{ \left\lfloor \frac{i}{E(M)} \right\rfloor * U_{inter} + \left\lfloor i - \frac{i}{E(M)} \right\rfloor * U_{intra} \right\} \beta(i) . \quad (9.9)$$

In the MIP and HMIP, the MN will update its registration for HA $\lfloor i/E(M) \rfloor$ times and for MAP $\lfloor i - i/E(M) \rfloor$ times. The total location update overhead of MIP and HMIP is

$$U_{MIP + HMIP} = \sum_{i=0}^{\infty} \left\{ \left\lfloor \frac{i}{E(M)} \right\rfloor * U_{mip} + \left\lfloor i - \frac{i}{E(M)} \right\rfloor * U_{hmip} \right\} \beta(i) . \quad (9.10)$$

The probability $\beta(i)$ of i moves between two incoming calls is written as [36]

$$\beta(i) = \begin{cases} 1 - \dfrac{1 - f_m^*(\lambda_c)}{\rho} & i = 0 \\ \dfrac{1}{\rho} \left[1 - f_m^*(\lambda_c)^2 \right] \left[f_m^*(\lambda_c) \right]^{i-1} & i > 0 \end{cases} , \quad (9.11)$$

where $\rho = \lambda_c/\lambda_m$ is the call-to-mobility ratio (CMR). λ_c is the call-arrival rate, and λ_m is the cross ASR rate. $f_m^*(\lambda_c)$ is the Laplace Transform of the MN residence time in a subnet.

Assuming that the MN residence time obeys gamma distribution, with the mean of $1/\lambda_c$ and the variance of V, the Gamma Laplace Transform is expressed as

$$f_m^*(s) = \left(\frac{\lambda_m \gamma}{s + \lambda_m \gamma} \right)^{\gamma}, \quad \gamma = \frac{1}{\lambda_m^2 V} . \quad (9.12)$$

If the variance is $V = 1/\lambda_m^2$, the MN residence time becomes the exponential distribution, and its Laplace Transform is calculated as

$$f_m^*(s) = \frac{\lambda_m}{s + \lambda_m} \; . \tag{9.13}$$

Then, substituting the $f_m^*(\lambda_c)$ into $\beta(i)$, we can derive

$$\beta(i) = \begin{cases} \dfrac{\rho}{\rho+1} & i = 0 \\[3mm] \dfrac{\rho}{(\rho+1)^{i+1}} & i > 0 \end{cases} . \tag{9.14}$$

Based on the above analysis, we will give the analytical performance results of the total signaling overhead. The parameter values are listed as follows: $c_{mt} = 6$, $c_{nt} = 1$, $c_{as} = 5$, $c_{ac} = 10$, $c_{at} = 1$, $c_{aa} = 5$, $c_{ss} = 1$, $a_n = 5$, $a_t = 6$, $a_s = 10$ and $N_{cn} = 5$.

Figure 9.6 illustrates the location update signaling overhead of HMM and HMIP + MIP. The total signaling overhead decreases as the CMR increases for both the HMM and HMIP + MIP. This is because when the CMR is low, the mobility rate is higher than the session arrival rate and the overhead of location update dominates.

Additionally, the total signaling overhead of the HMM is smaller than that of HMIP + HIP. The ASR and IDMS store AID-to-RID mapping information and know how to route packets, so they can take charge of MN to perform location updates. Since the distance of HMM's location update is shorter than the one of MIP + HMIP, the total traffic load of the HMM is lower than that of MIP + HMIP. Moreover, the MN in the HMM is not necessary to participate in

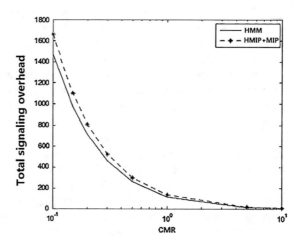

Fig. 9.6 The total signaling overhead versus the CMR. Reprinted from Ref. [2], with permission from Springer

mobility management, so it will be able to save much signaling overhead in the wireless links of HMM. Therefore, lower signaling overhead can be achieved in HMM.

9.4   Mapping Forwarding-Based Mobility Management (MFMM)

This section proposes a Mapping Forwarding-based Mobility Management (MFMM) scheme in the SINET architecture. In the MF scheme, the ASR is used as an agent of MN and keeps the MN's AID-to-RID mapping unchanged by setting up an MF chain. As long as the MN performs handoff in the same ASR, the MN's mapping information stored in the ASR of each CN (ASR_{CN}) does not need to be updated. Thus, the location update signaling overhead can be reduced. Meanwhile, the unchanged mapping guarantees the correct forwarding of packets and reduction of mobility-related disruption and enhances the location management's reliability.

9.4.1   Overview of MFMM

The key point of HFMM is the procedures of setting up the Mapping Forwarding (MF) chains shown in Fig. 9.7. Assuming that the ASRs are implemented at the first-hop access router and an MN attaches to the ASR_1, ASR_2,..., ASR_5 sequentially. If MN moves into the coverage area of ASR_1, the ASR_1 is used as the MN's current agent to maintain the MN's mapping entries in its local table and takes charge of MN to encapsulate or decapsulate the packets. When the MN moves into the coverage area of ASR_2, a tunnel will be set up between the ASR_1 and ASR_2. If the MN moves into the coverage area of ASR_3, ASR_3 will establish another tunnel to connect with ASR_2 [37]. Therefore, the MF chain's header is the ASR_1, and the packets are routed to the ASR_1. Then, the ASR_1 strips the header of RIDs and forwards packets along the MF chain.

In this way, the mapping entry in the ASR_{CN} and the IDMS does not need to be updated during the movement of MN. In the MFMM scheme, there is only one mapping update message between the neighbored ASRs. However, for the scheme without an MFMM strategy such as NMFMM, the MN's mapping in each ASR_{CN} and the IDMS should update messages between the ASR_1 and each ASR_{CN}. Thus, the MFMM scheme can reduce the location update overhead since the location update signaling overhead in MFMM is smaller than that in NMFMM.

Another benefit of the proposed MFMM scheme is the reduction of the blocking probability during the communication. In NMFMM, it is likely that the packets may be discarded because the MN's mapping entry in the remote ASR_{CN} is not updated quickly. While in MFMM, as long as the MN does not move out of the chain, the

Fig. 9.7 The procedures of setting up the MF chains. Reprinted from Ref. [3], with permission from Wiley

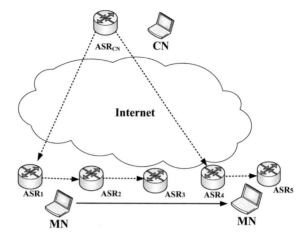

RID in the ASR$_{CN}$'s cache is unique. As a result, packets are first diverted to the agent and then forwarded to MN's location, so the MFMM scheme ensures that the packets are correctly routed.

However, a long MF chain will incur the delay and more transmission overhead. To address this problem, we set a threshold to limit the length of the MF chain. As shown in Fig. 9.7, we initiate the threshold of the chain to be 2. When the MN moves into the ASR$_4$, the chain's length will exceed the threshold. In this situation, the old chain will be deleted, and the ASR$_4$ will be the new agent of the MN. MN's RID changes to be the ASR$_4$ address, and the ASR$_{CN}$ directly forwards the packets to the ASR$_4$. Likewise, if the MN continues to move and attaches to the ASR$_5$, another MF chain is established between ASR$_4$ and ASR$_5$.

9.4.2   MFMM Solution

This section will introduce the operations of the MFMM scheme. Figure 9.8 shows the message flows of the MFMM scheme, which includes three procedures, i.e., the first access of an MN, the handoff under the same ASR$_A$ of MN and the handoff between two ASR$_A$s.

The First Access of MN. If an MN attaches to the ASR$_1$ for the first time, the ASR$_1$ assigns the MN's mapping information and stores it in the local table. After that, the ASR$_1$ sends a Map-Register message including the MN's AID and RID to the IDMS (step 1). The IDMS stores the MN's mapping entries and then responds with a Map-Reply message (step 2) to the ASR$_1$.

When a CN communicates with the MN, it sends packets to the ASR$_{CN}$ by using its AID as the packets' source address and the MN's AID as the destination address (step 3). The ASR$_{CN}$ queries the MN's RID from the IDMS (step 4). After acquiring the MN's mapping information (step 5), the ASR$_{CN}$ replaces the AIDs

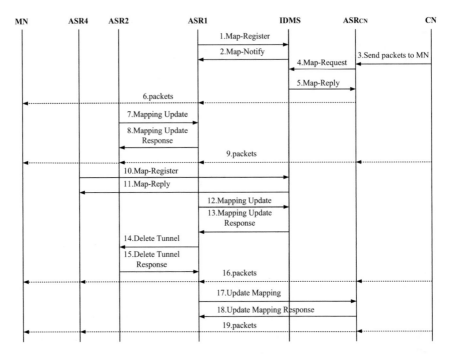

Fig. 9.8 Message flows of the MF scheme

with the CN's and MN's RIDs and forwards them to the ASR_1. At last, the ASR_1 receives the packets and sends them to the MN (step 6).

The Handoff under the Same ASR. As shown in Fig. 9.8, when the MN moves into the ASR_2, the ASR_2 sends a Mapping Update message to the ASR_1 to set up a tunnel (step 7). The ASR_1 replies a Mapping Update Response message (step 8) and establishes a tunnel with the ASR_2. If the MN attaches to the ASR_3, the tunnel will be established between the ASR_2 and the ASR_3. ASR_{CN} encapsulates data packets with the ASR_1 address as the MN's RID. The packets arriving at the ASR_1 are forwarded along the tunnels (step 9).

The Handoff between Two MF Chains. When the MN keeps moving and attaches to the ASR_4, the chain's length will exceed the threshold, and the ASR_4 will send a Map-Register message to the IDMS (step 10). The IDMS updates and sends the AID-to-RID mapping to the ASR_4 (step 11). Meanwhile, the IDMS also sends a Mapping Update message to the ASR_1 (step 12) to inform the MN of its new RID, and the ASR_1 sends the message to the IDMS (step 13). In addition, the ASR_1 as the old chain's header informs the ASR_2 to delete the outdated tunnel (step 14), and the ASR_2 sends a Deleting Tunnel Response to the ASR_1 (step 15). If the maximum of the MF chain's length is 2, the ASR_2 will send a deleting message to the ASR_3.

For an ongoing communication, packets are still diverted to ASR_1 since the ASR_{CN} reserves the old mapping information. Because ASR_1 has updated the mapping by the IDMS (step 12), the packets can be forwarded to the new ASR_4 to reduce the data loss. Then, an update message triggered by the packets is sent to the ASR_{CN} (step 17), which stores the new MN's AID-to-RID mapping and sends an Update Mapping Response message to the ASR_1 (step 18). After that, the ASR_{CN} can directly forward subsequent packets to the ASR_4 (step 19), which avoids the triangle routing. If no packet arrives at the ASR_1, it is unnecessary to send an update message to the ASR_{CN}. Thus, the data-triggered update scheme is able to avoid the redundant signaling overhead.

Selecting a Mapping Forwarding Agent. In the MFMM scheme, it is a critical challenge to detect whether an MN has moved into a new ASR_A. In the MF, the ASR sends the agent advertisement messages including its address. When an MN receives the ASR_1's agent advertisement message, it stores the ASR_1 address and sets the movement times as 0 in its local database. If the MN receives another agent's advertisement message, it compares the ASR address in these messages. If they are different, the MN assumes that it has moved to the ASR_2. Then, the MN checks the movement times to decide whether the value exceeds the chain length. If not, the MN sends an access request message with the type 1 to the ASR_2 including the ASR_1 address. Meanwhile, the MN sets the movement times as 1 and stores the ASR_2 address. The ASR_2 obtains the ASR_1 address from the access request message and then sets up a tunnel with the ASR_1. When the MN attaches to the ASR3, the movement times is set to be 2.

If the MN moves into the ASR_4 and the movement times exceed the threshold, it sends an access request message with the type 2 to the ASR_4. According to the message type, the ASR_4 will know that it is selected as the new forward agent of the MN and sends a Map-Register message to the IDMS. In addition, the MN adds the ASR_4 address instead of old ASR addresses and resets the movement times as 0.

The Design of the Timer. When an ASR is selected as an agent, it will contain two tables: the local table and the cache table. The local table stores the local users' mappings between AIDs and RIDs, and the cache table maintains mapping entries of CNs that local users are communicating with. However, if the ASR is selected as an access point (e.g., the ASR_2 or ASR_3 in Fig. 9.8), it only needs to maintain a local table for the users' AIDs and the established tunnel addresses. This is because the ASR just needs to forward the packets to an agent by the tunnel without encapsulating these packets.

There is a timer for deciding whether the ASR is an agent or not, and the timer is associated with each mapping entry in the local table. An MN sends update messages to the ASR periodically, and the timer will be set to the maximum T_l when the ASR receives an update message. Considering the probability of the update signaling loss, we set the periodic update time as $T_l/3$, which implies that there are three update messages during the T_l. As long as the ASR receives one of them, the timer will be reset. In this way, it reduces the probability of the fault deletion resulting from the packet loss. On expiration of time, the MN is supposed to be moving, and the related mapping entries are removed from the local table.

When the first packet arrives at the ASR_A, the ASR_A needs to query the IDMS to obtain the CN's mapping. In order to eliminate the need of the excess Map-Request messages, the ASR_A needs to cache the mapping entries. Then, the subsequent packets will directly be encapsulated and forwarded. However, if the session terminates, it is a waste of memory space to store the mapping entries in its cache table. Thus, it is necessary to set a timer for each mapping entry. If there is any session between the MN and the CN, the timer is reset to the maximum T_c. If no packet is received within the duration of the time-out, the ASR_A will remove the mapping entry from the cache.

As shown in Fig. 9.9, the ASR_{CN} receives the packets destined to the MN and forwards them to the MN's ASR_A. Then, the ASR_A forwards packets to the MN. The transmission delay between the ASR_A and the MN is t_{am}. Assuming that MN moves from the old ASR_A to the new ASR_A, t_u^r represents the residual update arrival time, which is the time duration from an intermediate moment to the next update arrival. After the T_l expires, the old ASR_{CN} detects that the MN has left, and the MN's mapping entry will be removed from its local table.

Figure 9.9 shows the case that the cache time-out T_c is larger than the sum of t_{am}, t_u^r and T_l. If a packet arrives at the ASR_{CN} during the T_c, the packet will be forwarded to the old ASR_A. It is likely that the old ASR_A has deleted the MN's mapping in its local table, which results in the packet's loss and communication is down. As a result, the cache time-out T_c should be shorter than the sum of t_{am}, t_u^r and T_l. In this way, if the subsequent packet arrives at the old ASR_A, they will be delivered to the new ASR_A because of the existence of the newest MN's mapping in the old ASR_A, which avoids packets loss and re-establishes the connection.

The t_{am} between the ASR_A and the MN is of the millisecond level, and it may be negligible compared with the second level T_l. In addition, when t_u^r takes its minimum value as 0, the T_l should be larger than T_c to make sure the connection is alive.

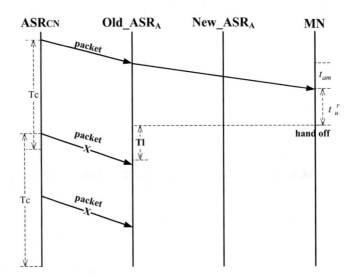

Fig. 9.9 The setting of timers

9.4.3 Evaluation

In this section, two analytical models are developed to study the packet blocking probability and the total overhead in the proposed mobility scheme. Table 9.4 shows the main parameters and their descriptions.

Blocking Probability Analysis. Blocking probability is analyzed based on the MFMM scheme. Figure 9.10 shows the timing diagram of the MN considering the location update sequence and the packet arrival sequence. Let $P_i(i = 0, 1, 2, \ldots)$ denote the i_{th} packet arrival time, and the destinations of packets are the same MN. The $t_{ni}(i = 1, 2)$ represents the interval time between two consecutive packets, that is, P_{i-1} and P_i. The probability density function (PDF), cumulative distribution function of the packets and PDF's Laplace transform (LT) of these packets are denoted as $f_{tn}(t)$, $F_{tn}(t)$ and $F_{tn}^*(t)$, respectively.

Let U_i denote the i_{th} update location for the MN. The t_u represents the update arrival interval time with the mean of $1/\lambda_u$. The PDF, cumulative distribution function and PDF's LT of t_u are $f_{tu}(t)$, $F_{tu}(t)$ and $F_{tu}^*(s)$. t_u^r is the residual update arrival interval time. According to the residual life theorem, the PDF of t_u^r is $f_{tur}(t) = \lambda_u[1 - F_{tu}(t)]$, and the LT of the PDF is $F_{tur}^*(s) = \lambda_u[1 - F_{tu}^*(s)]/s$.

Table 9.4 System parameters and descriptions

Notations	Descriptions
t_u	The update arrival interval time
t_u^r	The residual update arrival interval time
t_n	The arrival interval time of two consecutive packets
$f_{tu}(t)$	Probability density function of update arrival interval time
$f_{tur}(t)$	Probability density function of residual update arrival interval time
$f_{tn}(t)$	Probability density function of packet arrival interval time
$F_{tu}(t)$	Cumulative distribution function of update arrival interval time
$F_{tur}(t)$	Cumulative distribution function of residual update arrival interval time
$F_{tn}(t)$	Cumulative distribution function of packet arrival interval time
$F_{tu}^*(s)$	Laplace transform of $f_{tu}(t)$
$F_{tur}^*(s)$	Laplace transform of $f_{tur}(t)$
$F_{tn}^*(s)$	Laplace transform of $f_{tn}(t)$
λ_u	The location update rate
λ_s	The session arrival rate
$E(N)$	The average number of packets per session
T_c	The cache remove time
β	The packet blocking probability
L_{MF}	The average length of the mapping forward chain
h_{x-y}	The number of links hops between x and y
S_l	The average size of the location update message
S_d	The average size of date packets
N_{cn}	The average number of CNs that are communicating with an MN

In the ASR_{CN}, it is considered that a flow ended if no packet is received from or sent to the MN within T_c. If there is a packet sent by the MN arrives at the ASR_{CN} out of the duration of T_c, we will regard it as a new flow, and the ASR_{CN} will send a Map-Request message to the IDMS.

This section analyzes the packet blocking probability caused by the movement of MN without considering the expiration of lifetime. Therefore, the blocking probability is the percentage of packets that are discarded for the same flow. As a result, to avoid the time-out, the flow requires that t_n is less than the time-out T_c.

For the MFMM scheme, we assume that the threshold of the MF chain is k $(k > 0)$. The length of the chain is $j(0 \leq j \leq k)$ with an equal probability $1/(k+1)$ at the beginning. After the MN moves for $k-j+1$ times, it moves from the first chain to the second chain. If the MN performs the handoff for $2k-j+2$ times between two consecutive sessions, it will attach to the third chain. After that, if a packet arrives at the ASR_{CN}, the MN's RID in the ASR_{CN}'s cache table can only be updated using the second ASR_A address according to the handoff procedures between those two MF chains, denoting that $\varepsilon = t_{u1}^r + t_{u2} + \cdots + t_{u(k-j+1)} + t_{u(k-j+2)} + \cdots + t_{u(2k-j+2)}$ is the time interval of the $2k-j+2$ times movements. When the MN moves $2k-j+2$ times during two consecutive sessions, the packet is blocked. Thus, the blocking probability β_{MFMM} is calculated as

$$\beta_{MFMM} = \sum_{j=0}^{k} \frac{1}{k+1} p(\varepsilon < t_n < T_c) . \tag{9.15}$$

Then, the LT of ε's PDF is

$$F_\varepsilon^*(s) = F_{tur}^*(s)\left[F_{tu}^*(s)\right]^{2k-j+1} = \lambda_u\left[1 - F_{tu}^*(s)\right]\left[F_{tu}^*(s)\right]^{2k-j+1/s} . \tag{9.16}$$

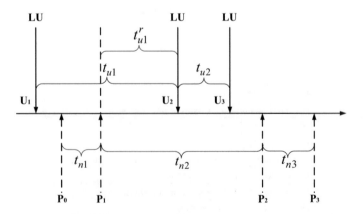

Fig. 9.10 Timing diagram to derive the blocking probability

Through the inverse LT of the $F_\varepsilon^*(s)$, the PDF of ε can be expressed as

$$f_\varepsilon^*(x) = L^{-1}\left[F_\varepsilon^*(s)\right] = L^{-1}\left\{\lambda_u\left[1 - F_{tu}^*(s)\right]\left[F_{tu}^*(s)\right]^{2k-j+1/s}\right\}. \tag{9.17}$$

Further simplifying Eq. 9.15, we have

$$
\begin{aligned}
\beta_{MFMM} &= \sum_{j=0}^{k} \frac{1}{k+1} \int_{x=0}^{T_c} f_\varepsilon(x) \int_x^{T_c} f_{tn}(t)\,dt\,dx \\
&= \sum_{j=0}^{k} \frac{1}{k+1} \int_{x=0}^{T_c} \{F_{tn}(T_c) - F_{tn}(x)\} L^{-1}\left\{\lambda_u\left[1 - F_{tu}^*(s)\right]\left[F_{tu}^*(s)\right]^{2k-j+1/s}\right\}dx.
\end{aligned}
\tag{9.18}
$$

Assume that the distribution of packet arrival obeys the Poisson process. Therefore, the interval time t_n follows an exponential distribution with the mean of $1/\lambda_p$. Therefore, it can be obtained that

$$f_{tn}(t) = \lambda_p e^{-\lambda_p t}, \tag{9.19}$$

$$F_{tn}(t) = 1 - e^{-\lambda_p t}. \tag{9.20}$$

Assuming t_u follows an exponential distribution, the LT of t_u can be written as

$$F_{tu}^*(s) = \frac{\lambda_u}{s + \lambda_u}. \tag{9.21}$$

By combining Eq. 9.21 with Eq. 9.16, it can be derived that

$$F_\varepsilon^*(s) = \left(\frac{\lambda_u}{s + \lambda_u}\right)^{2k-j+2}. \tag{9.22}$$

Then, the β_{MFMM} is

$$
\begin{aligned}
\beta_{MFMM} &= \sum_{j=0}^{k} \frac{1}{k+1} \int_{x=0}^{T_c} \{F_{tn}(T_c) - F_{tn}(x)\} L^{-1}\left\{\lambda_u\left[1 - F_{tu}^*(s)\right]\left[F_{tu}^*(s)\right]^{2k-j+1/s}\right\}dx \\
&= \sum_{j=0}^{k} \frac{1}{k+1} \int_{x=0}^{T_c} \{e^{-\lambda_p x} - e^{-\lambda_p T_c}\} \frac{\lambda_u^{2k-j+2}}{(2k-j+1)!} x^{2k-j+1} e^{-\lambda_u x}\,dx.
\end{aligned}
\tag{9.23}
$$

Blocking Probability in the NMFMM Scheme. For each movement, the operations of the handoff in NMFMM scheme are similar to the handoff between two chains in the MFMM scheme. When the MN moves two times between two consecutive sessions, the first ASR receives an update message from the IDMS and stores the second ASR address as the MN's RID. If a packet is sent from ASR_{CN}, it will be diverted to the first ASR since the old caching information is in the ASR_{CN}. Then, the first ASR sends an update message including the second ASR address to the ASR_{CN}. After that, the ASR_{CN} forwards the subsequent packets to the second ASR. However, it results in the packets being blocked since the MN has already attached into the third ASR. Thus, the blocking probability β_{NMFMM} is expressed as

$$\beta_{NMFMM} = p(t_{u1}^r + t_{u2} < t_n < T_c) . \tag{9.24}$$

The NMFMM's blocking probability is given by establishing a similar analytical model:

$$\begin{aligned}
\beta_{NMFMM} &= \int_{x=0}^{T_c} [F_{tn}(T_c) - F_{tn}(x)] L^{-1} \{\lambda_u [1 - F_{tu}^*(s)] F_{tu}^*(s)/s\} dx \\
&= \int_{x=0}^{T_c} (e^{-\lambda_p x} - e^{-\lambda_p T_c}) \lambda_u^2 x e^{-\lambda_u x} dx.
\end{aligned} \tag{9.25}$$

Total Overhead in the MFMM Scheme. In the MFMM scheme, the average length of MF chains $\overline{L}_{MF}$ can be given by

$$\overline{L}_{MF} = \frac{1}{k+1} \sum_{i=0}^{k} k = k/2 . \tag{9.26}$$

The session arrival process follows the Poisson distribution, and the arrival rate and cell crossing rate are λ_s and λ_u, respectively. Hence, the handoff rate between two MF chains during a session arrival interval is $\lambda_u/\lambda_s(k+1)$, and the handoff rate under the same ASR_A during a session arrival interval is $\lambda_u/\lambda_s - \lambda_u/\lambda_s(k+1)$.

The total overhead C_{MFMM}^{total} consists of the location update overhead C_{MFMM}^{lu} and the packet delivery overhead C_{MFMM}^{pd}. The protocol overhead is calculated by hops × packet size [38]. According to the message flows as shown in Fig. 9.8, the location update signaling overhead is calculated as

$$\begin{aligned}
C_{MFMM}^{lu} &= \frac{\lambda_u}{\lambda_s(k+1)} \times S_l \times (4h_{ASR-IDMS} + N_{cn} \times 2h_{ASR-ASR_{CN}}) \\
&+ (\lambda_u/\lambda_s - \frac{\lambda_u}{\lambda_s(k+1)}) \times S_l \times 2h_{ASR-ASR},
\end{aligned} \tag{9.27}$$

where S_l is the average size of the location update message. The first part denotes the overhead of the handoff between two MF chains. The second part denotes the overhead of the handoff in the same MF chain.

This part also introduces a performance factor called session-to-mobility ratio (SMR) to perform protocol overhead analysis. We assume that $\rho = \lambda_s/\lambda_u$, so the location update signaling overhead can be written as

$$C_{MFMM}^{lu} = \frac{1}{\rho(k+1)} \times S_l \times (4h_{ASR-IDMS} + N_{cn} \times 2h_{ASR-ASR_{CN}})$$
$$+ \frac{k}{\rho(k+1)} \times S_l \times 2h_{ASR-ASR}. \tag{9.28}$$

Assume that S_d is the average size of the data packet and $E(N)$ is the average number of packets per session. The packet delivery overhead per session is

$$C_{MFMM}^{pd} = E(N) \times S_d \times (h_{ASR-ASR_{CN}} + \overline{L}_{MF}) = E(N) \times S_d \times (h_{ASR-ASR_{CN}} + k/2). \tag{9.29}$$

The total protocol overhead can be calculated as

$$C_{MFMM}^{total} = C_{MFMM}^{lu} + C_{MFMM}^{pd}. \tag{9.30}$$

Total Overhead in the NMFMM Scheme. In the NMFMM scheme, when an MN attaches to another ASR, the entries such as the IDMS, old ASR and ASR$_{CN}$ need to be updated. Therefore, the location update overhead and the packet delivery overhead are shown as

$$C_{NMFMM}^{lu} = \frac{1}{\rho} \times S_l \times (4h_{ASR-IDMS} + N_{cn} \times 2h_{ASR-ASR_{CN}}), \tag{9.31}$$

$$C_{NMFMM}^{pd} = E(N) \times S_d \times h_{ASR-ASR_{CN}}. \tag{9.32}$$

The total protocol overhead in the NMFMM scheme can be expressed as

$$C_{NMFMM}^{total} = C_{NMFMM}^{lu} + C_{NMFMM}^{pd}. \tag{9.33}$$

Base on the aforementioned analysis, we will give the analytical results of the blocking probability and the total protocol overhead.

Analytical Results of Blocking Probability. According to Eqs. 9.23 and 9.25, it can be obtained that $\lambda_u = 0.02$, $T_c = 120$, and λ_p varies from 0.01 to 0.08. As shown in Fig. 9.11, the blocking probability decreases as the packet arrival rate increases in both the NMFMM scheme and MFMM scheme. When the packet arrival rate is rising, the interval time between two consecutive sessions is getting lower. For the short interval time, the probability that MNs move out of the range of the MF chain is low. Therefore, the blocking probability decreases with the packet arrival rate increasing.

For the same packet arrival rate, the larger the chain length is, the lower the blocking probability is. Therefore, it is more efficient to set a long MF chain in order to reduce the blocking probability. In addition, the blocking probability in the case of MFMM is lower than that in NMFMM regardless of the length of the chain.

Assume that $\lambda_p = 0.04$, $T_c = 120$ and λ_u vary from 0.01 to 0.08. Figure 9.12 shows that the blocking probability increases as the location update rate rises. Likewise, the blocking probability in the NMFMM scheme is higher than that in the MFMM scheme.

Figure 9.13 illustrates that the blocking probability changes with the cache time-out under different packet arrival rates. Assume that $\lambda_u = 0.02$, $k = 2$ and the T_c varies from 0 to 300; this shows that the blocking probability increases as the cache time-out rises. This is because of the same packet arrival rate and the location update frequency; the probability of MN's mapping entry timeout is large if the cache time-out is too long. Thus, it is necessary to set an appropriate cache time-out value.

Total Overhead. In order to compute the total overhead, assume that $h_{ASR-ASR} = 1$, $h_{ASR_{CN}-ASR} = 8$, $h_{ASR-IDMS} = 5$, $N_{cn} = 5$, $E(N) = 40$ and $S_l = S_d = 300$ bits. Let ρ vary from 0.1 to 10. According to Eqs. 9.30–9.33, Fig. 9.14 shows that the total overhead of the MFMM scheme and the NMFMM scheme changes with the SMR.

In the MFMM scheme, when the movement occurs within the same chain, the distance of the location update message is the hops between two ASRs. For the NMFMM scheme, mapping entries of MNs in the IDMS and the ASR_{CN} need to be updated whenever MNs move. The average update distance of the MFMM scheme is lower than that of the NMFMM scheme. Therefore, the MFMM scheme can achieve a lower update overhead.

As shown in Fig. 9.14, if the SMR is low, the total overhead of the MFMM scheme is lower than that of the NMFMM scheme. This is because when the SMR is low, the location update rate is high, which results in the frequent location updates. Therefore, the MFMM scheme is more suitable for MNs with a high mobility rate. While when the SMR is large, the packet delivery overhead also increases so that the total overhead of the MFMM scheme is larger than that of the NMFMM scheme.

Fig. 9.11 The blocking probability versus the packet arrival rate. Reprinted from Ref. [3], with permission from Wiley

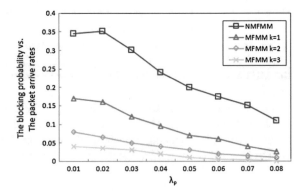

Fig. 9.12 The blocking probability versus the location update rate. Reprinted from Ref. [3], with permission from Wiley

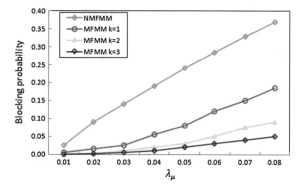

Fig. 9.13 The blocking probability versus the cache time-out. Reprinted from Ref. [3], with permission from Wiley

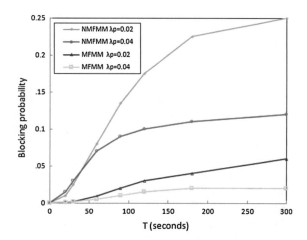

Fig. 9.14 The session-to-mobility ratio versus the total overhead. Reprinted from Ref. [3], with permission from Wiley

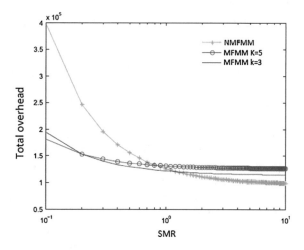

9.5   Indirect-Mapping-Based Mobility Support (IMM)

The SINET also introduces the Indirect-Mapping-based Mobility Support mechanism (IMM), which divides the network into many rendezvous domains (RDs) and
assigns a rendezvous point (RP) to an MN when it moves into an RD. Furthermore,
the mapping from the MN's AID to the RP's RID is registered into a mapping
system for the MN. If the packets are going to be sent to the MN, these packets will
first be sent to the MN's RP and then to the attaching egress ASR (EASR). In this
way, the AID-to-RID mapping for the MN remains unchanged as long as it roams
within the same RD. Thus, the proposed scheme can support host mobility
efficiently.

9.5.1   Overview of IMM

The IMM scheme introduces the idea of indirect mapping to support efficient host
mobility. Assume that the network is divided into many RDs. Whenever an MN
moves into an RD, we bind the MN's AID with the RP's RID instead of the RID of
the ASR in the RD and register the mapping information into the mapping service.
The AID-to-RID mapping registered into the mapping service for the MN does not
change as long as the MN roams within the same RD, regardless of which ASR the
MN is attaching to in the RD. In addition, when the MN roams to a new ASR in the
same RD, the ASR informs the MN's RP that the MN is attaching to it. When the
mapping service receives a map request for the MN, it returns the mapping from the
MN's AID onto the RID of the RP to the requesting node. The requesting node then
sends packets to the MN's RP by tunnel and uses the RP's RID as the destination.
When the MN's RP receives these packets, it sends them to the MN's attaching
ASR, which forwards these packets to the MN. When the MN sends packets to the
CN, these packets are first sent to the MN's ASR and then to the MN's RP. The
MN's RP then forwards them to the CN's ASR (or the CN's RP in the case that the
CN has an RP). This way, the number of mapping registrations sent into the
mapping service will be reduced largely. At the same time, the AID-to-RID map-
ping for an MN does not change since the MN roams within the same RD. It does
not need to inform the ASR of the MN's CN about the change of the MN's moving.
This makes it more efficient to support host mobility.

    Figure 9.15 shows the IMM architecture. Assume that ASR_4 is the RP of the
MN that is denoted as AID_{MN}. When the MN moves to ASR_2, ASR_2 registers the
mapping AID_{MN}-to-RID_2 to ASR_4 (step 1). Then, the mapping AID_{MN}-to-RID_4 is
registered to the mapping system (step 2). When ASR_1 sends a map request to the
mapping system (step 3), the mapping AID_{MN}-to-RID_4 is returned to ASR1 (step
4). ASR_1 then sends packets to ASR_4 by using RID_4 as destination (step 5). After
ASR4 receives these packets, it sends them to the MN's ASR (i.e., ASR_2) by using
RID_2 as destination (step 6). ASR_2 then sends these packets to the MN.

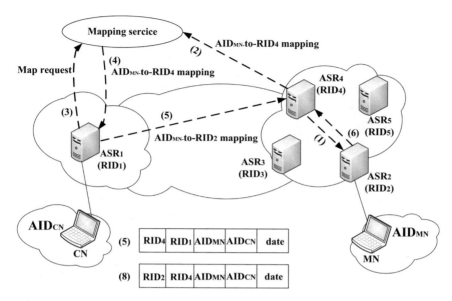

Fig. 9.15 The architecture of IMM. Reprinted from Ref. [4], with permission from IEEE

The IMM scheme is different from the two-level mapping system [39]. In IMM, the mapping registered into the mapping service for an AID is the mapping from the AID into the RID of the MN's RP.

9.5.2 IMM Solution

IMM can enable three types of handoff: (1) An MN roams within an RD; (2) either an MN or its CN roams across different RDs; (3) both an MN and CN roam across different RDs.

MN Roams Within an RD. When an MN roams within the same RD, the handoff process includes the following steps: (1) ASR detects the MN's attachment and binds the MN's AID with the new ASR's RID to update a new AID-to-RID mapping. (2) ASR sends the new mapping to the MN's RP. (3) When the MN's RP receives this new mapping, it updates the MN's AID-to-RID mapping table and tunnels packets to the new ASR; then, it forwards to the MN.

If the MN in Fig. 9.16 moves from ASR_2 to ASR_3, the MN's new ASR (i.e., ASR_3) registers the mapping AID_{MN}-to-RID_3 to the MN's RP (i.e., ASR_4) (step 7). After updating the mapping for the MN, ASR_4 then sends packets destined to the MN to ASR_3 (step 8).

It is unnecessary to register any new mapping for the MN into a mapping system, and it also does not need to inform the ingress ASR (IASR)/RP of the MN's CN about the change of the MN's location. Instead, the CN's IASR/RP still tunnels

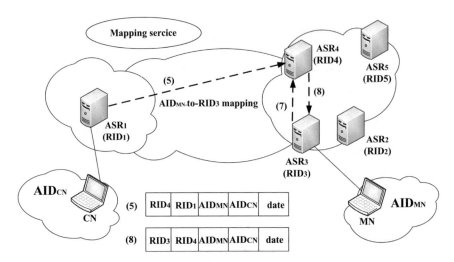

Fig. 9.16 Packet forwarding in IMM when the MN moves from ASR2 to ASR3. Reprinted from Ref. [4], with permission from IEEE

these packets to the MN's RP (step 5). In this way, it can significantly reduce the number of registration/resolution requests sent into the mapping service and makes the mapping services more scalable.

Either an MN or CN Roams Across Different RDs. Assume that the MN roams across different RDs but the CN corresponding to the MN roams within the same RD. We denote the MN's RP and the ASR attached by the MN in the old RD as RP_o and ASR_o, respectively. Similarly, when the MN moves into the new RD, its RP and attached ASR are denoted as RPn and ASR_n, respectively. When the MN moves into the new RD and is communicating with a CN, both ASR_n and RP_n do not know the CN's AID, and they do not know where to tunnel packets destined to the mapping system and to resolve an AID-to-RID mapping for the CN. As a result, this significantly increases the number of map requests sending into the mapping system, particularly when the MN communicates with multiple CNs. At the same time, the CN's ASR/RP may not know the MN's movement and still tunnels packets destined to the MN to RP_o, which leads to packet loss.

To resolve this problem, the IMM proposes the following handoff process as shown in Fig. 9.17.

- ASR_n detects the attachment of the MN (step 1).
- ASR_n sends a registration request to RP_n to register the mapping from the MN's AID onto ASR_n's RID (i.e., RID_2) (step 2).
- When RP_n receives the mapping from ASR_n, it stores the mapping in MN's AID-to-RID mapping table (step 3).
- RP_n registers the mapping from MN's AID to RP_n's RID (i.e., RID_4) at the mapping system (step 4).

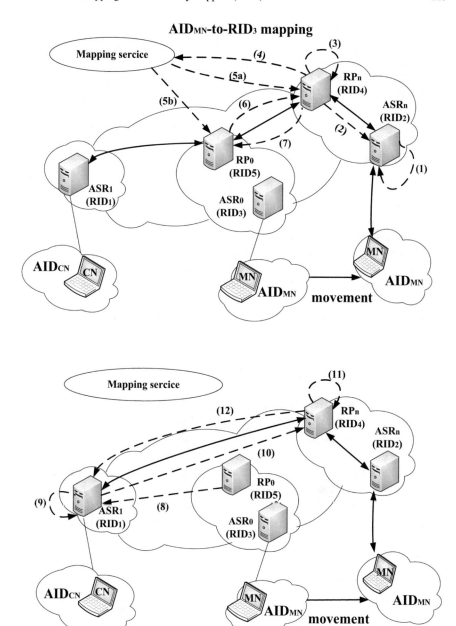

Fig. 9.17 Basic handoff process in IMM when an MN moves across different RDs. Reprinted from Ref. [4], with permission from IEEE

- The mapping system receives the registration request and sends RP_n a message informing RP_n of the old AID-to-RID mapping for MN (step 5a). At the same time, the mapping system sends RP_o a message informing RP_o of the new AID-to-RID mapping for the MN (step 5b). Moreover, the mapping system will update its AID-to-RID mapping table by storing the new AID-to-RID mapping for MN.
- RP_o checks whether the MN still attaches to its domain. If not, RP_o updates MN's AID-to-RID mapping table by replacing the mapping from the MN's AID to ASR_o's RID with the mapping from the MN's AID to RP_n's RID. Then, RP_o tunnels packets destined to the MN to RP_n (step 6).
- RP_n checks whether these packets are sent from RP_o. If so, RP_n tunnels these packets to ASR_n and then forwards them to the MN. At the same time, RP_n stores the mapping from MN's AID onto RP_o's RID locally (step 7).
- RP_o sends a notification message to the CN's ASR/RP to inform it of the newest AID-to-RID mapping for the MN (step 8).
- CN's ASR/RP updates the AID-to-RID mapping for the MN (step 9).
- CN's ASR/RP informs RP_n of the newest AID-to-RID mapping for the CN and directly tunnels packets destined to the MN to RP_n (step 10).
- RP_n stores the AID-to-RID mapping for CN into its CN's AID-to-RID mapping table and tunnels these packets to ASR_n, which sends the packets to the MN (step 11).
- RP_n receives packets destined to CN and directly tunnels them to the CN's ASR/RP instead of tunneling them to RP_o (step 12).

Both an MN and Its CN Roam Across Different RDs. In this scenario, we denote the MN's old ASR, old RP, new ASR and new RP as ASR_o^{MN}, RP_o^{MN}, ASR_n^{MN} and RP_n^{MN}, respectively. Similarly, we denote the CN's old ASR, old RP, new ASR and new RP as ASR_o^{CN}, RP_o^{CN}, ASR_n^{CN} and RP_n^{CN}, respectively.

When the MN and the CN both roam across different RDs, their handoff processes are operated independently. Assume that RP_o^{CN} receives the message from RP_o^{MN} earlier than RP_o^{MN} receives the message from RP_o^{CN} at step 8 in Fig. 9.17. With this assumption, RP_o^{CN} knows the new AID-to-RID mapping for the MN. Moreover, three subcases also exist:

- When RP_o^{CN} receives the message from RP_o^{MN}, it does not know the new AID-to-RID mapping for the CN.
- When RP_o^{CN} receives the message from RP_o^{MN}, it knows the new AID-to-RID mapping for the CN but has not sent the message to RP_o^{MN}.
- When RP_o^{CN} receives the message from RP_o^{MN}, it knows the new AID-to-RID mapping for the CN and has sent a message to RP_o^{MN}.

The handoff process in subcase A is shown in Fig. 9.18. In this case, RP_o^{CN} stores the new AID-to-RID mapping for the MN when it receives the notification message from RP_o^{MN} (step 9'). RP_o^{CN} sends packets destined to the MN to RP_n^{MN}, since it does not know the new AID-to-RID mapping for the CN (step 10'). RP_n^{MN}

receives packets destined to the CN and tunnels these packets to RP_o^{CN} (step 12′). When RP_o^{CN} knows the new AID-to-RID mapping for the CN, it notifies the RP_n^{MN} of this new mapping (step 13′). RP_n^{MN} receives the new AID-to-RID mapping for the CN and updates its CN's AID-to-RID mapping table (step 14′). Then RP_n^{MN} tunnels packets destined to the CN to RP_n^{CN} (step 15′). When RP_n^{CN} receives such packets, it takes the mapping from the MN's AID to the RID of RP_n^{MN} as the AID-to-RID mapping for the MN and stores it into its CN's AID-to-RID mapping table locally (step 16′). RP_n^{CN} acquires the new AID-to-RID mapping for the MN and then tunnels packets destined to the MN to RP_n^{MN}.

Figure 9.19 shows the handoff process in subcase B. RP_o^{CN} receives the new AID-to-RID mapping for the MN and stores this new mapping in its CN's AID-to-RID mapping table (step 8′). RP_o^{CN} directly notifies RP_n^{MN} of the new AID-to-RID mapping instead of the old one for the CN, since it knows the new AID-to-RID mapping for the CN (step 10′). RP_n^{MN} receives the new AID-to-RID mapping for CN and stores this new mapping in its CN's AID-to-RID mapping table (step 11′). As the RID in the new mapping points to RP_n^{CN}, RP_n^{MN} simply tunnels the packets destined to the CN to RP_n^{CN} (step 12'). Then RP_n^{CN} receives the packets from RP_n^{MN} as the AID-to-RID mapping for the MN and stores this mapping into its CN's AID-to-RID mapping table (step 13′). RP_n^{CN} receives packets destined to the MN and tunnels them to RP_n^{MN} (step 14').

The subcase C is shown as in Fig. 9.20; RP_o^{CN} or RP_o^{MN} sets up a bidirectional tunnel in (steps 8′) and (step 8″). In addition, RP_o^{CN} knows the new AID-to-RID mapping for the CN and sends it to RP_n^{MN} (step 10′). At the same time, RP_o^{MN} knows the new AID-to-RID mapping for the MN and sends it to RP_n^{CN} (step 10″). RP_n^{MN}

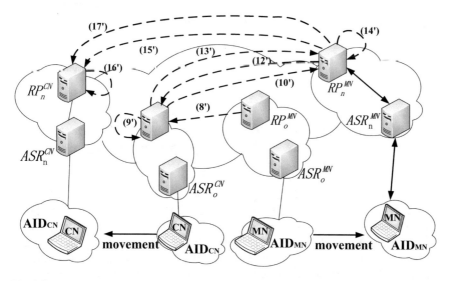

Fig. 9.18 Handoff process in subcase A. Reprinted from Ref. [4], with permission from IEEE

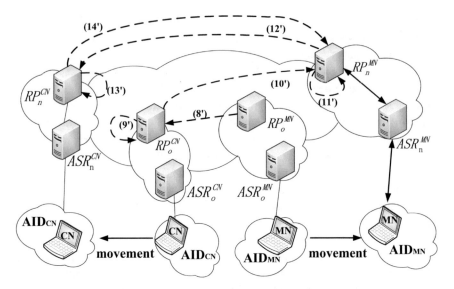

Fig. 9.19 Handoff process in subcase B. Reprinted from Ref. [4], with permission from IEEE

receives the new AID-to-RID mapping for the CN, stores this new mapping in its CN's AID-to-RID mapping table and then directly tunnels the packets destined to the CN to RP_n^{CN} through (step 11′) and (step 12′). Similarly, when RP_n^{CN} receives the new AID-to-RID mapping from the MN, it stores this new mapping in its CN's AID-to-RID mapping table (step 11″).RP_n^{CN} then directly tunnels the packets destined to the MN to RP_n^{MN}(step 12″).

From the preceding descriptions, we conclude that the proposed handoff process is able to support the handoff case that both an MN and its CN roam across different RDs.

9.5.3   Evaluation

This part presents evaluation results to demonstrate IMM's performance and analyzes how IMM reduces the number of mapping update messages sent into a mapping system and IASRs.

In IMM, when an MN roams across different RDs, it is necessary to send a mapping update message to the mapping system and the IASR of every CN of the MN. It is the key benefit of IMM to significantly reduce the number of mapping update messages sent to a mapping system and IASRs. This part analyzes the possible reduction in the number of mapping update messages using 24-day traces of 536 taxies collected at San Francisco, CA [40]. The traces are collected from the Global Position System (GPS) receivers that are placed in taxies, and every GPS

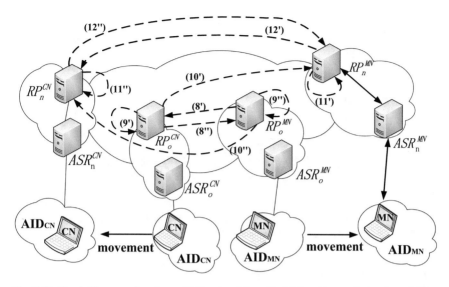

Fig. 9.20 Handoff process in subcase C. Reprinted from Ref. [4], with permission from IEEE

receiver takes a reading of its current position in terms of the latitude and longitude every 30 s and records them into a track log. We regard every person as an MN; whenever a taxi runs from one square to a neighboring one, we assume that a handoff occurs.

Figure 9.21 shows the total number of handoffs that all taxies would incur and the average number of handoffs per taxi per second. The average number of handoffs per taxi per second is about 3.72×10^{-3} (1.8×10^{-4}) when L = 1 km (L = 20 km). This implies that when L = 1 km the average number of handoffs per taxi per second is about 20 times that of the case when L = 20 km. Based on the preceding assumptions, this implies that the number of mapping update message sent to a mapping system and IASRs in the existing mapping service is about 20 times that in the IMM. Therefore, IMM can significantly reduce the number of mapping updates.

When MN communicates with multiple CNs, it may send a mapping update message to every CN's IASR. Assuming that a bandwidth of B_1 is required to transmit a mapping update message, the bandwidth requirement used to send a mapping update message per handoff is calculated as

$$BW_E = B_1 + p \times B_1, \qquad (9.34)$$

where p is the number of CNs that an MN simultaneously communicates.

For IMM, when an MN roams from an old EASR to a new one within the same RD, the new EASR first sends a message to the mapping system to obtain the MN's RP and then sends a new binding to inform MN's RP of the MN's newest point of attachment. In each of these steps, we assume that a bandwidth of B_2 is required.

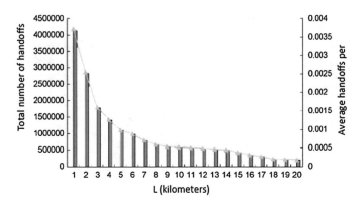

Fig. 9.21 Total number of handoffs and average number of handoffs per taxi per second. Reprinted from Ref. [4], with permission from IEEE

Fig. 9.22 Bandwidth gain of IMM over existing approaches. Reprinted from Ref. [4], with permission from IEEE

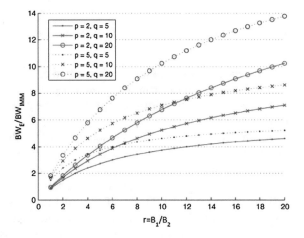

The total bandwidth requirement of $q+1$ movements is $q \times 3 \times B_2 + B_1 + p \times B_1 + 3 \times B_2$. The average bandwidth used to send update messages per handoff is

$$BW_{IMM} = \frac{q \times 3 \times B_2 + B_1 + p \times B_1 + 3 \times B_2}{q+1}. \qquad (9.35)$$

Let BW_E/BW_{IMM} be the bandwidth gain of IMM over existing approaches. Then,

$$\frac{BW_E}{BW_{IMM}} = \frac{(q+1)(p+1)B_1}{3(q+1)B_2+(p+1)B_1} = \frac{(q+1)(p+1)r}{3(q+1)+(p+1)r}, \qquad (9.36)$$

where $r = B_1/B_2$.

Figure 9.22 shows that BW_E/BW_{IMM} increases with the incensement of r. When $r = 1$, the benefit from IMM is very trivial; however, when r increases to 10, the bandwidth required by existing approaches is more than four times that required by IMM. Moreover, it is also observed that BW_E/BW_{IMM} increases with the increase in p and q. The bandwidth requirement used to transmit mapping update messages in MN is significantly less than that in existing approaches.

9.6   Conclusion

This chapter proposes four mobility management schemes, i.e., NMM, HMM, MFMM and IMM, to support the mobility in SINET.

NMM enables network operators to maintain the stability and reliability of the core network and make it independent of the customer network. It also provides a lower handoff delay than MIPv6 and satisfies most of the real-time applications. In addition, NMM's separating scheme raises a barrier against malicious attacks aimed at the provider infrastructure and provides an effective means of protection against privacy disclosures. Analysis and experiments show NMM is feasible and effective.

We also describe the handoff procedures of intra-domain mobility and inter-domain mobility for HMM in detail. In HMM architecture, it includes a management plane and user plane. The management plane maintains the AID-to-RID mappings, while the user plane is responsible for transmitting data packets. To evaluate the efficiency of HMM, we establish an analytical model to evaluate the signaling overhead. Numerical results show that the HMM scheme can effectively reduce the signaling traffic compared with MIP and HMIP.

In the proposed MFMM scheme, an ASR is selected as an agent that can keep the MN's AID-to-RID mapping invariable by establishing an MF chain. In this way, it can reduce the location update signaling overhead since the MN's mapping in the ASR_{CN} does not need to be updated. Meanwhile, the unchanged mapping assures the correct forwarding of packets. Therefore, the blocking probability can be reduced. When the MN moves between two MF chains, an effective data-triggered update scheme that can achieve route optimization is proposed.

The IMM scheme is proposed to map AIDs to RIDs in networks with locator/identifier separation to support efficient host mobility. IMM divides the whole network into many RDs and assigns the rendezvous nodes to MNs. When an MN roams into an RD, it registers the mapping from the MN's AID to the rendezvous node's RID into the mapping system so that the packets destined to the MN are sent to the MN's rendezvous node. In addition, when an MN roams within the same RD, the mapping registered into the mapping system is unchanged. This significantly reduces the number of mapping update messages sent to the mapping system and IASRs and therefore makes it efficient to support host mobility.

These proposed schemes can address the existing issues of MIP in mobility and also achieve the properties of location privacy, optimal signaling overhead, connection survivability, controllability and manageability. The evaluation results show that these schemes have low signaling overhead and handoff delay; they can support fast handoff under the high-speed movement.

References

1. Dong P, Yang. S, Zhang. H (2008) A network-based mobility management scheme. WiCOM'08, Dalian, China. doi:10.1109/WiCom.2008.8992
2. Qiu F, Li X, Zhang H (2012) Mobility management in identifier/locator split networks. Wirel Pers Commun 65(3):489–514
3. Qiu F, Luo H, Li X, Xue M, Dong P, Zhang H (2013) A mapping forwarding approach for supporting mobility in networks with identifier/locator separation. Int J Commun Syst 26 (5):626–643
4. Luo H, Zhang H, Qiao C (2011) Efficient mobility support by indirect mapping in networks with locator/identifier separation. IEEE Trans Veh Technol 60(5):2265–2279
5. Makaya C, Pierre S (2008) An analytical framework for performance evaluation of IPv6-Based mobility management protocols. IEEE Trans on Wirel Commun 7(3):972–983
6. Ma W, Fang Y (2005) A pointer forwarding based local anchoring (POFLA) scheme for wireless networks. IEEE Trans Veh Technol 54(3):1135–1146
7. Lam P, Liew S, Lee J (2005) Cellular universal IP: a low delay mobility scheme based on universal IP addressing. MSWiM' 05, Montreal, Quebec, Canada, p 323–332
8. Koodli R (2007) RFC 4882. http://datatracker.ietf.org/doc/rfc4882/. Accessed May 2007
9. Meyer D, Zhang L, Fall K (2007) RFC 4984. https://fl-test.rjsparks.org/doc/rfc4984/. Accessed Sept 2007
10. Johnson D et al (2004) RFC 3775. http://tools.ietf.org/html/rfc3775. Accessed Jun 2004
11. Xie J, Akyildiz I (2002) A distributed dynamic regional location management scheme for mobile IP. IEEE INFOCOM, New York, NY, USA, pp 1069–1078
12. Fang Y, Chlamtac I, Lin Y (2000) Portable movement modeling for PCS networks. IEEE Trans Veh Technol 49(4):1356–1363
13. Xie G, Chen J, Zheng H (2007) Handover latency of MIPv6 implementation in Linux. GLOBECOM'07, Washington, DC, USA, p 1780–1785
14. Han Y, Min S (2009) Performance analysis of hierarchical mobile IPv6: does it improve mobile IPv6 in terms of handover speed? Wirel Pers Commun 48(4):463–483
15. Fu S, Atiquzzaman M (2005) Handover latency comparison of SIGMA. FMIPv6, HMIPv6, and FHMIPv6. GLOBECOM'05, Louis, Missouri, USA, pp 3809–3813
16. Huston G (1994) Growth of the BGP table. http://bgp.potaroo.net/
17. Zhao X, Pacella D, Schiller J (2010) Routing scalability: an operator's view. IEEE J Sel Areas Commun 28(8):1262–1270
18. Zhang L, Wakikawa R, Zhu Z (2009) Support mobility in the global internet. MICNET'09, New York, NY, USA, pp 1–6
19. Jen D, Zhang L (2009) draft-jen-mapping-00.txt. http://www.ietfreport.isoc.org/idref/draft-jen-mapping/. Accessed Oct 2009
20. CRAWDAD. http://www.crawdad.org/index.php
21. Menth M, Hartmann M, Hofling M (2010) FIRMS: A future internet mapping system. IEEE J Sel Areas Commun 28(8):1326–1331
22. Valko A (1999) Cellular IP: a new approach to internet host mobility(ed). ACM SIGCOMM Comput Commun Rev 29(1):50–65
23. Ramjee R, Varadhan K, Salgarelli L et al (2002) HAWAII: a domain-based approach for supporting mobility in wide-area wireless networks (ed). IEEE/ACM Trans on Netw 10 (3):396–410

24. Perkins C (2008) IP mobility support for IPv4, revised. http://www.tools.ietf.org/html/draft-ietf-mip4-rfc3344bis-06. Accessed 11 Mar 2008

25. Johnson D, Perkins C, Arkko J (2004) Mobility support in IPv6. RFC 3775. http://www.ietf.org/rfc/rfc3775.txt. Accessed Jun 2004

26. Nakajima N, Dutta A, Das S, Schulzrinne H (2003) and measurement for SIP based mobility in IPv6. IEEE ICC 2:1085–1089

27. Koodli R (2007) IP address location privacy and mobile IPv6: Problem Statement. RFC 4882. http://datatracker.ietf.org/doc/rfc4882/. Accessed May 2007

28. Meyer D, Zhang L, Kall K (2007). RFC 4984. Report from the IAB workshop on routing and addressing. http://www.ietf.org/rfc/rfc4984.txt. Accessed Sept 2007

29. Khare V, Jen D, Zhao X, Liu Y, Massey D (2010) Evolution towards global routing scalability. IEEE J Sel Areas Commun 28(8):1363–1375

30. IETF Locator (2013). ID separation protocol. http://datatracker.ietf.org/wg/lisp/. Accessed Jan 2013

31. Quoitin B, Lannone L, Launois C, Bonaventure O (2007) Evaluating the benefits of the locator/identifier separation. SIGCOMM MobiArch'07. doi:10.1145/1366919.1366926

32. Farinacci D, Fuller V, Meyer D, Lewis D (2010) Locator/ID separation protocol (LISP). Internet draft. http://tools.ietf.org/html/draft-ietf-lisp-09. Accessed 11 Oct 2010

33. Moskowitz R, Nikander P (2006) Host identity protocol (HIP) architecture. RFC 4423. http://www.ietf.org/rfc/rfc4423. Accessed May 2006

34. Pan J, Paul S, Jain R, Bowman M (2008) MILSA: a mobility and multihoming supporting identifier locator split architecture for next generation internet. In: Proceedings of global telecommunications conference (GLOBECOM'08). doi:10.1109/GLOCOM.2008.ECP.436

35. Pan J, Jain R, Paul S, So-in C (2010) MILSA: A new evolutionary architecture for scalability, mobility, and multihoming in the future internet. IEEE J Sel Areas Commun 28(8):1344–1362

36. Farinacci D, Fuller V, Meyer D (2010). LISP alternative topology (LISP-ALT). IETF Draft. http://www.tools.ietf.org/html/draft-ietf-lisp-alt-05.txt. Accessed 18 Oct 2010

37. Lear E (2010) NERD: a not-so-novel EID to RLOC database. IETF Draft. https://tools.ietf.org/html/draft-lear-lisp-nerd-08. Accessed 6 Mar 2010

38. Menth M, Hartmann M, Hofling M (2010) FIRMS: a future internet mapping system(ed). IEEE J Sel Areas Commun 28(8):1326–1331

39. Luo H, Qin Y, Zhang H (2009) A DHT-based identifier-to-locator mapping approach for a scalable Internet. IEEE J Sel Areas Commun 20(12):1790–1802

40. Luo H, Zhang H, Zukerman M (2011) Decoupling the design of identifier-to-locator mapping services from identifiers. Comput Netw 55(4):959–974

Chapter 10
Security Technologies of SINET

In this chapter, we introduce three security enhancement solutions in SINET. First, related work on Internet security is summarized at the beginning. Then, we propose an Anomaly Detection Response Mechanism (ADRM) based on mapping requests, which is featured by the pre-alarming, detection efficiency and traffic control. Next, we present a scalable and efficient identifier-separating mapping mechanism, which is used to efficiently detect DDoS attacks and prevent DDoS attackers from controlling the botnets. Additionally, we systematically analyze the mitigation of worm propagation, and further give a quantitative comparison between the traditional network and SINET by using novel Analytical Active Worm Propagation (AAWP) and Susceptible-Infectious-Removed propagation (SIR) models.

10.1 Related Work

In recent years, security threats to the Internet and anomalous traffic events have been increasing dramatically, such as Distributed Denial of Service (DDoS) attacks and worms. Thus, identifying and preventing network anomalies are critical challenges. For different DDoS and worm attacks, researchers have proposed many new algorithms in the literature. In [1], the authors mainly focus on the spoofed address attack and propose detection approaches by exploiting spatial and temporal correlation of attack traffic. In [2], the authors focus on how to detect stealthy DDoS and advise a real-time detection approach based on time-series decomposition. In [3], the authors discuss the effects of multivariate correlation analysis on DDoS detection and propose a covariance analysis model for detecting SYNchronous (SYN) flooding attacks. Besides, in [4, 5], the authors propose many principal component analysis-based approaches, and these approaches can be used to detect DDoS attacks by decomposing the original traffic into the normal and abnormal proportions. Moreover, in [6], the authors summarize a number of different anomaly detection approaches. Although the existing anomaly detection approaches can

© Springer-Verlag Berlin Heidelberg 2016
H. Zhang et al., *Smart Collaborative Identifier Network*,
DOI 10.1007/978-3-662-49143-0_10

diagnose and identify the anomalous network behaviors, they cannot assure detecting and controlling the attack traffic in real time.

In order to effectively alleviate worm propagation, the worm propagation models that aim at characterizing the spread of worms have become an active research area. Up to now, two typical aspects exist in the study of basic worm propagation models. One is based on the epidemiology model, such as the Susceptible-Infectious-Susceptible (SIS) model [7], Two-Factor model [8], Kermack-McKendrick (KM) model [9] and so on. This type of model can provide a qualitative understanding of worm spread by adopting nonlinear difference equations. Particularly the KM model is also named the SIR model, and it can be used as background research for other worm propagation models. The other is mainly founded on the discrete time model, such as the AAWP model [10]. This type of model can describe the spread of active worms by taking advantage of deterministic approximation and can also explain why virtually most worms will be slow in global prevalence to some extent.

10.2   Anomaly Detection Response Mechanism in SINET

10.2.1   Anomaly Detection Mechanism

In the current SINET, when a host starts to establish a connection to another host, its Access Switching Router (ASR) must first send a mapping request to the corresponding Identifier Mapping Server (IDMS). Hence, it needs to consider whether the anomaly detection of the mapping requests can identify or diagnose the aberrant network behaviors, especially when a few network anomalies can have a dramatic impact on some servers or hosts [11]. With this consideration, this section proposes a mapping request-based anomaly detection mechanism, which can identify and diagnose some anomalous network behaviors by judging the mapping request traffic anomaly.

As shown in Fig. 10.1, we illustrate an example that is inspired by the mapping request anomaly flows. When a number of attackers aim at overwhelming a victim with an immense volume of useless traffic, their relevant ASRs first send the mapping requests to get the victim's mapping information. From this point, an anomaly detection mechanism is implemented in each IDMS to detect and diagnose the mapping request traffic anomaly for the Access Identifier to Routing Identifier (AID-to-RID) mapping items maintained by this IDMS. Furthermore, in order to raise an alarm in real time, a celebrated Cumulative Sum (CUSUM) algorithm is used for change point detection. Once the IDMS generates an alarm for some AID-to-RID mapping items, the IDMS can respond to control the attack traffic by cooperating with the ASRs or conditionally the incoming mapping requests.

We take a DDoS attack as an example to present the working process of the mapping request flow-based anomaly detection mechanism:

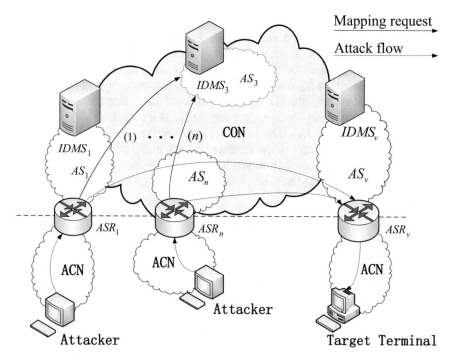

Fig. 10.1 Mapping request flow anomaly example

- When a large number of malicious attackers launch DDoS attacks to a target terminal, they first send the attack data packets to the ASR that they belong to.
- After the ASR receives the malicious data packets, it will send mapping requests to the corresponding IDMS to query the target terminal's mapping information.
- When the IDMS receives those requests, it detects the abnormal mutation point of the mapping request flow using CUSUM algorithm. If the point is found, an alarm will be generated; otherwise, the IDMS gives normal responses to those mapping requests and sends the target terminal's mapping information back to the ASR.

10.2.2   CUSUM-Based Abnormal Alarm Algorithm

The CUSUM algorithm is based on hypothesis testing. It is ascribed to the family of change point detection algorithms. The principle of change point detection is to estimate whether the observed random variables remain statistically homogeneous. If not, it can identify the change point in time [12, 13]. In essence, the CUSUM is based on the fact that, if the average value of a statistical process changes, the stochastic probability distribution will also change [14]. Unlike the high-dimensional network traffic, the mapping request traffic is simple and one dimensional. This means in order to generate an alarm we can directly apply the CUSUM algorithm. Besides, our ultimate purpose is to detect the mapping request traffic anomaly.

Here, we describe the CUSUM-based abnormal alarm algorithm as follows:

If we assume that the time sequence $x_1, x_2, ..., x_{k-1}$ shows independent identically distributed variables with the Gaussian distribution $N(0,1)$, then the time sequence $x_k, x_{k+1}, ..., x_n$ represents independent identically distributed variables with the Gaussian distribution $N(\delta,1)$. The value x_i represents the number of the mapping requests for some identifiers in the ith time interval, and k ($k < n$) is an unknown change point. If we suppose there is no change point ($k = \infty$), we can calculate the statistical value of the log-likelihood ratio (denoted by S_n) as Eq. 10.1:

$$S_n = \max_{1 \le k \le n} \sum_{i=k+1}^{n} \left(x_i - \frac{\delta}{2} \right). \tag{10.1}$$

If we suppose that t ($t > 0$) is a chosen threshold, which may be determined empirically through experiments, then, when $S_i \le t$ ($i = 1, 2, \cdots n$), the former $n-1$ values are under normal conditions, when $S_n > t$, anomaly happens and an alarm should be generated.

If the prerequisite is that we have assumed $\{x_n\}$ are independent Gaussian random variables, we can use Eq. 10.1 to illustrate the basic CUSUM algorithm. However, this is not applicable for network traffic measurements that relate to seasonality, trends and time correlations [15]. In order to remove such non-stationary behaviors, we can improve the basic CUSUM algorithm referring to [12], and S_n can be calculated by Eq. 10.3:

$$\begin{cases} S_n = \left[S_{n-1} + \frac{\alpha \bar{\mu}_{n-1}}{\sigma^2} \left(x_n - \bar{\mu}_{n-1} - \frac{\alpha \bar{\mu}_{n-1}}{2} \right) \right]^+ \\ S_0 = 0 \end{cases}, \tag{10.2}$$

where α is an amplitude percentage parameter, which corresponds to the most probable percentage for the case that the mean rate increases after a sudden change happens. δ^2 is the variance of δ. Meanwhile, referring to [16], the mean value of μ_n can be computed by using an exponentially weighted moving average of the previous measurements as presented in Eq. 10.3:

$$\bar{\mu}_n = \beta \bar{\mu}_{n-1} + (1 - \beta)x_n, \tag{10.3}$$

where β is the exponentially weighted moving average factor. Thus, we can calculate the conditions to generate an alarm as Eq. 10.4:

$$f(S_n) = \begin{cases} 1, & \text{if } S_n > t; \\ 0, & \text{otherwise.} \end{cases} \tag{10.4}$$

In Eq. 10.4, 0 indicates that the detected sequence $\{x_n\}$ is normal, while 1 indicates that the anomaly in the detected sequence $\{x_n\}$ is identified. If $f(S_n)$ is 1, an alarm will be generated.

However, there is a disadvantage existing in the CUSUM algorithm [17]. That is, when the anomaly or the attack is terminated, CUSUM still keeps on generating the false alarms for a long time. Then, in order to revoke an alarm, we can use Eq. 10.5:

$$f(S_n) = 0, \text{ if } S_n \geq t \text{ and } x_i < \varphi \bar{\mu}_{2k-i}, \tag{10.5}$$

where φ is the regulatory factor, $\varphi > 1$. If we assume that an anomalous behavior happens at time k, we suppose that x_i is the detected mapping request traffic in the i-th time interval, $i > k$.

Additionally, to revoke an alarm more accurately, the latter condition in Eq. 10.5 $(x_i < \varphi \overline{\mu_{2k-i}})$ can be improved by Eq. 10.6:

$$\sum_{j=0}^{n} 1_{\left\{x_{i+j} < \varphi \bar{\mu}_{2k-i-j}\right\}} \geq \theta, \tag{10.6}$$

where θ is a positive integer, $n > \theta > 1$.

Equation 10.6 expresses that, if the number of the times that satisfy the condition $x_i < \varphi \overline{\mu_{2k-i}}$ is larger than θ, the alarm will be revoked. Meanwhile, after the alarm has been revoked, we will further reset S_n between 0 and t.

10.2.3 Anomaly Response Mechanism

To restrain network anomalies in real time, we take defense mechanisms to respond to the alarms. As mentioned before, whenever the CUSUM algorithm detects a change point of the mapping request traffic, the proposed abnormal alarm algorithm will generate an alarm. Once alarming, the following two mechanisms can be carried out to control network traffic or the further attacks.

Cooperating with ASRs. On receiving the mapping requests that aim at resolving an RID for some victim AIDs, IDMS can inform each ASR who sends the corresponding mapping requests to limit the network traffic until the alarm has been revoked.

In the case of limiting network traffic, ASRs can recur to the rate limiting or packet-filtering mechanisms based on the intensity of the attacks or pre-defined response policies. Also, the foregoing response mechanism may need all the ASRs and IDMSs to cooperate with each other in the whole network. Additionally, we can also use the digital signature technique to guarantee the authenticity of the control information [18, 19].

Conditionally Answering the Mapping Requests for the Victim's AID. When it receives the mapping requests that aim at resolving an RID for the victim's AID, IDMS can employ either a random resolution algorithm or a pre-determined threshold algorithm to answer the mapping requests.

A random resolution algorithm is based on the idea that each IDMS can invoke a random rule to resolve an RID for the incoming mapping requests in order to indirectly reduce the attack traffic to the victim's AID.

A pre-determined threshold algorithm is based on the idea that each IDMS can set a threshold for the victim's AID first. Once the total number of the mapping requests for this AID is larger than the pre-determined threshold value, the IDMS will stop resolving the RID for the victim's AID for a period. In this way, the number of attackers can be restricted, and the attack traffic can be cut down as a matter of fact.

In general, each of the mechanisms mentioned before has its advantages and disadvantages. For one thing, although the first mechanism can efficiently restrain network anomalies or attacks, it is difficult to promote cooperation between all IDMSs and ASRs under current network conditions. For another, it is easy to carry out the second mechanism, but this mechanism may discard some legitimate communications. We must carefully consider how to implement the mechanisms mentioned before in accordance with actual experiences and network circumstances.

10.2.4   Performance Evaluation

In this section, we will evaluate the proposed ADRM mechanism in detail by a small-scale DDoS simulation in NS-2 and illustrate the advantages of the proposed ADRM by comparing it with the Anomaly Detection based on Network Traffic (ADNT) via alarm in advance, detection efficiency and traffic control.

In our simulation, we assume that six Provider Networks (PNs) are in the transit core and nine ACcess Networks (ACNs) under each of the first five PNs. Each ACN takes charge of one ASR and one host. Additionally, another host is regarded as a victim under the sixth PN. We suppose that the background traffic comes from 30 legitimate hosts and each communication is initiated at intervals of 1 s by each legitimate host lasts 2 s. Besides, the transmission rate from the legitimate host at 12 s is set to 5 Mbps to simulate a large traffic spike or surge caused by some legitimate hosts. Moreover, the DDoS attack from 15 malicious attackers starts at 23 s and lasts 5 s, while the average attack rate of each host is set to 1 Mbps. If the simulation begins at 5 s and ends at 35 s, then the network traffic received by the victim per 0.5 s can be presented as in Fig. 10.2.

Alarm in Advance. Unlike the general anomaly detection mechanism, which is based on network traffic, ADRM is able to generate an alarm in advance. In SINET, whenever a host wants to establish a connection to another host, it must first send a mapping request to the IDMS to resolve an RID for the destination host. Hence, if a

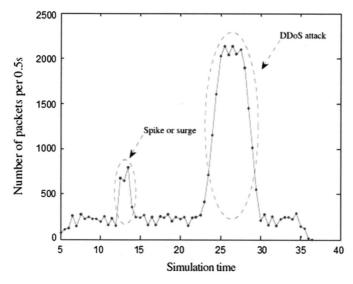

Fig. 10.2 Network traffic received by the victim per 0.5 s. Reprinted from Ref. [11], with permission from Wiley

DDoS attack or other attacks happen, the change point of the mapping request traffic detected by the IDMS is anterior to that of the attack traffic.

As shown in Fig. 10.3, the arrival time of the mapping request is earlier than that of attack flow. Here, the average arrival time of the mapping request and attack flow is at about 24.05 s and 24.29 s, respectively. Then, the average time difference of arrival is 0.24 s, and this time difference can be regarded as the alarm delay between ADRM and ADNT. Although the alarm delay in real network environments may be surprisingly small, this delay is still enough for the IDMSs to take the precaution to defend against further DDoS attacks.

In Fig. 10.4, we illustrate the mapping request delay of the 15 DDoS attackers. In our simulation, the average mapping request delay is 0.19 s. From Fig. 10.4, we can observe that the mapping request delay takes a major portion of the alarm delay. The mapping request delay may be different if we design other mapping services, but it will not affect the conclusion we achieved.

Detection Efficiency. ADRM is more efficient at identifying or diagnosing the aberrant network behaviors than ADNT since the network traffic is complicated and high-dimensional, and the background noises have a strong impact on the detection efficiency, while the mapping request traffic is simple and single dimensional, and it is convenient to detect network anomalies without decreasing the dimensions of network traffic. Moreover, our proposed mechanism is able to eliminate the influence caused by some large traffic spikes or surges. In our simulation, both ADNT and ADRM adopt the proposed abnormal alarm algorithm to generate and revoke the alarm.

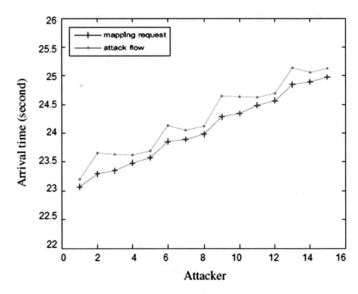

Fig. 10.3 Different arrival time between mapping requests and attack flow. Reprinted from Ref. [11], with permission from Wiley

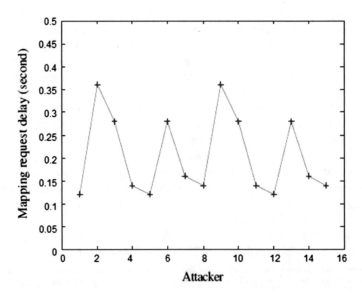

Fig. 10.4 Mapping request delay of the 15 distributed denial of service attackers. Reprinted from Ref. [11], with permission from Wiley

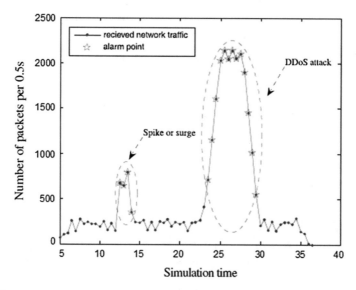

Fig. 10.5 Alarm points in the network traffic received by the victim. Reprinted from Ref. [11], with permission from Wiley

We can observe that the alarm points caused by the large traffic spike or surge in Fig. 10.5 are not shown in Fig. 10.6, while the alarm points caused by the DDoS attack are both shown in Figs. 10.5 and 10.6. Meanwhile, we can also observe that the first alarm point caused by the DDoS in Fig. 10.6 is recognizably earlier than that in Fig. 10.5.

Traffic Control. A real-time response is essential to protect the victim if network anomalies or attacks have been detected in advance. In Sect. 10.2.3, two response mechanisms were proposed, and both of them can be used to defend against malicious attacks by controlling the attack traffic. In this section, we carry out the second mechanism for ease of presentation. In Fig. 10.7, we present the change of the attack traffic under different random resolution values or predetermined thresholds. Here, the time period of the random resolution values or pre-determined thresholds is 5 s.

From Fig. 10.7, we can observe that when there is no response, the attack traffic is the largest. Besides, we can also observe that, when the random resolution value or pre-determined threshold decreases from 12 to 4, the attack traffic is also significantly reduced. By conditionally answering the mapping requests, our proposed response mechanism can efficiently cut down the attack traffic. However, this mechanism also has its drawbacks. As mentioned before, this mechanism may discard some normal or legitimate communications, and the smaller the random resolution value or pre-determined threshold is, the larger the negative effect will be. Hence, we should carefully consider how to implement the response mechanisms in accordance with actual experiences and network circumstances.

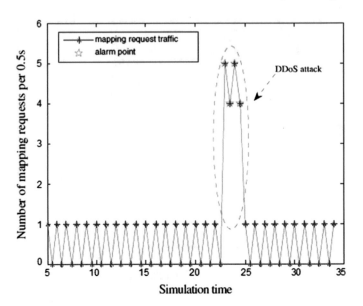

Fig. 10.6 Alarm points in the corresponding mapping request traffic for the victim. Reprinted from Ref. [11], with permission from Wiley

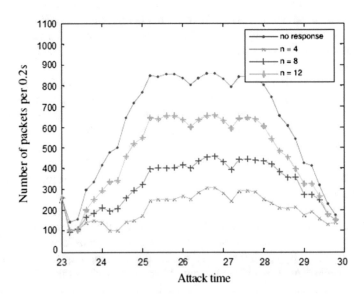

Fig. 10.7 Attack traffic under random resolution value or pre-determined threshold. Reprinted from Ref. [11], with permission from Wiley

10.3   DDoS-Preventing Mechanism in SINET

10.3.1   A Scalable Identifier-Separating Mapping Mechanism

In the current SINET, a service provider (server or the host servers as a server) registers the binding(s) from its Service IDentifiers [SID(s)] to the AID(s) into the Intelligent Service Resolution Server (ISRS). When a user (the host servers as a user) wants to obtain a service from the service provider, he/she first queries the AID corresponding to the service's SID, and then, he/she sends a request to the server that corresponds to the returned AID. Similarly, in peer-to-peer applications, some servers list the seeds and their corresponding AIDs. When a user wants to obtain a service, he/she needs to first connect to one or more seeds in order to obtain the AIDs of active peers. That is, if a server provides services to public users, the AID of the server needs be publicly available. Otherwise, it is not necessary to make the AID publicly available. Particularly, this fact can be used to help prevent DDoS attacks in our proposed identifier-separating mapping mechanism.

Let P represent the set of Provider Networks (PNs) in SINET; the basic ideas behind our proposed mechanism can be described as follows:

Let every provider network in P maintain one or more IDMSs. An IDMS is a server that stores AID-to-RID mappings and answers mapping requests.

For example, in the network demonstrated in Fig. 10.8, $P = \{PN_1, PN_2, PN_3\}$.

Every AID is associated with an IDMS that serves as the mapping server of the AID. This association may be configured when an AID is obtained from a network administrator.

For example, AID_A and AID_B in Fig. 10.8 may associate with $IDMS_1$ in PN_1 and $IDMS_2$ in PN_2, respectively. In addition, when the AID is associated with an IDMS, it is also assigned a key that is used to authenticate whether or not an AID is really associated with an IDMS by ASRs.

If a server needs to provide services, it will register its AID, the associated IDMS and the corresponding key into the Intelligent Service Resolution System.

For example, on the one hand, when server B in Fig. 10.8 wants to provide a web service to the specific users, it registers the binding from the service's SID to AID_B, the RID of $IDMS_2$ and the corresponding key to the Intelligent Service Resolution System, as illustrated by (1) in Fig. 10.8. On the other hand, if a server does not provide any service to the users, it is not necessary to register its AID, the associated IDMS and the corresponding key to the ISRS. Additionally, the server may even choose not to associate an IDMS for the AID of the server.

If a user wants to obtain a service from a server that provides the desired service, it will send an intelligent service resolution request to the ISRS, which will then return the AID of the server, its associated IDMS and the corresponding key.

For example, when user A wants to obtain the web service provided by server B, it sends an intelligent service resolution request to the ISRS, which then returns AID_B, the RID of $IDMS_1$ and the corresponding key to user A, as illustrated by

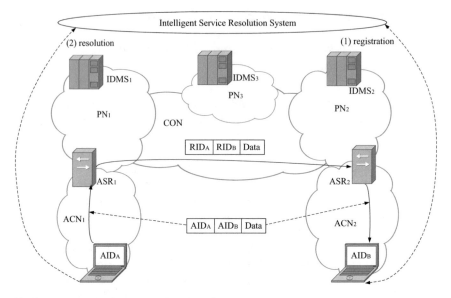

Fig. 10.8 Illustration of the identifier-separating mapping mechanism

(2) in Fig. 10.8. Then, user A sends a connection setup request to its ASR (i.e., ASR_1 in Fig. 10.8). The request should include AID_B, its associated IDMS and the corresponding key. When ASR_1 receives this request, it checks whether or not AID_B is really associated with $IDMS_2$. If so, it sends a mapping request to $IDMS_2$ to obtain the up-to-date mapping of AID_B. Whenever ASR_1 knows the mapping of AID_B, it modifies the receiving request by changing AID_A and AID_B to RID_A and RID_B. This modified request will be sent to ASR_2, and ASR_2 and will modify the receiving request by changing RID_A and RID_B to AID_A and AID_B, respectively. After that, ASR_2 will send this re-modified connection setup request to server B. In addition, ASR2 caches the mapping from AID_A to RID_A. Then, server B replies to user A, and ASR_2 can re-use the cached mapping of AID_A to send packets to ASR_1. In this way, user A can obtain the desired service provided by server B.

10.3.2   Preventing DDoS Attacks

In order to launch a DDoS attack, an attacker normally needs to control dozens of zombies as well as send attack commands to these zombies [20]. Next, we will explain how our proposed mechanism prevents attackers from recruiting zombies as well as sending attack commands to these zombies.

First, in order to recruit zombies, an attacker can use attacker tools to find vulnerable hosts. However, the prerequisite that judges whether a host is vulnerable is that the attacker can send packets to this host. In the traditional network, public Internet Protocol (IP) addresses are reachable, and any packets destined to a public IP address can be forwarded to the host using this IP address. However, with our proposed mechanism, the attacker's ASR can find only the RIDs of these hosts that provide services to users. For those hosts that serve only as users, it cannot know their RIDs. To this end, the attacker cannot find vulnerable hosts by directly sending packets to the hosts. However, the attacker is still able to send packets to the hosts that provide services. Fortunately, the number of hosts that provide services only amounts to a small fraction of the total number of hosts (less than 1 %).

Second, in order to recruit zombies, an attacker can embed viruses, Trojans, worms or other malware into data/web pages provided by the servers. However, the popular servers such as Google and Yahoo are unlikely to host malware. Although some unpopular servers may provide a platform for attackers to embed viruses, their user population is relatively small. Besides, according to the Trend Micro 2011 Threat Predictions [21], more than 80 % of top malware is delivered to the user's systems via the web. Moreover, after an attacker recruits many zombies, it still needs to send attack commands to these zombies. From this point, the attacker's ASR needs to know the RIDs or where to find the RIDs of these zombies. If a zombie does not provide service, the attacker's ASR cannot know its IDMS and RID if the zombie does not send packets to the attacker. However, the zombies may have some methods to "call home" and permit a return path, so that the attacker's command can also be sent to the zombies. Here, a critical point is that a "call home" packet from a zombie should be forwarded to the zombie's ASR first, which makes the ASR an ideal place to detect or identify whether or not a host is a zombie [22]. This prevents zombies from calling home as well as from port scanning.

By encoding the SID of the service provided by the server into the viruses, and making zombies simultaneously attack a target on a specific date and time, an attacker can still attack a server. However, this type of attack cannot be monitored by the attacker, and it is much less harmful than other attacks. Additionally, an attacker needs to resolve the RID of a victim by sending mapping requests to the IDMS of the victim, which makes the IDMS an ideal place to detect such attacks.

One may argue that an attacker may try to attack the IDMSs. However, in our proposed mechanism, the packets sent by the attacker cannot be forwarded to the IDMS. If the attacker sends a number of packets with different destinations aiming at overwhelming a server, the IDMSs of AIDs are selected by users and a block of AIDs may subscribe to different IDMSs. Additionally, a host's ASR is able to identify it if it sends packets to significantly more destinations than normal AIDs. Moreover, the caching mechanism used by the ASRs can further alleviate the traffic load sent to the IDMSs.

10.3.3   Numerical Analysis

In this section, we present numerical results based on the CAIDA "DDoS Attack 2007" Data set [23]. Relevant results show that even in the case of many zombies attacking a victim, our proposed identifier-separating mapping mechanism can help to detect such DDoS attacks.

As shown in Fig. 10.9, we can observe that during the period for 0 to about 1,530 s, the average traffic sent to the victim is about 378 packets per second. After that, the average traffic sent to the victim is increased to about 160,000 packets per second. This value is about 420 times higher than the average traffic load during the period of 0 to about 1,530 s.

We are focusing on the number of the mapping requests (per second) sent to the IDMS of the victim and how it helps prevent DDoS attacks. From this point, we assume that, for each ASR, if it receives a packet destined to the victim, but cannot find the mapping of the victim, it will send a mapping request to the IDMS of the victim. Whenever the IDMS receives the mapping request, it will send the corresponding mapping of the victim to the ASR. Then, the ASR will cache the victim's mapping and further set a cache timeout for this mapping. After that, the ASR does not need to send mapping requests to the IDMS when it receives subsequent packets to the victim. Besides, we assume that, if the ASR finds the mapping of the victim in its local cache when it receives a packet to the victim, it will update the cache timeout of the mapping to a default value (e.g., 1 min). In our analysis, we

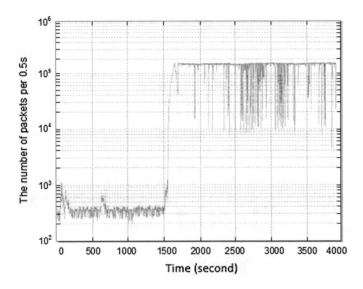

Fig. 10.9 The number of the packets that were sent to the victim per second versus time. Reprinted from Ref. [20], with permission from IEEE

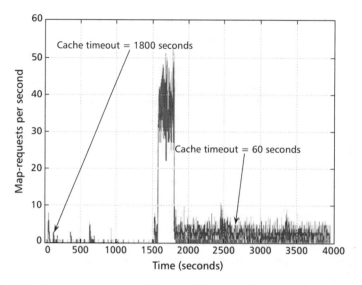

Fig. 10.10 Mapping requests per second. Reprinted from Ref. [20], with permission from IEEE

have 8,909 ASRs and count the total number of the mapping requests that were sent by these ASRs per second.

As shown in Fig. 10.10, we can find the number of mapping requests per second when the cache timeout are 60 s and 1,800 s. In this figure, we can observe that the number of the mapping requests per second is less than 10 during the period from time 0 to about 1530 s, while the number of the mapping requests per second is 1 or 0 at most of the time. After time 1530 s, however, the number of the mapping requests increases. Particularly when the number of the mapping requests is 8 at time 1,579 s, it suddenly increases to 32 at time 1,580 s. Then, the average number of the mapping requests is about 37 during the period from time 1,580 to 1,801 s. After that, the average number of the mapping requests reduces to less than 10 during the period from time 1,802 to about 4,000 s. Note that these trends are true in the cases that the cache timeout are 60 and 1800 s. Based on these observations, we can conclude that the number of the mapping requests per second is an adequate metric to detect DDoS attacks.

As shown in Fig. 10.11, we can find that it is likely to receive an earlier warning of the attack if we use the number of the mapping requests per second to detect DDoS attacks in CUSUM [24]. After we set the threshold to 1 (i.e., $g_n > 1$ indicates an attack), we can observe that g_n is larger than 1 only after time 1,583 s, if we use the number of the packets that were sent to the victim per second to detect DDoS attacks. However, if we use the number of the mapping requests per second to detect DDoS attacks, we will get three warnings of possible DDoS attacks before time 1,500 s. Besides, even if we increase the threshold to 10, we will get two warnings of possible DDoS attacks before time 1,500 s. Additionally, in the present example, compared to using the number of the packets that were sent to the victim per second, it is beneficial to use the number of the mapping requests per second to detect DDoS attacks, even if we only consider the case after time 1,500 s. Moreover, as presented in Fig. 10.11, if we use the number of the mapping requests per second to detect DDoS attacks, the time that g_n becomes larger than 1, 10, or 20 is time 1,529, 1,533, or 1,541 s. If we use the number of the packets that were sent to the victim per second to detect DDoS attacks, the time that g_n becomes larger than 1, 10 or 20 is time 1,584, 1,589 and 1,592 s, respectively. That is, compared with using the number of the packets that were sent to the victim, DDoS attacks can be detected 50 s earlier if we use the number of the mapping requests per second to detect DDoS attacks.

One may argue that an attacker is able to attack the victim by controlling the number of mapping requests and employing more hosts attaching to an ASR. In this case, however, the ASR is able to detect the attack easily by counting the number of the AIDs included in the packets that were sent to the victim.

In our analysis, we have collected the measurements for the number of the AIDs included in the packets that were sent to a victim during every minute for a 24 h period. These measurements were based on the normal network traffic traces that were collected from BJTU (Beijing Jiaotong University) campus network (collected on 12 October 2008).

Here, we assume M is a random variable, which is used to represent the number of the AIDs included in the packets that were sent to the ten most popular destinations. Then, we can use the histogram of the measurements associated with the ten most popular destinations to estimate the cumulative distribution of M (i.e., the solid curve in Fig. 10.12).

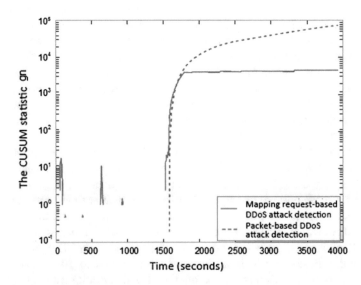

Fig. 10.11 Illustration of the benefits of identifier separation on DDoS attacks. Reprinted from Ref. [20], with permission from IEEE

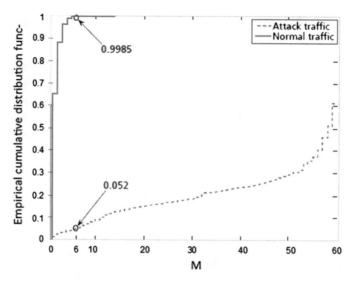

Fig. 10.12 The cumulative distribution function of M. Reprinted from Ref. [20], with permission from IEEE

From the solid curve in Fig. 10.12, we can observe that, for the normal network traffic traces, M is less than 6 with estimated probability larger than 99.85 %. Besides, a similar analysis shows that, for the CAIDA "DDoS Attack 2007" Dataset, M is less than 6 with estimated probability smaller than 0.52 %. That is, an ASR is able to easily detect such attacking cases.

However, according to the CAIDA "DDoS Attack 2007" Dataset, "only attack traffic to the victim and responses to the attack from the victim are included in the traces, and non-attack traffic has as much as possible been removed" [23], so the above results may be biased.

In order to verify the effectiveness of the above results, as well as verify the false-positive rate or the negative rate of using the number of the mapping requests per second to detect DDoS attacks, we have conducted extensive simulations since the network security community lacks thousands of suitable data sets of real large-scale DDoS attacks. Particularly, we use the packet traces destined to the ten most popular destinations as the background traffic and add DDoS attack traffic onto these traces. Meanwhile, in our simulation, we use the essential DDoS attack parameters in [25] (e.g., 5–10-min attack duration, 50–100 packets per second of attack flows and so on) and randomly choose the sources of the attack flows from the AID space within BJTU campus network.

From the simulation, we can find that using the number of the mapping requests facilitates early detection of DDoS attacks. Additionally, we can also find that, if the number of the mapping requests per second is used to detect DDoS attacks, the false-positive rate is 3.85 %, which is significantly smaller than the false-positive rate (37.2 %) if the number of the packets that were sent to the victim per second is used. Similarly, if the number of the mapping requests per second is used to detect

DDoS attacks, the false-negative rate is 1.28 %, which is also less than the false-negative rate (4.56 %) if the number of the packets that were sent to the victim per second is used.

In conclusion, once a DDoS attack is detected, our proposed identifier separation mechanism can make it convenient to prevent the DDoS attack. Once an ASR receives such a notification, it can use the results illustrated in Fig. 10.12 to detect whether there is DDoS attack traffic destined for the victim. If so, it can drop the offending traffic.

10.4   Mitigation of Worm Propagation in SINET

10.4.1   Worm Propagation

With the rise of the complex network applications, worms have become one of the major threats against network security [26]. They can infect millions of hosts in a short time, and the infected hosts can be recruited as the zombies that can be manipulated to cause unprecedented damage. For example, on 24 January 2003, Slammer rapidly spread throughout the traditional network because of its superfast scan rate (90 % of vulnerable hosts were infected within 10 min). Meanwhile, the enormous scan packets of Slammer caused a global-scale DDoS attack on the traditional network. Six months later, Blaster appeared and spread around more than 188,000 hosts within 2 h. Additionally, Witty, detected in 2004, infected 160 hosts in the last 30 s. Moreover, in order to spread faster, a routing worm appeared; it can use Border Gateway Protocol (BGP) routing information to decrease the scanning space without ignoring any potential hosts, and then its spread rate can be increased by two or three times. In recent years, many other worms (e.g., Conficker [27] and C-Worm [28]) have appeared. They are more intelligent and have caused much more substantial damage to the traditional network.

When the paradigm of SINET comes into being, it is worth discussing whether this new paradigm can provide better security capability than the traditional network. From this point, we study the damage of worm spread, which is inevitable in the traditional network and the incoming SINET and further model the mitigation of worm propagation in Sect. 10.3.2. Through the quantitative comparison between the traditional network and the incoming SINET, we can find that the incoming SINET can better alleviate worm propagation.

10.4.2   Modeling Mitigation of Worm Propagation

Up to now, two typical aspects in the study of basic worm propagation models have existed. One is based on the epidemiology model, and a typical instance is the SIR model [9]. This model can provide a qualitative understanding of worm spread by adopting different nonlinear equations. The other is founded on the discrete time model, and a typical instance is the AAWP model [10]. This model can describe the spread of active worms by taking advantage of deterministic approximation and can also explain why virtually most worms will be slow in global prevalence to some extent.

In this section, we model the mitigation of worm propagation between the traditional network and the incoming SINET and analyze the mitigation of worm propagation by using AAWP and SIR models. Our study is embodied with three aspects: address semantics, address space and mapping delay. Notice that we assume the address space size of SINET (AID space + RID space) is also 2^{32}, like that of the traditional network.

Address Semantics. Based on the AAWP model, we illustrate the influence of address semantics on worm propagation by calculating the number of infected hosts between the traditional network and the incoming SINET as follows:

In the traditional network, the IP address includes dual semantics (location and identifier). If we assume worms can define the size of scanning space as Ω, then the probability that any host is hit by one scan is $1/\Omega$. Besides, if m_i and n_i denote the total number of vulnerable hosts (including the infected ones) and the number of infected hosts at time tick i ($i \geq 0$), respectively, then the number of the newly infected hosts can be computed by $(m_i - n_i)[1 - (1 - 1/\Omega)^{sn_i}]$ (s is the scanning rate) [10]. Additionally, if we assume that d and p denote the death rate and the patching rate, then there will be $(d + p)n_i$ infected hosts that will change to either vulnerable host without being infected or invulnerable hosts on the next time tick. Meanwhile, the total number of vulnerable hosts will be reduced to $(1 - p)m_i$. Accordingly, on the next time tick, the total number of infected hosts (denoted by n_{i+1}) can be calculated by Eq. 10.7:

$$n_{i+1} = (1 - d - p)n_i + [(1 - p)^i N - n_i][1 - (1 - 1/\Omega)^{sn_i}], \qquad (10.7)$$

where n_0 is the initial number of infected hosts before worms spread ($n_0 = h$), and m_0 is the number of vulnerable hosts ($m_0 = N$).

In the incoming SINET, the dual semantics of the IP address can be resolved by the identifier separating; the location information of hosts (RIDs) can be sedulously concealed. Additionally, the feasible flat AIDs also make it more difficult for worms to surmise the AID space, because they have no idea of the corresponding addressing law. In order to achieve the consistency, we also suppose the size of the AID space is 2^{32}. Accordingly, on the next time tick the number of total infected hosts (denoted by n'_{i+1}) will change to Eq. 10.8:

$$n'_{i+1} = (1 - d - p)n'_i + [(1 - p)^i N - n'_i]\left[1 - \left(1 - 1/2^{32}\right)^{sn'_i}\right], \qquad (10.8)$$

where n'_i is the total number of infected hosts at time tick i $(i \geq 0)$ in SINET, and the assumption of other parameters is the same as that in the traditional network.

Address Space. Based on the AAWP model, we illustrate the influence of the address space on worm propagation by calculating the number of infected hosts between the traditional network and the incoming SINET as follows:

In the traditional network, the IP address space has been divided into the identifier space and the locator space. Particularly, we suppose that worms have no idea of the location information of the IP address, and they only use the random scanning to infect hosts. In order to spread effectively, worms need to scan the entire IP address space. Therefore, Ω in Eq. 10.7 is 2^{32}. Accordingly, on the next time tick, the total number of infected hosts can be calculated by Eq. 10.9:

$$n_{i+1} = (1 - d - p)n_i + \left[(1-p)^i N - n_i\right]\left[1 - (1 - 1/2^{32})^{sn_i}\right]. \qquad (10.9)$$

In the incoming SINET, a part of the address space is used as the RID that does not represent the identifier of the corresponding host. Therefore, it is meaningless for worms to scan the RID space. Note that the probability that any address is hit by one scan is $1/2^{32}$ during the random scanning. Accordingly, on the next time tick the total number of infected hosts will change to Eq. 10.10:

$$n'_{i+1} = (1 - d - p)n'_i + \left[(1-p)^i N - n'_i\right]\left[1 - (1 - q/2^{32})^{sn'_i}\right], \qquad (10.10)$$

where q denotes the probability that the scanned address is an AID.

In reality, q can be calculated by Eq. 10.11:

$$q = \frac{\text{size of AID space}}{\text{size of AID space} + \text{size of RID space}}. \qquad (10.11)$$

Mapping Delay. In the incoming SINET, when a worm tries to scan an AID, the ASR must first achieve the mapping information for this AID from the corresponding IDMS. Hence, the mapping delay may mitigate worm propagation in a manner. However, the AAWP model is a discrete time model that is not able to felicitously embody the influence on worm propagation. Therefore, we recur to the classical SIR model, which assumes that some infectious hosts can either recover or die by patching or closing during the worm spread, and these hosts are immune to the worm forever. Accordingly, each host will stay in one of the following three states at anytime: susceptible, infectious or removed.

The classical SIR model can be defined as Eq. 10.12:

$$\begin{cases} \frac{dJ(t)}{dt} = \beta(\tau)J(t)[M - J(t)] \\ \frac{dI(t)}{dt} = \beta(\tau)S(t)I(t) - \gamma I(t) \\ \frac{dR(t)}{dt} = \gamma I(t) \\ J(t) = I(t) + R(t) = M - S(t) \end{cases} \qquad (10.12)$$

In Eq. 10.12, J(t) is the number of infected hosts at time t, including the infectious and removed hosts. R(t) is the number of removed hosts from previously infectious hosts at time t. I(t) is the number of infectious hosts at time t. S(t) is the number of susceptible hosts at time t. N is the total number of vulnerable hosts. $\beta(\tau)$ is the infection rate that is determined by the impact of infection delay τ (τ is the time required by a worm to infect another susceptible host from some infectious hosts). γ is the removal rate of the infectious hosts.

To strongly indicate the effectiveness of the mapping delay, we can calculate $\beta(\tau)$ as Eq. 10.13, without regard for other factors:

$$\beta(\tau) = \beta_0 f(\tau). \tag{10.13}$$

In Eq. 10.13, $f(\tau)$ is the function of the infection delay τ. β_0 is the initial infection rate, and it is a universal and constant value.

In general cases, when the infection delay τ is longer, the infection rate $f(\tau)$ is lower. Accordingly, we can calculate $f(\tau)$ as Eq. 10.14:

$$f(\tau) = e^{-\eta\tau}, \tag{10.14}$$

where η is used to adjust the sensitivity of the infection rate, and $\eta = 0$ means the constant infection rate.

In the traditional network, in order to facilitate the analysis, we assume the infection delay (denoted by u) is constant. Accordingly, the infection rate of the traditional network (denoted by β_N) can be calculated by Eq. 10.15:

$$\beta_N = \beta(u) = \beta_0 f(\tau) = \beta_0 e^{-\eta u}. \tag{10.15}$$

In the incoming SINET, we also assume the mapping delay (denoted by v) is constant. Since the mapping delay in the incoming SINET is the additional time during the worm propagation, the corresponding infection delay can be calculated as $u + v$. Accordingly, the infection rate of the incoming SINET (denoted by β_S) can be calculated by Eq. 10.16:

$$\beta_S = \beta(u+v) = \beta_0 f(u+v) = \beta_0 e^{-\eta(u+v)}. \tag{10.16}$$

10.4.3   Numerical Analysis and Discussion

Based on the factual data, we give a quantitative comparison between the traditional network and the incoming SINET in this section. First, we analyze the numerical solutions of the above-mentioned equations and discuss the mitigation of worm propagation in the incoming SINET. Then, we discuss the worm detection based on computational intelligence in the incoming SINET.

Similar to Sect. 10.3.2, our simulation is also embodied in three aspects: address semantics, address space and mapping delay.

Address Semantics. Referring to [10], we use the real parameters that simulate the Code Red v2 worm in this simulation. We assume that 500,000 vulnerable hosts exist, and the worm starts on a single host ($n_0 = 1$). Additionally, we suppose that the worm performs two scans per second and takes 1 s to infect a host. We also set the death rate d to 0.00002 per second as well as set the patching rate p to 0.000002 per second. In the traditional network, we assume that the worm is able to use the information provided by BGP routing tables and Class A address allocations. Therefore, referring to [29], we can draw a conclusion that the size of scanning space Ω is 232/3.5 and 232/2.21, respectively. In the incoming SINET, since AID/RID separation has resolved the dual semantics of the IP address, the worm only uses the random scan, and the size of scanning space is 232.

According to Eqs. 10.7 and 10.8, we compare the different numbers of infected hosts as shown in Fig. 10.13.

From Fig. 10.13, we can observe that the total number of infected hosts in the incoming SINET is smaller than that in the traditional network, and the worm propagation rate in the incoming SINET is lower than that in the traditional network. Particularly, it takes 20 h for the worm in the incoming SINET to infect 300,000 hosts, while it only takes 4 h and 8 h for the worms in the cases of BGP routing information and Class A address space to infect the same number of hosts, respectively. If the worm also uses the unwise random scan, the curve of the traditional network will be the same as that of the incoming SINET. However, this

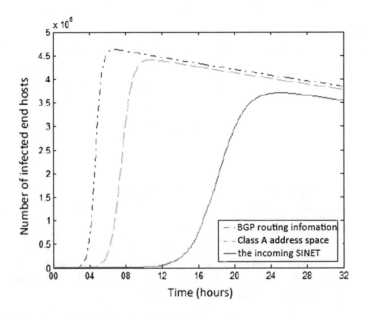

Fig. 10.13 Number of infected hosts with different scanning spaces

is a special case, and we believe that the sensible worm may try its best to avoid this situation in order to spread faster. Therefore, we can conclude that the change of address semantics in the incoming SINET can help to mitigate worm propagation.

Address Space. In this simulation, we also compare the number of infected hosts with different identifier probabilities. Here, we set the identifier probability q to 0.7, 0.8 and 0.9, respectively.

According to Eqs. 10.9 and 10.10, we depict the curves with different identifier probabilities, which is shown in Fig. 10.14.

From Fig. 10.14, we can observe that, in the traditional network, when the identifier probability q is 1, the number of infected hosts is the largest; when the identifier probability q decreases from 0.9 to 0.7, the number of infected hosts is significantly reduced. Accordingly, in order to rein in worm spread, we may attempt to reduce the identifier space. However, this method may be inapplicable to the scarce address space. Therefore, we should find a trade-off between worm spread and address space in practice.

Mapping Delay. As mentioned before, the mapping delay can help to reduce the infection rate as well as exert an influence on worm propagation. Referring to [8], we set $N = 1,000,000$, $\eta = 0.1$, $\gamma = 0.05$ and $\beta_0 = 0.8/N$. From [29], we can find that Slammer infected about 75,000 Microsoft SQL Servers, and the number of infected hosts doubled every 8.5 s. Thus, we assume the infection delay u is 8.5 s in the traditional network. Additionally, there are several mapping services, such as the Alternative Topology (ALT)-based mapping service, recursive-Distributed Hash Table (recursive-DHT)-based mapping service and iterative-Distributed Hash

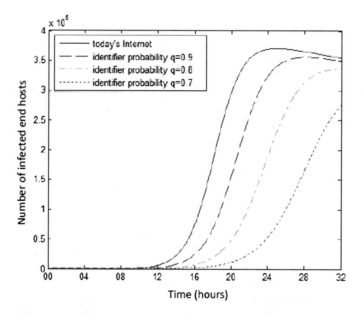

Fig. 10.14 Number of infected hosts with different identifier probabilities

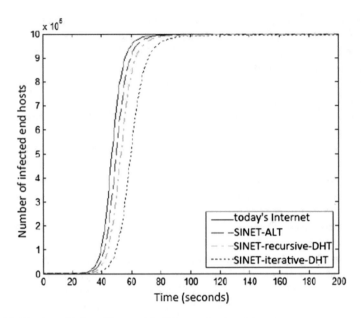

Fig. 10.15 Number of infected hosts with different mapping delays

Table (iterative-DHT)-based mapping service. The average mapping delay in each mapping service is significantly different. Therefore, we use the median mapping delay in [30] (0.5, 1 and 2 s) as the mapping delay v. Then, we calculate the infection delay in SINET-ALT, SINET-recursive-DHT and SINET-iterative-DHT as 9, 9.5 and 10.5 s.

According to Eqs. 10.12, 10.15 and 10.16, we compare the number of infected hosts with different mapping delays in Fig. 10.15 and compare the number of infectious hosts with different mapping delays in Fig. 10.16.

From Fig. 10.15, we can observe: when the mapping delay is longer, the number of infected hosts is smaller. For example, the number of infected hosts at time 60 s in the traditional network without any mapping service is about 950,000, while the number of infected hosts with an SINET-iterative-DHT mapping service is reduced to approximately 500,000. From this figure, we can also observe that the longer the mapping delay is, the lower the worm propagation rate becomes. Meanwhile, the number of infectious hosts is also affected by the mapping delay.

As shown in Fig. 10.16, the longer mapping delay makes the maximum number of infectious hosts smaller. The reason can be explained as: $\beta(\tau)$ is a main parameter that changes the number of infectious host $I(t)$. However, since the mapping delay has a significant influence on the normal and usual communication, we do not advocate controlling worm spread by increasing the mapping delay, although it can mitigate worm propagation.

To sum up, the characteristics of the incoming SINET, including the changes of address semantics, address space and mapping delay, play an important role to

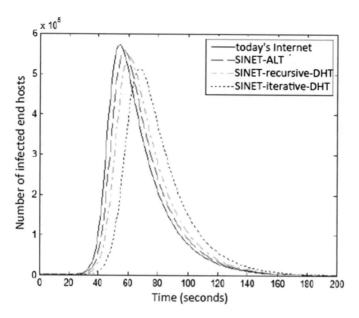

Fig. 10.16 Number of infectious hosts with different mapping delays

mitigate worm propagation. Meanwhile, the incoming SINET is more resistant to worm propagation than the traditional network.

Although worm propagation can obviously be mitigated in the incoming SINET, worms will still exist. The mitigation of worm propagation may result in some difficulties in detecting worms. However, worm detection based on computational intelligence can also benefit from the paradigm of the incoming SINET.

First of all, the ASR is the most crucial infrastructure in the incoming SINET, and nearly all the communications among hosts need to be accomplished with their help. Hence, multi-agent technology can be applied to the ASRs to detect worms. Besides, in order to make the ASRs more intelligent, we can also combine the multi-agent technology with other different fields (e.g., artificial intelligence, fuzzy logic). Moreover, by means of using cooperative intelligent agents distributed in the ASRs, worm detection will become more feasible and impactful.

Second, when worms or other threats want to launch an attack, the ASRs should send the mapping requests to resolve the corresponding RIDs first. Therefore, worms or other threats can be identified and diagnosed by the mapping request traffic. Meanwhile, since the mapping request traffic is simple and single dimensional, it is unlike the complicated and high-dimensional network traffic. The anomaly detection based on neural networks, machine learning or data mining could significantly reduce the false alarm rate.

Last but not least, the change of address semantics and address space in the incoming SINET can lower the detection limit of worm detection based on computational intelligence, which will further improve the detection efficiency.

10.5   Conclusion

First, this chapter proposes an anomaly detection response mechanism based on mapping requests. By using the cumulative sum algorithm to change point detection, this mechanism introduces the anomalous traffic detection of mapping requests to diagnose the aberrant network behaviors. Second, this chapter proposes a scalable and efficient identifier-separating mapping mechanism and explains how this mechanism makes it difficult for DDoS attackers to control botnets. Third, this chapter systematically analyzes the mitigation of worm propagation and indicates that the incoming SINET is more resistant to worm propagation than the traditional network.

References

1. Lu K, Wu D, Fan J et al (2007) Robust and efficient detection of DDoS attacks for large-scale internet. Comput Netw 51(18):5036–5056
2. Liu H, Kim MS (2010) Real-time detection of stealthy DDoS attacks using time-series decomposition. In: 2010 IEEE international conference on communications
3. Jin S, Yeung D S (2004) A covariance analysis model for DDoS attack detection. In: 2004 IEEE international conference on communications
4. Lakhina A, Crovella M, Diot C (2005) Mining anomalies using traffic feature distributions. ACM SIGCOMM Comput Commun Rev 35(4):217–228
5. Wang W, Battiti R (2006) Identifying intrusions in computer networks with principal component analysis. In: The 1st international conference on availability, reliability and security
6. Patcha A, Park JM (2007) An overview of anomaly detection techniques: existing solutions and latest technological trends. Comput Netw 51(12):3448–3470
7. Wang Y, Wang C (2003). Modeling the effects of timing parameters on virus propagation. In: The 2003 ACM workshop on Rapid Malcode
8. Zou CC, Gong W, Towsley D (2002) Code red worm propagation modeling and analysis. In: The 9th ACM conference on computer and communications security
9. Frauenthal JC (1980) Mathematical modeling in epidemiology. Springer
10. Chen Z, Gao L, Kwiaty K (2003) Modeling the spread of active worms. In: 22nd annual joint conference of the IEEE computer and communications
11. Wan M, Zhang HK, Wu TY et al (2012) Anomaly detection and response approach based on mapping requests. Secur Commun Netw 7(12):2277–2292
12. Siris VA, Papagalou F (2006) Application of anomaly detection algorithms for detecting SYN flooding attacks. Comput Commun 29(9):1433–1442
13. Wang H, Zhang D, Shin KG (2002) Detecting SYN flooding attacks. In: 21st annual joint conference of the IEEE computer and communications societies
14. Bu S, Wang R, Zhou H (2008) Anomaly network traffic detection based on auto-adapted parameters method. In: The 4th international conference on wireless communications, networking and mobile computing
15. Hellerstein JL, Zhang F, Shahabuddin P (2001) A statistical approach to predictive detection. Comput Netw 35(1):77–95
16. Lucas JM, Saccucci MS (1990) Exponentially weighted moving average control schemes: properties and enhancements. Technometrics 32(1):1–12

17. Takada HH, Hofmann U (2004). Application and analyses of cumulative sum to detect highly distributed denial of service attacks using different attack traffic patterns. http://www.ist-intermon.org/dissemination/newsletter7.pdf

18. Shamir A, Tauman Y (2001) Improved online/offline signature schemes. Advances in Cryptology—Crypto 2001. Springer, Berlin, pp 355–367

19. Srivastava A (2006) Electronic signatures: a brief review of the literature. In: The 8th international conference on electronic commerce: the new e-commerce: innovations for conquering current barriers, obstacles and limitations to conducting successful business on the internet

20. Luo H, Lin Y, Zhang H et al (2013) Preventing DDoS attacks by identifier/locator separation. IEEE Netw 27(6):60–65

21. Trend Micro 2011 Threat Predictions: mobile devices and diversity of operating systems will expand cybercriminal reach. http://trendmicro.mediaroom.com/index.php?s=43&news_item=851&type=archived&year=2010

22. Wang K, Luo H, Qin Y (2011). Identifier/locator separation: a worm detection and prevention perspective. In 2011 international conference on advanced intelligence and awareness

23. Hick P, Aben E, Claffy K et al (2007) The CAIDA DDoS Attack 2007 Dataset. http://www.caida.org/data/passive/ddos-20070804_dataset.xml

24. Brodsky E, Darkhovsky BS (1993) Nonparametric methods in change point problems. Springer Science & Business Media

25. Moore D, Shannon C, Brown DJ et al (2006) Inferring internet denial-of-service activity. ACM Trans Comput Syst (TOCS) 24(2):115–139

26. Wan M, Liu Y, Tang J et al (2012) Locator/identifier separation: comparison and analysis on the mitigation of worm propagation. Int J Comput Intell Syst 5(5):868–877

27. McMillan R (2009) Conficker worm sinks French navy network. http://www.pcworld.com/article/159224/conficker_worm_sinks_french_navy_network.html. Accessed 09 Feb 2009

28. Yu W, Wang X, Calyam P et al (2011) Modeling and detection of camouflaging worm. IEEE Trans Dependable Secure Comput 8(3):377–390

29. Costa M, Crowcroft J, Castro M et al (2005) Vigilante: end-to-end containment of internet worms. ACM SIGOPS Oper Syst Rev 39(5):133–147

30. Coras F (2009) CoreSim: a simulator for evaluating LISP mapping systems. Master's thesis, Technical University of Cluj-Napoca

Part III
Development and Applications

Chapter 11
System Development of SINET

In this chapter, the technical details of a SINET prototype are briefly summarized. We begin with an overview of the SINET prototype system with its basic design in Sect. 11.1. A description of the core functionalities of SINET, such as access identifier configuration, unified access authentication and access identifier mapping, is introduced in Sect. 11.2. Furthermore, we describe the key tactics of the subsystem implementation including the kernel network stack and the development of essential functional modules in Sect. 11.3. Lastly, we deploy the experimental testbed with a list of typical devices in Sect. 11.4. On these devices, we develop several applications to test the feasibility and reliability of the SINET prototype.

11.1 Overview

Each successful system relies on a solid foundation of architecture theories and engineering principles. Based on the general design mentioned in previous chapters, the SINET prototype system is developed as an integrated networking system that supports accessing multiple services and devices. We leverage a common set of programming languages and development tools as well as typical hardware platforms. The aim is to overcome the serious issues of the current Internet, such as poor scalability and security, poor support for mobility, low resource utilization ratio and energy harvesting.

The previous chapters have introduced the SINET principle as well as several of the supported mechanisms and technologies. In order to realize the advantages and check the rationality, we have built a primary prototype system of SINET. This prototype system can help to shorten the development time and reduce the costs of system development as well, which is one of the most important prerequisites for the industrialized promotion.

As illustrated in Fig. 11.1, the SINET prototype system consists of five parts: *the Access Subsystem, Routing Subsystem, Service Subsystem, Connection Subsystem*

© Springer-Verlag Berlin Heidelberg 2016
H. Zhang et al., *Smart Collaborative Identifier Network*,
DOI 10.1007/978-3-662-49143-0_11

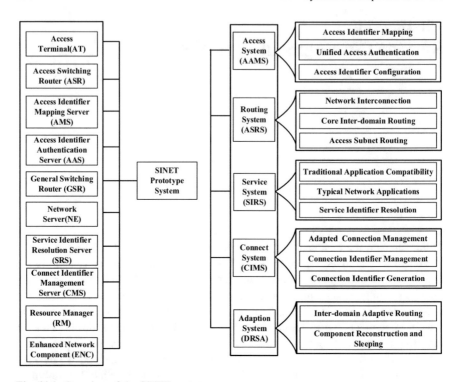

Fig. 11.1 Overview of the SINET prototype system

and *Adaption Subsystem*. The development work involves devices such as Access Terminals, Access Switching Routers (ASR), the Access Identifier Mapping Server (AMS), Access Identifier Authentication Server (AAS), General Switching Router (GSR), Network Servers, Service Identifier Resolution Server (SRS), Connection Identifier Management Server (CMS), Resource Manager (RM) and Enhanced Network Component (ENC).

11.2 Core Functionalities

As mentioned in the previous chapters, the SINET is comprised of three layers. The *Network Component Layer* is designed to perform the general switching and routing mechanisms and protocols. It realizes the unified access of heterogeneous terminals by introducing the variable-length access identifier theory. The inherent nature of the access authentication mechanism guarantees the legal utilization of network resources. The isolation mechanism between the access network and core network improves the network scalability. Meanwhile, the separation mechanism between identity and location provides better support for mobility. The *Pervasive*

Service Layer is responsible for the unified naming and description of services by introducing a *Service Identifier (SID)*. The support for the *Connection Identifier (CID)* and multiple connection mapping mechanisms makes the acquirement process of network services more flexible and provides guarantees for service quality. The *Resource Adaption Layer* dynamically adapts network resources and builds network families through perceiving service demands and network status so as to satisfy the service demands and improve the quality of experience. In order to realize the above advantages and verify the correctness of theories, the SINET prototype system will fulfill the core functionalities listed below.

11.2.1 Access Identifier Configuration

In SINET, the *Access Identifier (AID)* is an identification label assigned to each device participating in network communication, which is similar to an IP address in the traditional Internet. However, the length of the AID can be flexibly configured based on network demands or the processing capacity of nodes. (Byte is the unit of the AID in the SINET prototype system. The length of the AID can vary between 1 and 16 bytes).

The implementation of the access identifier configuration mainly consists of protocol stack development and specific functional implementation. In order to integrate more extensive functions, the SINET mapping protocol stack is developed in the Linux 2.6 kernel, which includes the access identifier configuration module.

11.2.2 Unified Access Authentication

Unified access authentication aims to realize a unified way for heterogeneous devices to complete the process of access and security authentication in SINET. It guarantees bidirectional trustworthiness between terminals and network. That is, only legal and registered users can access the network. Meanwhile, the specific network can merely provide access services, which can protect terminal users from fraud networks and cyber attacks.

In the SINET prototype system, unified access authentication is realized by the interactive process of access terminals, ASRs and AASs. It develops corresponding authentication protocol programs for each device. During the authentication process, the terminal identity can be obtained by extracting it from the inherent information or artificial specification. The access terminals cannot directly communicate with AASs; it has to go through the ASRs.

11.2.3   Access Identifier Mapping

Access identifier mapping, an outstanding feature that differs from the traditional Internet, is key in achieving the basic function of the SINET. It is mainly used to implement the AID-to-RID mapping mechanism of ASR on receiving data packets from legal terminals. Access identifier mapping not only separates the access network from the core network and achieves high network scalability but also provides better service continuity support for the nodes that perform handoff between different access points.

The access identifier mapping system, which is composed of ASRs and AMSs, is responsible for the AID mapping process in the SINET prototype system. ASR generates the specific RID and implements the mapping process from AID to RID when receiving the packets from the terminals with access privileges and then registers this AID-to-RID mapping item in AMS. In turn, when receiving packets from the core network, ASR performs the mapping from RID back to AID based on the known or queried mapping items and delivers it to the corresponding access terminal.

11.2.4   Access Subnet Routing

Access subnet routing is designed to solve packet routing issues when various kinds of devices join the access network. Due to the irregular, flat and differentiated nature of AID, a traditional routing protocol cannot meet the network's demands for mobility and quick convergence particularly well. However, the access subnet routing feature overcomes the above defects and implements unified routing for packets with different AIDs in the access network.

The implementation of access subset routing adopts a method that combines link state databases and distributed process modules. This routing mechanism is implemented at the application layer. We also develop a neighbor discovery module and a routing match and query module to implement the kernel-level packet routing. Applications import the calculated routing items into the kernel by the Netlink interfaces of the Linux system.

11.2.5   Core Inter-domain Routing

Core inter-domain routing is used for the cross-domain forwarding of the packets in core network. In SINET, the concept of virtual RID space appears on the foundation of existing inter-domain routing by introducing an AID-RID mapping mechanism. It is based on the original inter-domain routing mechanism but different from the traditional routing protocol. It can achieve rational utilization of network resources by reasonable planning and dynamically using virtual RIDs.

The core inter-domain routing protocol in the SINET prototype system employs the unified-length RIDs to make the packet routing process more efficient. Meanwhile, different levels and privileges of RIDs are defined to execute different strategies so as to guarantee the service quality of packet forwarding and reasonable allocation of inter-domain network traffic.

11.2.6   Network Interconnection

The interconnectivity with the traditional Internet is in some ways the most critical part in the process of SINET deployment under the condition of existing network infrastructures. It will directly affect the promotion and application of SINET. In addition, the interconnectivity solutions are constantly developed and optimized to adapt to the changing network scale and application scenes in different development periods.

The access identifier mapping in the SINET prototype system is compatible with existing IPv4 and IPv6, which ensures the data packets from the traditional Internet can be transmitted in SINET. Meanwhile, the tunneling support for the SINET packet is added to the original network protocol of the Linux kernel, which ensures SINET packets can be transmitted in the existing Internet.

11.2.7   Service Identifier Resolution

Service identifier resolution provides resource-oriented or service-oriented information resolution for users. SID brings a permanent, unique, time-invariant and location-independent identifier to network resources and services, which is useful for resource-oriented or service-oriented data query. Service identifier resolution generates SIDs by analyzing users' network demands and obtains the corresponding resource or service description, which is necessary for the subsequent nodes to establish an appropriate connection.

In the SINET prototype system, the service identifier resolution adopts a two-stage resolution mechanism, which is involved in distributed SRSs and the local node proxy. The former stores and maintains the SID registration information of all server nodes. It is also responsible for SID resolution queries from user nodes and the SID logging or updating operation from server nodes. The latter maintains its own registered SID items and executes its own service identifier resolution requests.

11.2.8   Typical Network Applications

Application is the ultimate criterion for testing theories. Only when meeting the requirements of network applications, the architecture can be accepted and used by the majority of people. Compared with the traditional Internet, the advantage of SINET lies in the specific service acquirement mechanism implementing the applications with the same function but more efficiently.

In the SINET prototype system, we have chosen to illustrate typical applications such as web browsing, file downloading, online video and voice call. The design of typical network applications is not only well supported for multi-services, but also shows its new features with high network performance to verify the correctness of SINET theories.

11.2.9   Compatibility with Traditional Applications

Based on the SINET protocol stack, the compatibility with traditional applications is an important precondition for SINET popularization and applications. However, there are numerous types of traditional network applications. It is impossible to replace them with the new SINET applications. For a long period of time, compatibility with traditional Internet applications is a necessity for SINET to become widely used.

In the SINET prototype system, the identifier mapping protocol stack develops a new network architecture and supports the traditional network protocol as well. The SINET service acquirement mechanism based on the extended socket realizes the characteristics of SINET while ensuring compatibility with traditional applications.

11.2.10   Connection Identifier Generation

CID is used to identify the process of obtaining services in the virtual connection module. Only the nodes with CIDs can acquire the subsequent network services. The specific CID is unchangeable in the service process, which makes handoff and service migration possible.

In the SINET prototype system, CID is created by CMSs. In the process of generating CID, CMS verifies the privilege of requesting terminals and generates a unique CID for them to identify the specific service acquirement process based on the real-time network status and network service mechanism.

11.2.11 Connection Identifier Management

Connection identifier management demonstrates SINET's good support for security and connection control features. The centralized CID management mechanism monitors the node behavior of obtaining services and provides opportunities to discover and eliminate malicious network behavior. Meanwhile, centralized authorization in the connection process facilitates the optimal utilization of network resources.

In the SINET prototype system, connection identifier management is implemented by the connection identifier management module, which fulfills functions of CID such as generation, authorization, storage, monitoring and status display. Any ongoing network connection can be broken by connection identifier management.

11.2.12 Adapted Connection Management

Adapted connection management is the negotiating process with the operable transmission protocol when nodes obtain network services. It enables the SINET architecture to expand to support new network transmission protocols in SINET. It provides abundant channel selection modes for data transmission between different nodes. Based on the adapted connection management mechanism, obtaining network services is independent of specific transmission protocol. The protocol can be used for data transmission as long as the service quality is guaranteed.

The design of adapted connection management is deployed by introducing the self-adapted connection protocol management module into the system kernel based on the SINET protocol stack, which makes the application connection establishment independent of the specific transmission protocol. It directly transmits the relevant QoS parameters to the kernel module. Then, the kernel module negotiates with the requesting nodes and service nodes according to the transmitted parameters.

11.2.13 Inter-domain Adaptive Routing

Inter-domain adaptive routing is one of the most important processes in the dynamic resource adaption mechanism. SINET selects the appropriate inter-domain network families and components for the service to optimize the inter-domain path adaptively by using multiple inter-domain traffic perceptive mechanisms and control algorithms.

Inter-domain adaptive routing is implemented by introducing a dynamic resource adaption management module on the SINET protocol stack. It can allocate the corresponding family identifier for various heterogeneous autonomous domains and collect the link status perceiving parameter in the inter-domain component so as to implement the inter-domain routing-forwarding mechanism of data flow.

11.2.14 Component Reconstruction and Sleeping

The design of the enhanced network component module requires that its sub-modules can be restructured to improve the flexibility of data transmission. Meanwhile, the separation mechanism between the control plane and data plane makes the components perceive their own conditions and regroup function modules in flexible ways so as to realize port sleeping and reduce energy consumption.

We employ NetFPGA10G as the development platform of network components and embed various functional modules into the online process to extend the functionality of network components. Meanwhile, a connection channel between the dynamic resource adaption management module and network components is established to control the behavior of the ENCs, such as port sleeping.

11.3 Subsystem Design

Based on the Linux operating system, the SINET prototype system is implemented by redesigning the kernel network stack and developing essential functional modules. The key development contents include seven parts: the SINET protocol stack, access authentication system, access mapping system, access subnet routing system, service identifier resolution system, connection identifier management system and dynamic resource adaption system.

11.3.1 Protocol Stack

The SINET protocol stack is the foundation for implementing a variety of device functions in the prototype system. The design of the SINET protocol stack is shown in Fig. 11.2.

As the core module in the SINET protocol stack, the *identifier-mapping module* is responsible for forwarding and receiving data packets over the Internet [1]. It has developed the following set of operating functions:

- *Receiving and forwarding packets.* It receives data packets from the network device driver and transmits the pending packets to the corresponding interface.
- *Packet encapsulation and decapsulation.* It adds or resolves the SINET packet header according to the relevant requirement.

Fig. 11.2 SINET protocol
stack

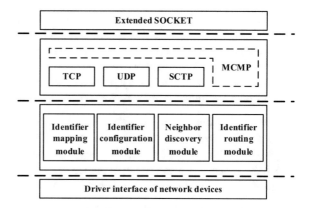

- *Forwarding packets.* It forwards the packets to the next hop according to the identifier routing information.
- *AID-to-RID mapping.* (Optional function, only required by ASR.) It employs predefined mapping functions to randomly select a suitable AID-to-RID entry.

As a relatively basic module, the *Identifier configuration module* provides interfaces for SINET nodes in the virtual network devices. This module supports the following functions:

- *Search and initialization of network devices.* It initializes essential attribute parameters of the SINET protocol stack for network devices.
- *Definition of* the *basic identifier strategy.* It supports appropriate identifier utilization for nodes in network communication.
- *Registering* the *SINET callback function.* It is used to handle NIC device affairs, such as registering, activating, renaming and closing.
- *Providing interfaces for user space.* It facilitates user configuration and identifier management.

The *neighbor discovery module* realizes the link negotiation process among neighbor nodes. It also provides AID items and interface information as well as the corresponding relationship between them. By imitating the development of ARP and the construction, transmission and receiving mechanism of the ND message in the IPv6 protocol stack, the neighbor discovery module modifies the message format and specific procedure and introduces a new secure neighbor identification mechanism to prevent neighbor fraud.

The *identifier routing module's* main duty is to maintain the kernel routing table and transmit data packets to the next hop based on the relevant lookup algorithm. This module fulfills the following functions:

- The *message interconnectivity mechanism* based on the kernel and application of Netlink implements the operation of user space and provides the interface for the kernel route configuration and management.

- *Hash tables and necessary interface functions* are appended to define a unified routing policy with variable-length identifier.
- The *device interface* is designed for classified routing lookup based on the configuration of the network interface.
- The *traditional routing query function* is inherited, which returns the next hop and relevant interface information according to the destination identifier.

The *Multi-Connection identifier Management Protocol (MCMP)* establishes a unified CID-based data transmission channel for the service requirements. It provides the mapping entries between network connections and relevant resource providers. Then, it is also used to negotiate the transmission procedure. In the frame of the SINET virtual connection theory, MCMP is developed as follows:

- The interface for negotiating, verifying, maintaining, controlling and managing CID information.
- The interface of transparent support for traditional transmission protocol.
- The new transmission protocol and congestion-controlled scheduling interface.
- The QoS-based self-adaptive scheduling mechanism.

Extended SOCKET is an optimal scheme for supporting the applications of SINET and the traditional Internet simultaneously. Through the research in the socket-calling mechanism, it judges and calls the parameters of unified kernel entry function sys_socketcall () again. Meanwhile, it adds the new socket protocol family AF_IDMP and supplies expansions and modifications to the relevant functions, such as socket (), bind (), listen (), connect (), accept (), sendto (), recv () and recvfrom ().

11.3.2   Access Authentication System

An access authentication system is one of the most important components that has to be developed in the SINET prototype system. Access authentication is the terminal access process used to realize the mutual trust between terminals and the network that needs to complete the access control protocol between the access terminal ASRs and AASs. The basic technical principle of the access mapping system is shown below. When the authenticated terminals send packets into the access network, ASR needs to match the mapping relation between AID and RID and implement the allocation of RID. Meanwhile, ASR realizes the registration, maintenance and lookup of the RID-to-AID mapping information in the AAS.

In the access authentication system of the SINET prototype system, ASR operates the access authentication protocol and maintains the accessing table of authenticated terminals by adding new authenticated terminals to the list and regularly removing the timeout items from the list. The authentication center stores the terminal identity information and verifies identities as they first access the network. When a terminal accesses the network, its identity must be authenticated, and it can

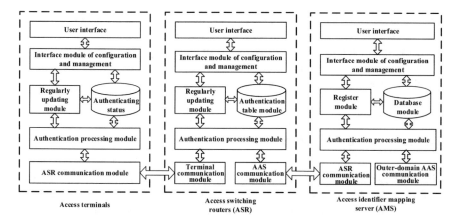

Fig. 11.3 Access authentication system

also authenticate the network reliability. Figure 11.3 describes the functions of each component of the access authentication system and their relationships.

The development of the access authentication system involves three of SINET's network entities: access terminal, ASR and AMS. These network entities have many similar functions in module design, and the developments of the following modules are nearly identical:

- *User interface module*: translates the operation of users into an instruction that can be received by the program and returns the program status back to the user interface.
- *Configuration and management interface module*: resolves programs or external instructions and implements the configuration and management of systems or programs.
- *Authentication processing module:* constructs and analyzes the authenticating messages of the access authentication protocol, handles the authentication messages and maintains authentication status.
- *Entity communication module*: transmits authentication messages to specific destinations on the basis of the SINET protocol stack, which is constructed by authentication programs. In addition, the SINET protocol stack receives the authentication messages and delivers it to the processing module for resolution.

In addition to the common modules of three network entities, network entities also have respective function modules. For access terminals, the regularly updating module handles the preset timed events. Terminals need to regularly communicate with the relevant ASRs. Authentication status is used to hold the current authentication identity of the ASR itself. The regularly updating module of the ASR frequently maintains the chain table of the access terminals in addition to handling preset timed events. The authentication table module maintains the table of authenticated access terminals and provides the interface for adding, searching, deleting and modifying the authentication items of access terminals. For AAS, the register module is used for the registration of new access terminals from the direct input of users or networks. The database module maintains the information of registered access terminals and provides the interface for establishing, adding, searching, deleting and modifying.

11.3.3   Access Mapping System

The development of the access mapping system mainly involves ASR and AMS. ASR maintains the RID for legal access terminals, registers the mapping relations to the AMS and looks up the mapping relations in the AMS, which it does not manage by itself. The AMS maintains the inter-domain mapping relations between the AID and RID. It responds to the query from the inter-domain ASR. Meanwhile, the AMS develops the inter-domain communication interface, which ensures the inter-domain queries of mapping relations between the AID and RID. All components of the access mapping system and their relations are shown in Fig. 11.4.

The development of the ASR includes two parts, the kernel and application. The kernel part implements the mapping between the AID and RID, and the application part mainly implements the allocation, maintenance and lookup of the mapping relationship. It also implements the interaction with users or other entities. The routing pool module in the application part maintains and manages the allocation and use of the identifier. The mapping table module maintains the mapping relationship between the AID and RID. The development of the AMS only includes the application part. Its service queue manages the received mapping query. The hash table maintains the mapping relationship between the AID and RID that has been registered in AMS. Remaining interfaces mainly implement the interaction with users or external entities.

In the access mapping system, the AID-to-RID mapping mechanism is implemented in the ASR's kernel mapping module. So, this module becomes the key

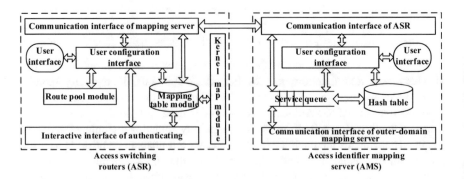

Fig. 11.4   Access mapping system

Fig. 11.5 Kernel mapping
design model of the ASR

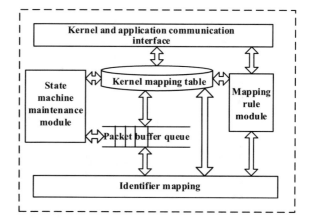

component affecting the performance and efficiency of AID mapping. Its structure
is designed as shown in Fig. 11.5. It includes six parts: the identifier mapping,
kernel mapping table, state machine maintenance module, packet buffer queue,
mapping rule module and application communication interface module. The
function of each component shown is as follows:

- *Identifier mapping*: This component mainly implements the mapping mechanism between AID and RID, including the mapping configuration of ASR, the
  selection of network interface type and classified mapping management.
- *Kernel mapping table*: This table mainly implements the storage and maintenance of AID and RID in kernel space, including the AID of nodes, mapping
  relation, priority, and weight. It provides the interfaces for adding, deleting,
  modifying and querying. Its design and implementation are more complicated
  than the mapping table module of the application part.
- *State machine maintenance module*: This module maintains the state migration
  of all items in the kernel-mapping table. It can modify the usage status by the
  condition of mapping relations. This is a mechanism that can retain the rea-
  sonability and correctness of mapping relations.
- *Packet cache queue*: This queue caches the packets that do not have the
  AID-to-RID mapping relationship and aims to reduce loss and retransmission
  due to the introduction of identifier mapping.
- *Mapping rule module*: This module mainly implements the storage of a
  user-defined mapping rule, which provides constraint conditions for identifier
  mapping.
- *Application communication interface module*: This module implements the
  communication interface between the kernel and application component.

Maintaining mapping relations in the kernel space is a complicated process. In
order to ensure the correct usage and maximum efficiency of the mapping relation,
the development process adopts the maintenance mechanism of the mapping state
machine-Map Information Detection (MID), as shown in Fig. 11.6.

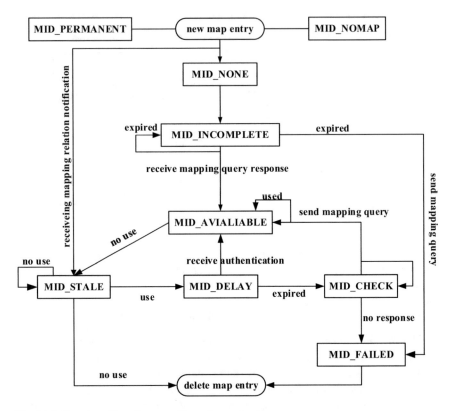

Fig. 11.6 State transition diagram of kernel mapping items

The status of mapping items include nine types, all of which are presented in the following:

- *MID_NONE*: the mapping relation is newly constructed without being labeled.
- *MID_NOMAP*: is used to label the AIDs or RIDs that do not need to perform identifier mapping.
- *MID_PERMANENT*: is the mapping relation of static configuration. It is permanently valid. State migration does not happen with the exception of artificial deleting.
- *MID_INCOMPLETE*: represents that the query request of the mapping relationship that has been sent when no response is received. The mapping relation only includes AID (or RID) while the corresponding RID (or AID) is null.
- *MID_AVAILABLE*: represents that the mapping relation is integrated and available. It will maintain the state if the mapping relation is used in the time interval that is set by the timer. Otherwise, the state will be migrated.
- *MID_STALE*: represents that the mapping relation is valid but has not been used for a while. The state migration will occur if the identifier mapping of the next

packet needs this item. Otherwise, such items will eventually be deleted by the system.

- *MID_DELAY*: represents that the mapping relation has already been used. It will return the MID_AVAILABLE status if the integrity confirmation of the mapping relation is acquired within a certain period of time. Otherwise, the state will be altered to MID_CHECK.
- *MID_CHECK*: represents that the request of the mapping relation will be limited in the condition of the available items. Its status will migrate to MID_FAILED if it does not acquire confirmation within the given time. Otherwise, its status will migrate to MID_AVAILABLE or continually issue queries of relation mapping with states unchanged.
- *MID_FAILED*: represents that the mapping item is unavailable. It will be removed on a regular or forced basis.

11.3.4 Access Subnet Routing System

The access subnet routing system is especially designed for access subnet adapting to the different access identifiers of different terminals. Based on the neighbor discovery mechanism of the SINET protocol stack, this system is developed by referencing the traditional OSPF protocol and the distributed Chord algorithm.

As shown in Fig. 11.7, the development of the access subnet routing system involves the kernel-forwarding plane and application control plane. The kernel-forwarding plane mainly implements the construction of the new routing table and forwarding mechanism of the Hash query in the kernel space. The application control plane mainly implements the interface management, link state database, routing computation and management, external routing interface and interface configuration.

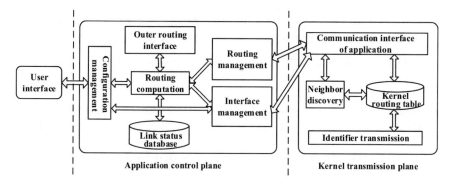

Fig. 11.7 Access subnet routing system

Specifically, the implementation of the application control plane consists of the following modules:

- *Configuration management module*: provides a configuration interface to users and implements user operations on the routing system.
- *Interface management module*: manages and collects the interface information of the access router, which facilitates the timely update of the link state database.
- *Routing management module*: delivers routing information between the applications and kernel space.
- *Link state database module*: mainly stores and maintains link connection states from the whole access network. It implements the operation interfaces for adding, querying, modifying and deleting link states.
- *Routing computation module*: performs the establishment and update of routing information, which is a key element of access subnet routing.
- *External routing interface module*: is responsible for the interaction with external routers.

The kernel transmission plane mainly implements the kernel routing table, identifier forwarding and application interface. The neighbor discovery module is the basic component of the SINET protocol stack. The implementation of access subnet routing merely calls its neighbor relations to establish a link state database on the application control plane.

11.3.5 Service Identifier Resolution System

The development of a service identifier resolution system includes a service registration and query system on the client side and a service identifier management system of SRS. The service identifier management system consists of a database module, message processing module, distributed maintenance module and foreground management interface module. The service registration and query system implements a foreground man-machine interaction interface, service identifier agent module, resolution cache module, external communication module, internal call module and so on. The relationships between the modules are shown in Fig. 11.8.

The following are the modules of the service identifier management system:

- *Database module*: implements the storage and maintenance of SID information and provides an external interface for adding, deleting, modifying, updating and so on.
- *Message processing module*: handles the input messages by foreground managers or the network and operates the SID database and returns relevant information.
- *Distributed maintenance module*: maintains the stored information of the service identifier of the distributed SRS.

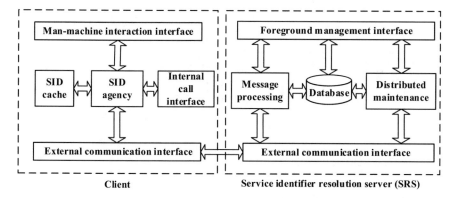

Fig. 11.8 Service identifier resolution system

- *Foreground management interface module*: provides the configuration management operations of SRS for users.

  The following are the modules of the service registration and query system:

- *Man-machine interaction interface*: provides the user interface for SID registration, query and display.
- *Service identifier agency*: represents all the operations of the SID registration and resolution on the client side and handles the messages between the SRS and other SID agencies.
- *Service identifier cache*: caches recently queried or used SIDs.
- *Internal call interface*: provides the interface of the SID resolution query for internal network applications.
- *External communication interface*: implements the communication with the SID agency and SRS.

11.3.6 Connection Identifier Management System

The overall framework of the connection identifier management system is shown in Fig. 11.9.

As shown in Fig. 11.9, CIMS fulfills the establishment and maintenance of the network connection for clients. The client/server establishes network connections by CMS based on the internal connection negotiation establishment mechanism and eventually implements the service process.

The following are the developed modules of CIMS:

- *User management interface module*: manages network connections for administrators.
- *Connection identifier generation module*: generates CIDs, which are used to acquire network services.

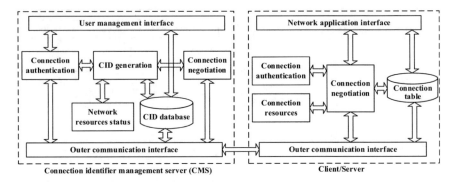

Fig. 11.9 Connection identifier management system

- *Connection identifier database module*: implements storage and maintenance of generated CIDs.
- *Network resources status module*: searches and monitors the status of network resources and provides a reference for the establishment of new connection requests.
- *Connection negotiation module*: negotiates with clients and servers to establish a new network connection.
- *Connection authentication module*: authenticates the validity of clients requesting initiation, cancellation or migration of connection.
- *External communication interface module*: implements the connection negotiation between the client and server.

The development of the client and server adopts a similar structure and function, since network services for nodes are always bidirectional. When nodes acquire network services, they may provide some kind of services, too. The development process includes the following modules:

- *Network application interface module*: provides service interfaces for network applications.
- *Connection negotiation module*: negotiates with CMS and correspondent nodes to establish network connections.
- *Connection authentication module*: authenticates the connection request from the network and ensures the validity of the network connection.
- *Connection resources module*: maintains the available resources of nodes for network transmission such as the AID and transmission protocol.
- *Connection table module*: maintains the connection that has been established for network applications.
- *External communication interface module*: is used for intercommunication with the CMS or interaction with other clients and servers.

11.3.7 Adaptive Resource Allocation System

The development of an adaptive resource allocation system includes the Resource Manager (RM) and Enhanced Network Component (ENC).

As illustrated by Fig. 11.10, RM is accomplished by integrating the major activities below: the query, mapping and forwarding operation of the service request message, monitoring the network state, topology management and NID clustering, FID encapsulation, SID-to-FID mapping and service adaptive allocation. The functions of each module are as follows:

- *SID table*: a table containing the mapping information from the SID to FID or intra-domain address.
- *PID table*: a table holding the ASN-to-FID mapping information.
- *GET packet processing module*: handles service requests and table queries and sends the resource adaption signal to the notification-processing module.
- *Topology manager*: manages and monitors network topology.
- *Network state information module*: carries out dynamic monitoring of the network status for dynamic resource adaption.
- *Notification processing module*: handles resource adaption signals and table queries and sends configuration instructions to the network components involved.
- *Path configuration module*: configures the corresponding network components following the upper-layer instructions.

As shown in Fig. 11.11, ENCs carry out the basic forwarding and sleeping function.

- *Component controller*: sends sleep/wake-up instructions to switch ports.
- *PCIEEP/DMA*: configures the communication connection between the component controller and network components.

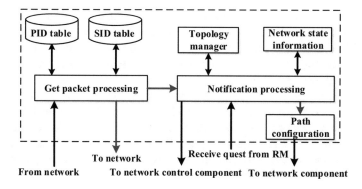

Fig. 11.10 RM design model

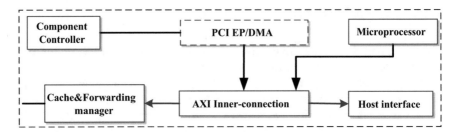

Fig. 11.11 ENC design model

- *Microprocessor*: polls EFLAGS and sets up sleep/wake-up instructions for ports.
- *Cache and forwarding manager*: sleep and caching function module of the network component.
- *Host interface*: resolves and executes specific instructions from the component controller such as adding, modifying, deleting forwarding entries and querying component status.

11.4   Prototyping and Tests

Through systematic analysis of key routing technologies in SINET, we establish a corresponding development prototype and related devices. We also build test environments and typical applications to verify the availability and structural advantages of SINET.

11.4.1   Prototyping and Products

The SINET prototype, as a pervasive service-oriented platform for long-term studies, makes it possible to compare simulation studies with real-world experiments. To facilitate the specification, execution and evaluation of experiments in complex scenarios, we deploy a core network domain and three access network domains as shown in Fig. 11.12.

Currently, the prototype consists of six or more software routers equipped with three GSRs and the same number of ASRs. The topology also includes several specific servers, such as RM, AMS, AAS and SRS. In addition, it includes various kinds of hosts and other devices. Using a Wide Area Network Simulator, we can fully simulate a real network environment. Figure 11.13 shows the actual appearance of the SINET prototype.

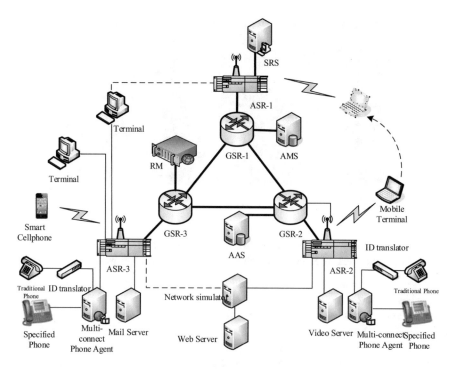

Fig. 11.12   The topology of the SINET prototype

Fig. 11.13   The SINET prototype system

To support both the increasing prototype system complexity and shorter design cycles, some of the essential SINET device products have been developed in close conjunction with related simulators and hardware emulators:

Access Switching Router (ASR). As shown in Fig. 11.14 Access switching routers (ASRs) are located between the core and access networks, connecting them.

Fig. 11.14 Access switching router

They are responsible for the access and packet transfer of the terminal users. The main functionalities of Access Switching Routers are the following:

- *Terminal user access control, including terminal verification and terminal state maintenance.*
- *Routing* the *ID assignment for the terminal users and reporting* the *mapping relationship to the Mapping Server.*
- *Handover of terminal users.*
- *Transfer of data packets from terminal users to the core network after analysis of the mapping relationship and substitution of their identifiers.*
- *Analysis of the mapping relationship and switching identifiers of the data packets sent to local terminals as well as transfer of data packets to local terminals.*

General Switching Router (GSR). As shown in Fig. 11.15, General Switching Routers (GSRs) are used to transfer routing information of identifier-based routing in the core network of SINET. They provide abundant configuration and display commands that are easy to operate. Users can readily analyze the operation of routing protocols and troubleshoot.

Access Identifier Mapping Server (AMS). As shown in Fig. 11.16, the Access identifier Mapping Server (AMS) is an important entity for location management in SINET. The device is responsible for the management of the mappings of the access identifier and routing identifier of all legal user terminals within a certain region. It also provides location inquiry for the Access Switching Router and other Access Identifier Mapping Servers.

Access Identifier Authentication Server (AAS). As shown in Fig. 11.17, the Access identifier Authentication Server (AAS) is used for access control, authentication and verification of the access network terminals intending to access the core network. When the mobile terminals need to connect to the core network, they first send access requests to the Access Switching Router. The Access Switching Router will then send a verification request to the Access Identifier Authentication Server. After verification, it will feedback related information to the Access Switching

Fig. 11.15 General switching router

Fig. 11.16 Access identifier mapping server

Fig. 11.17 Access identifier authentication server

Router. The mapping information will be created, and the terminals are allowed to access the core network. If verification fails, the terminals are blocked from accessing the core network.

Fig. 11.18 Multiple connection server

Multiple Connection Server. As shown in Fig. 11.18, the multiple connection server performs multiple connections and data transfers by employing multiple channel techniques in SINET. The use of this equipment can improve the network transmission performance significantly. In addition, it has the advantages of bandwidth aggregation and high reliability.

Multiple Connection Client. As shown in Fig. 11.19, the multiple connection client performs multiple connections and data transfers by the use of multiple channel techniques in SINET. The device can improve the receiving efficiency of the network significantly. Moreover, using multiple connection techniques has several advantages, such as preventing data interception.

Wide Area Network Simulator. As shown in Fig. 11.20, a wide area network simulator is used to simulate wide area network environments. They are capable of setting different network parameters, such as the bandwidth, delay, jitter and packet loss rate, and achieve accurate emulation of different network environments. This equipment can be used for verification and performance testing for related equipment by simulating a real network.

Fig. 11.19 Multiple connection client

Fig. 11.20 Wide area network simulator

11.4.2 Experimental Environments

Experimental environments are fundamental for the research of SINET's architecture, functionality and technological realization. In order to provide a network environment that satisfies all the system functions and performance indicators of SINET, the topology design needs to be close to the actual network deployment.

To test and verify each function of SINET, the network topology structure is designed in the SINET system prototype to be as similar as possible to the connection relations of the nodes in a real network. Limited by the number of hardware devices, different kinds of network topologies are established for testing. The role of nodes can be changed by installing different programs on the relevant hardware devices. The following are the network topology structures and application scenes:

Basic Function Scene of SINET. As shown in Fig. 11.21, the core network domain consists of three GSRs, three ASRs, an AMS and an AAS. The access network domains consist of three SRSs, a CMS, two application servers and a terminal device. This basic topology provides the below main functions:

- *Access authentications of terminal devices.*
- *RID allocation, the registration and query mechanism of ASR for authenticated terminals.*
- *The mapping mechanism of ASR between the source and destination identifier.*
- *The registration, maintenance and query of the SID.*
- *The acquirement process of basic network services.*

Access Subnet Routing Scene. As shown in Fig. 11.22, the topology consists of ten subnet access routers (AR), an ASR and three terminal devices. By setting different network parameters such as AID, we can test the working process of subset network routing and real-time status of terminal packets.

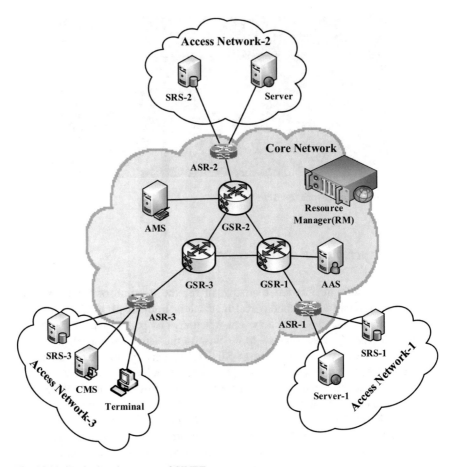

Fig. 11.21 Basic function scene of SINET

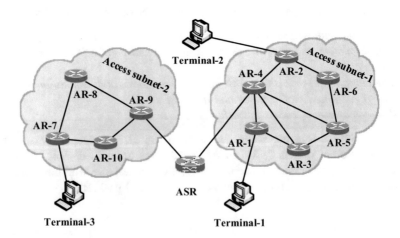

Fig. 11.22 Access subnet routing scene

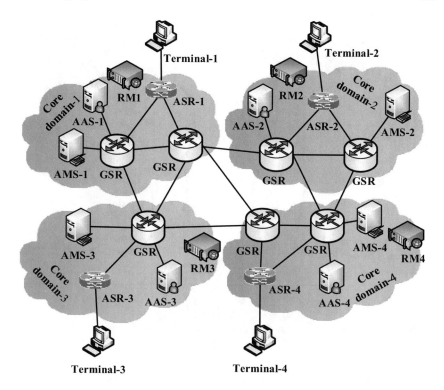

Fig. 11.23 Cross-domain routing scene

Cross-Domain Routing Scene. As shown in Fig. 11.23, the core network consists of four different core network domains.

Each domain has its own GSR, ASR, AMS and AMS. The access network domains consist of four terminals, which connect with core network domains separately. The topology scene can implement the following functions:

- *Intercommunication of inter-domain routing.*
- *Cross-domain cooperation among AMSs.*
- *Cross-domain cooperation between AMSs.*
- *Inter-domain adaptive routing.*
- *Component sleeping.*

Interconnection and Intercommunication Scene. In the topology design of the network interconnection and intercommunication, the SINET prototype system considers two stages:

In the first stage, SINET is used as an isolated island, which implements the cross-domain intercommunication across the current Internet domain. The topology is shown in Fig. 11.24. It shows that two simple SINET domains communicate with

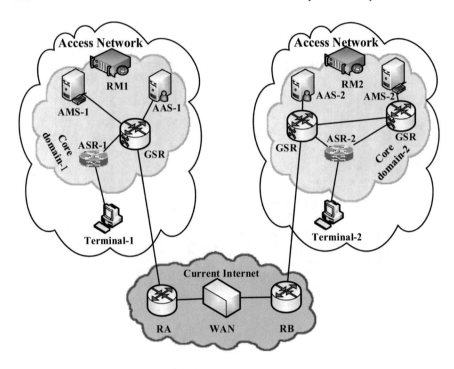

Fig. 11.24 The SINET domains' intercommunication across the existing Internet domain

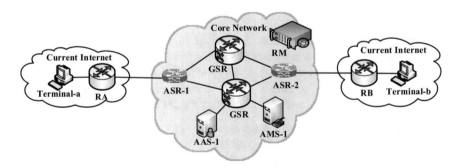

Fig. 11.25 The current Internet domains' interconnection by SINET

each other across the traditional Internet domain, which consists of a WAN simulator and two common routers.

In the next stage, the traditional Internet is used as the access network of SINET.
It can implement the intercommunication between traditional Internet domains
across SINET. The middle part in Fig. 11.25 is an integrated SINET. Two traditional Internet subnets access the SINET domain by the ASRs that lie on the
boundary.

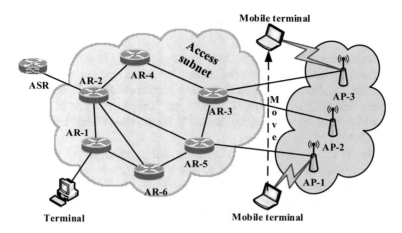

Fig. 11.26 Node mobility scene

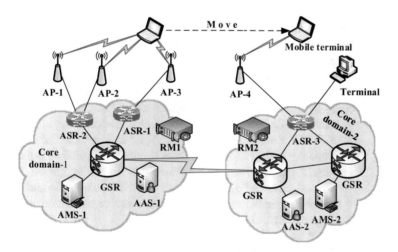

Fig. 11.27 Scene design of inter-domain and cross-domain handoff

The design of the two topology structures mainly aims to test two different tunnel mechanisms of the SINET protocol stack.

Node Mobility Scene. The node mobility scenes consist of two types: the first is the mobility within a subnet, which is shown in Fig. 11.26. The mobile terminals need to hand off between different access points of the same access router. They also need to hand off between different access points from different access routers.

In addition, the mobile terminals need to implement the cross-domain handoff between the access points from different access routers or in different core network domains. There are two small-scale SINET core domains in Fig. 11.27. The mobile terminal will implement the inter-domain and cross-domain handoff, respectively.

11.4.3   Typical Supported Applications

Implementing network applications is the most direct way to demonstrate network function and performance. Users can experience the advantages of SINET by the implementation of network applications. The implementation of applications also proves the feasibility of the SINET architecture. Therefore, a few of the typically supported applications are designed to verify the feasibility and structural advantages of SINET.

Mobile Video. In the mobility management mechanism of the traditional Internet, a new address will be allocated, which results in a longer handoff delay as well as interruption of the network connection. However, SINET ensures that their AID remains unchanged, while the user terminals are moving, which reduces the handoff delay. In order to show this feature, the SINET prototype designs the application instance of the mobile video to represent its better mobility support for terminals.

Webpage Browsing. Nowadays, webpage service is one of the most popular network applications in the traditional Internet. Users obtain services from Web servers by Web browsers, and the speed of Web browsing directly influences network efficiency and user experience. The SINET protocol stack adopts the MCMP (Multiple Connection Management Protocol), which has superior features on protocol negotiation, load balance and collective bandwidth. It improves the network utilization and efficiency of the data transmission. Meanwhile, it enhances network security by a multi-channel transmission mechanism.

File Downloading. File downloading is also a typical application in the present Internet. In the SINET prototype system, the application instance of file downloading also adopts the MCMP. With the same bandwidth limitation, a file of the same size in SINET can be downloaded faster than in the traditional Internet. Comparing download time and speed separately, SINET exhibits improved performance in transmission efficiency and network resource utilization in a more visually appealing manner.

Online Video. With the development of network technique, a multi-homed host (a host with more than two network cards) has become more and more popular in the existing Internet. Almost all laptops are multi-homed hosts (with wired and wireless network cards) but only one network card works, which results in a waste of hardware resources. Present network applications, especially online videos, place higher demands on the network bandwidth and delay. The multi-channel transmission mechanism makes up for the lack of limited bandwidth and higher latency.

Pervasive Phone. In the SINET prototype, a pervasive phone represents a design philosophy of a single network with multiple services. In other words, it can support data, video and voice services. CID makes it possible to migrate network services, and the pervasive phone is the most accepted application of service migration. In this instance, users are constantly changing, but CID remains the same. It verifies SINET's support for the mobility and connection management capacity.

In addition, the access network is separated from core network in the SINET prototype. Therefore, the devices in the core network are freed from the direct attacks of the access network, which enhances the security of the core network. Meanwhile, the privacy of the terminal identity and location can be well protected because of the AID-to-RID mapping in ASR. As for this characteristic, specific sniffer programs are also designed for testing network attacks and path information leakage to verify the security improvement in SINET.

11.5   Conclusions

In summary, this chapter introduces the design of key functionalities, subsystems, prototype and verification tests that are necessary to deploy a highly reliable, secure, mobile and service-rich SINET implementation system. The key development contents include seven parts: a SINET protocol stack, an access authentication system, an access mapping system, an access subnet routing system, a service identifier resolution system, a connection identifier management system and an adaptive resource allocation system. In addition, several essential SINET device products are introduced with the hope of being widely used in the future Internet area. These products have been applied in many security departments, campuses and several companies, including ZTE, BUPT, ChinaTelecom, China Electronics and so on.

Reference

1. Wang H (2012) Research on the identifier network mechanism and its key technologies. Dissertation, Beijing Jiaotong University

Chapter 12
Transition Schemes to SINET

The traditional network has millions of routers, and it would be extremely expensive to entirely replace them for the future network architecture. Hence, it is desirable to design a transition scheme to connect the traditional network and SINET. In this chapter, we discuss the transition schemes for SINET. The related work on the future Internet transitions is first introduced. Then, we give our consideration and analysis for SINET's transition solutions. Next, we propose a data-centric incrementally deployable transition scheme for SINET. The implementation of a proof-of-concept prototype is also presented. The experimental results obtained from the prototype indicate that the traditional network and SINET can simultaneously work together, and users in both networks can communicate with each other smoothly through the proposed schemes.

12.1 Related Work

In essence, SINET is a data-centric network architecture; several other data-centric network architectures have been proposed in recent years, e.g., DONA (Data Oriented Network Architecture) [1], Net-Inf (Network of Information) [2] and CCN (Content Centric Networking) [3–5].

In DONA, a unique and persistent name is assigned to all data or services. In order to provide data, the source needs to register the name of the data and the IP address of the source in a hierarchical resolution infrastructure. In order to obtain data, the consumer needs to send FIND to the resolution infrastructure, which further routes FIND by the name of the desired data and tries to find the desired data nearest to the consumer. Whenever the desired data are found, they are sent to the consumer through the standard IP routing mechanism. However, DONA cannot support a host-centric model, since it binds transport protocols to data names instead of IP addresses.

© Springer-Verlag Berlin Heidelberg 2016
H. Zhang et al., *Smart Collaborative Identifier Network*,
DOI 10.1007/978-3-662-49143-0_12

In NetInf, an IO (Information Object) is used to name data. Similar to DONA, in order to provide data, the source needs to register the IO of the data and the IP address of the node into an NRS (Name Resolution Server). Note that an IO may correspond to multiple IP addresses, since multiple sources may want to provide the same data. In order to obtain data, the consumer needs to send a request that contains the IO of the desired data to the NRS. The NRS then returns the IP address (es) of the desired data to the consumer. After that, the consumer can use the receiving IP address(es) to retrieve a copy of the desired data from the available source(s). However, NetInf does not solve the problem of how the host stack should be enhanced to support such a data-centric model.

In order to bring about a fundamental shift from the host-centric model to the data-centric model, CCN is proposed. In this network architecture, each content file/object can be split into multiple segments, and each of them is assigned a unique name. While names in DONA are flat and self-certifying, names in CCN are hierarchical. In order to obtain a particular content, the consumer needs to send out an Interest that contains the name of the desired segment. Whenever a router receives an Interest, if it caches the desired segment locally, it directly returns data that contains the desired segment to the consumer. Otherwise, it records the receiving Interest into the PIT (Pending Interest Table) and further forwards this Interest towards the original source of the desired segment. Whenever a router receives data, it forwards the data based on the PIT and further caches these data to satisfy the subsequent Interest.

In order to support host mobility and multi-homing, researchers have proposed network layer protocols such as HIP (Host Identity Protocol) [6] and LISP (Locator/Identifier Separation Protocol) [7]. However, these protocols are not able to support service mobility and data-centric service. Because of this, the authors in [8] proposed SIP (Session Initiation Protocol). However, the SIP-based approaches generally need to deploy a user agent, while we aim at realizing service mobility without agents.

12.2   SINET Smooth Transition Scheme

12.2.1   Smooth Transition Principles

To be compatible with the traditional network, SINET can use 32- or 128-bit AID (Access Identifier) and RID (Routing Identifier) to reduce the complexity of the actual deployment. However, SINET uses a series of new mechanisms, such as the SID (Service Identifier)/AID-separating mechanism, the AID/RID-separating mechanism and the CON (Core Network)/ACN (Access Network)-separating mechanism. Therefore, it is not practical to deploy a pure SINET architecture overnight, and SINET should be able to coexist with the traditional network. Thus, a transition scheme is needed to solve the connectivity problem between the

traditional network and SINET, and a smooth transition scheme should follow the
following design principles [9]:

- *In order to ensure that the traditional network can be used independently for a*
  long time, the smooth transition scheme should follow the principle of gradual
  deployment.
- *SINET should be able to coexist with the traditional network for a long time,*
  and the users in SINET should be able to communicate with the users in the
  traditional network.
- *The traditional network should be able to communicate with SINET without*
  modification, and the traditional network does not need to be aware of the
  presence of SINET.
- *In order to promote the deployment of SINET, the design of the smooth tran-*
  sition scheme should be as simple as possible and should provide enough
  benefits to users to select this new network.

The SINET smooth transition includes the following three stages:

The First Stage of SINET Deployment. At the first stage of SINET deployment, SINET is deployed on a small scale and becomes an island in the traditional
network. We can then return to tunnel technology (as shown in Fig. 12.1) to
connect each SINET island.

The Second Stage of SINET Deployment. At the second stage of SINET
deployment, the deployment scope of SINET is almost equal to the traditional
network. We can then adopt dual-stack technology (as shown in Fig. 12.2) and
tunnel technology to connect SINET with the traditional network.

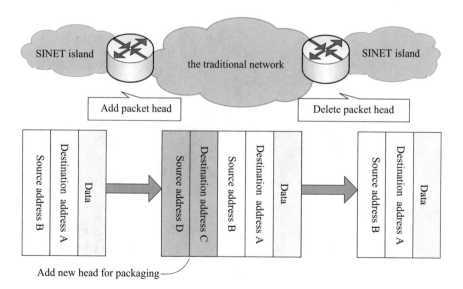

Fig. 12.1 Tunnel technology

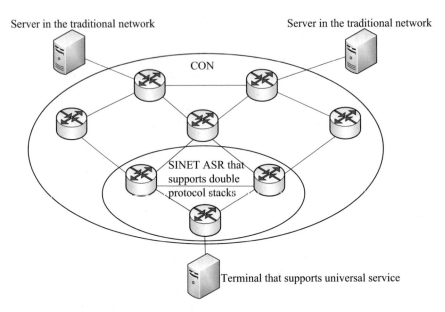

Fig. 12.2 Double protocol stack technology

The Final Stage of SINET Deployment. At the third stage of SINET deployment, SINET will be deployed on a large scale. We can then return to the RID/IP-address (Internet Protocol-address) translation technology (as shown in Fig. 12.3), double protocol stack technology and tunnel technology. Meanwhile,

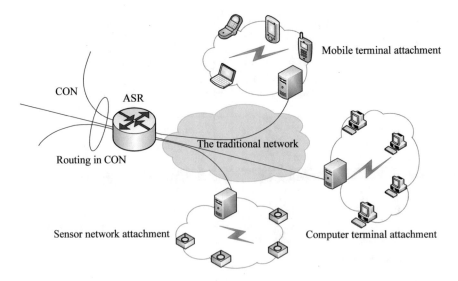

Fig. 12.3 RID/IP-address translation technology

we can treat the traditional network as the ACN in SINET. After that, all applications can run on the SINET platform.

12.2.2 Basic Idea

In order to meet the SINET smooth transition principles mentioned above, we propose a SINET smooth transition scheme based on ASR extension (as shown in Fig. 12.4).

In this scheme, SINET users can communicate with each other by adopting the AID/RID separating mechanism, while traditional network users can communicate with each other by adopting the traditional routing mechanism. In addition, these two types of network can be independent from each other and will not interfere with each other.

As shown in Fig. 12.4, Ex-ASR (Extended ASR) is deployed in SINET, which is extended with the following additional functionalities:

Handle the routing entries that were learned from the traditional network. First, Ex-ASR learns the traditional routing entries from the traditional network and regards each IP address as an AID. It then constructs the corresponding mapping information entry and further reports it to the relevant IDMS (Identifier Mapping Server) in SINET. Here, an additional flag bit is added to identify this specific mapping information, and the AID or RID in this specific mapping information entry is the IP address learned from the traditional routing entry, that is <Source IP address, Destination IP address>.

Moreover, once this mapping information entry has been learned, IDMS will advertise it to the CON in SINET. By treating the IP address in the traditional network as the RID in SINET, Ex-ASR is able to receive the packets from the

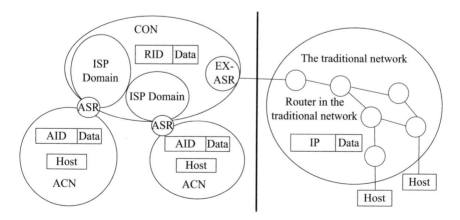

Fig. 12.4 The SINET smooth transition scheme based on ASR extension

traditional network. After that, the users in SINET can communicate with the users
in the traditional network.

**Handle the mapping information entries that were learned from the IDMSs
in SINET**. First, Ex-ASR learns the mapping information entries from the IDMSs
in SINET and regards each AID as an IP address. It then constructs the corresponding routing entry and further advertises it to the traditional network.

By treating the AID in SINET as the IP address in the traditional network,
Ex-ASR is able to forward the packets to the traditional network.

In this way, our proposed scheme connects SINET with the traditional network,
and SINET users can communicate with those in the traditional network.

12.2.3   Packet Processing

In the proposed SINET smooth transition scheme, packet processing in the Ex-ASR
can be divided into two situations: the packet is received through a CON interface
in the Ex-ASR (as shown in Fig. 12.5), and the packet is received through an ACN
interface in the Ex-ASR (as shown in Fig. 12.6).

The packet is received through a CON interface in the Ex-ASR. As shown in
Fig. 12.5, once the packet has been received through a CON interface, the Ex-ASR

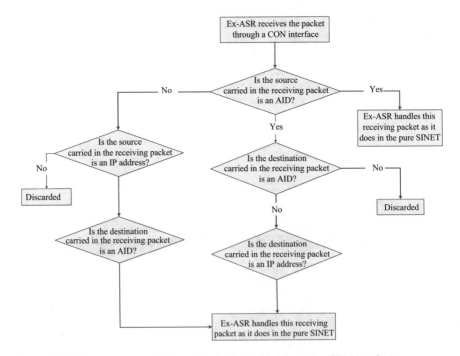

Fig. 12.5 Packet processing of the packet that is received through a CON interface

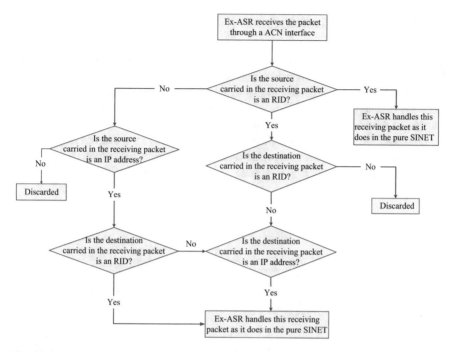

Fig. 12.6 Packet processing of the packet that is received through an ACN interface

will check the source and destination carried in the receiving packet. If the source or destination is not an AID or IP address, the Ex-ASR will view this receiving packet as illegal and drop the packet. If the source or destination is an IP address, the Ex-ASR will treat the IP address as a legal AID and further handle the receiving packet as if in the pure SINET. This also applies when both the source and destination are AIDs; the Ex-ASR will handle the receiving packet as if in the pure SINET.

The packet is received though an ACN interface in the Ex-ASR. As shown in Fig. 12.6, once the packet has been received through an ACN interface, the Ex-ASR will check the source and destination carried in the receiving packet. If the source or destination is neither an RID nor an IP address, the Ex-ASR will view the receiving packet as illegal and drop the packet. If the source or destination is an IP address, the Ex-ASR will treat the IP address as a legal RID and further handle the receiving packet as if in the pure SINET. This also applies when both the source and destination are RIDs; the Ex-ASR will handle the receiving packet as if in the pure SINET.

12.2.4   Communication Process

In this section, we present two examples to illustrate the communication processing in the proposed SINET smooth transition scheme. The first example is when the user in SINET sends a packet to the user in the traditional network (as shown in Fig. 12.7). The other example is when the user in the traditional network sends a packet to the user in SINET (as shown in Fig. 12.8).

The user in SINET sends a packet to the user in the traditional network. As illustrated in Fig. 12.7, the source AID and the destination AID of the packet issued by the user in SINET (user A) are AID_A and AID_B, respectively. Once this packet

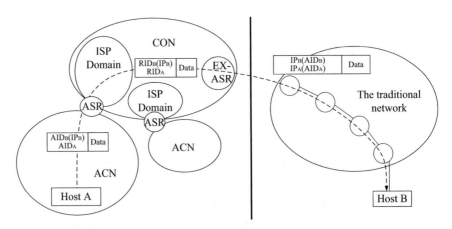

Fig. 12.7 The user in SINET sends a packet to the user in the traditional network

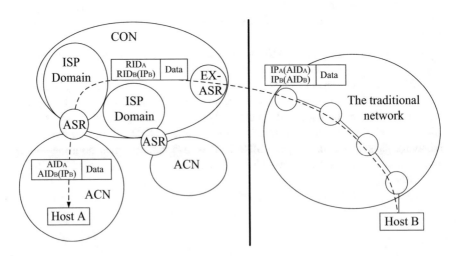

Fig. 12.8 The user in the traditional network sends a packet to the user in SINET

has been received, Ex-ASR will look up the mapping information entries for AID_A and AID_B and further replace AID_A and AID_B with RID_A and RID_B. Since the destination RID of the modified packet (RID_B) is an IP address, this modified packet can enter the traditional networking and will be forwarded to the user in the traditional networking (user B) through the traditional route ways.

The user in the traditional network sends a packet to the user in SINET. As illustrated in Fig. 12.8, the source IP address and the destination IP address of the packet issued by the user in the traditional network (user B) are IP_B and IP_A, respectively. Once this packet has been received, Ex-ASR will look up the mapping information entries for IP_B (equal to AID_B) and IP_A (equal to AID_A), and further replace IP_B and IP_A with RID_B (equal to IP_B) and RID_A. After that, the modified packet will enter SINET and will be forwarded to the ASR in the ACN where user A resides. Then, this ASR will look up the mapping information entries for RID_B and RID_A, re-modify the receiving packet (replace RID_B and RID_A with AID_B and AID_A) and further forward this re-modified packet to the user in SINET (user A).

12.2.5   Benefit Analysis

In this section, we analyze the following benefits of the proposed SINET smooth transition scheme:

- SINET and the traditional network are independent of each other. The traditional network can work as usual, unaffected by SINET.
- SINET and the traditional network can coexist, while the users in SINET can communicate with the users in the traditional network.
- The traditional network can communicate with SINET without any modification. That is, the traditional network does not sense the presence of SINET.
- The first batch of users or ISPs that deploy SINET can receive enough benefits, such as the CON of SINET will avoid attacks in the traditional network, the CON of SINET will avoid being attacked in the ACN of SINET, and the CON of SINET can provide mobility support for the users in SINET.

12.3   SINET Incrementally Deployable Transition Scheme

12.3.1   Basic Idea

In this section, we aim at designing a SINET incrementally deployable transition scheme that is data-centric by applying a CID (Connection Identifier) of SINET for service binding between the service layer and transport layer in the current Internet (denoted as DCID). Thus, in order to be incrementally deployable, the new hosts implementing SINET have to be compatible with the existing hosts implementing the traditional network. From the perspective of the new and existing hosts, it is desirable to make as few changes as possible to the host stack [10].

There are a few design choices to be made for the traditional network to move toward SINET while being incrementally deployable. One possible choice is for all applications in the application layer to be data-centric, just like in several newly proposed network architectures [2–5, 10–15]. For example, P2P (Peer-to-Peer) applications are data-centric, since the user does not need to know the location of the desired data or service. Instead, by using certain application-specific techniques, P2P applications can search the hosts that provide the desired data or service. However, as envisioned in the traditional network, the majority of applications are host-centric. For example, in the HTTP (Hypertext Transfer Protocol) application, we need to enter a URL (Uniform Resource Locator), and then the HTTP application resolves an IP address that corresponds to the domain name in the URL. After that, in order to obtain the desired data or service, the HTTP application sends requests to the resolved IP address. In the process mentioned above, the HTTP application sends commands or requests to a given domain name (contained in the URL). That is, it cares "where" the desired data or service comes from. However, in the data-centric model of SINET, we want applications to simply request the name of the desired data or service, without having to care about where the desired data or service comes from. If we want these applications to be data-centric, we have to revise them one-by-one, which is not efficient, because these revisions are tailored to the existing applications. Each time a new application emerges, the work needs to be repeated. It is more efficient to design a novel transition scheme that applies to all applications (including existing applications and future applications) instead of specific ones.

Another design choice is to design a new transport protocol that is both data- and host-centric. This choice can be used by all upper layer applications. However, this choice not only limits applications to a specific transport layer protocol, but also makes it impossible for existing applications to benefit from any novel transport layer protocol. As an example, in [16], the authors report that the SCTP (Stream Control Transmission Protocol) is superior to the TCP (Transmission Control Protocol). However, it is not widely used in the traditional network, since the SCTP is not compatible with the TCP, while many existing applications (e.g., HTTP) are bound to the TCP.

Because of the weaknesses of the above-mentioned design choices, we propose DCID, which inserts a shim layer between the application layer and transport layer of the traditional network architecture. Specifically, the inserted shim layer in DCID is called the SB (Service Binding) layer.

After the insertion of the SB layer, the functions of all the layers below it in DCID remain unchanged, just like in the traditional network architecture. In our implementation, we implement the network layer by employing an incrementally deployable identifier separating mechanism to further enhance the scalability of the routing system as well as to keep the function of the network layer unchanged.

The function of the application layer in DCID can be both backward compatible with the traditional network architecture and enhanced to benefit from a data-centric model. More specifically, the main function of the application layer is to identify the desired data or service that users want and to identify the location of the desired data or service. Particularly, we assume that all data or services have a unique name, a so-called SID (Service Identifier). The form of the SID may be similar to those in [1] or similar to these used in BitTorrent (e.g., the name of a data is the hash for the content of the data) [17]. As mentioned in [18–22], the name of a data packet (i.e., SID) in our implementation is a 160-bit hash for the content of the data, and the application layer will inform the SB layer in the same host as the SID of the desired data.

The SB layer is in charge of obtaining and caching the desired data or service for the applications. Based on the information received from the application layer, the SB layer can choose suitable transport protocols for applications. In addition, based on the QoS (Quality of Service) requirement of an application, the SB layer can also determine, based on how many sources it should obtain, the desired data or service. For example, if there are four servers that can provide the same desired data, the SB layer may choose to obtain the desired data from a single server, two servers, three servers or all four servers. Additionally, the SB layer needs to maintain a certain transport status so as to support efficient host mobility and service mobility, as will be discussed later in this section.

In the event that an application simply sends the SID of the desired data or service to the SB layer, the SB layer should also map the SID onto one or more IP addresses (the IP addresses of the hosts on which the desired data or service resides). In this section, we return to an approach similar to the one proposed in [1] to map SIDs onto IP addresses.

12.3.2   Consistent CID for Data/Service Binding

In DCID, we introduce a consistent CID (Connection Identifier) namespace in the SB layer. The CID uniquely identifies an application instance at a specific consistent period of time. In addition, in DCID, we define an application instance as each time an application in the application layer initiates a request for a given data segment or service. For example, if an application requires a data segment named SID_1, the SB layer considers it as an application instance, while if the same application requires another data segment named SID_2, the SB layer considers it as another application instance. For each application instance at a host, the SB layer of the host assigns it a unique CID. Additionally, this unique CID is not changed until the desired data have been obtained or the SB layer cannot find a host providing the desired data during a certain period of time (e.g., 10 s). Moreover, CIDs are locally unique. In other words, CIDs are used to differentiate application instances at a host, and they would not be used to differentiate application instances at different hosts. When assigning a CID, the SB layer allocates adequate physical resources to the

CID in order to cache data segments corresponding to the desired data or store the transport status. In DCID, the introduction of CIDs makes it possible to separate the upper layer application states and the transport layer states. Therefore, DCID is not only data-centric but also capable of supporting efficient mobility (including host mobility and service mobility) and multi-homing.

In order to link these layers efficiently, we use an interface (dubbed the NT interface) between the network and the transport layers, an interface between the transport and the SB layers, and an interface (dubbed the SA interface) between the SB and the application layers. In order to be incrementally deployable, the NT interface format and the TS interface format used in the proposed DCID are consistent with the interface formats used in the traditional network, namely, <source IP address, destination IP address> and <source IP address, destination IP address, source port and destination port>, respectively.

The SA interface format is <SID, source IP address, destination IP address, source port, destination port, ...>. There are several reasons for using this SA interface form. First, as mentioned above, we use the traditional network mainly to obtain services. If services are named by service identifiers (i.e., SIDs), applications may only know the SID of the desired service and do not know where the desired service is hosted. In this case, an application sends the SID of the desired service to the SB layer. Second, there are still specific applications that want to communicate with a given host. For example, when a person travels, he/she may want to access his/her personal computer (at home) in order to obtain certain data that are only hosted on that personal computer. Third, nearly all applications in the traditional network use the form <source IP address, destination IP address, source port, destination port> to communicate with the lower transport layer. Additionally, spare spaces should be reserved for future use, and we use "..." to represent the reserved spare spaces. Therefore, in order to be incrementally deployable, we should use the above-mentioned SA interface format.

However, in DCID, the application layer does not need to fill in all the fields of the SA interface. For example, if an application knows the SID of the desired data, it may only fill in the fields SID and source port. The purpose of filling in the field source port is to differentiate between two applications that require the same data. If an application knows the IP address of the host that provides the desired data, it may fill in the fields: source IP address, destination IP address, source port and destination port, just like in the traditional network.

12.3.3 Communication Processing

In Fig. 12.9, we illustrate how a destination host obtains the desired data from a source host in DCID.

In this figure, we assume that the destination host initiates the communication and the application only knows the SID of the desired data. Since this is similar to when an application knows the IP address of the host where the desired data resides,

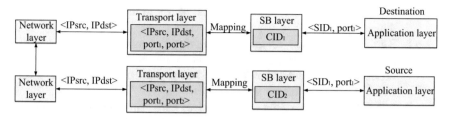

Fig. 12.9 Basic communication in DCID when an application only knows the SID

we will not elaborate on it. Hereafter, we will call a host requesting desired data a destination and a host providing the desired data a source.

Step 1. An application in the application layer of the destination fills in the fields of SID and source port (e.g., SID_1 and $port_1$ in Fig. 12.9) in the SA interface and sends a request packet to the SB layer of the destination. Specifically, SID_1 and $port_1$ indicate the desired data and the desired application, respectively.

Step 2. When the SB layer of the destination receives the request packet in Step 1, it first assigns it a CID (e.g., CID_2 in Fig. 12.9) that is not used by any other service. Meanwhile, the SB layer allocates physical resources to this CID. It then maps the binary $<SID_1, port_1>$ onto CID_2.

Step 3. Since the SB layer of the destination does not know which host(s) can provide the desired data, it should map SID1 onto one or more IP addresses of the hosts that provide the desired data.

Step 4. The SB layer of the destination fills in the TS interface by using the IP address of the source (e.g., IP_{src} in Fig. 12.9), the IP address of the destination (e.g., IP_{dst} in Fig. 12.9), the source port (e.g., $port_1$ in Fig. 12.9) and the destination port (e.g., $port_2$ in Fig. 12.9). It then maps CID_2 onto the filled TS interface and further sends the request packet to the transport layer of the destination. Specifically, the SB layer of the destination can choose the desired transport layer protocols based on the QoS requirement of upper layer applications.

Step 5. The transport layer of the destination adds a transport header to the request packet from the SB layer and further sends this encapsulated request packet to the network layer of the destination through the NT interface of the destination. This step is the same as what the transport layer does in the traditional network.

Step 6. The network layer of the destination adds a network header to the request packet and further sends out this encapsulated request packet to the source. Note that this step is also the same as what the network layer does in the traditional network.

Step 7. When the network layer of the source receives the encapsulated request packet in Step 6, it strips the network header of this request packet and further sends this decapsulated request packet to the transport layer of the source.

Step 8. The transport layer of the source strips the transport header when it receives the request packet from the network layer of the source and further sends this decapsulated request packet to the SB layer of the source through the TS interface of the source.

Step 9. When the SB layer of the source receives the decapsulted request packet in Step 8, it assigns a CID (e.g., CID_1 in Fig. 12.9) to the service if there is no CID corresponding to the quadruple of $<IP_{src}, IP_{dst}, port_1, port_2>$. Otherwise, the SB layer of the source simply maps the quadruple of $<IP_{src}, IP_{dst}, port_1, port_2>$ onto the existing CID.

Step 10. After that, the SB layer of the source maps CID_1 onto the binary of $<SID_1, port_1>$ if this is the first packet of the service. Then, the SB layer of the source sends the decapsulted request packet in Step 9 to the application layer of the source through the SA interface of the source by filling in the fields of SID and source port.

To facilitate the in-network cache, all packets need to carry the SID of the corresponding data. Whenever an old router receives a packet, it can ignore the SID field and further forward the packet to the next hop. Additionally, it is possible for data to be divided into multiple segments, and each of these segments can be represented by a unique SID. For example, if segment B is the subsequent segment of segment A, segment A's SID may contain a pointer to segment B's SID. In this case, the SB layer of the destination should map all segment's SIDs onto a corresponding IP address. Specifically, although both the SIDs for different segments and the corresponding IP addresses are different, once the SB layer has assigned a CID to the desired data, the CID remains unchanged until the desired data have been obtained or until no source can provide the desired data.

In the traditional network, an application (e.g., HTTP) requests data (e.g., a web page corresponding to a URL), while the web page often contains different data objects (e.g., pictures and text files). In this case, to enhance efficiency, the traditional network uses only a persistent TCP connection to obtain the data objects. In DCID, this could be achieved in a similar way, such as treating the URL as an SID and letting the SID point to other SIDs (each SID corresponding to a single data object contained in the web page). In this way, if an application wants the data, it only needs to send the SID corresponding to the URL to the SB layer. Then, the SB layer can use only one CID for this application. In addition, the SB layer may resolve the other SIDs onto corresponding servers or routers. If these SIDs are all mapped to the same server with the SID corresponding to the URL, the SB layer may also choose to use a common TCP connection to obtain the desired data objects for improved efficiency.

12.3.4   Implementation and Performance Evaluation

In this section, we evaluate the design of DCID by implementing a simple
Linux-based prototype with kernel version 2.6.28. In Fig. 12.10, we illustrate the
topology of the prototype, which comprises three CSRs, three ASRs, two mapping
servers, an RH (Resolution Handler), a multi-homed server implemented with
DCID, a server with DCID, a multi-homed host with DCID, a mobile host with
DCID and a traditional host.

The implementation of the hosts with DCID consists of about 22,300 lines of
code, which is comprised of the following main modules:

Application module. To verify that DCID can support both the host-centric and
data-centric model, we modify the Apache HTTP server (version 2.2), so that the
request packet can be sent to the SB layer, when we simply enter an SID instead of
a URL.

Session-binding module. The session-binding module is used to generate CIDs
for application instances as well as resolve IP addresses for SIDs and manage
transport layer connections that were used to obtain desired data.

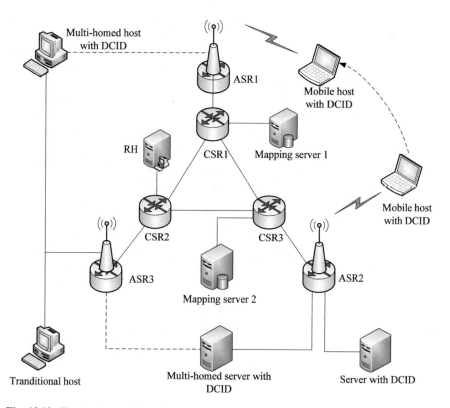

Fig. 12.10 The topology of the prototype

To improve routing efficiency in the traditional network, the ASRs are extended to split SIDs from IP addresses. In our prototype, the implementation of the ASRs consists of about 5,100 lines of code.

The mapping servers can be used to store the mapping items of the hosts. In our prototype, the implementation of the mapping servers consists of about 3700 lines of code.

The RH can be used to map SIDs onto IP addresses. Unlike the implementation of RHs in [2], in our prototype, we implement the RH by running a database in a Linux server. Specifically, this database is used to maintain the mappings from SIDs onto IP addresses.

We will now present the numerical results obtained from the prototype. Our results show that DCID can satisfy our design goals, namely, to be data-centric and incrementally deployable, and to provide support for mobility (host mobility and service mobility) and multi-homing.

Data-Centric. One of the most important merits of DCID is that it can support data-centric service. To illustrate this, we present an example shown in Fig. 12.11. In this example, we assume that a destination with IP_{dst} (i.e., IP address of the destination) wants to obtain a service with SID hosted by two sources (i.e., Source 1 with IP_{src}^1 and Source 2 with IP_{src}^2). Whenever the destination wants to obtain the service denoted by SID, its application layer will send a request packet to the corresponding SB layer. Then, the SB layer of the destination will assign an unused CID (i.e., CID_{dst}) and map the SID onto IP_{src}^1 (or IP_{src}^2 or both IP_{src}^1 and IP_{src}^2). After that, the destination will open a connection to communicate with Source 1 in order to obtain the desired service denoted by SID.

If we now assume that Source 1 fails, the SB layer of the destination would detect this failure. If the destination has obtained the IP address of Source 2 (i.e., IP_{src}^2), its SB layer will open a connection to Source 2. If the destination does not know IP_{src}^2, its SB layer should first map the SID onto IP_{src}^2 and further open a connection to Source 2. As illustrated in Fig. 12.11, in both cases mentioned above, the CID_{dst} remains unchanged. Hence, the upper layer application would not be affected by the failure of Source 1.

In Fig. 12.11, we have demonstrated DCID's support for data-centric services in our prototype. Next, we consider a case where the server is attached to ASR2 and the multi-homed servers host the same movie. Initially, the mobile host maps the SID of the movie onto the IP addresses of the two servers (i.e., the server attached to ASR2 and the multi-homed server) by querying the RH. Then, the mobile host obtains the movie from the server attached to ASR2. Nine seconds later, we manually shut down the server attached to ASR2.

In Fig. 12.12, we show the TCP segments captured using the WIRESHARK tool at the mobile host. From this figure, we can observe that the mobile host quickly detects the failure of the server attached to ASR2 and opens a new connection to the multi-homed server.

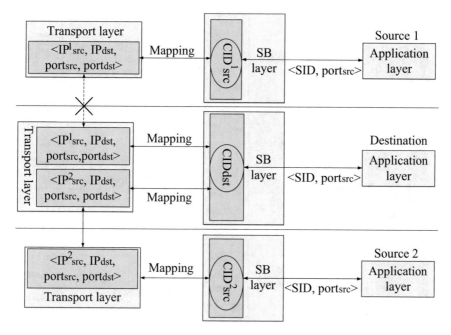

Fig. 12.11 DCID for data-centric service

Fig. 12.12 The size of the TCP segments captured using the WIRESHARK tool at the mobile host. Reprinted from Ref. [23], with permission from IEEE

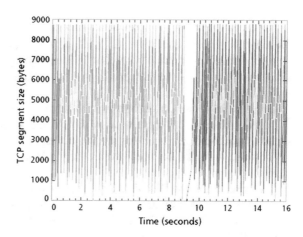

Mobility Support. Another important merit of DCID is that it can support mobility, including service mobility and host mobility.

Figure 12.13 illustrates how DCID supports host mobility when a source and a destination initiate communication using a SID.

When the source moves from one subnet to another, it changes its IP address from IP_{src}^0 to IP_{src}^n, and the source and destination simply:

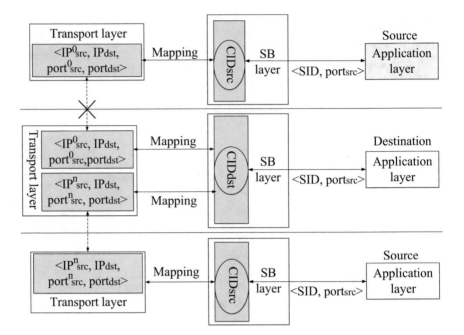

Fig. 12.13 Mobility support in DCID

Record the current transport status and tear down the old connection that is identified by the old quadruple $\langle IP^0_{src}, IP_{dst}, port^0_{src}, port_{dst}\rangle$.

Reestablish a new connection that is identified by the new quadruple $\langle IP^n_{src}, IP_{dst}, port^n_{src}, port_{dst}\rangle$ and further map the new quadruple onto CID_{src} and CID_{dst}, respectively.

Continue the communication from the recorded transport status.

In this way, the CIDs maintained at both the source and the destination can remain unchanged, as illustrated by the circles in Fig. 12.14. Hence, upper layer applications will not be interrupted when a host changes from one subnet to another.

We have evaluated DCID's support for host mobility. From this point, ASR1 and ASR2 work as ordinary IP routers in the traditional network, and the mobile host in Fig. 12.10 roams from ASR2 to ASR1 after 8 s. In our experiments, we observe that the movie continues after a short pause.

In Fig. 12.14, we show the TCP segments (to and from the mobile host and the server) captured by using the WIRESHARK tool at the mobile host. From this figure, we can observe that there are no packets to or from the server and the mobile host for a period of about 1.5 s. This can be explained by the fact that when the mobile host attaches to ASR1 it has to obtain a new IP address. Since a delay this long may be unacceptable for many time-sensitive applications, we conclude that DCID alone cannot efficiently support host mobility.

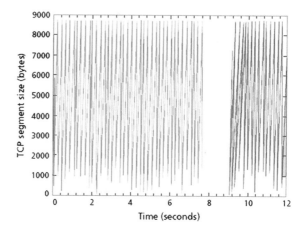

Fig. 12.14 Host mobility support in DCID. Reprinted from Ref. [23], with permission from IEEE

In our experiments, we have also evaluated DCID's support for service mobility. From this point, we assume that the mobile host knows the IP addresses of the multi-homed host and the multi-homed host also knows the IP addresses of the mobile host. What we need to do is move this session to the multi-homed host when the mobile host opens a session to obtain a movie from the server attached to ASR2. From this point, we manually send a command to the multi-homed host to inform it to open a TCP connection to the server. Keeping security in mind, we also send the TCP sequence number and the IP address of the mobile host to the multi-homed host. Once this command has been received, the multi-homed host opens a new TCP connection to the server. Meanwhile, we also send a message including the IP address of the multi-homed host to the server to inform it that we want to move the session to the multi-homed host. Once this message has been received, the server maps the TCP connection to the multi-homed host onto the existing CID, and then the server sends the movie to the multi-homed host. After a period of waiting, we move the session back to the mobile host. This process is repeated 300 times in our experiments.

In Fig. 12.15, we show the goodput before and after four consecutive mobility sessions. From this figure, we can observe that either the mobile host or the multi-homed host can stream the movie at about one megabit per second shortly after the mobility session.

In Fig. 12.16, we further show the handover delay of the 300 mobility sessions. In our experiments, we calculate the handover delay as the time interval between the time the server receives the message from the mobile host (or the multi-homed host) and the time the server receives the TCP ACK (Acknowledge) from the multi-homed host (or the mobile host) when the multi-homed host (or the mobile host) answers the TCP SYN (Synchronous) + ACK during the setup phase of a TCP connection. As shown in Fig. 12.16, the handover delay is upper-bounded by about 0.2 s, and the average handover delay is around 0.0631 s. Note that since the handover delay depends on the RTT (Round Trip Time) from the host to the server, we can conclude that the handover delay will increase when the RTT increases.

Fig. 12.15 The goodput from the server to the two hosts. Reprinted from [23], with permission from IEEE

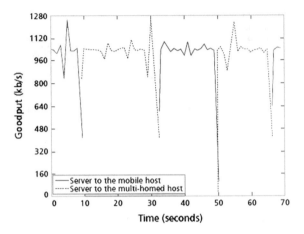

Fig. 12.16 The handover delay of the 300 mobility sessions. Reprinted from [23], with permission from IEEE

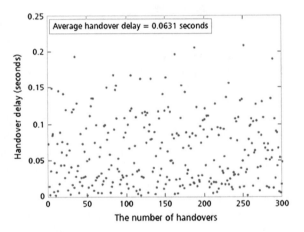

Multi-Homing Support. The third important merit of DCID is that it can support multi-homing. To illustrate this, we present an example in Fig. 12.17. Here, we assume that the source and destination initiate communication using the SID. Meanwhile, we suppose that the destination wants to obtain a service denoted by SID, hosted by a source whose IP address is IP_{src}, and assume that a destination is multi-homed to two subnets and has two IP addresses denoted by IP^1_{dst} and IP^2_{dst}. In this example, the destination may first establish a connection using IP^1_{dst} to the source. When IP^1_{dst} becomes unavailable, the destination can establish another connection using IP^2_{dst}. In this situation, multi-homing can be used for redundancy. In addition, the destination may simultaneously establish two connections using IP^1_{dst} and IP^2_{dst} to the source. It can then obtain a given percent of data from one connection and obtain the rest of the data from the other connection. In this situation, multi-homing can be used for load balancing. In both situations mentioned

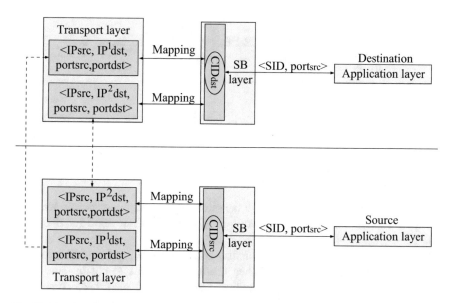

Fig. 12.17 Multi-homing support in DCID

above, the CIDs assigned to the service at the source and destination can remain unchanged.

In our experiments, we have evaluated DCID's performance in supporting multi-homing when it is used for redundancy. Initially, the multi-homed host (in Fig. 12.10) obtains a movie hosted by the server attached to ASR2 through the Ethernet interface connected to ASR3. About 10 s later, we disable this Ethernet interface. Then, the multi-homed host opens a new TCP connection to the server and further maps the existing CID onto the new TCP connection. Since the TCP segments captured by using the WIRESHARK tool in this situation are similar to those presented in Fig. 12.12, we omit this trace here for brevity.

Incremental Deployment. The fourth important merit of DCID is that it is incrementally deployable. To illustrate this, we present an example in Fig. 12.18. In this example, we show how a node with the traditional network architecture (a.k.a. old node) communicates with another node with DCID (a.k.a. new node). Since the source is an old node, it cannot support SID; thus, the destination node can only initiate communication using the IP address of the source. That is, an application in the application layer of the destination first fills in the fields IP_{src}, IP_{dst}, port1 and port2 in the SA interface and sends a request packet to the SB layer of the destination. The SB layer of the destination then assigns an unused CID (i.e., CID_1 in Fig. 12.18) to the service and sends the request packet to the transport layer of the destination. Since the SB layer of the destination does nothing to the request packet from the application layer, the transport layer of the destination further sends this request packet to the transport layer of the source through the network layer of the destination and the network layer of the source. After that, the application layer of

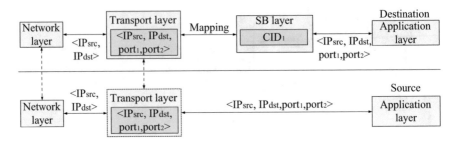

Fig. 12.18 Communication between a node with the traditional network and a node with DCID

the source receives a request packet in the same way as a request packet is sent from an application in the traditional network. In this way, the destination and the source can communicate with each other.

More importantly, a new node can also benefit from being data-centric when it obtains service from old nodes. When a new node wants to obtain data, it can establish multiple connections to multiple old nodes and map these connections onto the same CID assigned for the data. In addition, in case one of these connections fails, the new node can obtain service from the remaining old nodes.

12.4 Conclusions

This chapter has proposed a SINET smooth transition scheme. By extending Ex-ASR with additional functionalities, this scheme is able to solve the connectivity problem between the traditional network and SINET as well as bring great benefits to the users or ISPs that first deploy SINET. The chapter has also proposed a SINET incrementally deployable transition scheme that is data-centric and called DCID. By adding a shim layer between the application and transport layers, DCID is able to efficiently support service mobility and multi-homing, in addition to which it is incrementally deployable. However, there are still many open issues, including large-scale experiments; this work will inspire further research activities on the upcoming SINET.

References

1. Koponen T, Chawla M, Chun BG et al (2007) A data-oriented (and beyond) network architecture. ACM SIGCOMM Comput Commun Rev 37(4):181–192
2. NetInf project[EB/OL]. http://www.netinf.org/
3. Zhang L, Estrin D, Burke J et al (2010) Named data networking (ndn) project. Relatório Técnico NDN-0001, Xerox Palo Alto Research Center-PARC

4. Zhang L, Afanasyev A, Burke J et al (2014) Named data networking. ACM SIGCOMM Comput Commun Rev 44(3):66–73
5. Jacobson V, Smetters D K, Thornton J D et al (2009) Networking named content. In: The 5th international conference on Emerging networking experiments and technologies
6. Nikander P, Gurtov A, Henderson TR (2010) Host identity protocol (HIP): connectivity, mobility, multi-homing, security, and privacy over Ipv4 and Ipv6 networks. IEEE Commun Surv Tutor 12(2):186–204
7. Meyer D (2008) The locator/Id separation protocol (LISP). Internet Protoc 11(1):23–36
8. Shacham R et al (2009) Session initiation protocol (SIP) session mobility, IETF RFC 5631. Accessed Oct 2009
9. Dong P (2008) Research on the scalable routing architecture based on separating and mapping of identity and locator. Dissertation, Beijing Jiaotong University
10. Lagutin D, Visala K, Tarkoma S (2010) Publish/subscribe for internet: PSIRP perspective. In: Towards the future internet-emerging trends from European research, 2010 (Valencia FIA book 2010), pp 77–82
11. Choi J, Han J, Cho E et al (2011) A survey on content-oriented networking for efficient content delivery. IEEE Commun Mag 49(3):121–127
12. Pan J, Paul S, Jain R (2011) A survey of the research on future Internet architectures. IEEE Commun Mag 49(7):26–36
13. Jokela P, Zahemszky A, Esteve Rothenberg C et al (2009) LIPSIN: line speed publish/subscribe inter-networking. ACM SIGCOMM Comput Commun Rev 39(4):195–206
14. Seskar I, Nagaraja K, Nelson S et al (2011). Mobilityfirst future internet architecture project. In: The 7th Asian internet engineering conference
15. Beben A, Batalla JM, Florez D et al (2012) The content mediator architecture for content-aware networks. Spec Issue J Telecommun Rev Telecommun News 8–9:1192–1203
16. Dreibholz T, Rathgeb EP, Rüngeler I et al (2011) Stream control transmission protocol: Past, current, and future standardization activitie. IEEE Commun Mag 49(4):82–88
17. Cohen B (2008) The BitTorrent protocol specification. http://www.bittorrent.org/beps/bep_0003.html. Accessed 10 Jan 2008
18. Wu H, Gao D, Yang D et al (2010) A novel data-oriented name service. J Commun 5(9):684–691
19. Wu H, Lin F, Zhang H (2009) A novel data-oriented name service for next generation internet. In: IEEE international conference on communications technology and applications
20. Wu H (2011) Key technologies research on DHT-based Identifier mapping in universal network. Dissertation, Beijing Jiaotong University
21. Wang H (2012) Research on the identifier network mechanism and its key technologie. Dissertation, Beijing Jiaotong University
22. Huang D, Yang D, Song F et al (2011) SIDMAP: a service-oriented mapping system for Loc/ID split internet naming. J Commun 6(8):601–609
23. Luo H, Zhang H, Zukerman M et al (2014) An incrementally deployable network architecture to support both data-centric and host-centric services. IEEE Netw 28(4):58–65

Chapter 13
Applications of SINET

In this chapter, we introduce the real applications of SINET. As a new future collaborative Internet architecture, it provides a comprehensive and effective solution against the problems existing in the current Internet system, such as scalability, mobility, security, resource utilization and so on. Many advantages are introduced compared to the current Internet. With many years of efforts, SINET has been developed and extensively implemented. Thanks to these real applications, SINET has obtained several valuable feedbacks and awards. Lastly, we summarize and discuss the contributions, challenges and opportunities of SINET in the future.

13.1 Applications

13.1.1 Application in the High-Speed Railway Network

Nowadays, due to the low price, short waiting time and close distance to urban districts, HSRs have become a convenient and preferred transportation means in our daily life. It is obvious that specific wireless communications are required for such a high-speed mobility environment to satisfy these particular demands. By implementing the architecture and operating mechanism of SINET, passengers can be provided high-quality infotainment or entertainment services to make the long journey more pleasant. At the same time, some business activities, e.g., document transferring and video conferences, can also be performed as usual in HSR environments, realizing the notion of the mobile office.

Because of the outstanding performance, SINET has been tested and applied in the High-Speed Railway (HSR) networks. SINET is believed to be a technological breakthrough for promoting the development of challenging HSR networks. On one hand, as a revolution of mobile communication technology, SINET will be more suitable for communications for high-speed trains. On the other hand, the

© Springer-Verlag Berlin Heidelberg 2016
H. Zhang et al., *Smart Collaborative Identifier Network*,
DOI 10.1007/978-3-662-49143-0_13

high-speed railway will become an inevitability and significant application scenario for SINET. HSR provides a typical testing and application scenario to show the superiorities of SINET, which are specified in challenging situations, including "great service in a crowd," "best experience follows you," "amazingly fast," "super real-time and reliable connections" and "communicating ubiquitous things."

In SINET, to support the unified management of networks, the architecture is divided as three layers, namely: the Smart Pervasive Service Layer (L-SPS), Dynamic Resource Adaption Layer (L-DRA) and Collaborative Network Component Layer (L-CNC). The L-SPS is responsible for the naming, registration and management of various services. The L-DRA is designed to manage network function groups logically, which are in charge of optimal decision, task allocation and resource dynamic scheduling. In the L-DRA, different network function groups can be organized to adapt to the demands from both the L-SPS and L-CNC. The L-CNC is responsible for managing network components, storage and transmission of data and so on. This enables network devices such as routers, content servers, sensors, mobile terminals and interfaces to carry out a specific task collaboratively.

By implementing the architecture and operating mechanism of SINET, the triple bindings, i.e., resource-location binding, user-network binding and control-data binding, in the mobile network on the high-speed railway are broken, and numerous key technologies are also achieved including the network virtualization, the multilink data concurrent processing, the cross district fast switching, the heterogeneous network switching and so on. According to the survey of network users on the high-speed railway, it can be concluded that the SINET improves Internet access and user experience on high-speed mobile vehicles.

As shown in Fig. 13.1, a specially designed Wireless Multilink Mobile Router (WMMR) is deployed on the high-speed railway as the ASR. It merges multiple mobile network standards, including WCDMA, EVDO and Wi-Fi, and integrates the three dedicated networks into a CON. WMMR is able to perform the wireless link mapping, traffic shaping, dynamic monitoring and traffic scheduling to improve

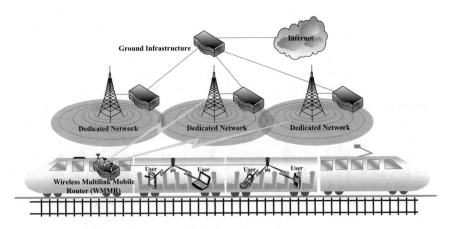

Fig. 13.1 SINET applied in a high-speed railway

the quality of experience. Moreover, it is also able to provide access to the mobile Internet in vehicles with high velocity based on the concurrent multi-path transmission control protocol in the mobile environment.

We have developed and tested a prototype system in a high-speed railway environment. In this experiment, we focus on a mobility-support function group, which is composed of one bandwidth monitor, one data link adaptor and six different wireless access components. The six components adopt different wireless technologies to support three main network operators, i.e., EVDO for China Telecom, WCDMA for China Unicom and TD-LTE for China Mobile. Each two components use one kind of wireless technology. All the components share the same name format, which has a prefix "nid." The components called nid 1 and nid 2 leverage the EVDO technology. The nid 3 and nid 4 use WCDMA. The nid 5 and nid 6 utilize TD-LTE. All these components are integrated on a small-form SAFG factor blade device with a Celeron mobile CPU.

To evaluate the performance, we tested the functions of our devices and the available bandwidth on a China high-speed bullet train from Beijing to Shanghai. The total distance is 1318 km. Its average speed is about 250 km/h, and the maximum speed is 300 km/h. The total experiment took about 6 months (from November 2014 to April 2015), including the data collection, performance analysis and optimal designs and so on.

Figure 13.2 shows the experimental results. We observe that the average bandwidth is about 10 Mbps and the peak value reaches 25 Mbps, which is much better than each of the solutions used in the three network operators (without the smart cooperation scheme). The main reason is that the proposed solution makes the data link adaptor select the appropriate wireless interface adaptively and concurrently, which is able to make the best usage of the network resources in the execrable mobile environment.

SINET is applied to promote efficient communications in the HSR environment. We conclude that SINET not only improves the quality of services in HSR

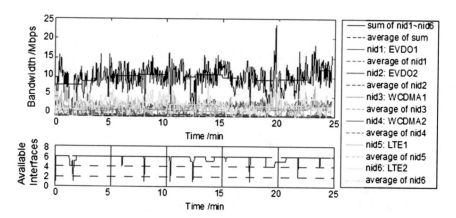

Fig. 13.2 Experimental results tested on high-speed bullet trains

networks, but also can be extended to provide great opportunities for more reconfigurable software-defined functions to promote 5G mobile communications in HSR. At the same time, SINET has great potential to provide flexible support for and close integration with existing heterogeneous network infrastructures.

13.1.2   Application in the Industrial Wireless Sensor Network

SINET has also been applied in the Industrial Wireless Sensor Network (IWSN) as shown in Fig. 13.3. IWSN is an emerging technology within the area of industrial automation, and it is considered as another technology hotspot after the fieldbus technology in the industrial control field. However, considering the special needs of industrial application, IWSN faces many new challenges, of which the two most important issues are reliability and real time. We built the Smart Wireless Sensor Networks (Smart-IWSNs) design by leveraging the idea of SINET as shown in Fig. 13.4. In Smart-WSNs, we could monitor and control different network components in different protocol layers. By optimally scheduling these network components in the cross-layer, we could also customize different applications providing different network performances. Since Smart-IWSN is inherited from WSN, the cross-layer design is necessary for Smart-IWSNs.

On the other hand, the Smart-IWSN adopts a new centralized control design in which it is easier to collect more communication resources in different protocol layers, so it is more suitable to implement a comprehensive cross-layer design. Currently, our platform supports at least the resources and requirements of different protocol layers. The application layer considers different data types and user demands, which is the final design objective of cross-layer centralized scheduling. The transport protocol and end-to-end transport layer ACK in the transport layer

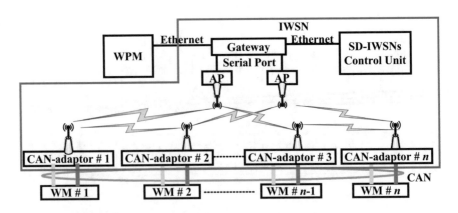

Fig. 13.3 SINET applied in the IWSN

Fig. 13.4 Smart-IWSN
practical system

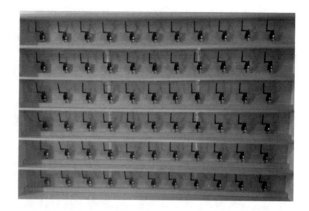

Table 13.1 TIME GROUP Smart-IWSN Product Size: MS02-09

Industrial products	Size	Workshop
DC welding machines	TDZ 4000/5000/6000	No. 1 assembly workshop
Plasma cutting machine	TDL 600/800/1000/1200	No. 1 assembly workshop
Semi-automatic gas shielded welding machine	TDN 3500/5000/6000	No. 2 assembly workshop
DC argon arc welding machine	TDW 4000/5000/6000	No. 3 assembly workshop
Pulse argon arc welding machine	TDW 4000M/5000M/6000M	No. 4 assembly workshop

provide the guarantee for high-reliability applications. Most of the schedulable communication resources are in the network layer and the data link layer, so these two layers are the main work space of cross-layer centralized scheduling. The physical layer provides basic physical channel resources and some necessary feedbacks of wireless communication to optimize the scheduling algorithm.

Table 13.1 shows that SINET is applied in TIME GROUP in Beijing and achieves good results.

13.1.3 Application in Smart Grid

The Current Smart Grid adopts the Internet architecture, which provides a great communication system to exchange information. With the vehicular network integrating traffic network, the electro mobile as an important component in Smart Grid will definitely increase the need for a communication system. Therefore, we also propose a clean-slate communication approach to boost the development of the smart grid in the respective of the Smart Identifier Network (SINET).

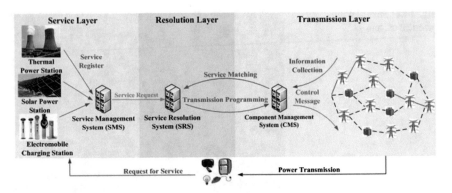

Fig. 13.5 SINET-based smart grid communication architecture

The primary purpose of SINET is to establish a reliable and efficient distribution method for content based on named entities, such as web pages, videos, files or other pieces of information. In light of this point, we regard the abundant electric services, including thermal power, solar power and electro mobile charging, and grid components, such as power lines and transformers, as the named entities. In this way, utilizing globally unique names to identify the services and components will improve the management efficiency and control efficiency of the smart grid to a large extent. Therefore, we propose the Service Identifier (SI) to name the electric service and Component Identifier (CI) to name the various components. Additionally, to better organize the communicational process, the SINET-based communication architecture is divided into three layers, i.e., the Service Layer, Resolution Layer and Transmission Layer. The overall communication architecture and workflow are shown as in Fig. 13.5.

13.1.4   Other Applications

Up to now, we have carried out a number of techniques and industry promotion projects. Here is an example of SINET-ZTE. With the assistance of SINET, in the mobile core network, we can avoid alternate routes, decreased network layers and simplified gateway configurations. In this example, gateway devices can be saved by 30 % and transmission resources can be saved by 18–64 %.

SINET also applies to the Beijing New Rail Technology Co., Ltd., including: (1) core series device "EMU mobile hollow axles ultrasonic testing machine," with a market share of more than 80 %; (2) applies to the high-tech equipment Langfang Development Zone monitoring and control system manufacturing based production workshop production line; (3) applies to high-speed rail maintenance and remote monitoring system overhaul equipment.

Table 13.2 Application cases of SINET

Year	Application cases
2008	Beijing Information Technology Institute
2009	ZTE Corp.
2009	Beijing Zhao Wei Electronic Corp.
2010	Institute of Sensing Technology and Business, BUPT
2010	China Academy of Electronics and Information Technology
2010	CSL Mobile Ltd.
2010	PT Smart Telecom
2011	Hi3G Sweden
2012	China Telecom, Institute in Guangzhou
2013	Cyberspace Great Wall
–	Other special departments

SINET not only provides important research ideas and a viable environment for future experimental research information networks around the world, but also for the fields of national defense, economic construction and scientific research. In future global information network research, SINET first realized the concept of the future information networks, systems and mechanisms, built a comprehensive test system prototype and began to promote national applications.

Additionally, SINET has been deployed and tested in many special areas. Table 13.2 lists the key application cases of SINET.

13.2   Contributions

SINET is a novel future Internet. The research has great importance for the development of information science and technology. The meanings of SINET research are concluded as the following four points:

Various kinds of serious disadvantages exist in the current network. Therefore, it is difficult to meet the demands of the development of the future information network. The existing information network is developed from the original mode in which one network supports one service. Although this mode had many benefits in the old days, it has been reported to have many benefits in recent years because of the proliferation of services and ever-increasing demands for quality service. For example, the telecommunication network is mainly designed for voice services. It is not able to provide users with high-quality broadband streaming media business. The Internet mainly supports the data service. With the increase of network users and applications, the problems of service quality, credibility and mobility of the Internet have gradually been exposed. Besides, the traditional

Internet seriously lacks support for an intelligent mechanism to perform the perception of network status and dynamic allocation of network resources. If the behaviors of the users or network are changed, it is difficult to perceive the changes and dynamically allocate the resources for the current Internet. So, the above problems lead to unreasonable network resource allocation, a low utilization ratio and excessive energy consumption. Considering the aspect of network link utilization, at the 2010 ACM SIGCOMM international conference researchers from Princeton University pointed out that the existing network backbone link utilization is only 30–40 %. At the 2011 ACM SIGCOMM international conference, researchers from the Spanish Telefonica pointed out that the access network link utilization rate of the existing network is less than 10 %. The network resource utilization rate is very low. From the view of quality of experience, according to the China Broadband User Survey released by the Data Center of the Chinese Internet in December 2011, less than 47 % of Chinese Internet users are satisfied with the broadband rate. At the same time, the Internet was originally designed for data transmission. It is a scale-free network with power-law structure, which makes the Internet vulnerable to malicious attacks. Therefore, it is urgent to break through the limitations of the existing network and design a new future network system and mechanism to effectively solve the problems of network scalability, mobility, security and so on.

Dynamic adaptation for services and the intelligent combination of resources will be the core of future network researches. The intelligence and universalization of services are the major objectives for future information network technology. However, due to the drawbacks of the original Internet, it is difficult to satisfy the above problems. Therefore, in-depth research on the theory and mechanism of dynamic adaptation of service and the smart service mechanism are necessary so as to achieve smart and universal service. In addition, the existing Internet lacks effective mechanisms to support the intelligence network, which leads to the problem of a low utilization rate of resources, high energy consumption of the network and so on. Therefore, it is necessary to further study the cognition and virtualization of network resources and establish mechanisms for the intelligent combination of resource and mapping theory to achieve cooperative network resources. It is also of great significance to improve the network resource utilization and achieve cloud computing, cloud services and a mobile Internet.

A complete theoretical system for the future information network is of great significance for its development. According to the current research status of the future information network, most of the research has been concentrated on improving one of the performances, such as mobility, security or cloud computing, and so on. Although the complexity and difficulty of the research can be greatly reduced, it cannot form a complete system for the information network because of the absence of systematic research. In this way, the demands of the future Internet cannot be satisfied very well. Therefore, creating a future network system should be assigned the first priority. Furthermore, the system should possess good scalability, mobility and security. It should also be able to be aware of the complex network behavior and support resources' dynamic adaptation so as to make the network more efficient and energy saving.

The SINET is supposed to break through the traditional network framework. It is of great scientific, economic and social significance for the development of our country. Recently, research on the theory of the new-generation information network system has been a research hotspot. However, no complete network system architecture has been proposed that can effectively support the network scalability, mobility and security and greatly improve the network resource utilization rate, energy consumption rate and quality of experience. Therefore, the fundamental research on the new-generation information network system has great prospects for development and potential opportunities. It is also an effective way to address the new problems and challenges of the development of the Internet. Therefore, conducting this basic and prospective research is urgent and necessary and will definitely cause great changes in the competition concerning the international information industry.

13.3   Challenges and Future Work

Although many researches and engineering developments have been carried out, there is still a long way ahead to achieve the large-scale implementation of SINET. Moreover, to achieve the large-scale implementation, several challenges have to be solved:

The first challenge is to achieve high-level intelligence of the SINET. In practical implementations, a realistic network environment is extremely intricate, and many complex cases have to be solved. For example, a network family will undertake multiple tasks and play different roles in the network. Meanwhile, a network component may be a part of different network families. Moreover, with the change of the network environment, the affiliation between the network family and network component is changeable. Therefore, how to efficiently schedule and manage these families and components is a very challenging and interesting research topic, which necessitates much effort from researchers from different disciplines.

The second challenge is the large-scale implementation of SINET. The current Internet is occupied and managed by multiple stakeholders and used by billions of users. They may not be willing to change the just-in-use Internet to the experimental testbeds. An available approach is to establish many small-scale platforms for certain areas without affecting existing Internet services greatly. Then, the SINET can be tested, validated and extended step by step before deploying the large-scale platform. Moreover, since the existing Internet has been developed to such a large scale, countless devices have been produced and deployed for the original Internet. It would be very expensive to reproduce new generation network devices so as to replace the old ones. Therefore, how to reuse these existing network devices in the SINET is another important and considerable problem.

The third challenge is the in-network caching mechanism. In-network caching is one of the important properties of information-centric networking (ICN). By implementing the in-networking caching, the ICN achieves good performance in terms of the data transmission. Moreover, SINET can be regarded as an ICN to a certain extent. The merge of the in-network caching property into the architecture of SINET will definitely further improve the performance data transmission. Therefore, creating an in-networking caching mechanism that can be operated in SINET is also an important research point.

The fourth challenge is the optimization of the proposed mapping mechanisms in this book. Since the mapping mechanisms are first proposed and implemented in SINET, many scientific problems and engineering difficulties have to be solved. For example, it is an important and urgent problem to efficiently achieve the fast operation of the four kinds of mappings, i.e., one to one, one to many, many to one and many to many, through the matrix transformation. Moreover, the accurate and complex mapping mechanisms will definitely increase the complexity of mapping algorithms during the engineering development phase. So, designing an efficient mapping algorithm with low time and space complexity is also waiting for study.

Besides the above challenges and research points, the future research and development directions will also include (but are not limited to) the following:

- the representation and dynamic perception of the complex network behaviors;
- the mechanism of dynamic allocation of network resources;
- intelligent service control;
- the mass deployment of the service adaption system;
- the scalability problems of the SID query system;
- the design of the smart service resource storage mechanism.

Based on the aforementioned descriptions, we sincerely hope that more researchers will join in the study of future Internet theory and technologies and address the difficult challenges that the information network is facing and will face. We also expect researchers to provide valuable comments and suggestions for SINET to further improve its performance and promote large-scale implementation.

Printed in the United States
By Bookmasters